Old Memories And Me

Charlie Craig

Aberdeen Bay
An Imprint of Champion Writers

Aberdeen Bay
Published by Aberdeen Bay, an imprint of Champion Writers.
www.aberdeenbay.com

Copyright © Charlie Craig, 2009.

All rights reserved. No part of this publication may be reproduced, stored in a database or retrieval system, or transmitted, in any form or by any means, without the prior written permission of the publisher. For information on obtaining permission for use of material from this publication, please visit the publisher's website at www.aberdeenbay.com.

PUBLISHER'S NOTE

Aberdeen Bay is not responsible for the accuracy of this book--including but not limited to events, people, dates, and locations.

International Standard Book Number
ISBN-13: 978-1-60830-019-8
ISBN-10: 1-60830-019-6

Printed in the United States of America.

Dedication

My loving wife, Betty Harrison Craig
I still miss you today, and I will miss you again tomorrow, but what a day yesterday was

My brother Bill, William Earl Craig
You were always my hero

Mama and Daddy, Clara Mae and John Benjamin Craig
The lessons I learned from you guided me down every road I have ever traveled

My sisters, Ruby Armstrong and Dot Sparks
When I think of you, I think of home

And to my lovely daughter, Dawn Craig and my wonderful grandsons, Kyle Smith and Del Primm
You are the strength I lean on now

ACKNOWLEDGEMENTS

There are so many people I need to acknowledge and thank for the opportunity to live out my dream of becoming a songwriter and sometimes recording artist. Without you this book would never have had a reason to be written. Without you there wouldn't be any songs of mine singing around the world today.

Bob Courtman: you paid for and produced my first recording session and it paved the way for all that I became in the music business.

Dr. Atkinson: you financed my first Nashville recording that introduced my songs to Nashville and that lead to my move to Music City.

Lou Stringer: you were my first music publisher and that year with you opened up so many doors for me. You got my first songs recorded by a major artist.

Howard See: in the first two years I was in Nashville you might be the single person most responsible for my survival. You gave me a job, paying me more that I was worth, and you bought my family groceries. Some people call you friend. You proved you are a friend. God Bless you.

The Dennys and Cedarwood Publishing: you were my second publisher and my first real opportunity to write for a major company. With you I had my first big cuts that established me as a known songwriter. You helped make me a professional.

Mel Tillis and Carl Perkins: you two were my first mentors and taught me so much, things that still help me to this day. Carl, RIP old friend.

Larry Butler: you produced so many of my songs in the late seventies and through the eighties. You produced my first top ten and award winning song, *I Would Like To See You Again*. What would I have done without you? You believed in me when not many still did.

Del Reeves: how many of my songs did you record? Sometimes I think you recorded some of my songs just to keep my career going. Hey, we had a few hits together though. RIP dear friend.

Moe Bandy: what can I say? You are one of the greatest honky tonk and cheating song singers in history. You gave me two top 10 singles in the eighties when I really needed them. You recorded several more of my songs in albums and kept me going through the eighties. You helped keep my name out there in this tough business.

Keith Stegall: the best co-writer and friend I ever had. We had a great run in the eighties and nineties. We laughed together and we cried some together. We made it through though because we believed.

Alan Jackson: where do I begin about you? I was the old pro when we first met in 1987 but you are the one that carried us to the top. I knew you would be a star from the beginning. I am so proud of you and what you have achieved. I already had some good hits when I met you, but when you started recording my songs it was a whole new world. Thanks for the ride and thanks for the friendship.

EMI Publishing: for 17 years you kept me on your writer's roster. I am certainly not the greatest writer you ever signed but no other songwriter ever appreciated all the things you did more than I. I am forever grateful.

Jesus: I should have mentioned You first but I saved You until last because You are the first and the last. You are my best friend, my strength and my Savior. Without You I would be nothing and I praise your name and thank You for all You have done for me in this life.

Charlie Craig

INTRODUCTION

    Looking back on my life in this dazzling world of country music, I sometimes wonder if I am somebody else and not that kid from Watts Mill, South Carolina that used to sit up on an iron rail across from the cotton mill and daydream about the life I have been living in this business of country music for more than forty years. How could I possibly have known that the Sears & Roebuck Silvertone guitar I got when I was about fourteen years old would lay the musical path to Nashville, Tennessee and pair me up with the likes of Alan Jackson, Travis Tritt, Dolly Parton, Johnny Cash and a lot of other great stars. It still amazes me how this all happened. I wasn't born with a silver spoon in my mouth. I didn't know anybody important. I didn't even have a rabbit's foot. So why me? I don't honestly know. I do believe that God gave me a gift and something inspired me to take that gift and make it my craft. Except for a poem, or a verse nobody would read, or a melody that nobody ever heard, *you* might have been me.
    I don't know why I got the breaks. They were not all easy of course. It never is when you stop dreaming and start walking up and down 16th and 17th Avenue South in Nashville, Tennessee in the real world.
    I entered two talent shows years ago back in South Carolina. I lost one to a little boy who forgot the words to his song and cried. I lost the second because my band was better than the professional band that was hosting the show. It was tough getting ahead in music, even back home.
    Over the years I have found it is about as difficult sometimes to get a song recorded by a major artist as it is surviving going over Niagara Falls in a barrel with both ends open. As hard as the road has been at times though, especially in the early days, I wouldn't really trade my life and career with anybody else, except maybe Alan Jackson or George Strait. They look good in cowboy hats. I don't wear one well and I always wanted to wear a cowboy hat. Other than that, and a number of songs I didn't get recorded that I thought should have been, I have had a wonderful and rewarding career.
    Not many people get to chase their dream, catch it, then live it. For some reason I have been able to do that. It wasn't always easy, but it was always there and I never let go, holding on even through the rough times that perhaps would cause any reasonable person to give up. Of

Old Memories and Me

course I had a rock to lean on for many years. That rock was my wife and I will tell you about Betty Craig throughout this story of my life and career.

I started this journey a long time ago. Along the pathway to get to where I am today, I performed in bars, honky tonks, movie theaters, high school auditoriums, lounges, cheap clubs, expensive clubs, plush country clubs, dinner parties, VFW's, American Legions, Shriner's events, old folk's homes, home for unwed mothers, prisons, beer joints, television shows, on the back of flatbed trucks in the rain, and finally on the stage of the Grand Ole Opry. If I haven't played there, then they either closed it or tore it down before my time.

I practiced a lot. You can't play in any game and compete well if you don't practice. I didn't come to that conclusion on my own. Back when I first started learning to play guitar and sing I learned the true meaning of that wisdom when I got into tough competition and realized I needed to be a little better. Learn all you can, then ask somebody else to teach you all that they know too. I have tried to live by that philosophy most of my life.

As a teenager I use to practice trying to sing through my nose. I wanted to sound like Webb Pierce. He was well known for his nasal-sounding vocal style. Then too, I would try to sing like Chuck Berry and Ray Charles. Believe it or not, I was able to pull both styles off. I used to listen to WLAC at night during the week. WLAC was a 50,000-watt radio station out of Nashville playing R&B music, and then rock & roll when it caught on around 1954. On Saturday night I would listen to the Grand Ole Opry on WSM, another 50,000-watt radio station out of Nashville. I still love several different genres of music, but country music will always be my first love.

I was always kind of witty, a quick thinker and fast to respond to somebody ribbing me, coming back with my own clever lines. I almost considered being a comedian for a while. I would get up in front of a few people, especially Betty and friends like Clyde and Connie Pennington, and Bradley Jones, and do little skits. They were pretty funny, at least they made my friends laugh and they suggested I do something with that talent. I never took it beyond my own entertainment and that of those few close acquaintances. I wanted to be in Nashville, write songs and sing on the Grand Ole Opry. That's all.

In 1968, 16th and 17th Avenues were known as *Record Row*, or *Music Row*, because that was where most of the recording studios were, along with the record labels, publishing companies, booking agencies, managers and etc. People walked those two streets every day for hours looking for a break, especially aspiring songwriters and recording artists. I use to see Chuck Woolery (Dating Game & Love Connection) there, and Kris Kristofferson. Both were looking for a "deal" like me, and it wasn't unusual to run into one of the stars like Bill Anderson or Waylon Jennings hanging out around their booking agent's office, or at their managers place, or maybe doing a session in one of the recording studios on *the row*.

Most people expect to see flashing neon signs, a Las Vegas-style strip when they first visit Music Row in Nashville. It is far from that. Most of the businesses, including some of the record labels, are in houses that once were homes before the area was commercialized. There are a few high rises and some of the record labels have built plush, multimillion-dollar buildings today. Mostly though, Music Row looks like any other part of town. It is anything but that though. Inside those houses and plush buildings dreams are fulfilled and rags can become riches. On the other hand, and unfortunately this is the norm, those rags stay rags and hearts are broken over dreams that won't ever come true. Most people that come to Nashville seeking a music career usually leave with those stars they were chasing still a distant glitter in their eyes. There is really no other place in the world like it. Country music is a huge business machine that operates kind of like a large family, yet it is as competitive as two boxers slugging it out in a ring. Over the years I have been here, some of the dirty politics and under the table deals have vanished and it is more professional and corporate now. It is still just as competitive though. It is a business of copyrights, contracts and royalty checks but for the most part we all trust each other, so to speak. You couldn't always say that when I first came to town.

It is sad, but back when I first came to Nashville we had a few of what was known as *couch producers*. I knew one record label head that told a stripper he was interested in signing her to a record contract. I was in his office and I witnessed that little conversation. I'm not saying she couldn't carry a tune, but she certainly wasn't another Tammy Wynette. She was a stripper, not a singer. That record executive had no real intentions of signing her to a record deal. He had other things in mind, thus the title, couch *producer*. This is a thing of the past now, at least with the major labels. Everything is business and handled properly, like any other big corporation. Most of the indie labels I am familiar with have good reputations as well.

If you want to find the best country singers, songwriters and musicians in the world, look in Nashville. There is so much talent in Nashville it is scary. Great singers singing demo sessions, or working gigs in the clubs and bars around town, unable to get record deals because a record label can only promote so many new acts a year. It's the same thing with musicians. Only so many get into the *click* for session work. The rest work the road with the artist, or play for nearly nothing in those same bars and clubs backing up those unknown singers, waiting for their break too. Those musicians that do work the recording sessions are so creative they are responsible for some of the great production and sounds you hear on the radio. Yes, Nashville has some genius record producers, but I think all of them will tell you how important the input of ideas coming from the musicians are.

Old Memories and Me

The Nashville Sound. There's nothing like it anywhere in the world. If you have the money, you can duplicate any great recording studio in Nashville, in any small town in America. Still, without the special breed of talented and creative musicians that work the recording sessions here, you would have nothing but an expensive recording studio and building.

Back then, in the late sixties and early seventies, RCA and Columbia Records both had two recording studios in their respective buildings. Along with Bradley's Barn out in Mt. Juliet, those five studios probably produced more hit records than any studios in the history of country music. Elvis cut most of his hits in RCA's Studio B. It is a tourist attraction today. Patsy Cline, Kitty Wells, Conway Twitty and Loretta Lynn cut most of their hits at Bradley's Barn, usually with the legendary Owen Bradley producing.

16th and 17th Avenues were both two lane, two-way streets back then. Now they are both two lane one-way streets. So much has changed, even the music. But I guess time does that to everything, changes things. We call yesterday the good old days. Tomorrow, we'll call today the good old days. Somewhere in between yesterday and today, for 41 years in Music City USA, my life changed too. And what a roller coaster ride it has been.

In the pages that follow I will try to put into words how I went from hoeing cotton in my daddy's cotton fields to writing and co-writing songs like *Between An Old Memory And Me* and *Wanted.* I will try to be open and honest, admit my mistakes and regrets, and share my success with humble awe. There will be hard times and heartbreaks, good times and laughter, success and failures, love and spite. There will be times I will step on somebody's toes, including my own, but if the shoe fits, I am sorry, we will all have to wear it. It is my life, my career, and I will tell it as it happened. I owe that to my honesty and integrity. Hold on for the ride, it gets rough sometimes.

* Some names have been changed to protect the privacy of certain individuals.

CHAPTER ONE

The sun came up over Watts Mill and spread out over the mill village to warm some of the chill of the fall season hanging in the air. Smoke was coming from most of the chimneys of the white-framed houses as people were beginning to stoke fires in their fireplaces and cook breakfast on wood burning stoves. All of the houses basically looked just alike. A few patches of fog were hovering above the small pond beside the cotton mill and smoke was pouring from the mill's smokestack. Dew glistened on the grass in the glare of the bright morning sun. The peaceful setting looked like a Norman Rockwell painting.

Just before 8 am the mill whistle blew and broke the silence, indicating it was shift-changing time. The graveyard shift was getting off work and the first shift was coming in. Inside the mill, the noisy weaving looms were vibrating the upstairs floors of the two-story brick building, weaving cloth from the spools of yarn that had been brought up from the first floor spinning room.

It was September 30, 1937. I was about to be born on Hammond Street, in one of those mill houses that surrounded the cotton mill in Watts Mill, South Carolina. Daddy gave my sister Dot a quarter to go buy candy at the Mill Company Store while my mama gave birth to me. Dot whined a little at first, wanting to stay and see a baby being born. She was 6 years old. They had allowed her to stay home from school that day because Mama had gone into labor and something special was going to happen. She had begged to be there to see me as soon as I was born.

"Git on now," my daddy told her and edged her toward the front porch steps with his gentle hands. "Your mama's about to have you a brother or a sister."

They didn't know what I was going to be until I came out of my mama's womb.

The Company Store was just a few blocks down the street, across from the cotton mill. At the Company Store Dot told Mr. Motes, the older man who operated the store for the mill company, that she wanted a quarters worth of the candy that was two for a penny. She got fifty pieces of candy.

"How come you're not in school little Dorothy?" Mr. Motes

Old Memories and Me

inquired.

"My mama's having a baby and Daddy let me stay home so I could see it as soon as it's born," Dot informed him.

When she returned home from the store Dot learned she had a baby brother, me, Charles Francis Craig. Ben and Clara Craig's clan was complete now.

Besides Dot, and now me, there was another sister, Ruby Nell, 9 years old, and the oldest child, my brother, Bill, who was twelve years old. There had been another boy, but he had died as an infant from pneumonia before I was born. His name was JB, named after my daddy, John Benjamin, and he would have been three years older than me.

Other than working in the cotton mill, as did my mama, my daddy worked part time at the Company Store. He had a bird dog named Jim and sometimes Mama would tell Jim to go down to the store, which was only a few blocks away from the house, "git on down to Benny, Jim. Go on," and she would point in the direction of the company store. That dog would take off to where my daddy was.

Daddy would tie a package around Jim's neck, whatever he wanted to send home to Mama from the store, then point and instruct Jim to go back home. That bird dog would run back up the sidewalk to the house and take Mama the package. Nothing could deter old Jim from carrying home the package tied around his neck.... nothing but a cat. Jim loved to chase cats. On one occasion Jim ran into a cat on the sidewalk between the store and home. Mama heard him barking and looked out the window to see him, with a package of hamburger meat tied and dangling around his neck, running after that cat. I think we had fried fatback and gravy for supper that night, instead of meatloaf.

There was a picture made of me with Jim when I was perhaps two or three years old. My hair is white as snow in that black and white photograph. I was a cotton top kid.

The house on Hammond Street looked just like all of the other houses that surrounded the cotton mill, which was owned by the J. P. Stevens Company, who also owned those houses, as well as the Company Store. Most of the houses were only four rooms with back alleys separating each row of back yards up and down each street. A mill owned garbage truck would drive up and down those back alleys emptying everybody's garbage cans once a week. All the houses were white and wood framed; none of them underpinned back in those days, with a porch and steps on the front and back.

I really don't remember living in the house on Hammond Street. Most of the things that happened while we lived there were told to me by family members, mostly by Mama and Dot.

Daddy bought a house on Fleming Mill Road when I was about two years old. Our new house was about a mile away from the mill. My mama's only brother, Carey Owens, and his wife Nell lived next to us. Carey and Nell had two daughters, Geraldine and Norma, my first cousins. Over the next few years I became very close to them. Dot and Geraldine were close to the same age, and Norma and I were only a year apart. A few years later Aunt Nell would give birth to a son, Bobby Owens.

My first real recollection of life was the ten years we lived in the house on Fleming Mill Road. It was a frame house too, but a lot nicer and larger than the house on the mill village, with three bedrooms, a living room, a den and a large kitchen. We had two fireplaces and an oil heater for heat. Mama cooked on a wood burning stove and heated water on it to pour into the bathtub in the bathroom, which was built out on the screened in back porch. Not many people had an inside bathroom in 1939, much less a bathtub.

Fleming Mill Road was still a dirt road back then. Ruby, Dot and I used to walk barefooted down towards the crossroads where the Prices lived and pick blackberries in a bucket to bring home for Mama to bake a blackberry pie.

"Charles, stop eating all of the blackberries," Ruby would scold me. "We ain't ever gonna get enough with you eating them all."

"I ain't eatin' any," I would say, but the smear of blackberry juice around my mouth always gave me away.

"Let me hold the bucket." That would be Dot. She wanted to sneak and eat some blackberries too.

"No, I'll hold onto the bucket," Ruby told her and held it behind her back as though protecting its content.

My mama made the best blackberry pies.

"Now, save your daddy some," Mama would tell us because we would eat it all if she would allow us to.

We had a couple of apple trees and Mama made apple pies as well. If there weren't many apples down on the ground, I would climb up in the tree and shake a limb so some would fall off.

My mama was one of the sweetest human beings God ever put on this earth. She was, as was my daddy, a self educated person. She had to drop out of school in the second grade to help farm their land when her daddy died of cancer. Mama was a strong woman, fairly tall for that day and time, perhaps 5 ft 8 inches, and a large boned woman, not overly large or overweight though. She was also a brave woman.

One night, while Daddy was working the second shift at Watts Mill, from 4 pm till midnight, Mama heard a noise outside. Bill had gone into the Navy by then and it was just Dot, Ruby, Mama and me at home that night. We didn't have a telephone to call Uncle Carey for help. He didn't have one to answer even if we did. Mama got a poker from beside one of the fireplaces and a flashlight from a drawer in the kitchen. She headed for the back door.

"Let's don't go out there," Ruby begged Mama. Ruby was probably 15 years old at that time.

"I ain't going out there," Dot whimpered. Dot was now 12

Old Memories and Me

years old.

"Y'all stay in the house," Mama told us.

"Uh uh." We weren't about to stay in the house by ourselves. I grabbed hold of Mama's housecoat and held on, scared to death. I must have been only 6 years old.

With my mama armed with that poker, me holding on to her housecoat, Dot holding on to my shirttail and Ruby holding on to Dot, the four of us went outside into the dark night.

"I know you're out here," Mama said in her best attempt to sound brave and shined the flashlight around.

My sisters and I trembled with fear, looking about, trying to see in the pitch-black night with a dim flashlight. Dot was holding on to me so tight I thought she was going to pull my shirt off.

Mama said to the would be intruder, "I've got a gun and I ain't afraid to shoot."

Dot whispered in a pitiful whine, "Mama, you ain't got a gun."

"Be quiet," Mama scolded her in a low voice. "He don't know that."

We rounded the corner of the house. "You better git out of here, if you know what's good for you!" Mama warned and raised the poker.

"I see him," Ruby gasped just loud enough for us to hear her, panic in her voice.

"Where?" Dot asked, not really wanting to know. She sounded like she was choking.

The dim glow of the flashlight passed over something dark just a few feet in front of us.

"I'm gonna shoot!" Mama warned. This time she didn't sound as convincing.

I think I peed my pants at that moment.

It was just a tree though.

Fortunately, we never encountered anybody out there in the dark yard that night. We never knew if somebody was there and took off, or if there was never anybody there at all, just the wind Mama had heard. I have never forgotten that night though. It was very frightful at the time, but thinking back, we must have looked and sounded pretty hilarious, like a mother hen and her three chicks.

That night may have been the incident that triggered it because not long after that Ruby started having nightmares at night. She and Dot slept together and Dot suffered the consequences of Ruby's bad dreams.

"He's out there," Ruby shrieked and sat straight up in bed one night. "I see him!"

"Who...where?" Dot cried out and sat up beside Ruby.

Their loud voices woke Mama and me up. I slept with Mama. We ran into their bedroom. Ruby had now grabbed Dot's hair and was pulling her head back and forth, frantically proclaiming, "I see him, I see

him!"
　　　Dot was crying and trying to free her long blonde hair from her sister's grasp. Mama and me were trying to get Dot's hair loose from Ruby's hold and at the same time attempting to convince her there was no one there, trying to calm her down.
　　　"She's gonna kill me y'all," Dot sobbed when we finally freed her. She glared at Ruby sitting upright beside her on the bed, wide eyed and still shaken from her bad dream. "Why do you have to pull my hair?"
　　　"Ain't nobody out there, Ruby." I said, and patted her on the shoulder for comfort.
　　　"Why are you petting her?" Dot exclaimed, rubbing her sore head. "I'm the one that's hurting."
　　　I gave Dot a hug too and she cried even more.
　　　"Now all of you stop it," Mama instructed, "and Ruby you quit having them nightmares."
　　　Now Ruby started crying, wiping big teardrops from her somewhat freckled face. "I can't help it Mama. I don't mean to."
　　　This happened several more times before Ruby finally stopped having nightmares. The bad dreams left just as suddenly as they had started. It's a wonder Dot had any hair left from those ordeals though.
　　　Grandpa Craig started staying with us at night during the week. His full name was Francis Marion Craig, named after the Civil War hero, Francis Marion, *The Swamp Fox*. I was named after my grandpa, thus Francis being my middle name.Grandpa Craig was already nearing his eighties, bent over and he used two walking canes, but he didn't want us staying by ourselves at night. I used to sit at the breakfast table and watch him pour his black coffee into a saucer and sip it from the saucer rather than the cup. He would swish the coffee around in his mouth before swallowing it.
　　　"Why do you do that grandpa?" I asked him one morning, both of my arms on top of the table and my chin resting in my palms.
　　　"Do what?" He wiped his white mustache with the back of his hand, stained somewhat from tobacco juice. His hair was white as snow too.
　　　"Why do you pour your coffee in your saucer? Why don't you just drink it out of the cup?" I inquired.
　　　"Don't taste as good like that," he told me matter of factly.
　　　"I don't see nobody else do that," I informed him.
　　　Grandpa just looked at me for a few seconds, poured more coffee into the saucer, and sipped it all out, swished it around in his mouth, then swallowed it. He smacked his lips together, lowered his gaze at me over the top of his wire-rimmed glasses resting on the bridge of his nose. "I ain't nobody else."
　　　Grandpa was right about that. There was nobody else like him. I loved the ground he walked on, but he was stubborn as a mule and

set in his ways. He sat in a pew right down on the front row at Lucas Avenue Baptist Church and if someone was in that seat he would tell them to move.

"You in my seat," he would snap, and nudge them with one of his walking canes.

I never knew Mama's parents, grandpa and grandma Owens. They both died before I was born. Mama had another brother besides Uncle Carey. His name was Russell but he had accidentally shot himself to death rabbit hunting, also before I was born. Now, there was just Mama and Uncle Carey.

On the other hand, the Craig clan was a large and close-knit family. Francis Marion Craig and Ella Fair Bobo Craig had eleven children. There was my daddy, Ben, his four brothers; George, Boyce, Sam and Wesley. There were six girls; Edna, Hattie Bell, Leila, Emma, Maggie and Lula, who died at a young age.

Granny Craig lived with my Aunt Edna and Aunt Leila on Simmons Street, down on the mill village. Grandpa Craig lived there too when he wasn't staying at our house while Daddy worked at night. Leila was confined to a wheelchair, having lost a leg in a car accident. Edna worked in the mill and supported the household, which also included my first cousins Sara and Buddy Craig. They were Wes's children but he was divorced and lived alone. I always admired my Aunt Edna for all that she took on.

When I turned six years old, in 1943, I started school in the first grade at Ford High School. Ford was about a half mile away from our house, so we walked to school, Dot, Ruby and me, along with our cousins Geraldine and Norma Owens. We called Geraldine, Jerry, most of the time. Ruby was in the tenth grade when I started first grade and she only had a year to go to graduate because back then you only had to go eleven years to school.

Sixteen years old by then, Ruby was really pretty. She had auburn hair and brown eyes. My brother Bill, who was now stationed at a naval base in Miami, Florida, also had auburn hair and brown eyes. Dot was thirteen and just as pretty as Ruby, with long blonde hair and blue eyes. Bill and Ruby got their brown eyes from Daddy, and Dot and I got our blue eyes from Mama.

At Ford High School you attended first and second grade in a building adjoined to the lunchroom and auditorium, then third grade through graduation in the larger building next door. None of the classes were large in number of students, perhaps anywhere from eighteen to twenty five in each class. We all pretty much knew each other. Our parents all knew each other as well. All of my cousins went to Ford High School, except Charles and Faye Marler, who were the children of my daddy's sister Emma Craig Marler, and Jimmy and Patsy Craig, my Uncle Sam Craig's children. Yep, we had our own Uncle Sam.

When I was in grammar school, Mr. Ford, for whom the school

was named, was the superintendent. We had a little recess and a big recess, as we called them. During little recess in the morning, around 10am, you could go to the canteen, which was on the first floor of the main building. You could buy snacks and take them back to your home classroom. Little recess lasted fifteen minutes.

Big recess was lunchtime and we had thirty minutes. You could eat in the school cafeteria for twenty-five cents, go down to Gossett's Café two doors away, or if you lived close enough to the school you could run home for lunch. I think it was mandatory that grades first through fifth had to stay on the school grounds and eat in the cafeteria. After big recess each class took ten minutes for prayer.I had never heard of atheist back then, so nobody tried to keep us from praying if we wanted to.

It was a unique experience going to Ford School. I think most of the students looked forward to going to school every day so we could see each other and be together. It was like one big family of kids and teachers.

There was a railroad track right behind the school gym and when a train would go by the teachers would have to stop talking until the train had passed so they could be heard. That would happen a couple of times a day.

There was a war going on across the Atlantic Ocean, World War II. The United States had not been directly involved until the Japanese bombed Pearl Harbor. President Roosevelt then declared war on Japan and we were in the war. We got word from Bill that he was being shipped overseas in a few weeks. Mama cried and Daddy said we were going to drive down to Miami and see Bill before he was shipped overseas. I didn't really know anything about wars, except that they were bad, and I was glad they were far off somewhere, away from Watts Mill.

Daddy had a 1941 Ford and him, Mama, Ruby, Edith Riddle, who was a close family friend, and I piled into the car and headed to Miami. I had no idea where Florida was, let alone Miami. I was now in the second grade and 7 years old. For some reason Dot didn't want to go. This was 1944.

Daddy drove all the way to Miami without stopping, except for gas and food. I slept in the back floorboard of the car. There was a hump in the floor and before we got back home I felt like my back had a hump in it too.

"You getting tired, Benny?" Mama asked Daddy as he drove, practically non-stop.

"Foot no," Daddy answered. He said *foot* a lot. "Besides, who else is gonna drive?"

"We can stop somewhere and let you rest," Mama told him.

Old Memories and Me

We didn't stop. Daddy kept going. If he was tired he wouldn't have admitted it. John Benjamin Craig was a proud man and he didn't take to what he thought might be a sign of weakness.

I remember going across a bridge on the way, a long flat bridge over a swamp or something. It was only two lanes and the road had holes in some places, not very big ones, but holes nonetheless. I looked out the window, my nosed pressed against the glass. I was scared to death. We met a Greyhound bus on that bridge and I thought the thing would break and we would all fall into the swampy water below. I held my breath until the bus was past us. We made it across safely.

"Can we go another way on the way back home, Daddy?" I asked, still feeling a quiver in my stomach. I didn't want to cross that bridge again.

"Ain't no other way," he told me.

We started seeing moss and palm trees. Driving down US Highway 1 we could see the Atlantic Ocean on our left just as the sun came up. The sun just rose right up out of the water, way over yonder somewhere. At least that is how it appeared to me. I had never seen an ocean before. Greenwood Lake, sometimes referred to as The Buzzard Roost, was the most water I had ever seen in my young life. It was a lake between Laurens and Greenwood.

We made it to Miami and moved our suitcases into the two rooms upstairs of a privately owned home Bill had been able to find for us. Miami was absolutely beautiful. I had never seen houses so pretty, with so many colored roofs, and rainbows of flowers everywhere. I couldn't get over the orange trees and coconuts growing about everywhere I looked.

"Look, Mama, them people's got oranges growing in their yard," I pointed out.

"Ain't that something," Mama agreed.

"I wonder if they would let us pick one from the tree?" Ruby said.

"I bet they wouldn't let us," Edith replied.

This was the first time I had seen my brother in nearly a year. He had been able to come home on a furlough for a few days before reporting to his present station there in Miami. When he had been home on that leave I had a picture made with him. He was in his white navy pants and top and white cap. I was sitting on his knee. He was my hero in that uniform and I would keep that picture for the rest of my life.

Bill showed us some of the sights in Miami. We went out on a glass bottom boat and it amazed me to see the fish and other water creatures right under my feet, right through the bottom of that boat. I was also in awe when I stood on the beach and looked out across that huge ocean. I couldn't understand why I couldn't see trees and land on the other side. I did see several ships out on the horizon. Bill pointed out to me that one of them was a naval vessel.

Wherever we went, I would stay as close to Bill as I could get. He was twelve years older than me and we hadn't got to spend that much time together. He had already graduated from high school by the time I started school. He went to Spartanburg Junior College for a year, then joined the Navy before he got drafted into the army. Now that we were with him, and him in his navy outfit, I was just so proud of him, I was about to burst with pride.

Bill was assigned to the infirmary on the naval base but on occasion he had to drive an ambulance to sites where naval planes had crashed during training, retrieving body parts. That had to be a tough job but Bill never talked about it to me.

We stayed in Miami with Bill for three days, then had to head back home. Mama didn't want to leave him, knowing he was about to go overseas where the war was going on. Daddy was strong enough to hold it inside but the rest of us cried when we told Bill bye. I think my mama cried all the way back to Watts Mill.

We had only been home for a few days when we got a telegram from Bill. His orders had been changed and he was staying in Miami. The Navy decided they needed him there in the infirmary treating the wounded and sick sailors and pilots. Bill was actually disappointed because a lot of the boys he had gone to Ford High with were overseas fighting in the war. Some of them had died in Europe, wherever that was. He felt guilty I guess that he was back in the states and safe in Miami.

It was a tough time during the war. A lot of grocery items were scarce, like sugar, which you had to have stamps to buy. Daddy had bought me a bicycle, with no fenders or chain guard, but I thought it was something and loved it. However, Daddy had to trade it, plus pay a few dollars to boot, for a pig, so we could have meat. I sure missed that bicycle but I enjoyed the pork chops and ham. Still, I didn't quite understand why I couldn't have pork chops and a bike too.

A lot of people couldn't get grass to grow in some parts of their yard, especially on the mill village. They swept the dirt spots with brush brooms. These were slender tree limbs from dogwood trees, with leaves left on one end for sweeping, tied into a bundle and held together by strings of strong cloth. You could buy these from the *brush broom man*. He was also called *Look Up*, because he wore a hat low on his head and was always looking up to see out from under his hat. Ruby, Dot I were scared to death of him.

Here comes Look Up.

We would all three run into the house.

Most of the yard at our house had plenty of grass, except some places in the back yard were bare. We made our own brush brooms. I used to help Mama sweep the back yard. We had chickens running loose in the yard and there was a lot of chicken *stuff* everywhere to cleanup, or step in.

Old Memories and Me

We kept up with the war by listening to the radio. We only had one radio and sometimes there was too much static to pick up many radio stations. It was a big Philco radio, and kind of looked like a chest of drawers from the front but the back was open and you could see a round cylinder-shaped thing. I never knew what that thing was but it would get warm when the radio had been turned on for a while.Late on Saturday night we were able to sometimes get a good enough signal to hear the Grand Ole Opry from Nashville, Tennessee. I would lie in the floor by the radio and listen. A lot of the country singers were in the military and just a few known performers were on the Opry. I loved the music but it never crossed my mind back then that I wanted to be a part of it.

One day the mill whistle started blowing. We were used to it blowing between shift changes but that day it kept blowing, over and over. Aunt Nell Owens ran to our house. "The war is over! It's over y'all," she exclaimed, jumping up and down with glee.

We all went down to the mill, people from the mill village, folks from all around, everybody hugging and dancing, shaking hands, anything to show their jubilation that the war was over. Finally, they turned off the mill whistle but most people stayed around a while longer, celebrating. When we got back home, Daddy, Mama, Ruby, Dot and me gathered around the radio and listened to President Roosevelt announce to the entire nation that Japan had surrendered.

"Will Bill be coming home now?" I asked.

Daddy patted me on top of my blonde head and grinned. "Won't be too long, I don't guess."

I loved living on Fleming Mill Road. We had about five acres of land, so I had plenty of room to run and play. I always did like to run. On one side of the house we had about a quarter acre up near the road that Mama and Daddy planted a large garden in. This was between our house and Uncle Carey's house. On the other side of our house, near the driveway, there was a patch of woods. I used to climb up as high as I could in the tall skinny trees and grab hold of a limb and jump. The green limb and tree would bend slowly, allowing me to glide down, sort of like having on a parachute. I kept the tops of those trees bent over all the time because they never would straighten back up after that. That part of the woods always looked like a storm had come through.

"Charles, you gonna break your neck climbing them old trees," Mama would say.

Out behind our house there was this big corral. Inside the corral there were three horse stalls on each side. Eventually Daddy bought some horses.That tickled Ruby, Dot and me to death. Daddy rented the horses out for horseback riding at 50 cents an hour. There was one horse he didn't rent out though. Its name was Major. He gave Major to us kids.

I learned to ride Major with Ruby and Dot standing about

twenty yards apart and me riding between them, from one to the other. I would walk Major to Ruby, she would turn him around and I would walk him back to Dot.

"I'm doing good, ain't I?" I felt proud of myself, although I was still a bit scared of horses.

Eventually, I got brave enough to ride him around the yard, then finally, down Fleming Mill Road with Daddy on a horse and Mama in a horse and buggy, sometimes with Miss Betty Richards riding with Mama in the buggy. Miss Betty ran the Watts Community Building. She had a horse she boarded in Daddy's corral.

Major was a beautiful horse, and very intelligent. However, he had one fault. Every time it rained he would take off to the house and his stall. He was petrified of the rain.

I was riding him one day down Fleming Mill Road, along with Daddy on a horse, my uncle George on another one, and Mama and Miss Betty in the buggy. We were well past the crossroads and the Price's place, about a mile or so from our house. It was a clear day when we had left the house.

All of a sudden a few drops of rain started falling. Daddy immediately got off of his horse to switch with me and ride Major. Before I could get off of him though, it thundered and the rain started coming down hard, like God turned a giant bucket upside down and poured it out on us. Major bolted and took off back down the road in a dead run. And he could run.

"Benny," Mama screamed. "Go help Charles!"

I was scared to death. I know, I got scared a lot back then.

Thank goodness I had sense enough to lay down forward over Major's neck, grab the saddle horn with one hand, a hand full of his mane with the other, and hold on for dear life. My legs weren't quite long enough to plant my feet securely in the stirrups, so I just dug my knees into Major's side.

I could hear Daddy and Uncle George riding somewhere behind me, both of them yelling for Major to "whoa!" I didn't dare try and look back. In fact, I closed my eyes and prayed, "Dear Lord..."

I knew the Lord was up there somewhere, but right then I needed Him down there where I was.

Major and I reached the house with me still in the saddle, barely. The corral gate was open and he headed straight to his stall. I lay as flat as I could to keep from hitting my head on the top of the stall doorway. We made it safely inside. I jumped off, breathing hard, and backed up against the stall wall, looking at Major. He turned and looked at me as though to make sure I was alright. As scared as I had been during the ordeal, and still was, I had to smile at him. I loved that horse and right then I knew he loved me too. He nudged me with his nose to prove it.

Daddy bought one horse that hadn't been broken. One day

Old Memories and Me

Daddy, Uncle George, and Uncle Wes, hooked that horse up to a plow. Mama and I stood on the screened in back porch watching as that crazy horse reared up, snorted, and took off running, pulling the plow from the ground, with Daddy pulling back on the reins as hard as he could, demanding, "Whoa!"

Daddy wanted him to pull the plow, just not through the garden and grape vines.

That wild horse pulled the plow and Daddy through a wooden grape vine frame that wound up hanging around the horses' neck like a collar as it uprooted, then he headed straight for the back porch where Mama and I stood petrified. He actually stomped both feet on the porch steps as though he were going to come through the screen door. Mama screamed and both of us ran into the house.

Daddy didn't buy any more unbroken horses after that incident.

Almost a year after the war ended Bill returned home. It was a happy time at our house.Mama cooked a big dinner and Ruby and Dot helped her. Bill loved Mama's fried chicken and macaroni and cheese pie, so we had plenty of that, and homemade biscuits. We all loved Mama's cooking. I guess everybody thinks their mama is the best cook in the world, but I swear, if anybody says they could make cream style corn and macaroni and cheese pie better than my mama could, then somebody's lying.

"Lord, thank you for this food and all the blessings we have received, amen."

Bill said a short blessing so we could get to eating.

CHAPTER TWO

Daddy had gotten promoted to loom fixer at Watts Mill and had changed over to the first shift, the same shift Mama was a weaver on. I was 12 years old now and just finishing 6th grade at Ford High. School would be out for the summer in a few weeks. Bill had gone to Columbia to attend the University Of South Carolina to study to be a pharmacist and would be getting out for the summer as well. Ruby had married Robert Armstrong a year after graduating from high school and Dot was dating a boy named Bobby Vaughn pretty regularly. My hair was no longer white, having turned to dishwater blonde. I was considered tall for my age, about 5' 9" but skinny as a rail.

Grandpa Craig had died and it was sad around our house for a long time, especially every Sunday when we would go to church at Lucas Avenue Baptist and see his empty seat down on the front pew. He was buried in the cemetery behind the church.

Daddy had sold all of the horses, including Major. He and Mama still had their big garden and Daddy was also still working at the Company Store for Mr. Motes for two hours on Fridays afternoons and all day on Saturdays. On Fridays after work Mama would ride home with her brother, Uncle Carey.

I had been making a lot of friends at school, people I already knew by name, but now I really was becoming close to some people that would become lifelong friends. Times were changing and things were good.

"I'm selling the house to Noel Frady," Daddy announced one afternoon at the supper table. Mama didn't even look up from her plate but Dot and I did.

"What?" I asked, surprised and a bit confused.

"Where are we gonna live, Daddy?" Dot asked. She was so pretty now I couldn't believe she was my sister. She had just turned 18 years old and was about to graduate from school. Her class was the last to go just eleven years.

Daddy looked over at Mama and it was all Mama could do to keep from spilling the beans.

"After we get done eatin' I want to take you and Charles and show you something," Daddy informed us and took the last bite of the biscuit covered with gravy on his plate.

Old Memories and Me

It was about five-thirty in the afternoon and still another hour or so of daylight left. Dot and I were anxious to see what Daddy was going to show us and wanted to go right then, but my mama never in her life left a dirty dish, or a messed up kitchen, before she went anywhere. Dot and I helped her wash and dry the dishes while Daddy went outside and watered the garden with a hosepipe. A hosepipe is the same as a garden hose. We just called it a hosepipe. You're going to get a country education reading my book.

"What's Daddy gonna show us," I prodded Mama. "Come on, now tell us, Mama." I was my mama's pet but she wouldn't budge. She smiled at me, put one arm around me and pulled me up close to her.

"You're my baby boy, but I can't tell you anything. Your daddy wants to surprise y'all."

Dot and I hurried up to help Mama get the kitchen cleaned up. Finally, we were done and the four of us got in Daddy's 1940 Ford and headed up dusty Fleming Mill Road toward highway 221. He turned left on 221 and drove the short distance to Setzler Road, which was almost directly across the road from Ford High School. He turned onto Setzler Road and drove to the top of the hill and pulled into the driveway of one of the nicest houses Dot and I had ever seen. We had seen the house from the outside before, knowing Jack Hammerick, the superintendent of Watts Mill lived there. Well, he used to anyway. We were surprised to find the house was vacant.

Daddy parked the car near the back door, which had cement steps and a little concrete stoop. We got out of the car and were surprised that Daddy had a key to the house. He opened the back door and we all went inside, Dot and I looking dumbfounded.

We stood in this big kitchen that had Formica top counters under the built in glass front cabinets, a double sink, and a booth built off to the side, like in a café.

"This is your new home," Daddy announced proudly.

Both mine and Dot's mouth's were wide open. We couldn't believe it. We went through the whole house. There were two big bedrooms and a smaller one, a living room, a den, the big kitchen and a bathroom, with a commode, a sink and bathtub, all inside the house. There was a huge attic fan in the front hallway to cool the house and a cellar with a coal furnace. I thought that was so cool, we were going to have a furnace in our house. The attic fan was neat too, but my favorite was the booth in the kitchen.

"It has twenty-two acres of land," Mama told us.

"You bought this house and land, Daddy?" Dot asked, somewhat amazed, as was I. "Can we afford this?"

"Why, foot yeah," Daddy laughed. "Me and Palmetto bank can."

After looking the house over on the inside, we all went outside to look around. There was a two car garage about twenty yards from the back door, across the driveway, and a big two-story barn, a small shed, and a long one-story barn back out behind that. Daddy told us there was a fenced in pasture with a water spring over in the back part of the twenty-two acres. It was a big place, at least to us it was.

Out in front of the house there was a brick wall about 1½ feet high that ran from the driveway to the other side of the front yard, with two little concrete columns on each side of an opening in the middle that had two brick steps to enter the front yard from the road. It was really neat. The front porch was big, and screen in, with a brick-colored concrete floor.

From the front yard you could look out across the Mill Company Pasture and see a lot of the mill houses on the other side, and the ballpark. The pasture used to be fenced in and people on the mill village kept cows there. Now the fence was gone and it was just a big open pasture. The mill company had also sold the mill houses to individuals and the Company Store was now privately owned by Mr. Motes.

About two weeks later we moved into our new house on Seltzer Road. I still slept with Mama, so Daddy took the first bedroom down the hall from the kitchen, the one nearest the bathroom. Mama and I had the next bedroom down the hall and Dot had the small room near the front of the house. You had to go through mine and Mama's room to get to Dot's. At eleven years old I was getting too big to sleep with Mama and I was trying to get up the nerve to sleep in a bed by myself. My sisters always told everybody my mama held me in her lap and fed me breakfast until my feet drug the floor. That is not so and I want to clear that up right here and now.

Mama and Daddy got up every morning at 5 am. Mama would cook a full breakfast while Daddy fed the pigs and his foxhounds. He had a big dog pen and pigpen a ways from the house so it wouldn't smell. Daddy wore overalls to work, like most of the other men that worked at the mill. I wore overall pants most of the time. That's like overalls without the tops.

"There are two boards loose on the back of the chicken barn," Daddy told me. "I want you to get some ten penny nails from the shed and nail those boards up tight."

He called the long barn out behind the shed a chicken barn because he was going to buy some chickens when he got the money. We were eating breakfast, fried eggs, grits and toast. There was always jelly and jam on the table.

"After that can I go over to the ball park and play ball?" I asked.

"I reckon so," Daddy told me. "Just be here when we get home from work. I need you to help me do some other things around here."

Mama had started taking plates off the table. Bless her heart; she would do that sometime before we finished eating.

Old Memories and Me

"You be careful and don't let that old ball hit you, Charles."

"Foot, Clara," Daddy said. "A few hard knocks'll help him grow up stronger." He looked at me seriously like he meant it and I am sure he did.

I looked at my mama. "I won't get hurt, Mama," I assured her. "Besides, I can catch real good now."I glanced back at Daddy. "I do need a new glove though."

"Maybe Santa Clause'll bring you a new glove for Christmas," he told me, then finished the last swigs from his coffee cup. "We got too much to buy right now."

"This is just July, Daddy," I sighed. "Christmas is a long time off." Then I added, "I thought I was gettin' a guitar for Christmas."

"You can't play no guitar, Charles," Dot grinned at me.

"But I'm gonna learn," I boasted. "Now that we live on a hill I can get the Grand Ole Opry real good on the radio and I been practicing singing." I grinned back at my sister.

Daddy got up from the table. "You're gonna be big enough to plow a mule before too long and you and me's gonna get that back 8 acres ready for plantin'."

"He ain't gonna plow no old mule," Mama told Daddy. She was cleaning the kitchen, getting everything spotless before she went off to the mill. Dot was helping her."He ain't big enough to plow no mule," Mama added.

One of Daddy's brothers, George, lived down the road from us, closer to the main highway, up on a hill on Patton Street, which you could get to by taking a short cut on a path from Setzler road. Uncle George, and Aunt Elizabeth's house was a mill house but made a little different from the other houses on the village and set off to the side from the others, up on that hill. They had four children. Betty Ruth was the oldest; she was a year younger than my sister Dot. Then there were three boys, Bobby, the oldest boy, Bill the next oldest boy, and Joe, the youngest. Bobby was my age and in my classes at school. Bill was a year behind us and Joe a year behind Bill. I was really close to them, along with another of my first cousins, Buddy Craig, who was Wes' son. Buddy and his older sister Sara still lived with Granny Craig, and Daddy's two sisters, Edna and Leila.

There was a creek or a branch as we called it that ran through the middle of the company pasture. I, Pete Estes and my cousins Bobby, Bill and Joe would dam up a wide place in the branch so the water would back up deep enough to skinny dip in. It was always muddy. We would jump in clean and come out dirty, but we didn't care, it was our swimming pool. We were a good ways from any of the houses so we would get butt naked, run and jump into the water, with our knees drawn up, making a big splash when we hit the muddy water. We spent a lot of time playing in that dammed up mud hole.

I recall on one occasion Pete and I were skinny-dipping by

ourselves.

"Oh my Lord," I cringed.

"What is it?" Pete asked.

"Something just slithered across my leg," I whimpered.

That's when the water moccasin popped its head up out of the water and glared at me.

"Shit!!" The moccasin immediately started swirling around on top of the water.

"He ain't so big," Pete forced a nervous laugh. "You grab his head and I'll grab his tail."

I caught it right off that Pete suggested I grab the snakes head.

"Not me," I yelped and headed for the bank, lunging through the muddy water. Pete wasn't so brave either; he was right behind me. It was some time before we got up the nerve to go skinny-dipping again.

I finally got my first guitar when I was fourteen years old. It was a Silvertone from Sears & Roebuck. While I was learning to make chords my fingers got so sore I nearly quit and just gave it up several times, but I stuck with it. Once I did learn to make several chords I took on another difficult task; learning to play rhythm and sing at the same time. Over and over I would pick and sing in the back bedroom of our house so I wouldn't drive everybody crazy while I learned. When I would learn something I thought would sound pretty good I would run into the den where Mama and Daddy would be watching television and ask them to listen.

"Let me show you what I just learned," I would blurt out with excitement.

"We're watching Arthur Godfrey," Daddy would say.

That was one of their favorite shows on television, along with Amos and Andy, and You Bet Your Life. Those were some of the popular shows on television then. Everything was still in black and white.

I remember the first television I ever saw. It was in the show window at Crews Music Store on the square in Laurens. Mr. Crews would leave it on at night for a few hours so people could come by and watch it. Daddy and Mama took me over there a few times and I would work my way through the crowd that gathered there and press my nose against the showroom glass and look in awe at the picture. I think it was about a 9-inch screen.

One of the first songs I learned to play and sing was *She'll Be Coming 'Round The Mountain*.

> She'll be coming 'round the mountain when she comes
> She'll be coming 'round the mountain when she comes
> She'll be coming 'round the mountain,
> she'll be coming 'round the mountain
> She'll be coming 'round the mountain when she comes

Old Memories and Me

Growing up I had to help Daddy on our 22-acre farm. One of the worst jobs I hated was hoeing cotton. I didn't mind picking cotton so much as I did hoeing it. Man, those rows of little cotton plants just got longer and longer after each row. Up one row, chopping the grass out from around the cotton leaves, then back down another long row. It seemed like a never-ending thing to me at times. If I didn't pay attention to what I was doing and chopped down a cotton leaf by mistake, Daddy would get on to me and raise Cain. That's what we called raising hell.

"You chopping down money," he would scold me.

One of the worst whippings I ever got happened in the field one day when Daddy was plowing his mule. He was fertilizing rows for something he was going to plant and I was sitting nearby in the cotton field beside the fertilizer sack and a bucket that I would use to carry fertilizer and seed to him when the feeder on the plow ran out. The cotton balls were still green and unopened. They were tall enough to provide a little shade for me. I was just sitting there glancing out toward the baseball field across the company pasture. I couldn't see them, but I could hear a bunch of my buddies yelling and having a good time playing baseball. I wanted to be over there with them.

We used to move the bases out into the outfield, and lay a jacket or shirt down for home plate, about twenty feet behind where second base would be so we could have a chance to hit the ball over the fence.

Watts Mill had a good baseball team and played in a very competitive textile league. A lot of the players were former major league players that had either gotten career ending injuries, or had been dropped from the team.

"Charles!"

Oh Lord. That was my daddy yelling for me. I had been daydreaming and hadn't heard him.

"I'm coming," I hollered back.

"Bring me some water too," Daddy said, not looking at me as he stumbled slightly behind the plow the mule was pulling.

I kept a Mason jar of water cool by digging a shallow hole in the dirt and laying the jar there and then covering it with a burlap sack.

"I'm coming," I called out and picked up the jar.

My daddy was good to me, I knew he loved me, but right then I thought he was mad at me because he had to call me a couple of times before I heard him, thinking about that ball field and wishing I was over there playing with my friends.

I took off running through the rows of cotton that separated me from the field where Daddy was plowing. Pop... Smack... Pop! The green, unopened cotton bowls were slapping against my overall pants as I ran. That stupid mule heard the sound and I saw him raise both ears, heard him go *whomp, ur whomp*, looking around toward the sound of me running. He bolted and took off running too.

Daddy always plowed with the lines tied and draped around his neck. Oh Lord. The plow was yanked out of his hands and thank goodness the force of the mule taking off pulled the plow line off Daddy's neck, but not before he fell down. I had stopped in my tracks, petrified. My daddy jumped back to his feet and chased that mule, still pulling the plow as it ran and snorting....*whomp, ur whomp.*

"Whoa!" Daddy yelled at the mule. He picked up a clod of dirt and threw it at him. He mumbled something I'm glad I didn't hear.

By then I was crying. I just knew my daddy was going to kill me.

"I'll catch him Daddy," I yelled and started running after the mule and the plow that was flopping left and right, bouncing up and down behind him.

I could really run fast but I couldn't catch that crazy mule.

Daddy took off to the house and got in his 1950 Ford pickup truck.

A little while later somebody was able to stop the mule down across from the cotton mill, in front of Eureka Drug Store. Daddy came back home with him tied to the tailgate of the truck, the plow in the back of the truck, laying in several different pieces. It was destroyed.

Daddy tore my behind up with a plow line. A plow line is a rope, similar to a lasso. I cried for an hour. It was the first and only time my daddy ever really whipped me that hard. It was also the first time I thought my mama was going to hit my daddy.

"Don't you ever whip him like that again," she snapped at him. She had come out of the house when she heard me hollering and crying. "I'll whoop you with that plow line and see how you like it."

I never heard my mama and Daddy have a real argument. And they didn't that day. Daddy never said a word back to her. He just took the mule down to the pasture. That was the end of it. I never knew for sure, but I think my daddy cried when he was at the pasture alone because he had whipped me so hard. His eyes looked watery when he came back to the house. He was a proud man, and a strong man. He never said a word about it again though.

My life went right back to normal. A little better educated in my rear end though.

On the 4th of July every year, the mill company would put on a big picnic with festivities at the ballpark. The two things I liked the most was chasing the greasy pig and trying to climb the greasy pole. Just about everybody turned out for the festivities that day.

The pig was always small, and really quick, greased with so much lard that he was too slick to get a good handle on even if you were lucky enough to grab a leg. Just us kids got to chase him and climb the greased pole, or at least try and climb it. There were refreshment

Old Memories and Me

stands set up to buy hamburgers, hotdogs, cokes, lemonade and iced tea. At the end of the day they would shoot off fireworks. Most folks called them firecrackers. Man that was a fun time back in the early fifties. Fun times and good times.

However, the most special event in my young life took place when I was 14 years old. I accepted Jesus as my savior and I was baptized one Sunday morning at Lucas Avenue Baptist Church. Even though I was that young, I knew who Jesus was and I knew what I was doing. It was totally my decision. Jesus was in my heart, my life, and I prayed to him every night, even sometime during the day. I looked to Him for guidance then and I would turn to Him for the rest of my life to show me the way. I wouldn't go through my life without sin but I knew He would forgive me now whenever I did sin because he said he would. All I had to do was ask.

Mama and Daddy always planted a big garden and once we had moved into the big house on Seltzer road, with a lot more land, we must have had at least a half-acre of garden, maybe bigger. We would plant potatoes, tomatoes, squash, green beans, turnip greens, a whole bunch of vegetables. We would pressure cook and then can or package a lot of vegetables for us to have for ourselves during the wintertime but Daddy would also sell a lot to vegetables to people on the mill village.

Daddy had traded his 1940 Ford car for a 1949 Ford pickup and I would go with him and sit on the back of the tailgate as he drove up and down each street on the village, stopping about every six or seven houses, and I would ring a big cowbell to let the housewives know we were there. We had a pair of hand scales to weigh the vegetables and brown paper bags to put the sold items in.

Daddy had also finally bought a bunch of chickens and raised them from little biddies, using electric brooders, until they grew into pullets, then he would kill them and we would dress them for sale. Now, for you folks that weren't raised in the country, dressing a chicken doesn't mean we put clothes on them. It means plucking their feathers off.

Daddy would dunk the chickens into a big tub full of scalding hot water, tested for just the right temperature by the biggest thermometer I had ever seen. The hot water would soften the feathers. He wouldn't allow anybody to do this but himself because you could actually burn the chicken in that scalding water. Then, using an electric plucker, which was a machine with a round cylinder full of rubber teats, that only he himself would use, Daddy would pluck all the feathers off the chickens.

There was like a small assembly line of tubs of water set up for us to get the plucked chickens ready for sale. After Daddy had all the feathers off, I got them next.

It was my job to *draw* them. Nope, I didn't use a pencil and paper to sketch them. Using a knife, I would cut open their rear ends and take out everything inside. Man, that was a messy job and I hated it. Dot and a black lady, Lois, got them next to finish cleaning them in tubs of cool water and making sure all of the pin feathers were off. After that the dressed chickens would be iced down in a huge icebox.

Daddy had regular customers that bought a chicken, or two, every weekend. One of my cousins, Bobby Craig, and I would wrap these chickens in white paper, seal the paper with tape, put them in the basket on our bicycles and deliver them to the customers on the mill village. Other people would come randomly to our house throughout the weekend and buy chickens as well. Back then most people had chicken every Sunday for dinner.

Pete Estes lived across the company pasture and I could see the back of his house from the front of mine. Pete was a year younger than me, a grade behind me at Ford High School, and he had become one of my closest friends, if not my best friend. That friendship would last a lifetime, as did a few others I made in those young days of my life. Pete and I used to play cowboys a lot together. He would come over to my house and we would use our cap pistols and ride sticks for horses. We nearly tore up Daddy's two-story barn shooting at the bad guys, even broke a couple of windowpanes out. Well, we had to make it realistic.

When I became interested in playing guitar and singing country music, Pete was one of my biggest supporters. Carol Hardin was another of my best friends and not only did Carol support my love for music, he learned to play guitar himself. When we were 15 years old Carol and I sang as a duet on the local radio station in Laurens, WLBG. The show was hosted by Red Webb and his Blue Sky Rangers. During the week Red was a disc jockey playing country music on WLBG and went by the name *Bashful Henry*. I remember he used to talk about strawberry gravy on the air.

One of the first songs Carol Hardin and I learned to sing together was *Peace in the Valley*. Carol would sing the lead and I did the harmony. I learned to sing harmony-singing hymns in church. It just came natural for me to sing either tenor or bass. Carol and I used to get cards and letters from people that listened to that Saturday morning radio show and it would tickle us to death when they would tell us how much they enjoyed our singing, and sometimes they would request for us to perform a certain favorite song of theirs. That was my first taste of fan reaction and I loved it.

I recall two young fellows coming to occasionally pick on that radio show. One was Buck Trent, from Ware Shoals, and the other was Bobby Thompson, from Spartanburg. Buck Trent would go on to play in Porter Wagoner's band years later and Bobby Thompson would become a session musician in Nashville and play regularly on *Hee Haw*. All that would be many years later though.

Carol Hardin and I played guitar and sang together quite a bit, mostly around either his house or mine. I recall us playing hooky from

Old Memories and Me

school one day and while walking up Smyth Street with our guitars, the principle, Mr. Elmore, came along and caught us. He put us in his car and took us to school, gave us a good talking to, then sent us to class. Besides being our principle Mr. Elmore was all the students' friend. That is the way it was at Ford High School and around Watts Mill.

You had to almost be a criminal to get expelled from school. I didn't know any criminals back then. Well, that is not exactly true. I knew Ted Weathers and he stole hubcaps and fender skirts. He also had a glass eye and he would sometimes take it out in school and tell the teacher he couldn't get it back in. That way he would get to go home, carrying his eye in his hand until he got outside, then he would put it back in. Ted Weathers wasn't really a criminal but he wound up in reform school, so at that age I wondered if he was a criminal.

Not only had I gotten really interested in music, I had started paying attention to girls too. I mean really noticing they were *girls*. I was getting pretty good at picking on the strings of my guitar and Polly Powers was getting real good at pulling on the strings of my heart. We would pass each other in the hallway at school, changing classes, and we would smile at each other. We had study hall together and I sat beside her most of the time. We would whisper and talk until Miss Scurry would hear us and make us hush.

Polly was a year behind me in school. When I was in the 11th grade, and she was a sophomore in the 10th grade, I asked her to go steady. She said yes. There was one problem though, Polly's daddy wouldn't allow her to date. He did agree to let me come to their house up on Barksdale Highway and sit on the front porch with Polly. He only agreed to that because Polly's older brother, Jim, went fox hunting with my daddy and they were friends. Okay then, so we would go steady on her front porch.

Her brother was a big man and I was scared to death of him catching me kissing Polly, or even holding her hand. I dared to anyway. I was getting tired of being scared of things. The first time I kissed her, her mama turned on the porch light, right in the middle of my lips pressed against Polly's. I jumped and almost fell out of the porch swing.

"It's gittin' late, Polly," her mama said, without actually opening the screen door and coming out onto the porch. Thank goodness for that. I wasn't *that tired of being scared yet*. Polly waited a few minutes then tiptoed over and reached inside the screen door and turned off the porch light.

"I got to go inside in a few minutes though," Polly told me in a low voice.

"Okay," I said and felt a lump in my throat, half of it because I wanted to kiss her again and half for my fear of her mama turning the porch light on again.

Polly was really pretty. I thought she looked a lot like Vivian Leigh, who played scarlet O'Hara in *Gone With The Wind*. She also looked a little like Elizabeth Taylor too. Well, Vivian Leigh and Elizabeth Taylor kind of look alike, so Polly resembled both of them.

Polly was my first real sweetheart. I was sixteen and she was fifteen. They called it puppy love but it sure felt like a big dog to me. I mean, I would go to sleep thinking about her and wake up thinking about her. I even cried over her a few times. Do puppies do that? I really wanted to kiss her again that night.

"Can we walk out in the yard for a few minutes?" I asked her. It was good and dark out there.

"I reckon," she smiled, knowing what I had in mind.

We stepped off the porch, held hands and walked around the corner of the house from the front porch. We didn't talk, just held hands and stopped and look at each other. My heart was pounding so loud I was surprised Polly couldn't hear it. I finally couldn't stand it and I kissed her. It wasn't just a lips pressed together kiss this time. I had never kissed a girl with our lips parted before. I had only heard about *French kissing*. I'm telling you, I felt hot and cold at the same time.

"Charles," she said real low, her hazel eyes sparkling from the moons reflection.

"What?" I asked and kissed her again before she could say anything else.

Puppy love, teenage crush, and call it whatever you want to, but it felt wonderful and being with a girl couldn't get any better than this. Boy was I in for a nice surprise. I would take my guitar with me sometimes and sing for Polly. Her favorite song for me to sing to her was *Secret Love*.

It wasn't too long before Polly's daddy let me take her out on a real date, go somewhere other than her front porch. I had to have her home by 10 o'clock though. Daddy had traded his pickup for a 1950 Ford car. It smelled like dogs half the time because he would haul some of his foxhounds in it. That was the only car we had so is what we dated in. That car became known to my friends as the *dog wagon*. I was the only one with a driver's license of the boys I hung out with, and the only one whose daddy would let drive his car at least one night a week. So, it was either the *dog wagon* or walk. Brush off the dog hairs and jump in boys.

Every day in school, when the bell would ring and we all changed classes, I would look for Polly in the crowded hall. We would spot each other and sometimes take just a moment to touch hands or do something to acknowledge each other. She was my sweetheart, we were going steady and I wanted everybody to know it.

We went to the Laurens County Fair together that year. There is just something really special about going to the County Fair with your sweetheart. We rode most of the rides, some of them twice, like The Rocket. The Ferris Wheel stopped with us right at the top. Doesn't it always. I hated that, way up there swaying in that little seat. Polly was

Old Memories and Me

laughing and waving to people below. I was sitting there stiff, holding on tight to that little bar and thinking, *get me down from here*. Why are the girls always braver than the boys on fair rides? They scream and yell but then say, "Let's ride that one again."

I must have spent half of my money trying to knock over three of those stuffed cats trying to win her a teddy bear. I finally won her one and she hugged it like it was something precious to her. That really felt good, winning her that little bear.

We got some cotton candy and got all sticky, giggling and peck-kissing with candy lips. Part of the time we were with Pete Estes and Anne Barnes. They were going steady too. Sometimes they would get on one ride and Polly and I another.

"Let's ride through the tunnel of love again," Polly said and tugged me in that direction.

"Again?" I laughed, actually looking forward to it because it was dark in there and you could snuggle up and kiss. Polly and I had a picture made together that day at the fair, a couple of teenagers on top of the world. When we looked at the picture we thought we looked like James Dean and Elizabeth Taylor.

Some people around Watts Mill still didn't have a telephone back then. We did though, and so did Polly. I used to call her every day. We couldn't talk long because we were on party lines. Most lines had to be shared with other people. Man that caused a lot of arguments and ill tempers to flare up.

"I was on here first!" one party would snap.

"No you wasn't, I was!" the other party would shout back.

Since I was a junior in school, Polly and I got to go to the Junior-Senior Prom. The prom was held in the school gym that was decorated with balloons and streamers. There were tables set up with white tablecloths for dinner and a stereo for playing music for dancing. We slow danced and did the Shag. We also did the Bunny Hop. I had on a rented tux, white coat and black pants with a black bow tie. Bow ties wouldn't stay straight on your neck back then either.

"I love this song," Polly sighed as we slow danced to *Sincerely*, sung by the Moonglows.

"Me too," I told her and held her close as we barely moved to the music.

We were crushing the corsage I had given her earlier between us. She was so pretty, especially on that night.

Carol Hardin was dating his sweetheart, Jackie Burgess that night. Pete and Anne were sophomores and couldn't attend the prom. I missed them. We were all really close. There probably weren't more than 100 to 125 people there because both the junior and senior classes were small at Ford High. If not for dates and faculty members there would have been only half that many.

We did the shag to *Work With Me Annie* by The Midnighters. We'd sing along with the chorus while we danced.
 For part of the song I would stop doing the shag and do my own thing, like jump up in the air a bit, and come down on one knee, then stand back up and twirl around, all the time swinging my arms and snapping my fingers to the beat. Polly didn't mind and laughed as she punched me playfully in my stomach. I doubled over and pretended it hurt for a few seconds, and then went back to doing the shag with her, grinning at my girl.
 It was a special night and I felt special being with Polly. If this wasn't love then somebody needed to tell my thumping heart before it exploded. I held her even closer when we danced to *Pledging My Love*. Johnny Ace sang that song and it was one of my favorites. For years I would sing that song, even when I finished school and worked clubs, on into the sixties and seventies. It was just a special song for me.
 After the festivities at the gym, everybody left to go somewhere with their dates. That meant either going up to Curry's Lake, or going to the Ranch Drive In Restaurant and parking to neck in the car. Polly and I went to the Ranch. They had speakers outside so you could hear the jukebox playing from inside and they had carhops. Somehow I had gotten a small bottle of gin. It was my first time to consume alcohol. Polly's too. We were into a little bolder kissing by then but I was still too much of a gentleman to try and go any further. You just didn't treat a girl like that. You kissed her with a certain amount of passion but never let your hands drop past her shoulders. Not on purpose anyway. Sometimes you would *accidentally* touch a girl's breast. Then it would happen again, *accidentally* of course. Maybe a few times you would cheat and break the rules and touch her knee. But you treated her with respect, even when you broke the rules. I know that doesn't make sense, but think about it, it's not supposed to.
 The Ranch had the best cheeseburgers around. We got a cheeseburger each and shared an order of French fries.
 Of course we got a little tipsy that night from our first daring attempt at drinking. I don't know how it happened, but the gearshift in Daddy's car got stuck in low gear somehow. Polly and I giggled all the way to my sister Ruby's house, the car stuck in that low gear and us having to stop every fifty yards or so and start off again. My brother-in-law Bob Armstrong got the gearshift working and we were on our way again. We didn't drink any more whiskey that night. I threw the half empty bottle into some brush alongside the road.
 Since it was prom night I didn't have to have Polly home until 11 pm. Polly was spending the night at her sister Dot's house so if we were a little late it was alright. Dot wouldn't tell Polly's daddy.
 With the gear shift acting up we were afraid to drive all the way up to Curry's Lake, so we went back over to the Ranch and necked some more in the car. We would talk a while and kiss a while.

Old Memories and Me

"Do you really want to be a singer, Charles?" Polly asked me, looking out at the full moon hanging far above us.

"Yeah, I really do," I assured her. "I want to get a band when I finish school next year, you know play clubs around Greenville, and Spartanburg, and maybe go to Nashville, Tennessee one day."

"You gonna take me with you," she smiled and looked at me with those hazel eyes.

"That would be cool," I smiled back and touched the tip of her nose with my finger. "Would you go with me?"

She sighed, "My daddy would kill me."

"Well, we could take him with us," I said.

We both laughed.

I just looked at her silently for a few minutes, thinking about how pretty she was and about how glad I was she was my girl. I put my arm around her and pulled her closer and she laid her head on my shoulder as we listened to the jukebox playing *Honey Love* by Clyde McPhatter and the Drifters through the speakers just outside the car.

I played on the Ford High boy's basketball team and Polly played on the girl's team. On all of the away games we rode the same school bus together but the coaches made the girls sit on one side of the bus and the boys on the other. I played both football and basketball but basketball was my real love between the two. I was already 6 feet tall my junior year and could jump pretty well. Back then the basketballs didn't have any grip on them and my hands aren't real big, so I couldn't palm the ball. I could jump high enough to get the ball to the rim but because I couldn't palm it I would lose it when I turned it over to try and dunk it. I nearly broke my neck trying to dunk the ball in practice. It was illegal to dunk in high school back then so even if I had succeeded it wouldn't have been allowed in games. It was kind of a waste of time to keep trying, but I kept trying. I don't like not succeeding, even when I was that young.

Bobby Brewington, a senior, was a little over 6 feet tall and he played center. That allowed me to play forward, which I preferred because I thought I played better facing the basket. Gene Madden was our best outside shooter and I was our best rebounder and inside scorer. We called Gene Madden *Polio* because he broke curfew a few years earlier when there was a polio epidemic and he got caught at the Watts Mill baseball park after curfew hours.

Henry *Dusty* Oates was our coach in both football and basketball. Ford High was his first coaching job after graduating from Erskine College. Of course we called him Coach Oates. He was a good-looking man, built solid and strong, and all the girls at school had a crush on him. Betty Blakely was the girl's basketball coach for many years at Ford.

Polio Madden and I didn't hang out much together, except for sitting on *the rail* at times, but we teamed up really well in sports. He was the starting quarterback on our football team our junior and senior years and I was the starting left end. Polio had an amazing arm for his size, which was about 5 feet 9 inches and 130 pounds. I was never much good at judging distance but I imagine he could throw the football somewhere between fifty and sixty yards with a pretty good zip on it. I had a lot of speed and good hands, so I was his primary target on most passing plays. At 6 feet and around 140 pounds, I could run like the wind. I wasn't the only one on our team that could run fast though. Carol Hardin was probably a step faster than me. Carol started at one of the halfback positions. Polio was pretty fast and so was Pete Estes. We had speed but we didn't have much size. Edwin Baldwin weighed perhaps 180 pounds and he was our biggest lineman. We called him *Hoochie* because he got caught slipping into a Hoochie Coochie show at the county fair. If you don't know what a Hoochie Coochie show is, I'm not going to be the one to tell you and make you blush.

    Nobody on our football team could kick field goals nor extra points. Therefore, we had to either pass or run the ball after a touchdown. Polio would usually call the play that sent me about three steps over the line of scrimmage, and then cut sharply to my right, and he would sort of toss the football up over the middle and let me go up in a crowd of defenders and get it. It worked most of the time because I could jump well and my height helped, plus Polio was very good at putting the ball right where I needed it to be. If we didn't run that play after a touchdown, we would run the option, where Polio would sweep around the end and either toss the ball to Carol Hardin or keep it himself. They both had excellent speed and that play worked a lot as well.

    One of the most jubilant feelings I ever got in football was when Polio would hit me on a long pass downfield. As I said, he had a great arm, and I had speed, so he would pump fake a couple of times in the opposite direction, then turn and throw the football long to me, allowing me to catch it in full stride. When that happened, nobody ever caught me. It wasn't unusual for that play to work for 60-70 yards a lot of times. It was a great feeling for both of us when that happened. I was number 49 in football and number 7 in basketball.

    Polly Powers was the first girl to win my heart and she was also the first girl to break it. She broke up with me in that summer of 1954 between my junior and senior year in school. I will never forget that painful feeling. There was no real reason for breaking up, except she said her daddy didn't want her getting serious with anybody and he felt we were getting too serious. I don't remember for sure now, but knowing me, I probably got my guitar out and sang *I'm So Lonesome I Could Cry*. That's the way people who like country music are. If you are sad, you want to hear a sad song.

    Polly and I remained friends but for a long while it was painful every time I would see her, especially if she was with another boy. I still

Old Memories and Me

would look for her in the hallway when we changed classes. As they say, old habits are hard to break.

Dot had married Bobby Vaughn and Bill had married Ruby Gillespie. Now we had two Rubys in our family. Bill was a pharmacist at Eureka Drugstore at Watts Mill right after he finished college. Later he worked at Poe Drugstore on the Square in Laurens. That summer, in 1954, he took a job with Eli Lilly as a pharmaceutical salesman and moved to Knoxville, Tennessee.

After Dot had married, Mama and Daddy decided to turn the front living room into their bedroom. We never used the living room and it would open up another bedroom for when one of my sisters or Bill needed to sleep over. I had taken the bedroom Daddy had been using, the first one down the hall from the kitchen, and near the bathroom. Yes, I stopped sleeping with my mama just before I turned 12, but not before Dot decided to join us unexpectedly one night.

We had mice in the house, especially in the wintertime, and one night one of those little boogers got in bed with Dot. She screamed and came running from her room and leaped over the footboard of Mama's bed. As soon as she hit the mattress the bed collapsed with the three of us. I awoke with a startled yelp, thinking the house had fallen in. After I found out what had happened I didn't blame Dot. I was scared of those little mice just as much as I was of the big field rats. Daddy got up and put a couple footstools under the bottom part of the bed where the slat had broken. Mama and Dot slept the rest of the night with their feet slightly down hill. I got in bed with Daddy but hardly slept from fear of a rat getting on our bed.

I continued to try and advance myself on guitar and improving my singing. I worked part time at the grocery store that was once the company store and was able to buy a little better guitar. It was an unknown brand but the strings weren't quite as high on the neck as the Silvertone, so fretting wasn't as hard on my fingers. I also bought a harmonica and one of those holders that put it right in front of your mouth. You could play guitar and harmonica at the same time that way. I use to play and sing *Hey Baby* all the time. I loved that song, mostly for the harmonica part. I never learned to play the harp very well though. I don't know why we called a harmonica a harp but a lot of people called it that back then. "Boy, you sure can blow that harp!"

"When you gonna take your guitar and go to Nashville, Charles?" Pete Estes asked me with a slight grin.

Most everybody really liked that new kind of music called *rock 'n roll*, including me, but I was still hooked on country music as my first love, and Pete knew that.

We were sitting on the rail across from the cotton mill. The rail was a long iron bar that ran atop a cement wall in front of the Watts Mill Community Building. It was right across the road from the cotton mill. Generations of boys and young men had sat on that rail, including my brother, Bill. We must have looked like a bunch of long legged chickens perched on a roost. No girls ever sat up on the rail, it wasn't proper, so just the guys sat there watching the girls walk past and the cars go by on highway 221, wondering if they were going to Spartanburg to the north, or Greenwood to the south. That's about as far as I had been in either direction back then, except for that trip to Miami to see Bill when I was in the second grade.

I sang a line of Webb Pierce's hit *There Stands The Glass*. I sang it in my best nasal sound.

"Don't that sound just like Webb Pierce?" I grinned at Pete. And it did too.

"I been telling you, you ought to go to Nashville, Tennessee and be on the Grand Ole Opry," Pete laughed, not *at* me but with me. Not only was he one of my best friends, he supported me and my desire to play country music.

"Who's Webb Pierce?" some smart Alec asked.

I didn't even answer him. You had to be stupid not to know who Webb Pierce was, as far as I was concerned anyway.

"Come on, Pete," I said. "Let's go shoot some pinball."

"You got any money?" He asked.

"I got sixteen cents," I told him.

"I got a nickel," he said.

We slid off the rail and walked the short distance to Wattsville Cafe. There was a pinball machine where you could put nickels in to try and win games and cash them in for money. It was illegal to gamble in South Carolina but Jimmy Hellams would payoff to people he knew, if nobody was looking. Jimmy owned the cafe and everybody liked him, especially the teenagers. If you wanted something and didn't have quite enough money, he would usually let you have it anyway. It was the same way with Yancey Gossett up the street at Gossett's Cafe. Back then a hotdog and cola cost a nickel each. That was my favorite cafe food, a hotdog, with mustard and chili, and an Orange Crush.

I loved playing a pinball machine. Three balls lined up in a row was good, four lined up was better, and five balls lined up paid twenty dollars. Twenty bucks was a lot of money back in the fifties. Still is to a lot of people. I lost fifteen cents and Pete lost his nickel. We had a penny left between us. I put that in the peanut machine and split them with Pete. We went home. I walked with Pete to his house on Copeland Street then I cut across the mill company pasture to my house over on Setzler Road.

Mama and Daddy were still at work at the cotton mill when I got home. They both still worked the first shift, from 8 am until 4 pm. I usually made my favorite snack, a peanut butter, mayonnaise

Old Memories and Me

and banana sandwich. You put a peeled banana on a saucer, spooned mayonnaise and peanut butter on it and used a fork to mash it all together, then spread it on two pieces of loaf bread. Loaf bread is sandwich bread, in case you didn't grow up in the south. This was called a Craig sandwich by my family. It was a tradition for years.

There was a railroad track less than a mile from our house and when I was a kid I used to like to stand and watch the freight train as it slowed to go around Horse Shoe Bend, waving to the engineer as it passed. Sometimes there would be a hobo or two sitting in the doorway of an empty boxcar and I would wave at them too.

I used to love to lie awake in bed late and listen to the train blow its whistle as it passed through the night. It was a lonesome sound but it also had peacefulness about it. There has never been another sound quite like a freight train blowing its whistle, especially in the stillness of a dark night. It made me imagine faraway places I had never been, or if I was away somewhere it made me think of home. Those old coal-burning locomotives are long gone now but they are memories in my mind that won't ever fade, another piece of history that won't pass this way again.

There were a lot of good memories to be made back then in Watts Mill, South Carolina. Some of my fondest years there were during the 1950's, when I was a teenager, and life was so good that I hardly noticed any bad times.

I wore a flat top that summer in 1954 and had to use wax to train my hair to lay down again. Man, that stuff was messy. It would get stiff from the cold in the wintertime and become a greasy drip from the heat in the summertime.

Black R&B singers were very popular, especially with teenagers. We still had segregation back then but music never seemed to have a color boundary. Music has always been universal. I loved the Moonglows and the Platters. They did mostly love songs. I have always been partial to love songs and ballads. But I could cut a rug, as some people called it, turn loose and really get down. I could rock 'n roll. I had some pretty cool moves, almost like I had no bones in my legs. I made up my own steps and style. I probably looked silly with everybody else around me dancing the Shag but I didn't care. I just did my own thing. I have always had a lot of showman in me.

Curry's Lake was a popular place for teenagers to hang out and dance. Bruce Cook, Monk Roberts and I used to go up there a lot together to meet girls. Curry's Lake was in Gray Court, just a few miles from Laurens and teenagers would come from all around to hang out there. There was a swimming pool, a building with a jukebox to dance, and a baseball batting cage.

Bruce Cook and Monk Roberts were my other best friends, besides Pete Estes and Carol Hardin. Pete and Carol weren't into dancing like Bruce, Monk and I were. Besides, Pete was still going steady with Anne Barnes and didn't mess with other girls. Monk's real name was Wayne. I am not sure where he got the nickname Monk but that is what everybody called him, except for the schoolteachers. They called him Wayne.

When we didn't have on jeans we were wearing pegged pants. That's where you have the bottom of your pants leg taken up so small it was very difficult to get them on and off, but they looked cool. We wore our hair in a ducks tail, blocked off in the back and combed back on the sides to form a ducks tail in the back where the long sides nearly touched. A lot of boys wore sideburns. I did too, even when I had a crew cut.

One night at Curry's Lake I met this older girl I had never seen there, or anywhere else before. She was very pretty, with shoulder length dark hair and dark eyes. She had on a dress that gathered at her narrow waist, then flared out over her hips to show off her great figure. I had never seen a female built like that, nor as pretty. I had watched her dance with a few other guys and wishing I could dance with her but I didn't have the nerve to ask her.

"Man, she is one good looking girl," I told Bruce and Monk.

"She's looking over here," Monk said.

"She's looking at me," Bruce laughed.

All three of us were gawking at her, but so was just about every guy there.

"She-it," Monk said, drawing out the word like it was two syllables. "She's coming over here."

She didn't walk, she glided over to the side of the dance floor where we were leaning against the wall, using every sway she had in her hips.

"Hello," she said and all three us just stared at her, caught up in her beauty.

"Cat got your tongue," she laughed.

She was looking straight at me.

"Nah," I said, trying to sound cool but knowing it really came out sounding like an idiot.

"What's your name," she asked and brushed back a strand of dark hair from her forehead.

"Bruce," Bruce said.

"Monk," Monk snickered.

"And you?"

"Charles," I said and managed to smile to try and hide how nervous I was.

"You want to dance, Charles?" she asked and I thought I was going to swallow my Adams apple. Before I could even answer, she took me by the hand and lead me out onto the dance floor. *Sixteen Candles* was playing on the jukebox. Man, that's how old I was and all 16 of my candles were burning right then, on fire inside my stomach.

"I fast dance better than I slow dance," I told her, already making excuses because I knew I was going to make a fool of myself

Old Memories and Me

holding this beauty in my arms dancing to that slow song. She put her right arm around my waist and pulled me close to her. I guess my male instincts just naturally took over and I put my right arm around her waist and we started moving slowly to the music.

"Where are you from, Charles?" She talked as smooth as my English teacher.

"Watts Mill," I managed to mutter. We were really up close to each other now.

"Where is that?"

She now had both of her arms around my waist, her hands locked together behind me. I followed suit and held her the same way. Our noses were almost touching. Man, she smelled good, like sweet violets.

"It's right outside Laurens," I told her and was surprised that I was beginning to relax a little.

"I know where that is," she smiled. "Never been there though."

"It's built in a square," I said, as though that was of some importance.

We were moving real good together, our bodies were touching from our knees up to our chest. Lord, did she ever have a chest.

"What's your name?" I asked her.

"Julie," she told me and laid her head on my shoulder and I got nervous again.

Oh man, that was a nice feeling though, holding her like that. At 16 years old I was naturally curious about girls and sex, wanting to learn and experience all I could, yet at the same time I was afraid to really try and learn, especially the sex part. I was scared to death of that.

When the song ended she stepped back from me, took my hand in hers and said as much with her smile as she did with her voice, "Let's go outside and get some fresh air."

Oh my goodness. What she is going to do once we get outside, I wondered. Even more frightful, what was *I* going to do. *If she kisses me I will just die. I'll have a heart attack at sixteen years old.*

"Ok," I said. Not that I had a choice. She had complete control of me.

I glanced over at Bruce and Monk as we walked toward the entrance to the dance hall. Both of them were grinning at me, like two mules eating briars.

Once we got outside Julie led me to the parking lot. She stopped beside a car and leaned against it, brushing back that dark hair from her lovely face again.

"How old are you, Charles," she asked.

"Nineteen," I lied.

She laughed. "You're not nineteen."

"How old are you?" I asked her.

"Twenty," she told me.

"You look twenty three," I said like a dumb ox. I suppose I said twenty-three because she looked grown up, like a young woman.

She laughed again, and then toyed with one of the buttons on the front of my shirt.

"If you were a little older I could really go for you," she told me. "You're cute."

I didn't know what to say to that, so I just smiled. No, I think I grinned. There's a difference you know. When you are happy you smile. When you are overwhelmed and speechless, you grin.

"Well," she sighed. "It won't hurt anything if we talk, will it?"

"No," I agreed and tried to control my excitement. "Not at all. I like talking to you."

"How tall are you?" she asked me.

"Six feet, I think."

"That's tall," Julie said. "I'll bet you play basketball."

I nodded. "I do, yes."

Julie stopped playing with the button on my shirt and reached up and draped her hand around my neck. She pulled my face down close to hers. I didn't try to resist. I couldn't anyway. I closed my eyes, waiting in nervous anticipation. I felt her soft lips barely touch mine, then withdraw. It wasn't what I had expected but it was nice.

"You kiss good," I told her, taking a deep breath, and daring to place my hands on each of her shoulders. I could get completely lost looking into those sensuous eyes of hers.

She laughed. "It was just a little peck."

Well, it had pecked all the way to the butterflies fluttering in my stomach. I wanted her to really kiss me, even though I wouldn't know quite how to handle it. I was like, cold from fear and hot with a kind of passion I had only imagined before.

"I shouldn't be kissing you at all," Julie told me. "You do look a little older than sixteen though."

In the movies, when a girl is going to kiss a guy, she looks at his lips. Julie was looking at my lips, then her pretty face came forward slightly. I shivered with anticipation again.

"Hey, Hightower, whatcha doing?" Hightower was a nickname Bruce and Monk gave me. It had something to do with me being kind of tall and playing basketball.

"What is it, Bruce?" I sighed. Monk was with him as they approached Julie and I.

"It's nine thirty," Bruce informed me. "I have to be home by ten."

I loved Bruce Cook like a brother but right then I wanted to stomp on his feet.

Well, that night I had almost learned what it was like to kiss a real woman. I never saw or heard from Julie again.

My senior year at Ford High School went by rather uneventful.

Old Memories and Me

I played football and basketball again. I was now 6 feet and two inches tall but still only weighed around 140 pounds. I dated a couple of different girls from school and I sponsored Barbara O'Bryant in the Homecoming Queen contest. Guess who was Homecoming Queen that year. Polly Powers.

There were two 10th grade girls that sat behind me in Mr. Brownlee's Algebra class that had a crush on me. They both would wait until Mr. Brownlee had his back to the class as he wrote an equation on the blackboard and they would use their pencils and run the eraser up and down the back of my neck. I have always loved for a girl to rub the back of my neck.

"What are you two girls doing to Charles?"

Oh Lord. Mr. Brownlee had unexpectedly turned around and caught them in the act of rubbing the back of my neck. He made us come to the front of the class and let the entire Algebra class watch as they had to repeat that maneuver on the back of my neck. Naturally, everybody laughed and the three of us were really embarrassed.

I was still set on becoming a singer after graduating from school. All I really cared about was sports and music and girls of course. My senior homeroom teacher, Miss Stevenson, told me if I kept on the course I was on, I wasn't going to amount to anything. She was probably right too. I barely made passing grades because I didn't study at night. I practiced on my guitar and learned new songs to sing. I was even beginning to write a few songs-- not very good ones though.

By then I had my own car, a 1951 Ford. I was still working part time at the former mill company grocery store, which was now owned by Mr. Ballentine and Mr. Pigg. I bought Mama and Daddy a new television with the money I made working there.

At the end of the school year I had failed Geography. It was rather surprising because Geography was my favorite subject. I didn't have many favorite subjects in school. I was suppose to go to a summer class for six weeks before I could receive my diploma but the teacher that taught the course called Mr. Elmore at Ford High after three weeks and told him she thought he should go ahead and give me my high school diploma because I had made a hundred on every test she had given me. Mr. Elmore complied and I went to Ford High for the last time and got my diploma. When I left the school grounds that day I felt a little sad, knowing I was through at the school I had gone from 1st grade through 12th and now it was over. No more walking those halls with so many friends I cared so much about, no more basketball and football, and no more being a schoolboy. I was now a young man going off on my own. Now, my real journey in life would really begin.

I wasn't afraid of the future though, just a little scared of having to leave the past behind me that all of a sudden felt like leaving home.

CHAPTER THREE

In 1956, along came Elvis Presley. He started the long sideburns craze and rock 'n roll started a new trend of attire. Boys started wearing their collars turned up and girls really got into bobby socks and jeans. *Billy Haley and The Comets* had a huge hit with one of the first rock n roll classics called *Rock Around The Clock*. Then, another huge hit came out on the radio and rock n roll was really on its way. It was *Blue Suede Shoes*.

Carl Perkins had written and recorded *Blue Suede Shoes*, having a hit himself with the song, then Elvis recorded it and had an even bigger hit with it. Everybody was rockin' and rollin' to Elvis, Bill Haley, Carl Perkins, Gene Vincent, Chuck Berry and a host of other new artist that were taking over radio airwaves by leaps and bounds. As much as I loved country music, I was into the rocking beat as well. I had learned to play and sing *Blue Suede Shoes* and *Honey Don't*. I became a huge Carl Perkins fan as soon as I heard him the first time.

It was about this time that I met Wister Todd. Wister would become my mentor for the next few years, teaching me to play electric bass and a lot about music in general. Wister worked the third shift at Watts Mill, from midnight till 8 am, the graveyard shift as it is sometimes referred to. He lived on Woodrow Street in Laurens in a small house with his mother. Wister had a piano, a set of drums, a really classic electric Gibson guitar, an electric bass, an upright acoustic bass, and a saxophone. He could play them all.

Clyde Pennington had introduced me to Wister. Clyde played drums, guitar and sang.I also got to know Johnny Meeks about this time. Johnny lived in Laurens, as did Clyde, but Johnny had attended Ford High School for a little while. Clyde and Johnny were about my age and Wister was probably 12 years old than we were and had played professionally in California for a few years, I think back in the late forties. His musical background was mostly pop and classical music. Mine, Clyde's and Johnny's were country and rock n roll, as of late. Of course we hadn't played professionally before like Wister had.

"You boys are gonna kill me," Wister would say, standing in his doorway, in his shorts and t-shirt, wiping sleep from his eyes.

Johnny, Clyde and I would wake him up about 10 or 11 o'clock

Old Memories and Me

in the morning, right after he would get into bed for sleep after working all night in the mill as a loom fixer.

"Let's jam and pick a ditty or two, Wister," Meeks would grin. Wister would always let us in and we would play music for a couple of hours. Wister would play piano, Johnny electric guitar, Clyde drums and me on electric bass, mostly learning as I went. Before Wister's mother passed away, we must have driven her crazy with all that loud music in that little 3 room house.

Johnny played a fender electric and had gotten really good. Eventually he went out to California to try and get with a rock n roll band or land a gig in the Hollywood area. Clyde and I stayed around home, jamming with Wister. After a while Clyde was getting really good on drums, as I was on bass.

Most of the guys I had graduated from school with, especially the ones I hung out with, including Carol Hardin, had gone into the Air Force right after graduation to avoid being drafted into the Army. Since I was still 17 when they all joined, Daddy had to sign for me but he didn't feel right about it. He said he was afraid I wouldn't like it, or if something happened to me he would feel it was his fault. He wanted me to wait until I was 18 and could sign for myself.

Besides making music with Clyde, Johnny and Wister, I was still hanging around with Bruce Cook and Monk Roberts. They were seniors at Ford High School now. We still went up to Curry's Lake and sat on the rail a lot, along with Pete Estes, who was also a senior in school now. I turned 18 in September, 1956 and joined the Army National Guard because I didn't want to get drafted, nor did I want to join the Navy or Air Force by myself.

Sundays were always special at Mama and Daddy's house. Mama cooked a big dinner and our whole family would be there to spend the day with Mama and Daddy.

My mama made everything from scratch, no cans or boxes. She always fixed a lot of different dishes, homemade biscuits and cornbread, and banana pudding. She would set all the food around on the counter tops, like a buffet. We would all help our plates and find a seat at either the kitchen table, in the booth, or go into the den. Folks didn't eat out much back then.

On most of those Sundays my two sisters, my brother and I would sing as a quartet. Mama played the piano and that was really something because she couldn't read music, and even more amazing, she had no idea what key she would be playing in. If she could hum it she usually could play it on the piano.

We would switch the lead and harmony around between us, depending on which song we were singing. Mostly I would sing either the high tenor part or the low bass. Big difference in range but I could do it. So could my brother, Bill.

I used to try and get them to lets record and make a record, but

Dot was too shy, Ruby giggled too much and Bill was too busy being a pharmaceutical salesman, now in Charlotte, North Carolina. He and his wife, Ruby, and their children, would drive down early on Sundays. Ruby and Bob Armstrong, and their children, would drive over from Honea Path, South Carolina where Bob was the high school principle. Dot and Bobby Vaughn lived in Laurens, with their children. I was still living at home.

"Don't you think we sound good enough to make a record, Daddy?" I asked him. He loved to listen to us sing.

"Why foot yeah," he grinned. He always said that, *aw foot*, or *foot yeah*. I never knew exactly why he said that but he said it a lot.

"You wanna go fishing, Daddy?"

"Foot yeah."

In February of 1957 I got my first professional job in music when I went on the road with a band that traveled throughout South Carolina and Georgia. I had met the guy that managed and booked the band at radio station WLBG in Laurens one day.

"Can you play a doghouse bass, son?" he asked me.

A doghouse bass was an old term for describing an upright acoustic bass.

"Yes sir," I lied. I had never touched an upright bass in my life. I had only played an electric bass but I knew Wister Todd had an upright bass so I figured I could learn real quick.

"Can you sing too?"

"Yes sir." I didn't lie that time.

The man hired me on the spot to play bass and do some of the singing. We left for a weekend in Georgia two days later so I didn't have time to learn to play an upright bass. Wister Todd did let me borrow his to take on the gig. We laid it across the top of the seats inside a station wagon and took off to Georgia.

The band included a lead guitar, steel, piano, drums and me on bass. There was another singer in the band that was the feature and he played acoustic guitar when we brought him out to perform. I did the singing when he wasn't on stage. He was billed as a Hank Williams sound alike. He did sound quite a bit like Hank Williams but nobody is as good as Hank was.

As far as my upright bass playing, I just got on one string and ran up and down the neck on the fast songs. I faked the heck out of it most of the time but on some of the ballads I was able to figure out where most of the chords were on that fretless thing, well close most of the time anyway.

The first show we did that Friday night was in Waynesboro, Georgia, at a schoolhouse out in the country. People seem to come out of the woodworks to see our show. I guess they were hungry for

Old Memories and Me

entertainment. I opened the show singing a Carl Smith song, *Are You Teasing Me.*

I was nervous as an alley cat amongst a bunch of stray dogs. I thought I was in the big time though. When I finished that first song I got a good response and I thanked the audience.

"Thank y'all very much," I said and kind of got carried away. "I'm Charles Craig from up in Watts Mill, South Carolina. I appreciate y'all being so nice." I was grinning from ear to ear.

Our manager got my attention by waving his arms from the side of the stage and then making a rolling motion with his hands to tell me to get on with it. I went into my next song, disappointed that I didn't get to say more. I knew right then though that I was going to like getting up in front of a crowd and performing.

My singing was fine but naturally my doghouse bass playing wasn't really all that good. Somehow I got through that first show without making too big of a fool out of myself. The next morning we moved on to Statesboro for a Saturday night show. This one was at the local movie theater. Georgia Southern College is in that town and there were a lot of girls in the audience. I sang a lot of rock n roll songs that night because I figured they would like that better than country music. I had talked to a few of those college girls before the show and really wanted to do well in front of them. I had told them I was Carl Perkin's cousin to really impress them. I don't know what made me do that but it worked though. I was doing real well until right in the middle of *Honey Don't* the wooden bridge that holds the four strings up on the bass broke. I guess I was slapping the strings too hard, getting into it for some of Georgia Southern's finest. When the bridge broke it made a loud pop and nearly scared heck out of me. The audience must have thought it was planned and part of the show because they laughed and applauded. We had to finish the show without a bass though. I switched over to rhythm guitar.

I didn't know what in the world I was going to say to Wister Todd about breaking his upright bass. However, after the show I wasn't thinking about that too much. There was a blue-eyed brunette that thought I did very well, especially since I was Carl Perkin's cousin.

"You're really good," she assured me.

"Thank you very much," I beamed. I wondered if she wanted my autograph. I had never signed an autograph before.

"Do you make records?" she asked and I could tell she was intrigued with the fact I was an entertainer.

"Not yet," I told her, but quickly added, "but I plan on going to Nashville soon and make a record."

"Wow," she cooed.

I smiled at her and wondered if I looked like an entertainer. I don't know why I wondered that. I guess because I wanted to be one so badly.

"Are you staying the night here in Statesboro," she asked.

"Well, our manager said something about going back home tonight," I informed her and was wishing we were staying over the night here now that I had met her.

"Awww," she pouted. "I wish you didn't have to go back tonight."

"Me too," I told her.

It was kind of cold, even way down there in southern Georgia. We both put on jackets and walked outside the theatre to the parking area, away from the streetlights. She slipped her arm around my waist, so I put mine around hers. I turned her so that she was facing me. She was my age, 18, and I could tell her heart was racing like mine.

I kept thinking maybe I should kiss her but I had just met her and I was afraid that would be too bold and forward and she might slap the heck out of me.

"So, you're Carl Perkins's cousin?" she asked, her blue eyes beaming.

"Yeah, but I don't get to see him much though," I replied. I was wishing I hadn't lied about that because I was afraid she was going to ask me something about Carl Perkins I couldn't answer.

"I bet you meet a lot of girls traveling around playing and singing, don't you?" she asked and I could see a little vapor coming from her mouth in the chilly night air. I didn't want her to know this was only the second show I had ever played before.

"Yeah," I lied again. "But not many as pretty as you." At least that part was the truth.

"Oh, you're just saying that," she smiled and poked me playfully in my chest. She started glancing at my lips and I was starting to think it was now expected of me to kiss her.

"No I'm not," I laughed and lowered my face to give her a little kiss.

"Whoa," she laughed and turn her head away, "You move fast."

Now I was embarrassed. "I'm sorry. I thought you wanted me to do that."

"Well, I do," she informed me with a cute little pout. "But let me get to know you a few minutes first."

"How many minutes?" I laughed and jokingly looked at my watch, as though I were timing her.

"Umm," she cooed again, then smiled. "I guess it's been long enough for just a little one."

I gave her a little one. We kissed gently, pressing our lips together, then away, then back again. Then, she gave me a big one. She must have been chewing spearmint gum because her deep kiss tastes like spearmint. She withdrew her lips from mine a little and looked straight into my eyes. She giggled and I did too. Then, we kissed again,

Old Memories and Me

a long wet one.

Now, I don't mean to sound dirty or anything, but this girl was now in complete control of my sensitive emotions that Webster might describe as being horny.

"Hey, Charles," somebody called out.

Darn it. I jerked my lips from hers as though I had been caught stealing something. I turned and saw it was one of the guys in the band.

"What cha doing man?" he asked like some moron.

"Uh, nothing, just talking to, uh, what did you say your name was?" I asked her.

"Susan," she told me, frowning a little. "I thought I told you."

"You probably did," I said and smiled apologetically.

"We need to pack up man," the guy told me. "They are going to cut the lights and lock up the place in a few minutes."

"Ok," I said. "I'll be right there." I turned back to Susan. "I'm sorry, I have to go." I sure didn't want to though.

"Well, I wish you didn't have to," she smiled almost pitifully. "After you pack your things can you go get something to eat?"

"I guess we will stop somewhere and eat," I told her. "I don't know where though."

"I suppose I won't see you again," she sighed. "I sure do wish you could stay a while longer."

"Yeah, well, that would be nice," I assured her. "But I can't."

I had only known this girl for just the short time since we had finished the show, but she was easy to get to know, and it was easy to like those eyes and that smile, not to mention those kisses, and that spearmint taste was suddenly my favorite flavor. I walked her back to where two of her girlfriends were waiting by their car. She introduced me but I don't recall their names. She gave me a sweet little quick kiss, more like a peck.

"See ya," Susan told me, squeezed my hand, then turned it lose reluctantly.

"It was nice meeting you," I told her. "And you too," I said to her two friends, giving them a little wave.

I looked at Susan one last time and then walked away. Man, I was going to think about this little brunette all the way back to Watts Mill, and then some. Of course it wasn't love but I develop feelings for people easily, especially pretty girls. I suppose feelings were not the right word with Susan, maybe emotions.

After I returned home I switched over to electric bass but only stayed with that band for another two weekends. It was hard to get the manager to pay us what he had promised. On the last gig I played he took off and didn't pay us at all. I stayed home in Watts Mill and went to work at Mr. Pigg's Red and White Supermarket, in the meat department. My short stint as a professional musician and singer was over before it got started good.

I would listen to the Grand Ole Opry a lot on Saturday night, lying in the floor in front of our large radio that was the size of a small jukebox. Some of the stars back then were Roy Acuff, Bill Monroe, Carl Smith, Webb Pierce, Minnie Pearl and Marty Robbins. During the week I would tune the radio to WLAC in Nashville and listen to disc jockey's Gene Noble, Hoss Allen and Big John R play rhythm and blues and rock 'n roll. Some of my favorites were Chuck Berry, Fats Domino, Clyde McPhatter, The Moonglows, The Drifters, LaVern Baker, and of course Elvis and Carl Perkins. There was no era that had the music we had back in the fifties. As far as I am concerned it was the best era to grow up in, not for just the music, but also the clothes we wore, the hairstyles, and the culture.

I still spent a lot of time sitting on the rail across from the mill, even in the winter months. So did my friends, Bruce Cook, Pete Estes, Polio Madden, James Baldwin and others.

"I thought you went off somewhere playing with a hillbilly band," Robert Gray said. He was my friend but he also liked to rub my love for country music in.

"I did," I told him sarcastically. "But I missed sittin' up on this rail with you guys so I came back." Everybody laughed, except Robert Gray. I had only been gone for three weekends and Robert knew that.

"He broke Wister Todd's bass," Bruce Cook informed everybody and laughed. "Didn't you, Charles?"

"Man that scared me to death when that bridge popped. I must've jumped two feet off the stage floor," I told them and joined in the laughter.

"You need to stick to playing that guitar," Pete said. "I been telling you how you need to go to Nashville. I want to hear you singing on the Grand Ole Opry."

"He ain't gonna be on the Grand Ole Opry," Robert said."He's gonna wind up over there in the mill like most everybody else."

"We'll see," I remarked and slid off the rail.

"Come on, Pete," Let's go shoot some pinball."

I was about to fall in love again. Her name was Barbara Lester and she was from Spartanburg, South Carolina. Barbara looked like actress Janet Leigh. I guess it sounds like all my girlfriends looked like movie stars, but she really did. I met her at Curry's Lake, and we were attracted to each other immediately, openly looking back and forth at each other until I finally got up the nerve to approach her and ask her to dance. She had on a pair of short shorts and a pullover top. She had a great figure with really nice legs. Using an old descriptive phrase, *she nearly knocked my eyeballs out.*

We did the shag a couple of times, then slow danced. That did it, the slow dance. She was blonde quicksand and I was sinking fast as

Old Memories and Me

we moved to the mood of *Earth Angel*.

"You dance good," she told me, her head resting against my chest.

"So do you," I said.

Barbara was eighteen and so was I but she had been around and had dated a lot more than I had, and I was still pretty naïve, especially when it came to the serious stuff.

"You're tall," she said and looked up at me from her 5 foot 1 inch frame with her brown eyes slow dancing too, the sound of her voice sending me signals I was too dumb to recognize at the time. It would take some courage for me to kiss a girl like her. I mean, I already could tell, she would know how to really kiss. She was going to be as much, if not more, than Julie what's her name had been. I had to take it slow. Man, I was from Watts Mill and certain kind of kissing was considered a sin by members of Lucas Avenue Baptist Church. Barbara Lester didn't know those rules though. Not that she was a bad girl, she was just already a woman at age eighteen. I was still a virgin.

For the next hour or so we danced and then we would talk for a while, and then dance again. The way we looked at each other, especially when we slow danced, I knew I was going to get to kiss her. I was nervous, but I was daring. How could I not be, getting attention from Barbara Lester. She was locked onto me, more than just physically, but with an emotion that touched me inside and captured every tingle and spark I had ever felt. Finally we walked outside and Barbara leaned against my car, looking up at me for a few seconds with those beautiful brown eyes, then reaching up and pulling me toward her, her lips already parting slightly.

That first kiss was tender and really nice. I had kissed like that before, so I relaxed and felt at ease. We stopped for a moment, not saying anything, then we kissed the second time, or rather she did. Holy cow. It must have lasted five minutes, or it seemed like it. However long it was, it was too short. Wow. Do that again. I don't mean to sound overly excited here, but this girl knew how to kiss a guy into volunteering to lose his mind. Susan from down in Statesboro, Georgia could take kissing lessons from Barbara Lester.

"You kiss very good," she informed me.

"I do?" I must have sounded surprised, because I was.

"Umm huh," she purred and kissed me again.

With my eyes closed, I could see sparklers and roman candles going off, like at Christmas, but it was March.

You know how you move from one stage of your life to another, gradually? You know, learning things and developing? Well, if those stages were rated from 1-10, Barbara Lester took me from a 3 to a 10 in fifteen minutes that night. For the rest of that evening I just floated wherever she wanted to take me.

I fell head over heels for her. I could tell she really liked me too.

"You want to sit in the car and listen to the radio?" I asked her.
We sat in my car, with the radio tuned to WLAC in Nashville, but we hardly heard it. We didn't talk a lot either. I had never kissed so much without stopping in my life. I didn't complain though. I just followed Barbara's lead and learned a lot about falling in love.

When it came time for us to leave, her going back to Spartanburg with the friends she had rode there with, and me back to Watts Mill with Bruce Cook, I asked her if I could call her. She gave me her telephone number. I called her the next day and asked her for a date. She said yes. After two dates I asked her to go steady. She said yes again. Well, I could handle that. I had gone steady before.

I started going to Spartanburg about every night. Barbara liked for me to bring my guitar along and play and sing, mostly rock n roll. She didn't like country music too much. She said she liked it when I sang it though. Her favorite song for me to sing was *Sincerely*. It wasn't a country song and I did it like the Moonglows' version of it. She really believed I would make it as a singer one day. She used to tell me I was going to be a star.

Love feeling like this scared the heck out of me. I mean, I certainly enjoyed kissing the way we did, setting fireworks off in the skies of my mind, and nearly taking my breath away. But what was I supposed to do next? Barbara knew how to light a fire in a boy that only the fire department or going too far could put out.

Those intimate moments never felt dirty, or made me think less of her. They made me love her more. I just wasn't able to find the courage to break the rules of my upbringing. I wanted to make love to her, oh Lord did I ever. And we almost did a few times, parked in my car out in front of her house, touching places I had never touched before, and being touched where I had never been touched before as well. Later, driving back home I would get upset with myself for not making love to her. I didn't know what I was sorry for the most, not doing it or for even trying. Man, it was tough becoming a man, not to mention how guilty I felt knowing God was probably upset with me too.

When Barbara and I dated we either went to Curry's Lake to dance, or to a drive-in movie around Spartanburg. We used to have to watch out for her former boyfriend. They called him *Freight Train* because his car got hit by a train and left him with a limp. Anybody that could survive that didn't need to be catching me with his former girlfriend.

On one occasion we drove over to Greenville and saw a rock n roll show that starred Bo Diddley, The Coasters, Etta James and a few other R&B acts. Bo Diddley came off the stage and performed in the isles, near the first rows of people. I thought he must have a mighty long guitar chord. I learned later he had some type of cordless receiver and that was unheard of back in the fifties.

Old Memories and Me

Wherever Barbara and I went on a date, we always wound up parked in front of her house talking and fooling around until way after midnight. Every night I got braver but not brave enough.

One night while we were parked in front of her house, her 19-year-old sister had come out and got in the back seat of my car with us. The three of us talked for a while, then Barbara kissed me. Her sister reached up and removed my arm from behind Barbara's head and took my hand and placed it in her own. Then she started messing around with my hand, teasing me, pressing it to her breast.

"Shit!" I gasped and jerked my hand away, and my lips came away from Barbara's.

"What's wrong?" Barbara asked, surprised.

I glanced at her sister in the back seat, who was laughing.

"Nothing," I told Barbara, looking back at her "I think I need to go. It's getting late and I have to get up early in the morning." I didn't know what else to say.

Barbara suspected something. She looked back at her sister.

"Did you do something?"

"Who me?" her sister giggled.

"You little shit," Barbara snapped. "What did you do to him?"

Barbara was close to her sister and they were always pulling something on each other like that, kidding and clowning around. Barbara didn't think it was funny right then though. Her sister was always telling me I should be dating her instead of Barbara. I always thought she was just joking with me. After that night though, I wasn't quite sure anymore. I wasn't about to fool around with her sister. Barbara would kill me. Besides, I was in love with her. Barbara and I both really thought this was it, true love. I bought her an engagement ring on credit and proposed.

"Will you marry me?" I asked her and I know my voice was trembling. I didn't get on my knees when I asked her because they were shaking too much. Besides, we were in my car again. We spent half our time in my car. It was a sharp 1955 Victoria Ford, aqua with white interior.

Barbara said, "Yes."

Oh my goodness. I just got engaged.

I continued working at Pigg's Red and White Supermarket on North Harper Street and being in the meat market, to me my hands always smelled like fish and hamburger meat. You had to weigh everything up for the customers back then, a pound of this, two pounds of that. Weigh it, and then wrap it up. Put the price on it with a felt pen.

The man I worked for was Claude Simmons, the butcher in the meat market. One of his sons was Brad Simmons. Brad went to Laurens High School and we had met before, but now we had became close friends. Brad started dating my high school sweetheart, Polly Powers. They were planning on getting married and I was going to marry

Barbara Lester. Still, even though I was in love with Barbara, for some reason it bothered me a little that Brad was dating Polly. I don't guess you ever completely forget your first sweetheart.

I used to drive back from Spartanburg and Barbara's house, which was about 35 miles from Watts Mill, at two or three am in the morning. Sometimes I would fall asleep and not even remember most of the drive. It was a wonder I didn't wreck. I guess God was looking after me, even though I might not always have deserved it.

Clyde Pennington, Wister Todd and I had continued to play music together. Johnny Meeks had gotten a job playing lead guitar with rock n roll star Gene Vincent, who had a monster hit with *Be-Bop-A-Lula*. "Hey, Charles," Clyde called and said with excitement to me one day. "Man, Meeks called me last night and he's got me a job drumming for Gene Vincent."

"Wow," I exclaimed. "You're kidding."

"No shit, man," Clyde told me. "I leave day after tomorrow."

"Does he need a bass player?" I laughed.

"No," he informed me. "I already asked and Vincent has a bass player."

Well, at least two of my picking buddies, Clyde Pennington and Johnny Meeks, had now made it to the big time in the music world. My time would come. I was sure of that.

Barbara called me on the phone one day and said she wanted to come down to my house and talk to me. I don't recall her girlfriend's name but she was going to drive her down. I could tell something was seriously on her mind but she wouldn't tell me over the phone.

She and her girlfriend drove to Watts Mill that afternoon and Barbara and I sat on the front porch steps at my mama and daddy's house and talked. The friend waited in the car. In so many words Barbara told me she felt like she was too mature for me, saying she still loved me but maybe it just wasn't the right thing for us. I looked into her brown eyes and knew she was doing something she didn't really want to do, letting go of something she wanted to hold on to but for some reason, and I never really understood why, she gave me back the engagement ring. We both had tears in our eyes. I knew why I did but I didn't know why she did. She was the one letting go.

"I am really sorry," she said and wiped the tears from her cheek.

"I don't understand," I said, tears in my own eyes. "Was it something I did?" *No, it was something I didn't do.*

"No," she assured me. "I just think it is not going to work out, I mean, you are a wonderful guy, Charlie, but I feel like I am too old for you."

"We're the same age," I reminded her. I couldn't believe this was happening.

Barbara sighed and bit her lower lip. "Not really," she said softly, and then she seemed to search for words. "Maybe in years but... but not in...you know, not in maturity. I am sorry and this wasn't an easy decision for me."

"Yeah, well I am too, Barbara," I responded while everything inside of me that could possibly be hurt was emotionally bleeding at that moment.

It was only for a minute or so, but it seemed a lot longer, the two of us just sat there in silence looking at each other with tears still in our eyes. Finally, she wiped her eyes. "I have to go," she told me with her voice quivering.

"Barbara." I said her name, and then stopped.

"What?" she asked and I could have sworn her eyes were pleading for me to say, *don't go, talk me out of saying goodbye*. I might have been wrong and misread her feelings. I don't think so though.

"Nothing," I said and took a deep breath to try and gain control of myself.

She hesitated, then, "Bye," she said and managed a sweet smile.

"Goodbye, Barbara," I told her and smiled back.

To this day I can't tell you why she did that, call off the engagement, nor why I didn't try and talk her out of it. Perhaps things were happening too fast in our young lives, especially mine because I was still so naive. I think my small town ways frustrated her. She had practically come right out and said as much when she said she was older than me and more mature. I didn't want to let her go, but I did because I didn't know what to do with her. When we would hold each other, and kissed the way we did, and we touched the way we did, for me it was like walking into heaven and running from hell at the same time. It broke my heart to let her go. I can still picture her looking back at me as she walked to her girlfriend's car, wearing that same pretty smile she wore the first time I saw her at Curry's Lake. She was still a bit misty eyed though. So was I. That was the last time I ever saw Barbara Lester.

Polly Powers was my first sweetheart. Barbara Lester was my first real love. They both wound up breaking my heart. But I would soon learn that time and someone very special heal all wounds. I didn't know it then but my true soul mate was just a song and a pair of roller skates away.

CHAPTER FOUR

One night in May of 1957, while I was roller-skating at Mineral Springs Park in Laurens, the jukebox was playing *Searching* by the Coasters. I remember that because as I skated I was singing along with the Coasters when I first laid eyes on Betty Joyce Harrison. She was one of the prettiest girls I had ever seen. I know, I said that about Polly Powers and Barbara Lester too. This was different though. Don't expect me to be able to explain it. I can't. It *was* different though.

Betty didn't look like any particular movie star but Lord she could have been one herself. Barbara Lester had a great figure but Betty Harrison was built like no girl I had ever seen. Every boy there had his eyes on her.

I caught up with her and skated along beside her. "Hi."
She looked over at me and smiled. "Hello."
I introduced myself and she told me her name was Betty.
"Is it alright if I skate with you?" I asked her.
"Sure," she told me and her lips curled into another smile.

Chills went all over me. I have had chills from girls before but I had never been where the sight of Betty Harrison took me that very first moment I saw her.

Her dark hair was short, shaping her pretty face almost like an ebony frame. Her deep brown eyes just reached out and pulled me in like I was home for the first time in my life. She had on a pair of black shorts and a plaid shirt, not tucked in, but the bottom tied into a bow in front, with the collar turned up.

We skated together and laughed as we darted in and out between slower skaters, holding hands once as we glided around the circle at one end of the rink. We circled the floor a few more times and then took a break. I bought a couple of Dr. Peppers for us and we sat on a bench inside the skating rink with our skates still on. We just made small talk and enjoyed being with each other.

"Are you from Laurens?" she asked, then took a sip from her bottle of Dr. Pepper.
"Watts Mill," I told her. "And you?"
"Clinton," she replied.

Clinton was only eight miles from Laurens and about ten miles from Watts Mill.

Old Memories and Me

I was nineteen but when she told me she was twenty I lied and said I was twenty also. Something just told me it was best that I do that. Back then girls were funny about dating guys younger than themselves, even just a year's difference.

We went back out on the wooden floor of the rink and skated some more. We were both excellent roller skaters and we danced as we skated to Fats Domino singing *Blueberry Hill*.

We danced-skated side by side, arms around each other's waist, then I twirled her around so she was skating backwards, facing me. Once around the rink we switched and I was skating backwards, facing her. We were good together. Everything was just so natural between us. I can't explain it but I felt like I had known her all my life. I swear, I knew after thirty minutes with her that I was going to marry her. I didn't even know I was looking for her, but I had been, and now I had found her. Yes, I was nervous and excited, but this time I wasn't afraid I wouldn't know all the right things to do. I knew this time was going to be different. I would know what to do and what I didn't know Betty Harrison would show me.

I had experienced strong feelings for two other girls but this was something beyond that. This was something else and it was telling me I was looking at the girl I was meant to spend the rest of my life with. I can't explain how but I knew that. I would never be the same again. A new kind of tingling in my stomach, a new kind of anticipation in my excitement, a new need I had never known before came over me, not to mention what was happening to my heart. It was so excited it nearly jumped out of my chest and got into hers to beat with her heart. From first love, to real love, and now, the right love. I knew Betty Harrison was the right one.

After another twenty minutes we took off our skates. Betty owned her own but I turned my rented skates in at the counter. We went outside and walked down to the swimming pool. We sat down on a bench. It was getting late and there wasn't anybody else at the pool. We were alone.

We talked for a while, sipping on Dr. Peppers again and telling each other a little more about ourselves. When I finally got around to kissing her I could taste the Dr. Pepper on her lips.

We sat there holding hands, looking at the moon. I turned and looked at her, she looked back at me and neither of us said anything for a moment. Off in the distance, from the jukebox inside the skating rink, we could hear Sonny James singing *Young Love*.

"I think I've been looking for you for a long time Betty Harrison," I told her and was so happy I felt like I would burst. It was unreal.

She smiled mischievously. "Well, you found me, Charles Craig."

I leaned over and kissed her again, softly, like the warm

emotions I felt inside, as though I wanted to slowly consume every part of her into my soul. Something wonderful was happening between us. We didn't have to rush things. Somehow we both knew we were going to have a long time together.

"I feel like something special has happened tonight," she said with a soft smile and looked into my blue eyes with her brown ones like she was bonding her feelings with mine.

Something special was happening. It was more than just a boy and girl meeting and liking each other a lot and kissing. There was a feeling between us that mattered more than just the heat of the moment.

"I feel that way too," I told her and knew I was falling more in love this time than I would ever be able to fall out of.

She tucked both of her hands under my arm and nestled closer to me, laying her head on my shoulder, like she felt warm and safe there. We both looked up at the night sky. There were a million stars out and two of them were ours.

As though right on cue, in the distance we could hear Ivory Joe Hunter singing on the jukebox.

Since I met you baby

I asked her for a date for the next night and she accepted. We went ice skating in Greenville. It was my first time ice skating and only her second time. We fell a lot on the ice but we fell even more in our hearts. Love was being born at a rapid pace but she and I were taking our time, savoring each moment we were together. I couldn't do anything without thinking of Betty. Every night we were seeing each other, and every day talking on the phone. With her, I knew I had discovered what forever is for. Betty made me feel like there wasn't anything I couldn't do. When I looked into her eyes I was king of the hill. She put me up on a throne and wouldn't let anything or anybody knock me off. She told me I was the most special person she had ever met and she said she thought about me every minute we were apart. If there ever was a perfect match, we had struck it.

A week or so after we met and started dating I confessed I was only nineteen and she pitched a fit and told me she would never have started dating me had she known I was a year younger than her. I thought that was funny but she didn't. She pouted about that for a long while but she finally forgave me. Betty and I were dating every night. Sometimes we double dated with one of her best friends, Ruth Butler, and the boy from Watts Mill that Ruth went with, Bruce Hughes. One night when Bruce and I were on our way to pick them up we stopped at Spec's Place, a beer joint. I didn't drink but Bruce did and he wanted a beer. We stayed there too long and we were late picking Betty and Ruth up. They were not there waiting for us. They had gone on without us. I was upset because I knew we should have already been there and I

Old Memories and Me

knew Betty was upset with me or she would have waited.

Bruce didn't want to, but we were in my car, so I drove around looking for them. We found them at a drive-in restaurant in Clinton that had a cement dance floor built outside with speakers to hear the jukebox inside. As soon as Betty saw me, she got up and started dancing with some guy. I knew she loved me and she was doing it to spite me because she was upset that I didn't pick her up when I said I would. Seeing her dancing with another guy made me both mad and hurt. I went directly to the dance floor and took her by the arm and pulled her away from him, gently of course. Before I could say anything to Betty, the guy said, "Hey, butt out, fellow!"

I didn't say a word to him. I gave him a quick glance and a stiff middle finger. I pulled Betty to the side. "I'm sorry I'm late," I said.

"Late?" she said with sarcasm and pulled away from me. "I think over an hour is a little more than late."

"I'm sorry," I told her again. "Come on, let's go somewhere and talk. It isn't my fault. Bruce wanted a beer. I should have said no."

The guy she had been dancing with tried to interfere.

"Who is this guy," he asked her, looking at me like he was her guardian.

I wasn't a tough guy but I felt tough at that moment. I wanted to talk to my girl and he was interfering. "She's my girlfriend," I told him. "So get lost."

"Well, she's with me right now," he boasted. He looked like a sissy to me and that gave me a little more courage.

"Not anymore she's not," I informed him and took Betty's arm again and led her away.

That impressed Betty and evidently depressed him. He left and so did we.

We went to my car. I explained to her about Bruce and I stopping at Spec's. She didn't like me going there but I finally convinced her it wasn't a place I went often and I assured her I hadn't talked to any girls there nor had I even had a beer or anything.

"Maybe I over reacted but I don't like being stood up," she told me, some of her anger subsiding. "I had waited all day to see you."

"I have missed you all day long too," I told her and meant it.

We kissed and made up. Then we drove back to Laurens, leaving Bruce and Ruth on their own after dropping them off at Bruce's car. Betty and I went to Mineral Springs where we first met. We went down to the pool and sat on that same bench and held hands, just being in love.

"Look at that moon," I pointed. "I wonder if there really is a man up there." I chuckled at my own remark.

"Probably," she said. "And he's watching us right now."

"He better close his eyes then," I said and kissed her.

When our lips had parted she drew her knees up to her chest

and wrapped her arms around her legs, looking at the moon, just thinking to herself for a moment, and then turned her head to look at me. "I'm glad we came here. I could sit here with you all night and just talk."

I just looked at her, my breath increasing and feeling a bunch of butterflies fluttering in my stomach. She had on jeans that were rolled up at the bottoms, bobby socks and loafers. She was so pretty. I knew I would love this girl the rest of my life. I know I keep saying that but it was so true. Then, she reached over and punched me playfully. "But you better not cheat for those Watts Mill girls in softball again."

"Do what?" I asked, puzzled by her remark.

Betty told me I had umpired a game between the Watts team and the Clinton team that Betty and her twin sister Bobbie had played on.

"I didn't umpire that game, honey," I assured her. "I would remember you if I had."

"Yes you did and you cheated, especially for that Polly Powers." She gave me an accusing look. She knew Polly had been my sweetheart in school.

"I did not," I laughed. "You got me mixed up with somebody else."

"No I haven't," she ribbed me. Then she looked at me real serious. "You ever think about that girl from up in Spartanburg?"

I had told her about Barbara Lester too. I didn't want anything to come back and haunt me. "No, not anymore," I told her and rubbed the side of her face softly with my hand. "Not since I met you."

She pinched me lightly again and wrinkled her nose. "You better not."

After a while we decided to go over to the Ranch Drive-In and get a cheeseburger. We got back in the car and as I was starting to pull away from the parking lot, Betty asked me, "What would you do if I said I love you more than anything in the whole world?"

"I'd probably fall out of the car," I laughed and felt a tingle run over me just hearing her say that.

"Well," she said and smiled at me, those brown eyes soft and serious. "I love you more than anything in the whole world, Charles Craig."

I kept my word. I opened the car door and fell out. We weren't moving fast, still in the Mineral Springs parking lot. Betty shrieked and grabbed the steering wheel. She also managed to hit the brake and turn the car off. I know it was crazy but love does that to you. Besides, I was kind of goofy and silly sometimes. I had almost overdone it a bit this time though.

"Are you alright?" she asked with concern written on her face, laying across the seat and leaning out of the driver's side door and looking wide eyed down at me sitting on my rear on the ground.

Old Memories and Me

"I think so," I groaned and then smiled. Of course I was alright. Betty Harrison loved me more than anything in the whole world. But my butt was aching and I had skinned the palms of my hands a little and they were burning. I crawled over to where she was leaning from out of the car and kissed her. After that night we always said, "I love you more than anything in the whole world," whenever we were telling each other how much we cared. When I got back in the car and we were just sitting there laughing about me falling out like an idiot. I just blurted it out. "Will you marry me?"

"Yes, yes, yes," she laughed, gooching me three times, once for every yes.

"Good," I told her "'Cause I am going to just follow you around the rest of your life if you don't. I ain't letting you go."

Then we kissed again, and this time it was long one, and different. I can't really explain it. It was just different....a little bit sweeter, a little more belonging. A kiss was never like that before.

I gave her all the love in my young heart and she gave as much back, perhaps even more. I couldn't hang wallpaper, let alone the moon, but Betty thought I hung the moon and would tell me that for years to come. Everything I would become, Betty would be both the reason and the strength behind it. It was like two souls had merged into one. We became one shadow, one feeling, one being, truly, soul mates.

Right from the beginning, we were inseparable. We did everything together. We liked each other as much as we loved each other. This was the beginning of a true love story. We would have our ups and downs, nothing is perfect I guess, but Betty and I sure came close with our love for each other.

I had left the grocery store and gone to work on the third shift at Palmetto Worsted Mill. I was with Betty every night. I would usually go to bed by 10 am after getting off work at 8 am. Back then you didn't have to worry about locking the doors, especially in the daytime. Betty used to slip into my mama and Daddy's house while I was asleep and pick up the phone and dial our number, then hang up and let it ring. You could do that on telephones back then. I would get up in my shorts and t-shirt and answer the phone, but of course nobody would be on the line. Betty would have sneaked out on the back porch and hid from me, giggling.

One morning, I was asleep and something woke me up. It was Betty. She was sitting on the side of the bed looking at me. She had never done that before, just ringing the telephone and playing tricks on me. We had become very passionate on dates but we had never been in a bedroom together before. But there she was. I don't think we really said anything, we didn't have to. We made love for the first time and I was no longer a virgin. Maybe it wasn't right in God's eyes, but I didn't feel guilty and I just don't see how it could have been wrong. It was more than just sex, it was beautiful and I'd be lying if I didn't say it was the most wonderful thing that ever happened in my life. As much as I already loved her, I loved her even more after that. We just held each other for a long time afterwards. This was going to last forever. It almost did.

Betty was a very considerate person but she was also one of the most outspoken people I had ever met. She would say exactly what she thought. She always took offense when somebody treated me unfairly but she also had one of the sweetest personalities. She had an identical twin sister who was just like her. Her name was Barbara Bolt. They called her Bobbie. Both of them were highly competitive and couldn't stand to lose at anything, and seldom did.

Back then you could not tell them apart. Betty was right handed and Bobbie was left handed.

Doctors said it was like looking in a mirror, raise your right arm and the left comes up in the mirror.

I remember on my first date with Betty, the night we went ice skating, they tried to trick me afterwards. At least Bobbie did.

After I had dropped Betty off at home, I went to work at Palmetto Worsted Mill on the third shift. Bobbie worked the second shift in the spinning room. The coffee machine in the drawing room where I worked was out of order so I had gone to the one in the spinning room when I arrived for work that night. I couldn't believe my eyes when I saw Bobbie.

"What are you doing here?" I asked, thinking it was Betty.

Bobbie just laughed and said, "I had a good time tonight."

"Me too but how did you get over here so fast?" I was dumbfounded. "I didn't even know you worked here."

Then I started noticing some things. Yarn was all over her clothes and in her hair. And her hair looked a little longer. I began to realize something wasn't right. There was something a little different about the shape of her face, not much different than Betty's, but just enough to make me suspect something, and then I noticed she was left handed.

"You're not Betty," I said and wasn't quite sure I believed it fully myself.

She laughed and told me, "No, I'm Bobbie, her twin sister."

They never fooled me again but they did a lot of other people.

When I first told Betty I played guitar and sang I didn't know how she would react to me singing country music. It 1957 and every young person was digging rock n roll. The first time I played my guitar and sang for her she said she loved it. I did some rock n roll songs too but she actually liked the country songs I did as well. But when I would do one of Elvis's songs she wouldn't hesitate to tell me, "Honey, I love your singing, but you need to leave Elvis's songs alone. Nobody can

Old Memories and Me

sing 'em like he does." Like most of the girls she loved Elvis. I was a big fan too. I think everybody knew Elvis was really something special, even early on in his career. After Elvis, I was Betty's favorite singer. That is probably the only time I ever came in second with her. Her favorite song for me to sing to her was *Pledging My Love*, the Johnny Ace song I had always loved to sing.

My mama and daddy really liked Betty from the start, especially my daddy. He really took to her. I remember the time Betty and I drove up to Fort Mill for me to meet her mother for the first time. Miss Jessie, that's what everybody called her, worked at the cotton mill in Fort Mill and didn't get off until 10 pm. I told Daddy it was an hour and a half drive each way and I would be late getting back. I was 19 but still living at home and still living by my daddy's rules. I always told him and Mama where I was going and when I expected to be back.

Miss Jessie was a small lady, less than 5 feet tall, but had a big heart and was very strong willed. She seemed to like me right off. She, Betty and I talked for a long time. She was a plainspoken woman, just like her twin daughters, and she told me what she would expect out of me as far as her daughter was concerned. I assured her that I loved Betty dearly and would never mistreat her.

"You got a job, haven't you?" Miss Jessie asked seriously.

"Mama!" Betty shrieked, but laughed.

"Yes ma'am," I told her and laughed too.

Things went well with Miss Jessie. I learned that she would be a no nonsense woman when it came to her daughter's happiness and well being. She loved country music too. After God and Elvis, Marty Robbins was next in line with Miss Jessie.

By the time Betty and I left her mama and started the drive back from Fort Mill it was a little after midnight. Betty loved my 1955 Victoria Ford. It would scat. I let her drive back. That was a mistake. Somewhere between Whitmire and Clinton there was a long flat stretch of two-lane road and hardly any traffic that time of night. It was around 1:30 am by then and we came up on a 1950 Ford coupe. Betty flashed her lights and pulled around to pass the car, hesitating in the left lane because nothing was coming in the opposite direction on that long stretch. She honked the horn. She was picking for a race with the Ford coupe. She got it.

"No," I exclaimed loudly.

Too late. We were in a race and when I looked at the speedometer, I thought, "Holy shit!" We were doing a little over 110 miles per hour. We were still in the left lane and about a half car length in front of the coupe.

"Go Baby," Betty laughed, talking to my car. Then, like a quick flash of lightening, the coupe left us like we were standing still. Souped up coupe with a 4-barrell carburetor. "Damn it!" Betty was ticked. I told you she couldn't stand losing.

"Why did you do that?" I asked, a little anger showing. "And get back in the right hand lane." That was the first time I had ever snapped at her.

She looked over at me. There was enough moonlight to see that she was now smiling. "We've got to get a faster car."

I managed to smile back, but I rolled my eyes. "What kind of girl have I got here?"

"A cool chick, baby" she said and laughed. "A real cool chick."

"Yeah," I said and felt relaxed again. "I sure do have myself a cool chick alright, and a good-looking one too."

As usual, she had on a pair of tight shorts. Man, did she ever have nice legs and I reached over and laid my hand on her thigh. Well, not boldly. Ok, a little boldly. I leaned over and gave her a kiss on the cheek. She turned to face me just long enough to give me a quick kiss on the lips then she faced the highway again.

After that we rode along in silence for a little while. Betty was probably thinking about that souped up coupe and I was thinking about having to get up real early and get to the weekend National Guard meeting I had to attend starting in a few hours. I was also wondering what Daddy was going to say.

He was sitting out on the back porch stoop when we pulled in about 2 am. Betty had left her car at Mama and Daddy's house. He had on his pajamas and robe. "What are you doing keeping this girl out till this time of morning?" he scolded me.

I told you he liked her. "We talked to her mama for quite a while and we didn't get started back until after midnight," I told him. I was thinking too, *if Betty hadn't drove a hundred and ten miles an hour part of the way it would be later than this.*

He wouldn't let Betty drive home by herself and he wouldn't let me take her. He told her to stay with us. She slept in a spare bed that used to be my sister Dot's room. Somehow I managed to drag out of bed about 6:30 am and get to the National Guard Armory by 8 am. I had to stay in the Guards eight years to fulfill my military obligation. I had to attend meetings every Monday night, several weekend drills, a couple of weekends at the Fort Jackson firing range in Columbia, South Carolina, and a two week summer camp at Ft. Stewart, Georgia.

It was during one of these two-week training periods that I got word that one of my daddy's brothers, George, had died from a stroke he had suffered a few weeks earlier. I was allowed to come home for the funeral. That was the first time I ever saw my daddy with a lot of tears in his eyes.

I had planned to get Betty an engagement ring but she wouldn't allow me to because it would cost too much money. She said we needed to save money to get married. She wore my high school ring instead.

Betty scared the heck out of me one night. I was waiting for

Old Memories and Me

her to arrive at Mineral Springs Park when her friend Betty Lou Parrish came inside the skating rink and told me Betty was outside and wanted to see me.

"Why didn't she come in?"

"She can't," Betty Lou informed me.

"Why?" I asked as we walked outside.

"She's hurt," Betty Lou told me. "She had a car wreck."

"What!"

I took off running to where I could see Betty's car parked. She was sitting inside, with a bandage around her head and I could see that it had been bleeding. One of her knees was bandaged too. I flung the door open in a panic.

"What happened? Are you alright?"

"I had a wreck," Betty said meekly and looked at me so pitiful.

"Oh, my Lord," I gasped and almost broke into tears. I wanted to hold her but was afraid I might hurt her injuries. "Where did you wreck, how, I mean what happened?" I was so upset and concerned. I knelt down beside her in the open car door.

"Can we go down and sit beside the pool," she asked.

"Can you walk?"

"If you help me I can."

"Of course I will sweetheart."

I helped her from the car.

"You want me to carry you?" I asked her.

"No, just help me and I can hobble," Betty told me.

I was as careful as I could be, halfway holding her up and assisting her to walk. I was baby talking to her, "Oh, honey" and "you poor thing."

Betty started looking away from me. Then, I heard her trying to muffle a laugh. I looked at Betty Lou. She was laughing too, holding her hand to her mouth to try and hide it.

"What are you two laughing....?" Then it hit me. This was all a hoax. I couldn't believe it. The bandages looked so real, and the blood beneath. "What in the world is going on here?" I was still confused enough to be cautious though.

Betty straightened up and looked fine, unwrapping the bandage from her forehead. "Just paying you back from when you and Bruce stood Ruth and me up," she laughed.

"I didn't stand you up," I reminded her.

She was referring to the time Bruce Hughes and I had stopped at Spec's Place and were late picking them up. Betty and Betty Lou couldn't stop laughing.

"You scared the heck out of me, Betty," I told her. In case you're not from the South, getting the heck scared out of you is the same thing as getting the hell scared out of you.

"I'm sorry," she said and was trying to stop laughing. "You

have to admit though, it looked real."

It did look real. Turned out the blood was catsup.

Betty put her arm around me. "Don't be mad honey."

I wasn't mad, just a little ticked off, but more than anything I was relieved that she was alright. Pretty soon I was laughing with them. It was a good trick, like something I might have come up with myself.

Betty and I finally got in my car and went to the Laurens Drive-In Theater. We didn't pay much attention to the movie. There was nothing quite like necking in the car at a drive-n theater. We didn't care about the movie. We crawled into the back seat and practically disappeared.

On June 29, 1957, at 2 o'clock on a Saturday, just six weeks after we first met that night at Mineral Springs Park roller-skating, Betty and I were married. She would become my most loyal supporter and never once stop believing in me. Every time I faced a mountain, she would help me climb it. If I had trouble climbing, she would climb for both of us. She was one of the strongest willed and most determined women I have ever known. If I wandered into the dark, she was my light. If I stumbled she caught me and kept me from falling. She was wonderful and she was mine. And I was hers.

For our wedding she wore a white dress and a white hairpiece. She was so beautiful that day that I was afraid I couldn't measure up to being good enough for her. It was the most wonderful day in my life. We only invited our families and a few friends. Ruth and Betty Lou were there. Bradley Jones, my lifelong friend, who had also become Betty's friend, was my best man. Bobbie, Betty's twin sister was her bridesmaid.

There was a reception at my mama and daddy's house and afterward we had changed into blue jeans and shirts and were off to the beach for a week's honeymoon. However, before we could go, we had to drop off Miss Jessie at the blockhouse in Clinton. That's what they called the house where Betty had lived with her brother Clarence before he moved to Fort Mill. Miss Jessie still owned the house.

Miss Jessie wanted to stop and eat somewhere. She said she had only eaten a little bit of our wedding cake. We wound up at a restaurant in Clinton, eight miles away, and got food. Betty and I kept looking at each other, holding hands and trying to be polite to her mother, but we wanted to get on down the road to Charleston. Miss Jessie was a wonderful and sweet lady but at the moment I wanted to leave her and get on with our honeymoon. She would become a precious and dependable mother-in-law to me. However, as I said, like her twin daughters, she did have a temper. You make Jessie mad and she was like a little pit bull. So we let her eat and fidgeted the whole time.

Finally, we dropped my new mother-in-law off at the blockhouse right outside Clinton and Betty and I were on our way to

Old Memories and Me

Charleston. There was no interstate then, just two lane roads most of the way there. We got into Charleston late at night and crossed over the Cooper River Bridge to the Isle of Palms and stayed at a motel there. I wanted it to be like I had seen it in the movies, carry my bride across the threshold. The doorway was kind of narrow and turning sideways, my lean 140-pound frame struggled a bit carrying her shapely 105-pound body, and I nearly dropped her. Well, alright, I admit it. I did drop her.

"Charles!" she shrieked and fell to the floor.

I fell on top of her, breaking my fall so I wouldn't crush her.

"Oops," I laughed. "Are you alright, honey?"

Betty laughed too. "Yeah," she told me, looking up at me laying over her. "But next time let me carry you."

"We gonna get married another time?" I kidded her and gave her a little peck on the lips.

She giggled. "Get off of me."

It wasn't a very plush room or anything but it was our honeymoon suite and the most wonderful night in our lives. We made love, went out and got burgers and fries to bring back to the room, then after eating we made love again. Sometime after midnight we fell asleep in each other's arms.

We spent the next day sightseeing in Charleston, looking out at historic Fort Sumter from the battery, touring some of the beautiful old plantations with all the most amazingly colored flowers we had ever seen. The next morning we drove up to Myrtle Beach. First thing we did when we arrived there was have a flat tire. As Clint Eastwood might sarcastically say, *marvelous*. A state highway patrol officer helped me change the tire.

We checked into a motel and then went swimming in the ocean. Later we strolled up and down the beach holding hands. We were so happy. There was nobody in the world right then but the two of us.

"You're the best looking girl on the beach," I told Betty. She looked great in a bathing suit. She tanned easily too because she was already naturally dark skinned.

"You're the best looking guy here too but you've also got the skinniest legs here as well," she laughed. She was probably right about the legs but I threw a handful of sand at her anyway and chased her into the ocean. I caught her about waist deep in the water and pulled her into my arms and kissed her. Life was wonderful. I probably had less than a hundred dollars left to my name but I felt like the richest man in the world with Betty belonging to me.

Back then, in 1957, compared to today, Myrtle Beach was mostly a two-lane, one strip resort. We had a ball though and especially loved the seafood places. We made a lot of pictures, getting other people to take some of us together. One was the two of us in a makeshift jail where you put coins in a slot and snapped the picture yourself. We looked like *Bonnie and Clyde*. One afternoon, just before sunset, we sat on the beach, looking out across the Atlantic and talking about our future together.

"One day I want us to go to Nashville and let you sing on the Grand Ole Opry," she told me.

I chuckled. "I don't think we can just go to Nashville and they will let me sing on the Opry, I mean, not just like that."

"Why not," she asked, seriously.

"Well," I shrugged, not sure of the answer myself. "I don't know. Maybe I will have to audition or something."

Betty picked up a handful of sand and let it trickle through her fingers to the ground, thinking. "I think you're good enough to sing on the Grand Ole Opry."

I cupped her pretty face with both of my hands. "I love you Betty Craig." It was the first time I had called her by my last name. I liked the sound of it.

"I love you too," she smiled and gave me a sweet kiss.

Nashville was a long way off, probably as far away as across the ocean we were looking at. It was a dream of mine to be a country singer but at the moment I was happy just being with my new bride. She was real, not a dream.

"Let's go get something to eat," I said.

"Ok," she replied. "I'll race you to the car."

I let her win.

Betty and I lived with my parents until we could get a house of our own. I was still working third shift at Palmetto Worsted Mill and Betty got a job on the first shift there. We were making $40 apiece a week, unless we worked overtime on Saturday, which we seldom got to do at that time.

Mama and Daddy loved to play a card game called setback. Betty and I would play with them about every night. Betty and Daddy would be partners, and Mama and me were partners. When somebody would trump Daddy's high card, he would say, foot. There was that expression again.

Betty started sitting down with Daddy at the kitchen table every month and writing checks out for him to pay his and Mama's monthly bills. That was something she would do for the next 10 years or so for my daddy.

After a few months living with Mama and Daddy, Betty and I moved into a housing project in Laurens to have our own place. It wasn't much, just three rooms, a bedroom, a kitchen, a den and one bath. I had switched jobs and was working the second shift at Watts Mill, the same mill across from the rail that I had sat on with my high school buddies. Betty was still on the first shift at Palmetto Worsted Mill. I was still in bed when she left for work and she was usually in bed

Old Memories and Me

when I left for my shift. We always left each other a little note.

I left you a Dr. Pepper in the refrigerator and there's a Moon Pie in the cabinet. Love you lots.
Charlie

I miss you so much every night. I am going to try and get on the second shift tomorrow so we will be together when we are off. I go crazy without you every night. I love you, Betty

Our families used to tease us about acting like two teenagers still in love, even after we had been married for years. We held hands a lot and she would sit in my lap frequently when we were all sitting around talking. Betty and I did just have something really special.

At least once a month we would go up to Fort Mill for Sunday dinner at Miss Jessie's duplex, which she now shared with Betty's brother Clarence and his wife Sadie. We would all go in one car, Betty, me, Bobby, Jack and their daughter Robin. Betty's other sister, Juanita McGuirt, and her family, along with her other brother, David, and his family, would all be there. Betty had another brother Lloyd who died not long after we were married. He had been editor of *The State* newspaper in Columbia.

I would take my guitar a lot of times on those trips to Fort Mill and play and sing for everybody. Whenever I would play *Do Lord*, everybody would sing along.

"Do Lord, oh do Lord, do remember me..."

Another song her family liked for me to sing was Stonewall Jackson's *I Washed My Hands In Muddy Water*.

I didn't realize it back then, but things were happening in my life for a reason. Some of them were just little things, but still, things were happening that would later cause me to look back and remember them all as stepping stones to the unbelievable musical career that was waiting a few years down the road for me.

I played my guitar around the house all the time, singing the songs I would hear on the radio. I kept dreaming about singing on the Grand Ole Opry one day. Sometimes when Betty and I would go over to Mama and Daddy's house I would take my guitar and sing for Mama. She always liked for me to do that. I don't think she ever visualized that someday I would ever do anything more than just play and sing around home. Not many other people around Watts Mill did either. Betty did though, and that kept me believing it too.

After 6 months living at the housing projects, Betty and I moved into a rented house on Smythe Street at Watts Mill, just two streets over from where I went to school at Ford High, and within walking distance to my mama and Daddy's house. The house was wood framed, and wasn't underpinned so the pipes froze a lot in the winter, then they would burst. We came home from work with water all over the kitchen floor many times. We had an oil heater that didn't put out much heat but we liked to sleep close together anyway, so we kept warm cuddling up and fell deeper and deeper in love.

    Little mice would get into that house, especially in the wintertime. I was scared to death of those things. I knew they couldn't hurt me but they could make me hurt myself. One would run across the floor and Betty and I both would jump up on the bed.

    "Get the broom and kill it!" Betty squealed.

    "You kill it," I told her, trying to keep my balance standing in the middle of the bed. "I ain't gettin' down from here."

    I wouldn't get down off that bed and face that little mouse but I would face up to a grown man that flirted with Betty. Like the time the guy that ran the miniature golf course came on to her one afternoon while she, Bobbie, Jack and I were playing miniature golf there. Betty didn't tell me at the moment but after a game was over she said, "Let's go."

    "Why?" I asked. "Ain't you having a good time?"

    "Yes, but I want to go" she informed sternly me and headed for the car.

    I knew something was wrong and began to suspect what it was.

    "Did Mr. Carter say something out of the way to you?" I questioned her, looking over to where he was. He was the owner of the place-- a man probably in his fifties.

    It wasn't until after Jack and Bobbie had dropped us off at our house and we were inside that Betty finally told me what had happened. Mr. Carter had indeed said something to her, about how good she looked in the shorts she had on and he had told her she could come up there anytime and play golf for free in those shorts. I hit the ceiling.

    "That son-of-a-bitch," I said and stomped around the room, huffing and puffing. "I knew it!"

    I rarely cursed but I had lost my temper and was furious. It really ticked me off. What made his rude and uncalled remarks even worse was the fact that I had been going up there even before I married Betty. I used to shoot pool up there a lot. I had known him for a long time, considered him a friend, and now he would say something like that to my wife. I was burning up more by the minute.

    "Calm down, Charles," Betty said. "We just won't ever go back up there."

    "Oh, I'm going back up there alright, like right now," I told her. I was madder than a hornet. "Where's the car keys?"

    "I hid them."

    "Gimme the keys!"

    "No. You'll just get in trouble."

Old Memories and Me

"Betty, gimme the car keys." I held out my hand.

She shook her head no. "Come here," she said and held out her arms.

"Betty?" I said but eased into her arms. I was still mad, not at her of course, at Mr. Carter.

"Wait until tomorrow," she suggested. "After you have cooled off some and then talk to him."

"Oh, miss cool," I mocked, raising my eyebrows for emphasis. "You wouldn't wait until tomorrow if this situation was reversed."

She sighed. "I know, but I don't want you to get into any trouble. I don't blame you for being upset but promise me you will wait until tomorrow before going up there and talking to him, ok?"

She ran her hand over the side of my face. I took a deep breath. Then another one.

"Alright," I finally agreed. "But gimme the car keys. I need to go to the store. We're out of Dr. Pepper."

"No," Betty laughed and playfully punched me in the stomach.

I waited until the next morning and then I went up to see Mr. Carter. He was outside doing some work. He was digging a hole or something. He had a digging pick in his hand. He looked up as I approached.

"Hey, Charles," he greeted me, like he had no idea anything was wrong.

I was only 21 years old, and as I have said, he was in his fifties. I admit, now that I was facing him, I was a bit nervous. However, I had to speak my mind about what he had done. "Betty told me what you said to her last night," I informed him. I looked at him, and then glanced at that pick in his hand.

"What?" He tried to sound as though he had no idea what I was talking about.

He wasn't that big of a man, medium height, maybe 165 or 170 pounds. I was thinner, maybe a 150 pounds, but I was several inches taller at 6'2". Still, he was older, and had that pick in his hand.

"Well, you made some bad remarks to her," I said as sternly as I could. "Don't you ever say anything to my wife again."

"I don't know what you're talking about, Charles," he said to me. "If she said I said something out of the way, well, she's lying."

That did it. When he called Betty a liar I lost all fear and caution. I pointed my finger at him. "Listen you son-of-a-bitch, don't you call her a liar," I told him furiously. I even took a step closer to him. "And if you ever say anything to her again, even hello, I'll do my best to stomp your ass in the ground!"

My Lord. Did I just say that to a man with a pick in his hand? He changed his attitude.

"I don't remember saying anything out of the way, but if I did say anything to offend your wife, I apologize," he offered. He really didn't look worried, or afraid of me, his expression was that of guilt and embarrassment.

"Well, Betty wouldn't lie about it," I assured him, still angry.

"I'm sure she wouldn't," he said awkwardly.

I just looked at him for a moment. "Ok then, that's what I wanted to say to you," I told him. I had spoken my mind and he had apologized. I left him standing there without saying another word. Once in the car I talked to Jesus and asked him to forgive me for the way I had acted, but I was still upset.

It was about this time that I was offered a job playing bass with Gene Vincent. My friends Johnny Meeks and Clyde Pennington were still touring with him but I turned down the job because I didn't want to go on the road and leave Betty. The pay was a lot of money for back then but I had rather be home with her. Gene Vincent had a huge hit called *Be-Bop-A-Lula* and I remember his whole band wore blue caps, thus *Gene Vincent and the Blue Caps*.

Betty and I were so much in love and still did everything together. We spent most weekends with Bobbie and Jack Bolt. We pitched horseshoes, played badminton, and played a lot of spades. Betty and Bobbie were always partners and Jack and I were. Betty and Bobbie also like to play serious bridge but Jack and I never quite got that serious with it. We played to make them happy but we would talk a lot back and forth because we didn't understand the bidding and what it was telling your partner about each other's hand. So we just told each other aloud.

"How many clubs you got, Jack?"

"Charles!" Betty would scold me.

"If y'all are gonna cheat I'm quittin'," Bobbie would threaten.

"Good," Jack and I both would respond, laughing.

Usually, after a while we would wind up playing spades again.

Jack and Bobbie had a boat and in the summer we spent a lot of weekends at Lake Greenwood water skiing. It was tough learning to get up out of the water on two skis. That took a lot of strength. Then, after we learned to ski on two, we learned to drop one and ski on just one. Man, we took a lot of tumbles learning that. Once you learned to ski on just one ski it was a great feeling gliding back and forth over the boat's wake.

There was a guy skiing somewhere, I always heard it was on a lake in South Carolina, and he swung way out behind the boat that was pulling him as it circled into a cove and back out to let him swing wide and glide ashore. The story was he didn't let go of the rope soon enough and being on one ski he skied right into the shallow water and hit bottom near the bank. It threw him, end over end, head over heels ashore and tore his hide up something awful. Somebody wrote a song about it and put out a record that was a hit, at least in that part of the country. It was called *Ski King*.

Later, my daddy bought a boat too and I went bass fishing with him. I think in all the times I went fishing in that boat I caught

Old Memories and Me

one bass. I did better from the bank catching carp. We used to go to a commercial fishing pond where you paid to fish, Betty, Mama, Daddy, Granny Craig and me. What fish we caught we would take them home, clean them and Daddy would pan fry them and make sand gravy.

No, we didn't bring in dirt from the yard. Sand gravy is where you use the dripping from the fish and corn meal to make the gravy. Now that was some good eating.

Those were some good times. Betty and I had fun doing about anything, as long as we were together. We would take a piece of paper and draw a big 7 on it and make up a word. We would put a line of dashes beside the seven, one for each letter in the word and the other one would guess letters and try and guess the word before the other could draw a man hanging from the 7. We did that for an hour or more sometime. We played double solitaire, Chinese checkers and scrabble. It didn't take much to make us happy. We had each other and that was all we really needed.

There was a sad time too, though. Granny Craig died and she was buried behind Lucas Avenue Baptist Church right beside Grandpa Craig. Most of my relatives would be buried in that cemetery.

Just by chance one day I happened to run into Pete Simmons. Pete and his mother ran Mineral Springs Park, the same park where Betty and I had met. Pete knew I was trying to get started into music and told me he needed a band for Saturday nights.

I put a band together of my own.

That first band consisted of several musicians from over in Anderson and Wister Todd and me. Later on, after Clyde Pennington left Gene Vincent's band and was drafted into the army, I took my bass, and Clyde's drums that he had left in my care at my house, and somehow taught his younger brother Kenneth how to play drums. Some of the neighbors on Smythe Street called the police a couple of times because of the loud noise. It's amazing how far the sound of a bass and set of drums will carry.

"You boys need to quieten down some," Mr. Sprewell told us. He was the only policeman at Watts Mill. He was more like a constable I suppose.

Later on I put Kenneth Pennington on drums in the band playing at Mineral Springs. We played on Saturday nights at the park, playing square dance music, country and rock n roll. People danced out on the same wooden floor where people roller skated Monday through Friday and on Sundays. Saturday night was live music though. I was having a ball. I looked forward all week long to Saturday night. I would still perform *Honey Don't* and *Blue Suede Shoes*, along with *Don't Let The Stars Get In Your Eyes* and various other songs. We had a female singer in the band that was the sister of the lead guitar player.

We would play country music and rock n roll for about thirty minutes, then do a square dance set. We had a guy that would get up with the band and call the square dance. After that we would take a fifteen to twenty minute break, then go back and repeat the same routine again. We played from 8 pm till midnight. I think we made $20 apiece.

CHAPTER FIVE

I just couldn't find my place in this world, my niche in this life, except for when I found Betty, so I changed day jobs again and went to work at Firth Carpet as an inspector. Betty was still working at Palmetto Worsted Mill, also as an inspector. It was nice to be back working the same shifts again so we could be at home together at night.

It was at Firth Carpet that I was reunited with a high school friend, Cecil McCauley. Cecil was also an inspector, and along with Carl Poole, who was actually the head inspector, we crawled around on the finished carpet after it had been run through the latex backing process, looking for tears and stains. From 8 am till 4 pm, Monday through Friday, and sometimes on Saturday, I inspected carpets, and on Saturday night I continued playing the gig at Mineral Springs with my band.

Sam Wallace was the supervisor over the maintenance department at Firth Carpet and he started using my little band at suppers he would have for his maintenance crew. My co-inspectors, Cecil McCauley and Carl Poole would usually get invited. Cecil started calling me Bass. That nickname was kind of like his tribute to me as a singer and musician. Cecil had become one of my loyal music supporters when a lot of people around home never thought my musical ambition would ever amount to anything.

Kenneth Pennington got introduced to waking Wister Todd up to rehearse, just like his brother Clyde and I used to do. I don't know what I would have done without my good friend and mentor, Wister Todd.

The Saturday night job at Mineral Springs ended and I changed some band members as well. I kept Kenneth on drums and added Roger Williams on piano, Joe Huffman on lead guitar, and a young kid named Johnny Phillips that played both saxophone and trumpet. I played bass and did the singing.

We worked the NCO Club at Donaldson Air Force Base in Greenville a few times. A few months later Clyde Pennington was discharged from the army. He could already play some lead guitar but he had always played drums. Now that his brother Kenneth was playing drums Clyde started working on improving his guitar skills.

Clyde had married Connie Cox, from Woodruff, and they

Old Memories and Me

stayed with Betty and me at our house on Wallace Street in Watts Mill. Lifelong friend Bradley Jones had bought the house as an investment and rented it to Betty and me. I got Clyde a job at Firth Carpet on Sam Wallace's maintenance crew.

It wasn't long until Clyde felt he was ready to play gigs on guitar so he joined the band, replacing Joe Huffman on lead guitar. Huffman had built a recording studio in Greenville with his two brothers and didn't play many clubs after that. Eventually Clyde's wife's cousin, Johnny Cox, would join the band and we had two saxophones, with Jonny Phillips doubling on trumpet at times. We had the best band around, maybe one of the best bands in the entire south. We were that good.

Our first gig was the Cascade Lounge in Greenville, 32 miles from Laurens. The Cascade Lounge was more of a honky tonk than a lounge. Making music my fulltime job was always in my dreams and on my mind. Other than those few weekends I had toured down in Georgia with a band, and the Saturday night gig at Mineral Springs, I hadn't had much opportunity at that point in my life to expand my musical career. And if I had, I have to admit I didn't have the guts to just pull up roots and go. I surely had Betty's support but still I wasn't ready to give the big time a shot yet.

The Cascade Lounge was my first real regular paying music job after meeting Betty. It was a Friday and Saturday night gig at first. Later we added Sunday night. We made $25 apiece per night, playing mostly rock n roll, R&B and some country. We did it all. The twist songs were popular then; *The Twist, Peppermint Twist, Let's Twist Again Like We Did Last Summer*. We also did songs like *Soul Man, So Fine, Bo Diddley, Sixteen Candles*, you name it and we played it. Clyde and I would use extended chords and leave the stage, me with my bass and him with his guitar behind our necks, and twist on the dance floor with the dancers. We played the *Limbo Rock* a lot too because it was the mini skirt days. I would fib and announce, "We have another request for the *Limbo*," so we could watch the ladies get down and try to go under the limbo stick that two people would hold low to the dance floor. I guess we all have a little mischief in us.

Betty went with me a lot when I played clubs. I admit I was a jealous guy. With Betty being so pretty and having a great figure she drew a lot of looks from men but the looks didn't bother me so much. It was when she got flirted with and a guy came on really strong to her that would make me mad. One guy did that at the Cascade one night. He was drunk and went over to the table where Betty was sitting with the other band member's wives and girlfriends. He asked her to dance and she declined but the guy then tried to pull her to her feet anyway, attempting to put his arm around her. I was onstage playing but when I saw him grab her arm I practically threw my electric bass off and jumped down from the stage and went after him. The bouncer got to him first and had him in a headlock. I don't recall my exact words but I flat called him a couple of names I wouldn't want my preacher to have heard me say. The guy apologized and things settled down. The three or four buddies he was with escorted him back to his table.

We always had fifteen or twenty airmen from Donaldson Air Force Base come to the Cascade every night we played. South Carolina didn't allow drinks to be sold in clubs and bars back then, so everybody brown bagged. That's where you bring your own whiskey in a brown bag and buy a beverage at the club to mix it with. You could buy beer on the premises, just not mixed drinks. The Air Force guys usually brought pure, 100% alcohol, and mixed it with orange juice. They would get stoned on that stuff, whatever it was. When the guy tried to grab Betty that night, and I had came off the stage, they were ready to defend the USA and Betty and me too. Everybody likes the band, except drunks who want to dance with a band member's wife or girlfriend.

When I got back on the stage and we were playing another song, maybe ten or fifteen minutes after the incident, the guy came to the front of the stage and looked up at me and yelled over the loud sound of the music, "Screw you," and shook his fist at me.

I kicked at him from the stage but missed. However one of the United States Air Force's finest didn't. He had jumped to his feet and raced across the floor, through the crowd and knocked the guy to the floor with one punch. All hell broke loose then. The bouncer, the club owner and a few more sober customers finally got things calmed back down. They threw the guy and his buddies out of the place.

Driving home that night Betty told me I was her hero. At 6' 2" and 150 pounds I looked more like a scarecrow than I did a hero.

I had another scary episode at the Cascade. I was using a four speaker Fender Baseman amplifier and one of the speakers burst one night in the middle of a set. When a speaker burst like that it makes a rattling noise when you play. We took a break and I got some big cotton balls from somewhere and stuffed them into the busted speaker. When we resumed playing my amplifier sounded fine for a while, until that cotton got hot and caught on fire.

It was mostly smoke at first but somebody tried to help my bad situation out and splashed an alcohol beverage onto my smoking speaker. *Swoosh!* The thing burst into instant flames. Without thinking I ran my hand between the metal slits that framed the speaker and pulled the burning cotton balls out. It wasn't until a few minutes later I realized my fingers were wet. They were bleeding. I had cut myself pretty bad on that hot and sharp metal in the back of my amplifier. Betty took me to the emergency room and it took seven stitches to close the wound. I still carry a scar from that incident today. I didn't know picking and grinning could be so dangerous.

With the pipes freezing and bursting so much in our rented house and with the weekends at the Cascade Lounge bringing in $75 a

Old Memories and Me

week, along with both our regular day job salaries, Betty and I decided we could afford a house that was underpinned. We moved into a house in Laurens on Hillcrest Drive, just down the street from Hillcrest Baptist Church where Reverend Buck Word had married Betty and me.

I hadn't consumed much alcohol back in those days but one night I had way too many beers working at the Cascade. I got drunk. Betty had gone with me again that night and drove us home. I was sitting on the front porch steps at 3:30 am, sick as a dog, and moaning about being hot. It was wintertime, freezing cold. Betty got disgusted with me and poured a bucket of water over my head. "Here, this will cool you off!" I nearly froze to death. Good thing I didn't though because a few days later Betty told me I was going to be a father.

Betty's mother, Miss Jessie, was a wonderful mother-in-law to me. She worked in the cotton mill in Fort Mill for a while longer after Betty and I were married, but later she became a nurse at a hospital in Charlotte, N.C., just a few miles from Fort Mill. She was there when the great NASCAR race driver, Fireball Roberts, was brought in with burns from a terrible crash at Charlotte Motor Speedway. She helped treat and take care of him. He died from those burns. Miss Jessie wasn't a racing fan but she took it hard when Fireball died because she had been with him, taking care of him while he fought for his life. She was less than five feet tall but she stood much taller with her caring heart and the strength to raise all those children, most of the time by herself. Betty's daddy died of a heart attack when she was 6 years old. Miss Jessie's first husband was killed by a train. Betty's other sister, Juanita McGuirt, and two of her brothers, David Harrison and Clarence Huntington all still lived in the Fort Mill/Rock Hill area. We still went up there about once a month, usually driving up with Bobbie and Jack.

Like my mama, Miss Jessie was a marvelous cook, making everything from scratch, vegetables from the garden and meat from the freezer, or a chicken from the yard.

Sometimes we would all go over to Betty's sister Juanita's house but I was always a bit cautious there at dinner time. Juanita's husband, Dee McGuirt, would often cook and he was bad about serving us what we thought was beef from a cow, then later confessing it was actually goat meat, or a turtle stew.

Betty called me at work one day at Firth Carpet.

"Charles, President Kennedy has just been shot," she told me and I could tell she was almost in tears. "They think he is dead."

"What?" I asked. Did I hear her correctly. "John Kennedy is dead?"

"They think he is," she said. "It happened down in Dallas just a while ago."

"Hey y'all," I turned and called out to Cecil McCauley and Carl Poole. "President Kennedy has been shot."

Like everybody else in America and around the world, Betty

and I followed the news on television vigorously the next few days. It was unbelievable what had happened. Lee Harvey Oswald had been arrested on suspicion of assassinating the President of the United States.

A lot of Sundays we still all gathered at my mama and daddy's for dinner. We were having dinner there the Sunday that Jack Ruby shot Lee Harvey Oswald. I was watching television when that happened and saw it live. I couldn't believe what I had just seen.

"Hey, everybody come in here," I called out to those in the kitchen. "Jack Ruby just shot Lee Harvey Oswald!"

It was a dark time in American for everybody.

One of my favorite things to do, even after high school, was play basketball. Firth Carpet sponsored a basketball team and I coached and played on it. We got in an industrial league and I still remember some of those games. Betty, like most of the wives and girlfriends would come and watch us play. I always wanted to do good in front of her. She just had a way of bringing out the best in everything I did.

There was no doubt she was the woman I was supposed to meet and live my life with.

I started getting better at writing songs when I was near my mid-twenties. I was still working clubs and honky tonks around the Greenville area. I was always a pretty decent singer, even considered by some to be a good singer. Modestly, I admit I sang pretty well and did harmony really well. There was no doubt I had put together probably the best band around. I had renamed us The Checkers, the Cascade Lounge band still intact, except Johnny Phillips had left and Donny Wilson had taken his place to twin with Johnny Cox on Saxophones.

Betty and I, along with Kenneth Pennington, went down to Atlanta to try and get The Checkers a job playing there full time. We found one place willing to talk to us. It was a strip joint. I don't think I need to tell you what Betty had to say about that. We returned home to Watts Mill.

I had changed day jobs like the seasons change. I still couldn't find my *niche*. From Palmetto Worsted Mill to Watts Mill, to Firth Carpet, to a Palmetto Life Insurance salesman, I worked somewhere during the day for eight hours and played the clubs and joints on weekends. Betty worked at Laurens Mill for a while but quit and went back to Palmetto Worsted Mill. By then I think she was up to $1.55 an hour.Our rent was now $45 a month.

I was still in the National Guard and we were having a weekend drill when Bobbie Bolt called the armory on Sunday and told me I better come home. Betty had gone into labor. I rushed home and at 4:30 pm we took her to the Laurens County Hospital. For the next 8 hours I was a nervous wreck.

Betty would have sharp labor pains and she knew I was wringing my hands every time that would happen, scared to death. She would tell me to leave the room. I would leave and she would send for me to come right back in. She would send me out of the room again, then she would want me back beside her. Back and forth I went. I must have walked ten miles that night.

It was July 30, 1962, and at 12:28 am Betty gave birth to our daughter, Barbara Dawn Craig.

I was 25 years old. Betty was 26.

I was waiting with Miss Jessie out in the hallway just outside the delivery room. We heard a baby cry, then another one. I thought the sounds came from the same direction.

"Oh, Lord," I gasped. "She's had twins!"

It turned out another baby was born in the next delivery room within a matter of minutes after Dawn was born. Barbara Dawn Craig was named after Betty's twin Bobbie, whose real name was Barbara. Betty and Bobbie had made an agreement when they were younger that when they got married and had children, if they were girls, they would name them after each other. Bobbie's daughter was named Robin Joyce because Betty's middle name was Joyce, so Dawn was named Barbara Dawn after Bobbie, or Barbara.

Betty had an acute kidney disease when she was a little girl and it flared up again from having Dawn. She nearly died and had to be hospitalized for a while. The doctors said she used up most of her good kidney and having another baby could kill her. We never had another child. Like most fathers I wanted a boy at first but Dawn turned out to be a beautiful tomboy, so I got the best of both worlds.

Thankfully, God answered our prayers and Betty got better. She still had to watch her intake of sodium and she wasn't supposed to drink any alcohol. She took care of herself and got her strength back and everything went back to normal in our lives.

With the help of Betty's mother, Miss Jessie, we bought our first house. It was on Lee Street in Laurens, just outside the Watts Mill unincorporated sign. I also changed jobs again and went to work for GAC Finance as an adjuster.

Dawn was just a toddler, and I would hold her in my arms and walk around in the yard saying things like, "Now this is grass, and this is a tree." Man, I was so proud and happy. We lived in a four room frame house that we were buying, not exactly a mansion, but it was ours and I had beautiful Betty and her love and the most precious daughter in the whole wide world. I mean, I felt like, *you can have the dollar, I can be happy on a nickel.*

Each year that passed Betty got prettier and prettier. She was letting her dark hair grow out a little longer. There's only one thing better than a man waking up in the morning with a pretty woman lying beside him and that's waking up being married to her. I was a lucky man and I knew it.

I started trying to write rock n roll as well as country songs.

I wanted to record in a real studio but didn't have the money or the means. It was really a bad time for me musically. I continued to work clubs for another year or so and finally got tired and was ready to just give up music. Lately the band seemed to always have problems. There was jealousy, petty differences, musicians were always quitting and sometimes the club owner didn't want to pay what he was supposed to if it was a slow night. It was always something. I got so frustrated I just quit.

"I can't take this anymore, honey," I told Betty. "It's always something." I walked away from music.

With extra time on my hands from not playing clubs on the weekend, Betty and I decided to add on a room across the back of our home, 30 feet by 14 feet. Betty and I did everything ourselves. We couldn't afford to hire it done. We got a small home improvement loan from Palmetto Bank.

Betty helped me pour cement and lay down the concrete blocks for the foundation. She held the boards and studs while I nailed them in place. We were a sight, building that room ourselves. We had never built something as simple as a rabbit box, let alone a room onto a house.

"Hold it straight, honey" I told Betty. I was trying to nail a stud in place and she was holding it.

"I am holding it straight," Betty said. "You're just nailing crooked."

We both laughed. She was so cute trying to hold and balance that big two-by-eight. I just had to stop nailing and give her a little kiss.

"Nail it, honey," she panted. "We can kiss later. This thing is hard to hold in place."

Dawn was old enough by that time to be walking and running around everywhere. She always wanted to help, so we would let her pick up small blocks and little pieces of wood and pretend she was building something too.

Most afternoons we would work on that room until after dark, using a long drop cord for the buzz saw and the light to see by. If Betty was too tired to cook I would run out and bring back burgers and fries. Sometimes she and Dawn would go with me and we would eat in the car, parked at The Hub or some other drive-in restaurant.

Somebody at the lumberyard had sold us green flooring lumber and after we laid the tile the wood dried out and the tile started separating. Where we joined the new roof onto the old roof didn't work out to well either. The first time it rained it leaked there and the next morning we awoke to find water standing on our new $125 pool table. We gave up carpenter work after that project.

I started out as an adjuster for GAC Finance, which is nothing but a chase man going out to people's homes and trying to collect on past due accounts. That can be a hazardous job at times. Like the rainy night I was sent out to this guy's house way out in the country to try and get him to pay on an account he hadn't paid on in nearly three

Old Memories and Me

months. It was pouring down rain and his yard had no grass, all dirt, and this rainy night it was mostly mud.

I climbed the wooden steps to the wooden front porch. It was summertime and the frame door was open, just the screen door was between me and the hallway. There was a bare light bulb hanging from the ceiling in the hallway and it was difficult to see beyond that point inside the house.

I knocked on the door, a bit apprehensive, having dealt with this man before. He was a drinker and he was a pretty good size guy. They didn't have a telephone and I was glad. My manager back in the office was a tough talking guy and when I would put a person on the phone to talk to him about their delinquent bill, with me in their house, he would make them mad and there I would be to face their fury while he was safe back in the office. I hated that.

I knocked again and finally his wife came to the door. I asked if her husband was home. Darn, just my luck. He was home. When he came down the hall he was more of a huge shadow with the bare light bulb glaring behind him.

"Evenin', how are you tonight?" I smiled and tried to sound friendly and polite.

"You're from that finance company, ain't cha?" he asked with his gruff voice.

"Uh, yes sir," I acknowledged. "You've gotten behind on your payments again," I continued, searching for any kind of lingo that would tell him why I was here, and at the same time not make him angry. "You are...." I started to say.

"I ain't got no money," he snapped and cut me off in mid sentence.

I cleared my throat nervously. I could tell he was drinking, if not indeed fully intoxicated. "I am afraid we have to have at least a partial payment sir."

Without any warning he shoved the screen door open and I stepped backward very quickly. He advanced toward me, snorting something I didn't understand. I backed up more until I fell off the porch. I wound up on my butt in the mud. "Shit." Now anger overruled my fear but not by much.

"Get the hell out of here 'fore I whoop your ass!"

I got to my feet, soaking wet. It was still raining hard. "I tried to be nice about this," I told him and tried to sound a little tougher than I knew I was. I pointed a trembling finger at him. "Now, you have attacked me. That's against the law, you know." I was muddy and rain was running down my face.

He didn't care about the law. He stumbled down the steps mumbling again, angrier than ever. His wife came out onto the porch and screamed at him to stop. He didn't stop. He took a step toward me and swung. I stepped back and he missed, losing his balance. This time he fell in the mud.

I left him there cursing and slipping down every time he tried to get up. I got in my car to leave, yelling at him through the window I had rolled down just a little bit. "You better have a payment in the office by noon tomorrow."
Yeah, right.
I wondered if Hank Williams started out like this.
Thank the Lord I made assistant manager at GAC. That meant I could sit at a desk in the office calling people on the phone and trying to collect past due accounts and feel a lot safer. We hired another adjuster and he took over my hazardous job.

Betty opened up a dress shop just a few doors down from where I worked at GAC. We would drive up to Walhalla to a dress factory, about 2½ hours away to get our station wagon full of casual dresses on consignment. We weren't getting rich with our new business but it was ours and it started making a little profit after a month or so.

We did have shoplifters at times and on one occasion Betty chased a woman out the door that had gone into a dressing room with two dresses and emerged with only one. There was no doubt the woman had the other dress on under her own clothes. When Betty told me about the incident that night and how the woman weighed well over two hundred pounds I couldn't help but laugh as I pictured Betty, at 105 pounds, confronting a woman that size.

"It's not funny," she said to me. "That dress cost ten dollars."

By the way, Betty never caught her, thank goodness. No, not for Betty's sake but for the other woman's sake.

A short time later GAC transferred me to Aiken, South Carolina. We had to sell our little home with the new addition we had struggled building ourselves and give up our dress shop as well.

Aiken was about an hour and a half away from Watts Mill. It was my and Betty's first time to move away from the Watts Mill, Laurens and Clinton area, a radius of only about eight miles we had lived in all of our lives.

In Aiken most GAC's accounts were from Ft. Gordon, an army base across the river in Augusta, Georgia. They were harder to keep up with than a rabbit in a briar patch, always getting transferred or discharged. Every so often we were required to work so many P&L accounts. P&L stood for profit & loss. These were accounts that hadn't been paid on in quite some time. You have to find these people. It is called *skip tracing*. It is almost hysterical what some people will say when you finally reach them about a long past due account.

I found this one guy up in Ohio. He hadn't paid on his account in almost a year.

"Mister Johnson, this is Charles Craig, with GAC in Aiken, South Carolina."

"Oh, hello there Mr. Craig," he beamed over the phone. "How ya doin? I was just thinking about you guys today. I am putting a

Old Memories and Me

payment in the mail first thing in the morning."
Yeah, right, about like I'm going to be President first thing in the morning.

There were only three things about Aiken that Betty and I really liked. One was our neighbors, another was a drive-in restaurant that had great hamburgers and homemade style chocolate milk, and the other was a little hole in the wall fish place that got fresh fish in every day from *Little River,* near the coast. They would gut and clean the fish you picked out from the iced down case, filet it upon request, then deep fry it in a huge black pot. They would wrap it in newspaper so it stayed hot until you could drive home. Our favorite was the Red Snapper.

Every day at the finance company was mentally exhausting. Trying to find the borrowers that had skipped town, plus help my adjuster with the ones he was trying to collect from out in the field was sending me home every night ready to pull my hair out.

I couldn't take that kind of work any longer. I answered an ad in the newspaper and applied for a credit sales manager position with Lerner Shop, a chain of ladies dress stores. I got the job and after training across the river in Augusta, Georgia for six weeks, they transferred me to Columbia, South Carolina. I still wasn't playing in a band anymore but I had kept my bass and guitar. As frustrated as I had gotten, I still missed playing and singing. I always played the radio when I was in my car and sang along with my favorite country singers.

The job at Lerner Shop was going pretty good. They were thinking about making me a state supervisor. I was starting to think that maybe I had found my calling after all. Of course it ended up not being my calling but I was trying to make the best of it. It helped that my sister Ruby, her husband Bob, and their four children now lived in Columbia as well. At least we had family there. We had a nice brick home in a good section of the city, a nice yard and a screened in side porch. Betty was working at J.C. Penny and we were bringing home decent money. Still, something was missing in my life.

One day at lunch I went to a cafeteria by myself. It was very crowded and finding a table was difficult. There were two young men sitting at a table with two empty chairs. They noticed me with my tray of food looking for a seat.

"Would you like to join us?" one of them asked.

As the old southern saying goes, *I have never met a stranger,* so I accepted the invitation.

"Thanks," I said and sat down.

We introduced ourselves to each other. One of them was named Bob Courtman, an ex-songwriter from Philadelphia. During our conversation it came out that he had written a big pop hit called *One, Two, Three.* He had used his royalties to move down to Columbia and go into a business with the other young man seated at the table with us. I was really impressed that Bob Courtman had written a song that had actually been recorded and was marveling over the fact it had become a well known million-seller in the pop field. I had heard of the song.

"I use to play in a band and sing. I write a little too," I told them. It sounded kind of dumb saying I wrote songs sitting at the same table with a guy who had written a #1 hit. My songs were all stuffed in a box somewhere gathering dust.

"Really?" Bob Courtman sounded interested. "What kind of songs do you write?"

"Some rock n roll but mostly country though," I informed him. I had to throw in the rock n roll, I mean, he was a pop writer.

"I would like to hear them sometime," Bob told me seriously.

I was surprised. "Really?"

"Yes, I'd like to hear them sometime," he told me again.

"I have never had a song recorded before and I am not a great singer or anything," I told him. I didn't want him to expect anything fancy or really good. We exchanged telephone numbers and I gave him my address and he said he would come out Thursday night. That was that. Man, a hit songwriter was coming out to my house to hear my songs and listen to me sing. What in the world was Betty going to say!

"You met him a cafeteria?" she asked when we both were home after work.

"Yeah, downtown at Morison's Cafeteria. He and his friend offered me a seat at their table," I explained and shrugged with a slight grin. "He wants to come out here Thursday night."

"You don't even know him, Charles," she reminded me. "How do you know he wrote that song he said he wrote?"

I hadn't thought about that.

"I don't," I admitted. "But I bet he did. I could just tell. He was a nice guy and well, I just believe him."

Betty was skeptical but she wanted anything that would make me happy, within reason of course. Ok, sometimes not within reason. Betty and I didn't do everything by the book. Actually, we didn't do anything by the book. We did it by love and on instinct. She was 31 and I was 30 but we still acted like teenagers in a lot of ways-- fairly intelligent teenagers, though. Actually, Betty was extremely smart. She had been told she had the IQ of a genius. If you recall, I failed geography my senior year in high school.

She agreed to let Bob Courtman come out on Thursday. I was excited and it rubbed off on Betty. After going to the A&W Root Beer for burgers and a milkshake we went back home and after we got Dawn to bed we stretched out on the carpet in the den. We did that a lot, lay on the floor and talked rather than on the couch or in a chair. That way we could roll over and lay in each other's arms. We always held each other a lot; maybe just hands sometimes, but we made contact. We had that kind of relationship, that kind of need to always share with each other.

After the excitement about me going to be able to show my

Old Memories and Me

songs and singing to a professional had subsided a little, we got into another mood. We made love a lot when we were celebrating something, no matter how small a deal it was. Actually, we just made love a lot, then we would celebrate that.

I had Wednesday afternoon off so I got out my guitar and rehearsed, trying to pick out some of what I considered to be my best songs. I must have changed my mind ten times. I was excited but I was also nervous as heck. Doesn't excitement and nervousness go together though? Yeah, it's called nervous anticipation.

I called Betty at work several times to ask her what songs she thought I should sing for Bob Courtman. She wasn't supposed to receive calls at work but I wanted her opinion so I called anyway.

Bob Courtman came over around 7:30 that Thursday night. Betty had made supper and he ate with us. He was a nice looking young man and nicely mannered. Betty was as impressed with him, as I was. Later, the time came for me to perform. Center stage, or rather center living room floor. I wasn't nervous anymore, just excited.

I sang a song called *Over the Rugged Mountain* first. Betty was watching me and beaming proudly. Bob Courtman was nodding and smiling as I performed the song.

>   *Over the rugged mountains*
>   *Across the valleys below*
>   *From my house to your house*
>   *That's where I have to go*

"Charles, that song is really great," Bob told me and I could tell he meant it. "And you sing great. You have your own style. Your voice is rich and full."

I thanked him modestly. Then I sang several more of my songs. Before the night was over Bob Courtman told me he would like to take me into a studio and record me on two of my songs, *Over The Rugged Mountain* and *Show Me*. He said he would pay for everything.

We knew it was just going to be a local project but Betty and I were excited that somebody was willing to pay for me to record and was even going to press up records for the radio stations around the state and surrounding areas.

I couldn't sleep that night. Betty finally fell asleep after we talked for an hour or so lying in bed. Before she fell asleep though, she said, "I love you more than anything in the whole world."

"I love you more than anything in the whole world, too," I answered back and kissed her goodnight.

I will say it again. I was a lucky guy. I was lying beside one of the most beautiful women God ever put on this earth, I had a beautiful and darling little girl too, a good job, and now I was going to cut a record. Even horses don't have it that good and they get to go to bed with their shoes on.

We recorded the record at a Columbia radio station. It was a makeshift recording studio of course. We hired a lead guitar player, a piano player and a saxophone player. Bob Courtman was a good drummer. I played electric bass and sang the songs at the same time. Besides the lead vocal I stacked four different harmony parts.

Bob Courtman had 500 records pressed and put it on a label he made up the name for, *Shot Gun Records*. I hated that name but he was paying for it so we used it.

We didn't mark an A or B side. *Over The Rugged Mountain*, a country ballad, was on one side, and *Show Me*, more pop oriented, was on the other.

Right off we got both country radio stations in Columbia playing *Over The Rugged Mountain* and surprisingly a local pop station started playing *Show Me*.

Larry Garr was a disc jockey at WLBG in Laurens. The little radio station where I first performed when I was 15 years old kept coming to my rescue over the years. Larry Garr was originally from New York and he not only played both sides of the record at WLBG but he sent the record to a friend of his in New York, who also was gracious enough to play *Show Me*. A radio station in Charlotte, N.C. started playing *Over The Rugged Mountain* as well as WESC in Greenville, S.C. We had ourselves a little wonder hit on a very limited scale but still we were on the air.

Meanwhile, back at Lerner Shop my newfound recording success was causing some problems on my job. I had to talk by phone with the girls at the Columbia Credit Bureau on a daily basis, checking the credit reports on new charge account applications. Naturally, they knew my name was Charles Craig and when they started hearing a Charles Craig being played on the radio they knew it was me. Of course I had never met these ladies, just over the telephone. So, being curious, they started dropping by Lerner Shop to check out what they thought was a new recording star. Little did they know I was only being played at a few radio stations. I didn't tell them any different. I won't lie, I was eating the attention up. It got crowded back at the credit department at Lerner's sometimes. At times there were four or five females there at once wanting my autograph, a picture made with me, things like that.

After about a week of this, Mister Maddox, the store manager called me into his office. He gave me an ultimatum. Get out of the music business or get out of Lerner Shop.

"Did you talk this decision over with my supervisor?" I questioned him. My Southeastern supervisor really liked me and the job I was doing.

"Yes," Maddox assured me. "And he agrees with me."

"Oh," I said meekly.

Betty and I talked over that choice. Naturally, it affected her life too so I wanted to know what she thought.

Old Memories and Me

"Get out of Lerner," she told me emphatically. I knew she would say that.

So I quit my job at Lerner Shop. I guess I was finally in the music business, ready or not.

Betty kept her job at J.C. Penny while we waited to see what would happen with my record. In the meantime, a well-known record promoter in Texas had gotten one of my records and called me. He said the songs and vocals were good but the record sounded like an amateur recording as far as the quality was concerned. He wanted us to send the master to him in Texas and let him do some overdubbing, including adding black female backup singers on *Show Me*. He also wanted to manage and book me. He sent me a contract in the mail. When it arrived, Betty and I read it.

"He must think we are stupid and I will tell him so," she exclaimed, clearly upset. In a telephone conversation with him she told him so. I told you she was very outspoken and she was my strength and my brains.

The way the contract read, this guy could send me to say, Mobile, Alabama on a promotional tour at my own expense. It also had him making a lot bigger percentage than me off the record and my songs. I didn't know anything about royalties and managers. Bob Courtman had known enough to tell me I needed to affiliate myself with either BMI or ASCAP so I would get paid for my songs being played on the radio. I chose to sign with BMI. I don't know why I picked BMI. It just sounded good. That was 1966.

I turned the guy from Texas down. Looked like not only was I out of a regular job, but I was also back out of the music business after a short stay. One thing that hurt was that the pop star, Joe Tex, came out with a single with the same title as my *Show Me*. His was a national hit. Needless to say mine wasn't.

We couldn't make it on what Betty was making at her job so we packed up and went back to Watts Mill. We moved back in with my parents. We hadn't advanced very far. That is where we started out when we first got married nine years before, living with Mama and Daddy. Well, that is not quite true. We had Dawn now and that was quite a lot. She was a little platinum haired doll, 4 years old now.

Our plan was to save as much money as we could and just take a chance and move to Nashville once we had the funds to do so. I got a job at Palmetto Mobile Homes stapling molding in mobile homes on an assembly line. Betty went back to work at good old dependable Palmetto Worsted Mill. Everybody had about stopped playing my record by then. Larry Garr still played it a few times at WLBG.

"We'll save what money we can and then move to Nashville," Betty said with determination.

You would think she would have given up on my dream by now.

CHAPTER SIX

     I was still bursting with the desire to sing and perform, and now writing songs had become important to me as well. I teamed up with my old friend, and former band member Clyde Pennington, along with another former band member, sax player Donny Wilson, and we opened up a little recording studio on the Princeton Highway, just outside of Laurens. Donny's daddy let us use an old store building he owned. We put empty egg cartoons on the walls and got some old carpet somewhere for the floors. We had two reel-to-reel tape machines, both two tracks. I managed to get two microphones, both inexpensive. It was all we could afford.
     Our intentions were for me to write songs and we would record them and send them to Nashville. However the first thing we recorded was a jingle I had written for Cox's Gulf Station in Watts Mill. I made $20 and they played it on WLBG. I had made my first money as a songwriter.
     Like me, Clyde and Donny had day jobs so we only got to work in the studio late afternoons and nights. We knew a man who called himself Tennessee Ralph and he had written a song called *Sixteen Women In A Limousine*. It was a funny song about piling sixteen women into a limousine. He wanted us to record it. We did two versions of it. I sang one version and Clyde sang the other.
     We had no engineer, so one of us had to put the machine in record mode and run around into the next room and grab our instrument and we would all three start playing. It was hit and miss with nobody to watch the recording levels.
     We got our reverb by running the sound through an empty septic tank. Hey, we might have been hillbillies, but we were creative hillbillies. Tennessee Ralph pressed up some records of my version of *Sixteen Women* and we made a picture with me sitting in a Cadillac with sixteen young girls everywhere inside the car and outside, lying on the hood, the roof and hanging out the windows. Local stations played the record some and Ralph sold copies at his used car lot in Hickory Tavern. Later he released Clyde's version of the song too. Neither of us sold many records but caused a lot of talk and got some attention around the area.
     Some time later, Betty's two brothers, Clarence Huntington

Old Memories and Me

and David Harrison put up the money for me to record my third record. I was going to record at Arthur Smith's studio in Charlotte, N.C. This was the same Arthur Smith that wrote *Guitar Boogie* and would later write *Dueling Banjos*. We recorded two songs I had written, *Let's Talk It Over* and another one that I cannot recall the title to. The label was named after David and Clarence, thus DaClare Records. Again, I got a little airplay locally but that was about it.

  The little studio Clyde, Donny and I had up on the Princeton Highway didn't last long. I wanted to record in Nashville. I knew Nashville was the only place to record a country record with high quality and competitive standard. I dedicated myself to writing better songs, so when the opportunity presented itself, I would be ready. It happened sooner than I expected

  I had been talking for a few weeks to Tommy Hill, a record producer with Starday Records in Nashville. He had also written the Webb Pierce hit, *Slowly*. Tommy told me to call him collect, he would then refuse the charges and call me back on the record labels watch line.I had sent him a few of the songs I had been writing lately.

  "I think you are going to be a great songwriter," Tommy Hill told me over the phone. "I like your singing too."

  "Thank you," I said graciously.

  "Can you come to Nashville?" he asked me. "At least for a couple of days so I can get with you and see what we can do?"

  Go to Nashville, Tennessee? Man that would be a dream come true, even if it was just for a couple of days.

  I talked to Betty about it. Where would we get the money for the trip? Betty's mama, Miss Jessie, and her twin sister Bobbie, came to the rescue.Between them and what little Betty and I could come up with we had enough for gas, meals and two nights in a cheap motel. Betty had to work overtime that Saturday at Palmetto Worsted Mill making time-and-a-half per hour and we needed the money. Also, we couldn't afford for both of us to be off work two or three days the following week so I got a guy to ride with me and we took off for Nashville. His last name was Alford. He had been my adjuster at one time at GAC when I was assistant manager there in Laurens. He paid his own expenses.

  Betty and I had a 1965 Mustang now, dark blue and a beauty. It was a Sunday and traffic was heavy. The interstates between Marietta, Georgia and Nashville weren't finished so it took quite a while, having to get off on two lane roads a lot where they were still working on the interstate. Finally, we arrived in Nashville late Sunday afternoon. The sign read, *Music City USA*.

  I can't begin to tell you how excited I was. My hands were actually trembling on the steering wheel. I kept thinking, *what if I meet Webb Pierce or Marty Robbins?* I guess I would just have gone into convulsions.

  We checked into a motel on Murfreesboro road. As soon as I

got into the room I called Betty collect. "I'm here, honey."
"You sound excited," she told me and she sounded excited for me.
"I am," I beamed. "Tired but excited."
"How long did it take you to drive up there?" she asked.
"About eleven hours," I told her. "There was a lot of construction and detours everywhere."
We weren't used to being apart. "I miss you," I told her.
"I miss you too," she said, then added, "Don't you be flirtin' with any girls up there."
"I won't, you know that honey," I said, laughing a little. "I ain't gonna look at nothing but for a record deal."
"Yeah, well, you better not, or I'll bop you one." Betty warned with a laugh, but I knew she meant it.
We talked for a few a little while then I talked to Dawn for a minute. When back got back on the line we said what we always said when we were about to hang up the phone.
"I love you," I told her.
How much?" she asked, already knowing what I would say.
"More than anything in the whole world."
"I love you, too," she replied.
"How much you love me?" I prompted her, smiling on my end of the line.
"More than anything in the whole world," she assured me and I could tell she was smiling on her end as well. Hearing her say that could get me through anything.
That night Alford and I had burgers and fries for supper then drove around looking for record row. Naturally, we got lost. When we finally did find record row, with directions from someone, I was disappointed. There were no glittering lights, no flashing neon's, no Las Vegas atmosphere. Of course it was dark and we couldn't see much anyway.
"This is it?" I asked myself as much as I was asking Alford.
That was it. Two streets: primarily 16th and 17th Avenues. The tallest building I saw was 3 stories. Most of them were one and two story brick buildings and remodeled homes turned into offices. Broadway, downtown was lit up like a Christmas tree. We went in *Tootsies* for a few minutes and I saw all of the stars pictures hanging all over the walls. It was getting late and being Sunday night, Ernest Tubb Record Shop was closed. We drove by the historical Ryman. That gave me chills.
When I got back to the motel I called Betty again. I forgot it was an hour later back home. I woke her up but she didn't mind. I just had to tell her I had driven by the Ryman and up and down record row. We just talked for a few minutes, said we loved each other again and said goodnight.

Old Memories and Me

The next day I found my way out to Starday Records, out of town a little way, on Dickerson Road. Tommy Hill had set aside some time to see me. He was just as nice in person as he had been on the telephone. I went inside, taking my guitar along with me.

"So, when did you get into town?" Tommy asked, smiling as we went into his office and he offered me a chair across from his desk.

"Last night," I told him.

We exchanged some small talk for a few minutes.

"I like that record you made of *Over The Rugged Mountain*," he told me. "It's different. Where'd you record that?"

"At a radio station in Columbia, South Carolina," I told him. "It wasn't a real recording studio or anything."

"Yeah, the quality isn't quite up to par," Tommy said. "But it's not that bad. You did a pretty good job."

"Thank you."

Tommy Hill was easy to talk to.

"You wanna get that guitar out and sing me a couple of tunes?" He said.

"Sure," I responded and tried to act like this was something I was used to doing, singing for big record producers like him. Actually, I was pretty relaxed though.

I took my inexpensive Harmony guitar out of its cheap case. I strummed a few chords. "I don't play guitar that great," I informed him. "I mostly play electric bass."

"That's alright," he assured me with a pleasant smile.

I would later learn that Tommy Hill was an excellent guitar player. I settled in on a G chord. "I wrote this one about a week ago," I told him.

"Okay," he smiled.

Tommy Hill smiled a lot. I liked him. I sang the song for him.

The way you hold my hand
When you walk with me
The way you look at me
When you talk to me

The song was called *Just By Watching You*. I had written it about the way I felt when Betty did certain things, things she did without really saying much but I could tell, just by watching her, how she felt.

"That's a good little song, Charlie Craig," Tommy complimented me when I had finished. He smiled again too.

That was the first time anybody had ever called me Charlie. I liked the sound of it. It sounded more like a country singer than Charles did. At his request I sang him another one I had just written, called *Willow Bend Springs*.

"I think you've got a special talent, Charlie," he said. He picked up a tape from his desktop. "I've got your tape here of *Over The Rugged Mountain*. I haven't played it for Don Pierce yet 'cause I wanted to hear you sing live first. I want to play it for him now though. I really like your songwriting and your singing."

Tommy had told me about Don Pierce. He was the owner of Starday Records.

Tommy took my tape and disappeared into another office down the hall. A few minutes later I could hear my tape playing of *Over The Rugged Mountain*. When the tape finished I heard voices. They got louder. It was Tommy Hill trying to convince Don Pierce to sign me to Starday Records.

A short time later Tommy came back into his office.

"I couldn't convince him," he said almost apologetic and shaking his head. "I told him *Over The Rugged Mountain* was either another *Winchester Cathedral* or a piece of nothing."

I couldn't tell if that was a compliment to me or not. I think it was, kind of anyway.

I didn't get a record deal that day. Tommy Hill still encouraged me to try and move to Nashville as soon as I could. He said he felt confident that I could make it as a songwriter even if I couldn't get a recording deal.He told me to stay in touch and if I did move to Nashville he would help me any way he could. Tommy Hill would soon become one of my biggest supporters and best friends.

Alford and I messed around the record row area the rest of that day and just by chance I met a guy named Lou Stringer. Lou had a publishing company and I showed him the same songs I had showed Tommy Hill.

"Those are really good," Lou told me sincerely. "I will sign them right now to my publishing company and pitch them for you and try to get 'um recorded."

I didn't know what to say. I didn't know anything about publishing. Lou Stringer explained to me that a publisher signed a contract with a writer for a song, or songs, which would give the publisher exclusive rights on the song and in return the publisher played the songs for all the record labels and producers and tried to get the song recorded by a major artist. If a song got recorded the publisher made 2 cents a record which he split 50-50 with the writer. If it became a single, then the publisher and writer each received an equal share from whichever performing rights organization licensed it. It my case it would be BMI because I had recently signed with them even though I wouldn't be officially affiliated until I actually had a song recorded and released.

"Two cents," I said, "That ain't much."

"I know," Lou agreed. "But if the album sells a million copies then that's $20,000."

Old Memories and Me

"Wow," I said, somewhat amazed.

I had never seen two thousand dollars, let alone twenty thousand.

"Let me ask you something," said Lou. "Do you want to record these songs yourself? You sing really good."

"Well, Yeah," I nodded.

"Well, if you can raise the money I will take you in the studio and produce you on these songs." Lou told me. "I have a record label called Pick City and I will put you a record out on it. But I don't have the money in my budget to do it myself, or I would pay for it."

"How much will it cost?" I asked him.

"I will have to figure it up," he said.

Later, Lou told me it would cost somewhere around $2,000 to record three songs. I told him I didn't have that kind of money and had no idea how to raise it. My two meetings had left me with mixed emotions. Both Tommy Hill and Lou Stringer liked my songs and my singing. Evidently Don Pierce didn't like either. Lou Stringer wanted to produce me in a Nashville studio, with Nashville musicians, the very thing I had dreamed about doing. However, neither Lou nor I had the $2,000 it would cost for the recording session.

I called Betty.

"I'm coming home."

Betty, Dawn and I continued staying with my parents until we could either make the move to Nashville, or just give up on the whole idea and me settle down to some other profession.

One morning about 7 a.m. something woke Betty and me up. Suddenly, we realized it was my daddy yelling and we could tell the hollering was coming from outside. We pulled on some clothes and told Mama to come on. We all three ran outside and found Daddy on the ground near the dog pen where he kept his foxhounds. Daddy had been feeding his dogs and had gotten down on his back and couldn't get up.

"Ohhh, I can't move," he groaned and looked really pitiful lying on the ground in so much pain.

"What happened, Papa?" Betty asked and knelt down beside him. Both of my daddy's daughter-in-laws called him Papa.

"My back just give out on me," Daddy said and grunted as he tried to hold his back with his hand to get some relief.

"Let me try and help you up," I said and gently tried to help him to his feet.

"No, no, no..." Daddy gasped in agony. "Stop, Charles."

We had to get him to the house somehow. I suggested calling an ambulance but Daddy wouldn't have any of that.

"Just let me lay here a minute or two," he told us, lying on his side. Betty held his head off the ground.

Mama kept saying, "Now Benny, let us help you."
I knew his back was out and wasn't going to get any better by him just lying there. We had to get him to the house, which was about a hundred yards away. I had an idea. "I'll be right back," I told them.
I ran to the shed where Daddy kept his tools and things. I got a wheelbarrow. Well, we had to have something to roll him back to the house in. I pushed it back to where they were.
It wasn't a funny situation but Betty couldn't help but laugh a little when she saw me run up with that wheelbarrow.
"What are you doing with that?" she asked me.
"We're gonna put Daddy in it and roll him to the house," I explained and shrugged, "What else can we do?"
"No, no," Daddy protested and shook his head. "You can't move me yet."
"We can't leave you here, Papa," Betty told him kissed his forehead. "It'll be alright."
"That's cause it ain't you hurting," Daddy said and tried to laugh through the pain.
"Lordy, what a mess," Mama proclaimed. "You want me to call Hubert Matthews to come and help?"
Hubert Matthews was Mama and Daddy's good neighbor that helped them do a lot around the house and in the fields. He sort of looked after them. I don't know who looked after Hubert.
"No, we can do it," I told Mama. "You hold the wheelbarrow for us."
"Charles, just wait now," Daddy said and gave me a look that tried to put himself in control of the situation. I felt so sorry for him. I have a bad back too and when it goes out I know the terrible pain it causes. You can't walk. You can't even crawl.
"We can't leave you here all day, Daddy," I said.
"Yes you can," he groaned.
We had to move him despite the added pain we were going to cause him.
I got his upper body and Betty got his legs. Mama held the wheelbarrow. Daddy yelled. Somehow we got him in that wheelbarrow. Betty was only 5' 2" and 110 pounds but she was stronger than her size would indicate. I was 6' 2" and around 150 pounds. Daddy was 5' 10" and perhaps 160 pounds. Mama was actually bigger than any of us but she was holding the wheelbarrow so it wouldn't tip over as we loaded him. We must have looked like the Three Stooges, plus one.
"Ohhh," Daddy moaned, cramped up in that thing with his legs hanging over the sides.
He might of weighed only 160 pounds but trying to roll him in that wheelbarrow across a dirt patch of land and then over the grass in the backyard, it felt like he weighed 260 pounds. We finally got him to the back porch stoop.

Old Memories and Me

I hope you know what a stoop is cause I don't know exactly how to describe it. Well, I'll try. It is like a small, uncovered porch made of concrete with steps. In this case it was what you stepped up on to get to the back porch which Daddy had walled in and made into a covered porch.

Now, how to get him from the wheelbarrow onto the stoop.

"How are we gonna get him out of the wheelbarrow?" Betty asked.

"As careful as you can," Daddy suggested.

As careful as we could we dumped him onto the stoop.

"Ohhh!"

"Be careful y'all," Mama cautioned, pity showing in her voice for my daddy.

Betty and I were out of breath. We both smoked. Daddy was glad we had to rest a few minutes.

"How we gonna get him in the house?" Betty panted.

"I don't know," I confessed.

"Can we get the wheelbarrow up on the back porch and let's roll him into the house?" Betty asked.

"No," Daddy protested. "I ain't getting back in that thing." I thought he was going to cry. I had never seen my daddy really cry.

Mama was wringing her hands with worry. "You want me to call Hubert Mathews, Charles?"

"No Mama, I don't want you to call Hubert."

I don't know which one of us thought of it but we got a blanket and spread it out and somehow got Daddy on it and the three of us, Betty, Mama and me, pulled Daddy from that stoop, across the framed in back porch, across the kitchen floor, through the den, and finally into the front bedroom.

"Now, how are we gonna get him on the bed?" Betty wondered.

I called an ambulance.

The medics arrived and got Daddy on a gurney, raised it to bed level and helped him ease off of it onto the bed. Bad backs are a medical mystery. Two days later Daddy was up and around again.

I continued working at Palmetto Mobile Homes and Betty at Palmetto Worsted Mill. We were trying to save money but we weren't doing too good at it. We had talked and talked about how to raise the money for a recording session in Greenville. It wouldn't be as good as the Nashville sound but it would be cheaper.

I had a sore throat and went to see Doctor Atkinson in Watts Mill. It turned out to be a blessing in disguise.

"How is your music coming along?" Doctor Atkinson asked me, looking into my open mouth at my throat. I don't know how he expected me to answer him with that stick pressed down on my tongue, gagging me, and my mouth wide open.

"It unt unning oo ood," I muffled.
"What?" the doctor asked, taking the thing out of my mouth.
I swallowed hard, and then told him, "It ain't doing too good. My music, I mean"
"Oh," Doctor Atkinson said, "Why not?"
"I went to Nashville the other week," I began. "They liked me, well two people did, and they think I should record and cut a record in Nashville."
"Well, why don't you?" he asked.
"It cost two thousand dollars," I told him. "And I don't have two thousand dollars.
"Is that all that's stopping you?" Doctor Atkinson asked.
"Well, yes," I confessed.
"Are you any good?" he wanted to know.
He actually knew nothing about my music. He just knew I played and sang around the area.
"Well, some people say I am," I told him modestly. Then I added, "Yeah, I'm pretty good."
"Then I'll put up the money," he told me without batting an eye.
My mouth fell open again, this time on its own.
"By the way," he said. "You have tonsillitis."
In May of 1967 I made my second trip to Nashville, along with Betty, my mother Clara, and Betty's mother Jessie. Bobbie kept Dawn for us.
Trust me, don't ever go anywhere with two mothers-in-law at the same time. God love them but one wanted to do this and the other one didn't and vice versa. Back and forth we went trying to keep both of them contented.
We made the trip for me to record on Pick City Records. Lou Stringer, produced the session and we recorded at Columbia's famed Studio A. Bobby Hardin, of the Hardin Trio, sang harmony with me and some of Nashville's most prominent musicians played on the session and it really flattered me that Jimmy Capps, the acoustic guitar player, and Roy Husky, the bass player, who was considered one of the best upright acoustic bass players in the world, stayed over and listened to the tracks long after the session was finished. Famed steel guitar player Lloyd Green played on the session too. Willie Ackerman was on drums. The Ackerman Family and the Craig's would become close friends later on.
That session was some big time stuff and I knew I would be back. I became close friends with most of the musicians from that session, including my harmony singer Bobby Hardin. Junior (Roy) Husky would always call me Big Charlie. I found that funny because he was a little taller and lot heavier than I was. I was 6' 2" and probably still weighed only 150 pounds, so don't ask me why he called me Big

Old Memories and Me

Charlie.
        We had recorded on Friday. The next night, Saturday, Lou took me backstage at the Grand Ole Opry. It was still at the Ryman then. He made Polaroid pictures of me and some of the Opry stars together to use as promotion for the record. I kept running upstairs to the balcony to show Betty, Mama and Miss Jessie the pictures. Man was I proud to be in photos with Porter Wagoner, Ernest Tubb and Dolly Parton.
        Betty got a little upset about the picture with Dolly. "She's got her boobs all over you," she accused.
        "I couldn't help it," I told her. "No matter where I stood they were all over me."
        I couldn't believe I was actually backstage at the Grand Ole Opry. Tex Ritter sat in the shoeshine chair and told some road stories while he got his boots shined by an elderly black man. I stood there looking at him and listening in awe. One story Tex told was about songwriter Kent Westbury traveling with his band. Kent had a habit of rocking back and forth and just could not sit still. He rocked to and fro, not side to side. Tex Ritter told how Kent got on his nerves when it was Kent's turn to drive the car out on the road, rocking back and forth driving down the highway. Tex went through the motion to illustrate as he sat on the shoeshine stand getting his boots polished and shined. Later I would have the opportunity to meet and get to know Kent Westbury. Even sitting in an office chair he would do that same rocking motion. It didn't hurt his songwriting though. Kent Westbury was an excellent writer.
        They only had a couple of dressing rooms at the Opry then. At the back of the stage were different backdrops they kept changing, depending on the sponsor for that segment of the Opry. One would go up and one would come down. Stagehands did it by hand with ropes and sandbags. It's a wonder nobody got hit in the head.
        Grant Turner was one of the announcers. I had listened to him for years on WSM, coming on the air at 2 a.m. in the morning just as Ralph Emery went off. On Friday and Saturday nights Grant would work the Grand Ole Opry as one of the featured announcers. Grant Turner was a radio legend to me and I am sure to many others as well.
        That night I spent some time talking to Loretta Lynn backstage and having my picture made with her. She was a pretty lady and extremely nice. She talked just like she sang, with that heavy southern drawl. Roy Acuff was there and without a doubt he was one of the crowd favorites. After all, he was *The King Of Country Music*.
        I really enjoyed Bob Luman's performance that night. I couldn't believe Jimmy Dickens. His guitar was as big as he was. Minnie Pearl was there too and as usual she was a hoot. I got pictures made with just about everybody. I felt like I already knew all of them personally from listening to them on the radio for years and watching some of them on their television shows. I had seen a lot of them perform

in package shows in Greenville, South Carolina. They called them package shows because back then a show would consist of four or five acts on the same billing.

Lou Stringer and I took a mastered version of my record to Ralph Emery and I thought I was king of the hill when Ralph played *Just By Watching You* on his late night radio show at WSM. I was scared to death of Ralph Emery but somehow I got through the interview and he must have liked me because over the years he would have me on his show many times and played my songs regularly.

Betty, Miss Jessie, my mama and I returned home to Watts Mill. I didn't go back to playing clubs. That just wasn't working for me anymore. Donny Wilson's daddy had sold the building where our little studio was so that was gone. Not long after coming back from recording in Nashville I met a man named Sherwood Burton that had built a pretty nice studio near Watts Mill. At about the same time I learned that a longtime family friend, Edith Orr Riddle, had three daughters that sang beautifully. They were Susan, Peggy and Beth. They ranged from 14 years old to 19. We started rehearsing together with me singing my songs and them singing backup. It sounded really good with the Riddle girls harmonizing with me. Sherwood Burton let us record in his studio. He didn't charge us anything because he used us to get his studio set up better. He needed live recordings for that and naturally we were willing. Clyde Pennington, Kenneth Pennington and Wister Todd helped out as musicians. I played bass on the sessions.

Lou Stringer released a single by me on his Pick City Records. The A side was *Just By Watching You* and the B side was *Lyda Don't Think I Should*. Both were songs I had written back in Watts Mill. Never in my wildest dreams did I think I would record them in Nashville, Tennessee.

After visiting Nashville, recording in a famous studio, with famous musicians, going backstage at the Grand Ole Opry, and meeting so many country music stars, and Ralph Emery playing me on his radio show, I was really inspired to write more songs. I would write songs at least three or four times a week. My record, *Just By Watching You*, was getting more airplay than any of my previous records but it still wasn't setting the world on fire. It was getting airplay at some stations across the country but not nearly enough to bring it in the national charts. Still, I was excited and Betty and I were making plans for me to have a full time career in music. I was still afraid of just turning loose of everything and making that jump. I don't know why though. There wasn't much to turn loose of.

Betty was my soul mate, the love of my life, but Dawn was my pride and joy. Her hair was platinum blonde and couple that with her pretty brown eyes and she looked like a little movie star. She was

Old Memories and Me

5 years old now and I took her to the grocery store about every time I went. People were always making over her and buying her candy and things. Mama and Daddy treated her like she was the Queen of Sheba, especially my mama. I was a proud daddy. I treated her like a little princess and to me she was just that.

Betty and I helped Mama and Daddy in their garden and Daddy always had a huge one. We would pick beans, turnip greens, dig up potatoes and pull weeds. Betty would still sit down with Daddy a couple of times a month and write out checks for him to pay bills. He treated Betty like she was one of his daughters. They really got along well. He was also crazy about my sister-in-law Ruby, Bill's wife. I had a sister named Ruby and a sister-in-law named Ruby and a brother named Bill and a first cousin named Bill. It doesn't end there. I have another first cousin named Betty Ruth and I married a Betty. I have a first cousin named Charles and of course I was a Charles. I guess our family minds didn't have to travel very far to pick out names.

Time was passing by and I was miserable working at the mobile home place. I felt lost and unsure of myself. I would sit around at night picking my guitar and trying to write songs but I was getting discouraged.

Betty and I still hadn't been able to save much money to move to Nashville. My record was completely over with. Nobody was playing *Just By Watching You* anymore. Not even WLBG in Laurens.

One night Betty told me to sit down at the kitchen table. She wanted to talk to me. Mama and Daddy had already gone to bed. We always did that. Talk. It was our bond that got us through a lot of tough times.

"If you're ever going to give music a real try now is the time to do it." She just came right out and said it. "Let's move to Nashville. Just sell or give away what little furniture we've got and go."

"Are you crazy?" I asked her, my eyebrows raised in surprise.

"Yes," she said.

We both laughed. Then we talked very seriously for a long time. I took her hands in mine and thanked her for believing in me so much. I remember thinking again how beautiful she was and how lucky I was to have her. Sometime after midnight the decision was made. We would move to Nashville as soon as we could sell some things and raise a little money. Betty put in her notice at Palmetto Worsted Mill and I did the same at Palmetto Mobile Homes.

One Friday Betty and I drove up to Charlotte, N. C., about 90 minutes from Watts Mill, to try and meet Tammy Wynette. There was a show that night at the Auditorium with Tammy in the show and a Charlotte disc jockey named Mike Clore had gotten me two backstage passes. Mike was originally from Columbia, South Carolina and I had met him when Betty and I lived there. Not only was Mike Clore a disc jockey but he was a singer as well. When he still lived in Columbia I rode up to Charlotte with him to appear on the Arthur Smith television show. It was taped to be broadcast later and on the drive back to Columbia Mike stopped in several small towns and mailed postcards to the television station back in Charlotte saying how well his performance was liked on the show. He signed each card with a different name. The only problem was a baseball game superseded the show he was on and the postcards arrived a few days before the show was actually broadcast. It was quite embarrassing to Mike to say the least. However, I couldn't help but get a laugh out that situation. Later Mike Clore would learn to laugh about it too.

    Betty and I had gone up early that Friday because Tammy Wynette was doing a promotion thing for a Charlotte car dealership. We had hoped to be able to talk to her there. We hung around and finally got lucky. I found an opportunity to introduce myself to Tammy Wynette and told her I was a singer and had written a few songs. I had a tape to give to her if she would accept it.

    "Do you have a guitar with you?" Tammy asked me.

    "Yes I do," I told her. I was nervous as a fox being chased by a pack of hounds.

    "We can go out to your car and you can play me a couple of things," Tammy told me.

    Wow. Tammy Wynette was going to sit in my car and let me sing for her. I couldn't believe it. I was just hoping to hand her that tape.

    Tammy, Betty and I went out to our Mustang. Tammy and Betty sat in the two bucket seats in front and I sat in the back with my guitar and sang two songs for her. I was so nervous my voice was trembling and I kept missing some of the chords on my guitar. I must have done pretty good though because Tammy was impressed.

    "You need to get yourself to Nashville," she advised me sincerely. "You sing good and your songwriting talent really has a lot of potential."

    "You really think so?" I was grinning from ear to ear. I looked at Betty and she was grinning too.

    Tammy Wynette gave me her record producer's office number in Nashville. "Tell him I told you to call."

    I was excited about her thinking I had enough talent to possibly make it in Nashville and I was pumped about calling her producer but the thing I was mostly excited about at that very moment was I couldn't wait to get back to Watts Mill and tell everybody Tammy Wynette had sat in my car and listened to me sing. What a thrill and a time in my life I will never forget.

    That night Betty and I attended the Charlotte country music show backstage. We met the legendary Lefty Frizzell. Meeting and talking to Tammy Wynette and Lefty Frizzell both in the same day was an incredible experience.

    That Monday I called Tammy's producer and left a message.

Old Memories and Me

He didn't call back but his secretary did and told me to call her when I got to Nashville. I had told her we were coming there to try and make a go of it. Just a few weeks later, on Saturday night, July 29, 1968 I performed at Greenville Municipal Auditorium in a country music package show hosted by radio station WESC. I had gotten to know several of the disc jockeys at the station, especially Wally Mullinax and the program director, Bob Hooper, and they put me on the show to try and help jump start my career. They had been playing my records quite regularly.

The Riddle girls sang with me that night, Susan, Peggy, and Beth. There was somewhere around 9,000 people there. When I peeped out from behind the stage and saw all of those people I got so nervous I could barely swallow. I thought I was going to choke.

I did manage to perform though and I was sandwiched between David Houston and Conway Twitty. I did three songs, *Just By Watching You, Lyda* and *Willow Bend Springs*, the three songs I had written and recorded in Nashville. The Wilburn Brothers band backed me. Doyle Wilburn remembered meeting me backstage at The Opry when I was in Nashville to record. Teddy Wilburn was a nice guy but Doyle and I just hit it off and became pals. Loretta Lynn was part of their show back then so I got to visit with her again.

The next morning we packed everything we had in our 1965 blue Mustang and headed for Music City USA. It was Dawn's birthday. She was 6 years old. We had $900 and what clothes and a few utensils we could carry in the car.

We were on our way and it would be a long way. I had never even had a song recorded by anybody other than myself and that was on small independent labels. I didn't even look like a country singer, or songwriter. I had short hair and no sideburns anymore. My ears stuck out. I was thirty-one years old.

We listened to country radio stations all the way to Nashville. We were thrilled to death and listening to country music just made it seem like we were a part of it now. When one station would fade out we would turn the dial until we found another. We talked about being up in Charlotte a few weeks earlier and Tammy Wynette sitting in the car with us and me in the back with my guitar singing for her. Both Tammy Wynette and Tommy Hill had said I had talent. Well, we would soon find out. Nashville, here we come.

CHAPTER SEVEN

Interstates 40 and 24 West were still not complete. We went by way of Marietta, Georgia, the same route I had taken on my first trip to Nashville. It took a long time again with all of the construction going on, the heavy traffic around Atlanta, detours and still a lot of two lane roads, plus Dawn having to go to the bathroom every 30 or 40 minutes. We finally pulled into Nashville late Sunday afternoon around 6pm. The cheapest motel we could find was $20 a night. Throw in gas and meals and $900 wouldn't last long.

We were tired from the long drive and Dawn was getting irritable and understandably so for a 6 year old. That first night we made bologna sandwiches in the motel room. I just had to drive up and down 16th and 17th Avenues' *record row* before going to bed. I know it was our first night in town but man I was now living in Nashville, Tennessee. I know it doesn't make any sense but I actually already felt like I belonged, like I was home.

Betty and I slept in one of the queen size beds and Dawn in the other one.

"I can't believe we're finally in Nashville," I told Betty, lying on my back with my hands clasp behind my head, just looking up at the ceiling. She didn't say anything.

"Honey?" I said and looked over at her. She was asleep.

I leaned over and kissed her on her forehead.

It had been a long and tiresome drive. Betty had kept Dawn occupied by playing little games with her, like seeing who count the most Volkswagens we passed and looking for clouds that formed faces and pictures. Well ok, I played too.

I couldn't sleep that first night. I have always been a night owl but the biggest reason was my excitement about now being a resident of Nashville. However, mixed in with that excitement was some fear of not being good enough to make it with my music.

Lou Stringer had promised to sign me to write for his publishing company for $25 a week as an advance and I signed a two-year contract the next morning. It was my first writing deal. He had a bi-weekly country music paper called *Countrypolitan* that went out to radio stations around the country and I made another $25 a week working for him trying to sell ads to recording artists and collecting

Old Memories and Me

unpaid bills from the ones who hadn't paid him for previous ads. That's how I met Del Reeves, among others.

"I don't owe him no money," Del told me over the phone and hung up. I had a strange and uncomfortable feeling like I was working for a finance company again, calling about overdue accounts. I called Del Reeves back and this time I talked to Ellen, his wife. She calmly explained to me the mix up and I was satisfied Del didn't owe Lou any money. After discussing the situation with Lou he agreed there had been a misunderstanding too. I didn't like calling about any past due bills and told Lou I preferred not to do that. I felt I was getting off on the wrong foot with some of the stars. Lou complied to my request and I started only calling artist about selling them space in his *Countrypolitan* paper.

Calling the stars to sell ads in Lou's paper really set up some nice friendships for me that would last for years to come. Those conversations led to relationships with Jim Ed Brown, Faron Young, Billy Walker, Jack Greene, Carl Smith and Bill Anderson, as well as mending the misunderstanding with Del Reeves.

Betty and I had found a duplex in the Melrose area near record row. We had gone to a salvage company and bought what little cheap furniture we could afford. Our dinette was a card table and three fold up chairs. Dawn slept on a folding cot. Betty and I had an old bed with a hard mattress, a small table and lamp and a chestier drawer. In the front room we had a soiled couch and chair that didn't match. We had a 13" television that Lou Stringer let us use. We made do with an ice chest until we could get a refrigerator.

We hadn't had a whole lot back in Watts Mill but it was like living high on the hog compared to what we started out with in Music City USA. I guess it was what you would call life in the slow lane.

When I wasn't working the phones for *Countrypolitan* I wrote songs for Lou's Stringberg Publishing Company. About a month after we had arrived in town I sit down one night and wrote a song called *Turn Ole' Nothing Loose*. After we demoed it Lou took the song to RCA Records and played it for producer Danny Davis. Danny liked the song and cut it on Hank Locklin, of *Send Me The Pillow That You Dream On* fame. Wow, I had my first song recorded by somebody beside myself and it was by a star on RCA Records. It was never a single but it was on Hank's next album and I thought I was going to set Nashville on fire. The day after Hank Locklin recorded that song we had a party at Lou and Carolyn Stringers house to celebrate my first song being recorded.

Everybody in Nashville was calling me Charlie, like Tommy Hill had done. It was weird at first but even Betty started calling me Charlie.

Lou Stringer had signed another writer, L. E. White, and he and I shared a couple of demo sessions, usually doing two of my songs and two of his. Woodland Sound Studio was one of the newest recording studios in town and we did most of our demos there. It was a beautiful studio with multi tracks and it was hard to comprehend that I was actually recording in a place that plush and modern with as wonderful a sound as you could get anywhere in the world. The musicians just blew me away with how fast they learned songs they had never heard before.

"How do you guys learn these songs so fast?" I asked guitarist Jimmy Capps.

"Well," Capps informed me, "It's really pretty simple to learn the chords because of the number system we use. "

He was referring to a system all musicians in Nashville were using to chart songs by using numbers 1 through 7 rather than writing out the actual notes, such as A, B, B-flat, C, etc. It is too complicated to explain how it works here but it is actually pretty simple once you learn it as a musician. It certainly saves time and also allows a singer to change the key they want to sing a song in without having to change the charts. The legendary Jordonaires came up with the system to use on background vocals in recording sessions. Famed harmonica player Charlie McCoy started thinking if it works for background singers then why not musicians as well.

Lou Stringer's partner in Stringberg Music was star singer Sonny James. Sonny had had a huge crossover hit in the late fifties called *Young Love*. Sonny never came around the office so I never saw him except on the Grand Ole Opry on occasions.

Lou eventually moved his office a little further down 17th Avenue and rented office space in a house owned by Central Songs, a highly successful publishing company with songs in their catalog written by Buck Owens and Harlan Howard, among others. I recall Billy Mize also wrote for Central Songs and he would come in from California to record. Billy was on Imperial Records.

I soon learned that Mel Tillis had an office next door. Mel had already written several hits for other artist and was now trying to build his own recording career. I was a big Tillis fan as a songwriter and when L. E. White and I shared another demo session I really loved one of his songs from that session called *I Love You More Today (Than He Can From Now own)*. I thought it would be a great song for Mel Tillis to record, but I admit, I was thinking that it would give me a chance to really meet Mel if I took that song to him. I had spoken to Mel a few times but didn't really know him.

Back in those days you didn't always have to have an appointment in advance to see somebody. If they weren't busy they would just say, "Come on in."

"Cu-come on in," Mel told me that day when I went next door to his office to pitch him L.E. White's song.

I had been in Nashville now about five months and being around the stars still made me a little nervous. Even though Mel wasn't

Old Memories and Me

the singing star he would later become he was already a songwriting star in the business and one of my heroes.

"Mel, I don't know if you remember me or not," I said, a little apprehensive. "I'm Charles Craig." I forgot to call myself Charlie.

"Uh, uh, no, bu..but come on in anyway," Mel stuttered.

I told Mel I had a song that L.E. White had written that I thought was a hit. I handed him the little reel-to-reel tape and he played it.

"I r-r-really d-do like it," Mel informed me and gave me that little flip of his hand sign he became so famous for.

I was tickled pink. It made me feel like I had formed some kind of bond between Mel Tillis and myself. It also made me feel like I was a little more a part of the Nashville family especially when Mel put the song on hold to record.

I was writing about every day now and writing some pretty good songs. I tried co-writing with a couple of people, including my new friend L. E. White, but I just couldn't get my mind to be creative writing with someone else. I don't know why that was but it just didn't work for me, so I continued to write alone.

I got by second song recorded and this time the singer was Nat Stuckey, also on RCA Records and again produced by Danny Davis. It was *Willow Bend Springs*, one of the songs that I had previously recorded myself on that first session I did at Columbia Studio a year or so before we moved to Nashville.

Man, I was on a roll for a new kid in town. Two cuts in the first six months I was here.

Betty and I had become friends with a couple our age that lived near the duplex where we lived. It was close enough to walk from our place to theirs. They invited us over one night to play cards. They had children as well and we took Dawn along. I had a beer that night and Betty had a mixed drink. About an hour later Betty started swelling in her face, hands and lower legs. We both knew right off it was her kidney disease reacting from the alcohol. We went home.

"Are you alright, honey?" I asked her as she laid down on the couch.

"Yeah," she said and tried to sound convincing.

She had experienced this kind of reaction before, sometime after getting too tired, other times from too much sodium or from alcohol, even after just one drink. Right at that moment her face was puffed up so much that even her eyes looked swollen. Her lower legs looked like they were going to crack open. It scared me.

"Come on," I told her. "I am taking you to the emergency room."

"No," she shook her head. "We don't have the money. I will be alright."

She was right, we didn't have the money and naturally we

didn't have any health insurance. I worried about her all night and kept her awake for hours by constantly asking her if she was okay. The next morning the swelling had gone down a lot and I felt a little relieved.

I stayed home to write that day so I would be near her. I was writing better and more commercially, as they say in the business, and a few months later I got another cut, *Bring The Woman Out In Me*, by Judy Lynn on Columbia Records, produced by Frank Jones. It was a B-side single and enough radio stations started playing it that it charted in Billboard. Even though it didn't chart very high I was ecstatic. I finally had a song in the national charts, me, Charles Craig, from Watts Mill, South Carolina. Well actually, Charlie Craig did. I had to get used to being Charlie.

Ralph Emery let me come on his late night radio show again at WSM and interviewed me and played the record by Judy Lynn. I also met Jon Riggs that night, the shaven head guy that answered the request line for Ralph's show.

"So, you've moved to Nashville now," Ralph said to me as he talked to me on the air.

"Yes sir," I replied, a bit nervously. I leaned in closer to the microphone. "About nine months ago."

I was going out all over the country on 650 WSM, from Nashville, Tennessee and I wanted to make sure everybody heard me. I had listened to that station for so many years back home in Watts Mill and it was hard to believe I was sitting there talking to famed disc jockey, Ralph Emery.

"You came here from North Carolina I believe," Ralph remarked.

"South Carolina," I corrected him.

"Oh, sorry," he smiled. "What town in South Carolina?"

"Watts Mill," I told him, then added, "that's a little mill village about two miles from Laurens."

"Well, Charlie, let's play this song you wrote and Judy Lynn has recorded," he announced. "It's called *Bring The Woman Out In Me*." Then, as an afterthought, he asked me, "Where did you get the idea for this song?"

I shrugged my shoulders and gave him a look I suppose was goofy and replied, "I just made it up."

Ralph Emery chuckled. "Let's give it a listen to."

Ralph had liked my recording of *Just By Watching You* and after hearing *Bring The Woman Out In Me* he told me that night that if I stuck with it he thought I had the makings of becoming a hit songwriter. That made me feel really good, coming from an industry giant such as himself.

"Thank you, I appreciate that," I said to him with a broad grin.

The next night Lou and Carolyn threw another party for me. Having three songs recorded within the first year I was in Nashville

Old Memories and Me

might not have been a big deal to the country music industry but it sure was to me. Heck, three songs recorded and one of them charting in Billboard Magazine was a big deal for about any songwriter. Curly Putnam had written the other side of the Judy Lynn record, a song called *Here Comes The Judge*, and to be on the same record with the writer that had written the classic *Green Green Grass Of Home* put me in high cotton, as far as I was concerned.

Then nothing. All of a sudden I couldn't buy a cut.

Since I played bass, I was told I could pick up some extra money playing demo sessions in the studios. I got a couple of chances at that but it didn't work out that well. I was a good stage bass player, however, playing bass, or any other instrument in the studio is quite different than playing on stage. I didn't realize I popped my bass strings until I did a session. Besides that, I just wasn't as good as the bass players playing sessions and making records with Conway Twitty, Loretta Lynn, Dolly Parton and all the other hits coming out of Nashville. It didn't take me long to realize I wasn't going to pick up extra income playing bass on recording sessions. I couldn't make a living on $50 a week either. Besides, Betty's kidney problem was acting up really bad again and we still had no insurance. Dawn needed school clothes and I couldn't buy her any. Our personal life was falling apart, just like my songwriting and singing career.

"You want to go back home?" I asked Betty. Things were looking bad and I was losing faith in myself again.

"No," she told me adamantly. "We came here to make it and we will."

I knew she would say that. Betty was a fighter. I was the weak one. I was strong in a lot of ways but ironically I was a bit doubtful about my songwriting ability. I knew I could write and sing pretty good but getting someone outside my immediate family thinking it was good was tough some times. Betty would get me back to believing in myself though. Seems like every time we started sinking she would get tough and right the boat again. Even sick in bed, with her face, arms and legs swollen with fluid from her kidney disease, she was still the strong one. She was also getting prettier and prettier. Her dark hair now down to just below her shoulders.

I had to get her to a doctor though. We had no money to pay a doctor and barely enough to buy a few groceries and pay rent. Someone told me about a kidney specialist at Vanderbilt University Hospital. I called and finally go through to him and explained Betty's condition and or financial situation. He generously agreed to see her. He put her on a medication for the fluid building up and causing the swelling. I paid him what I could every few weeks or so. We never did get him completely paid but he never sent us any demanding bills.

One day Mel Tillis called me and asked me to come next door to his office. When I met with him he told me Porter Wagoner was getting ready to record and needed a great ballad. Mel asked me if I minded Porter recording L. E. White's song, *I Love You More Today*, rather than him doing it himself. Mel said he had several ballads and Porter didn't. I told him that would be fine. I knew L. E. and Lou wouldn't mind because Porter Wagoner was a big singing star already and selling more albums than Mel at that time.

I already knew Porter and he thanked me for the song. Then, he turned around and got upset with me. Oh Lord, Porter Wagoner getting upset with me wasn't a good thing for my music career. It bothered me personally too because I liked Porter.

What happened was, L. E. White went out on the road and played in a few package shows that promoter Carlton Haney allowed him to perform in. Conway Twitty was on those package shows as well and L. E. spent some time talking with Conway and eventually played him *I Love You More Today*. Conway loved it and kept the tape L. E had played him.

A couple of weeks later Porter Wagoner walked into Mel Tillis' office.

"I was just up at RCA Studio B," Porter told Mel and it was clear to Mel that Porter was upset. "Conway Twitty is cuttin' my song."

Porter wasn't upset with Conway, nor Mel. He was upset with me. Mel called me and told me what Porter had said. It was all news to me. I had no idea how Conway had gotten the song and told Mel that. I promised I would find out. After confronting L E. White he told me he had played it for Conway. I then went back to Mel's office and told him how L. E. had played the song to Conway.

Right then I wished I were back in Watts Mill sitting on the rail. Nashville was getting too complicated. All I had tried to do was help a few people out and now Porter Wagoner was upset with me. Not some neighbor down the street, but *the Porter Wagoner*.

I went to Porter's office, scared to death, to explain to him about what had happened.

"It's alright," Porter told me. He had on a baseball cap and peered out from under the bib at me with eyes and an expression that didn't quite convince me *it was all right*.

"I really am sorry, Porter," I told him as pitifully as I could. "I didn't know Conway had the song."

I left Porter's office feeling still down and depressed because I felt Porter was still upset with me. I really couldn't blame him. I couldn't blame Conway Twitty for recording the song either. I don't think he even knew Porter had the song. Should I blame L. E White? Not really. L. E. said he just played it for Conway to hear because he had become friends with him.

A few weeks right after all of that happened Mama and Daddy came up to visit Betty, Dawn and me. I took them around town. Mama loved the Wilburn Brothers so I took her by their office. Teddy

Old Memories and Me

was there and signed a picture for her. Then, I took them by Porter Wagoner's office. Dolly was really nice and friendly but Porter seemed a little distant, not to Mama and Daddy, he was real nice to them, but kind of chilly toward me.

Later, I saw Mel Tillis.

"I apologized to Porter about the mix-up on the song but I think he is still upset with me about it, Mel."

"W-well," Mel stuttered, using a hand for emphasis. "Don't w-worry about it t-then. Y-you apologized."

"I don't want Porter mad at me," I told Mel.

"C-Charlie, you c-can't keep every b-body happy."

I didn't want everybody happy. I just wanted Porter Wagoner happy again.

Conway's next single was *I Love You More Today*. It was an instant hit. Oh well, I knew it would be for somebody.

In the coming weeks Porter went back to laughing and cutting up with me whenever I visited him or saw him at the Opry. All was well again and I was really glad because I liked Porter.

All was well, except for my songwriting career.

I started returning glass Coke and Pepsi bottles to the store and getting the deposit back to buy a can of pork and beans. If I had enough bottles I would buy some saltine crackers too. If we weren't poor we were standing at the door begging to get in. I had to get some kind of job and fast.

Lou Stringer used a printing company owned by Howard See to print his *Countrypolitan* paper. Howard was also a Church Of Christ minister. He gave me a job at his printing company doing paste up and artwork. I was a pretty good artist. I give two of my lifelong friends from back home credit for teaching me to draw during our school days. They were Marion and Wayne Crowe, brothers that were as good at drawing characters as some professionals like Al Capp, who drew the Lil' Abner comic strip.

A friendship grew between Howard See and me. He paid me more than the job was worth because he knew I needed the money. A lot of people say they are your friend. Howard See proved he was a friend.

Late one evening there was a knock on our door. It was Howard See and he had a box of groceries. Betty and I both nearly cried. If not for Howard See I might not be writing this biography. I might have had to go back to Watts Mill and work in the cotton mill and leave my dreams lying on the sidewalks of 16th and 17th Avenues. There were a lot of dreams all up and down music row from the footsteps of other songwriters and singers that finally had to give up and leave Nashville. You can't see them with your eyes, but they are there, invisible footprints of lost dreamers. Sometimes, when I would walk down the streets of music row I feel like I am stepping on some of those fallen dreams.

Howard See thought I had a real talent and that I needed to get with a big publisher with my songs. A bigger publisher could also put me on a larger advance. Lou Stringer owed Howard a modest bill for some printing work and Howard offered Lou a deal on my behalf.

"Let Charlie out of his contract and I will mark your bill here paid."

I never knew how much Lou owed Howard See but whatever it was Lou agreed to the deal. In fairness to Lou, I have to say he really tried to get my songs recorded and also pitched me all over the row as an artist. It just wasn't happening after those first three cuts. We were dead in the water as a team.

I will always be grateful to Lou Stringer for signing me to my first publishing deal and getting me my first cuts by major recording artist.Although they never became big hits, those cuts actually launched my songwriting career. Lou and I would remain friends and I am thankful for that too.

I will also be forever grateful to Howard See too for what he did for Betty, Dawn and I. As I said earlier, without him, I might not be writing this book today because there probably wouldn't be a story to tell.

Old Memories and Me

CHAPTER EIGHT

In 1969 I signed an exclusive songwriting contract with Cedarwood Publishing, the largest publisher in Nashville at the time. Cedarwood was owned and operated by Bill and John Denny, along with their stepmother, Dolly. They had great staff writers like Wayne Walker (*Are You Sincere?*), Carl Perkins (*Blue Suede Shoes*) and my new friend, Mel Tillis (*Detroit City*). The Cedarwood catalog included other standards like *Long Black Veil*, *Waterloo*, and *The Battle Of New Orleans*. I was already in awe of Mel Tillis, and now meeting Wayne Walker and Carl Perkins was just as awesome. They all became my friends, and gave me advice on how to improve my writing. They helped guide me with their experience, advice and encouragement. I was surrounded by some of the greatest songwriting talent in the history of country music.

In the first weeks at Cedarwood, among all of those classic songwriters, I wondered, *what am I doing here*? Meeting Carl Perkins after telling those girls back in Statesboro, Georgia I was his cousin was a little frightening. Eventually, I got around to telling him about that and he laughed about it. Carl Perkins was a great guy.

"It's a wonder it hadn't done you more harm than good," Carl told me modestly.

One of the first things that caught my attention when I first went with Cedarwood was a check underneath a glass top desk. It was a royalty check issued to Mel Tillis. It was for 22 cents as I recall.

"T-t-that is m-m-my first r-royalty check," Mel told me, stuttering as usual and gesturing with his right hand.

It certainly wouldn't be his last royalty check. He now was also becoming a star as a recording artist.

Mel was a lot of fun to be around. I use to look for him during the day, hoping he would come by Cedarwood so I could talk with him. We became pals and to this day I still think about him and the friendship he gave me back then. Mel Tillis is one of my all time favorite people in the music business. He has written some big time hits, some classics, and my favorite Mel Tillis song is *Mental Revenge*. Just think about what that title says about someone trying to get over a lover that has left them for someone else. That is such a well-written song and some of the lines are so unique, like, "*I hope that the train from Caribou, Maine, runs over your new love affair.*" Some writers go a lifetime and

Old Memories and Me

never come up with a line like that. Mel Tillis was brilliant with coming up with unique lines and ideas.

Cedarwood put me on $150 a week draw. That was really good in 1969, especially for a new writer who had never had a top ten hit. Heck, I hadn't even had a top 40.

I loved those days at Cedarwood. It had a family feel there. A lot of the stars came by, like Minnie Pearl stopping by to sit and chat with Dolly Denny in the lobby just inside the front door. Brenda Lee came by a lot, and Waylon Jennings, Carl Smith and Webb Pierce. Carl Smith and I became pals and we use to talk on the phone from time to time. I couldn't believe I was talking to the man that recorded *Are You Teasing Me*, the song I use to sing in clubs back in home. Lucky Moeller had his booking agency in the Cedarwood building for a while and he booked a lot of the stars back then. I was fortunate to get to know most of them.

I talked it over with Betty and decided to play in bands again. I started working clubs in and around Nashville, making $35 a night, Friday and Saturday nights. I was bringing in $220 a week total. We felt like poor rich people. Betty and I had never made that much money before. We moved to Hermitage, a suburb twenty minutes east of downtown Nashville, into another duplex, but this one was a lot nicer, and we got better furniture, most of it on credit. Now Dawn had a real bed too.

Betty and I had joined a music business-bowling league on Sunday nights in Donelson. Hermitage was a lot closer to Donelson than where we had lived in the Melrose area. Jerry Reed and his wife, Prissy, bowled in the league for a while. Charlie McCoy, the famed harmonica player, had formed the league and a lot of well-known musicians, songwriters, producers and engineers bowled. Willie and Jeannie Ackerman were our partners that formed our team. Willie had played drums on my first session when I had recorded *Willow Bend Springs* during that second visit to Nashville.

We had a blast bowling but it was very competitive. I bowled a 665 three game series one night. Scratch. Most of the time though I had less than a 500 series for 3 games.

Things were getting better, especially financially. I didn't have to take bottles back to the store for deposit returns to get food anymore. Betty and I bought our own bowling balls and shoes. Dawn had some new clothes. She was seven years old now and going to school at Dodson Elementary in Hermitage. We bought a used Chevet for Betty. Now we had two cars, with me driving the Mustang.

The first song I got recorded after signing with Cedarwood was *Window Number Five* by Johnny Duncan. It was on Columbia Records and Frank Jones produced it. He had produced my song *Bring The Woman Out In Me* on Judy Lynn at Columbia too. Along with Danny Davis at RCA, Frank Jones had become one of the first record executives to believe in my songwriting. He invited me to Johnny Duncan's session and I was awed. It was in Columbia's Studio A, the same one I had recorded in on my first trip to Music City. They recorded everything live that night.

Besides the basic instruments, bass, drums, piano, acoustic guitar, lead guitar, and steel, there was a large string section and a couple of cellos, plus the famous Jordonaires singing background. It was an awesome sound and I wrote the song this large session was set up for. That seemed so awesome to me. I felt ten feet tall even before the first note was played.

Frank Jones had told me he thought *Window Number Five* could make Johnny Duncan a star and he went all out for it. Although it only made it into the thirties in the Billboard charts, the song did actually help excel my and Duncan's careers to a higher level. Johnny would hit later with *Strangers*, with Janie Fricke singing with him. I was still a few years off from my first big hit. It was 1969 and I had been in Nashville less than two years.

I was around a lot of great songwriters every day, but I didn't co-write with anybody those first few years. I did try and position myself around as many successful people as I could. I asked questions about the business and I listened a lot as well. I made some lifetime contacts and friends in the music business bowling league.

One of those friends I came to know so well from that league was Charlie McCoy. As I said earlier, Charlie is one of the greatest harmonica players in the world. He started that bowling league and it lasted perhaps three decades. Charlie moved to Nashville from Miami in the early sixties, a few years before I got to town. One of he first hit records he played on was Roy Orbison's *Candy Man*. Charlie's harmonica part on that song was the signature sound of that hit record.

There were other great musicians in that bowling league. Wayne Moss, who created the guitar lick on Waylon Jennings's smash *Only Daddy That'll Walk The Line*, was in that league, with his wife Jerry. There was famed drummer Buddy Harmon, and his wife Marsha, and Curly Chalker, the well known steel guitarist, and his wife Barbara. Jim Colvard, another fabulous session guitar player, and his wife Laura bowled. There was Kenneth Buttrey, one of the best drummers in pop, rock and country music and his wife Delores. The list goes on and on.

The Colvards lived just around the corner from us. Laura and Betty became good friends, as well as Jim and I. He played guitar on most of my demo sessions back then. Our families became close and we visited a lot. Jim was one of the fastest picking guitar players I had ever seen. His fingers moved like lightening on those strings. He played country music for a living, but his first love was playing jazz. A lot of people didn't know it, except his closest friends, but Jim Colvard was a frustrated musician. He couldn't really show his skills on guitar in the studio playing three and four chord country songs, and in the late

Old Memories and Me

sixties and through the seventies most country songs were pretty simply structured and didn't have many chord patterns. As I said, Colvard loved jazz but that music wasn't in demand then, not in the studios. I don't know exactly what kind of drugs Jim got on, but he was on something, I could tell that a lot of times I was around him. And I was around him a lot.

Spider Wilson, another well-known guitar player also lived just around the corner. Spider played in The Grand Ole Opry staff band.

Betty's hair was really long by then and the older she got the more beautiful she became. I was writing good songs, starting to get a few cuts again and people in the music business were beginning to know who I was. I had a gorgeous wife, a precious little girl and I was gaining some respect as a songwriter.

I felt good about things.

Gene Kennedy was Decca Record's national promotion man and he also loved to work clubs and sing. He didn't play an instrument so he hired me to play bass in the band when he booked the job at the American Legion in Madison, a suburb of Nashville. It was a big room and we had great crowds. Being Decca's promo man Gene knew all the stars on the label, like Conway Twitty and Loretta Lynn. I knew both of those mega stars pretty well myself. Since I had arrived in Nashville I had tried to meet and get to know as many industry people as I could, producers, record label executives, other songwriters and the stars.

Loretta Lynn had a younger sister that was about 15 or 16 at the time. At that age she was too young to be in a club but she wanted to be a singer so we slipped her in a couple of times and let her sing a few songs. Her name was Crystal Gayle. Of course she would go on to record *Don't It Make My Brown Eyes Blue* and many more hits.

One weekend, in the early seventies, when our guitar player was on vacation, I had called every guitarist I knew, and some I didn't know, to fill in on guitar for that Friday and Saturday night. Dale Sellers, a well-known session guitar player, the man behind the lick on *Baby's Got Her Blue Jean's On*, told me about a guy I had never heard of. I called him and he said he would be glad to work the gig. It paid $70 for the two nights. I told him I would pay him $60 for both nights. That way I would make $10 extra. I didn't lie to him, I just told him how much I would pay him and he accepted it. He came out and worked those two nights on guitar. He also played fiddle. We did a lot of fifties songs, mixed in with country and he played them all very well. I was impressed.

"I sing a little if you need for me to," he told me during a break.

"Gene and I have a lot of requests," I informed him. "If we have time you can sing a couple."

We never did let him sing. Gene Kennedy and I were hogging the microphone and the attention for ourselves.

His name was Charlie Daniels. Nobody knew who he was back then but they sure do now. To this day, I feel like I owe Charlie Daniels $10 and an apology for not letting him sing.

A word of advice here; *be kind to everybody you meet in Nashville. You never know who the next star is going to be.*

That was the only opportunity I ever got to spend any time with Charlie Daniels but after he started recording I loved his music, his sound and the man. I became one of Charlie's biggest fans and still am to this day. I think Charlie Daniels brought country music a new generation of fans. He also stood up for America, long before many recording artists did. He is a very patriotic man. He had a new kind of music and a new attitude. I think of Charlie Daniels as a pioneer. He set a trend and opened some new doors.

I kept working clubs to supplement my songwriting income. We only made about 2 ½ cents a unit sold for a song in an album back then and my advance was still only $150 a week. If you were lucky enough to have a single and it went to #1, you might make $30,000 to $40,000 for the airplay. If you co-wrote the song, you made only half of that.

Gene Kennedy decided to get out of the band and I regrouped, bringing in a new lead guitar player and piano player. I had already started using a young drummer, Mike Copas, the son of the late Cowboy Copas. Mike stayed with me playing drums and doing some lead vocals and harmonies for seven or eight years. I hired Willie Rainsford on keyboards, and he also sang lead and harmonies. Willie worked recording sessions during the day.

I got lucky and found one of the best guitar players in Nashville to play in my band. He would play all my club gigs and also on all my demos throughout the late seventies and into the eighties. His name was Paul Yandell and he also worked with Jerry Reed and later with mister guitar himself, Chet Atkins. Paul Yandell had his own style and sound and to this day I still consider him one of the best guitarists to ever play that instrument. Paul played on some of Jerry Reed's early hits such as *Alabama Wild Man* and *When You're Hot You're Hot*. I used a few other musicians over the years, but Mike Copas and Paul Yandell were always there for me and the three of us became very close friends. The band and our sound was always built around the three of us.

The first song I actually co-wrote with anybody was with Betty. She wasn't really a songwriter that could sit down and construct a song by herself, but she did have a good knack with coming up with lines and structures of how the verses might go. If she didn't have the right line, it might inspire me to come up with the one that was right.

I remember the night Betty and I wrote our first song together. We were sitting on the couch talking. We had moved into the

Old Memories and Me

duplex on Terry Lane in Hermitage in 1969. Dawn had already gone to bed and Betty had made herself a rum and coke. I was drinking a beer. We were reminiscing about some of the good times we had had together.

"Remember building that room on to the house on Lee Street," Betty said. "It was hard work but I loved that little house, especially after we put so much of ourselves into it."

"Yeah, I loved it too," I said, remembering as well.

"The only house we ever owned," she reminded me.

"We'll buy another one someday," I promised her. I put my arm around her.

Betty had her legs stretched out, crossed at the ankles and her bare feet resting on the coffee table. She laid her head on my shoulder.

"I know one day you will have a bunch of hit songs, Charlie," she told me. "And we might have a little money then, but you know what, I don't think we'll ever be any happier than we are right now."

I kissed the top of her head and snuggled her closer. "You're right about that," I agreed and smiled. "You know, money can't buy love anyway."

"True," she said and took a sip from her rum and coke. "Money *can't* buy love."

"Ummmm," I said and took a swig of beer. "Sounds like a song title."

Betty set up straight. "Yes it does," she said. Then she sang, "*Money can't buy love, no money can't but love,*" and swayed her pretty head from side to side. It was a terrible melody but the idea was sure there.

"Well I'll be damned," I laughed. "My little wife is becoming quite a songwriter."

"Go get your guitar and let's write it," she smiled broadly. Betty had a shy way of smiling with her lips pulled back a little when she was in certain moods. Sometimes shy, sometimes sly, but always beautiful.

I went into the closet in our bedroom and got my Alvarez guitar. I got a legal pad and a pen and sat back down beside her on the couch.

Ok, some people call it a sofa, some even call it a settee. We call it a couch at our house.

Betty was singing some lines she was thinking.

"*It ain't the house that makes the love, it's the love that makes the house, and that's why I know, money can't buy love,*" she sang, all out of meter, but she was cute as heck sitting there singing and sipping on her rum and coke. She didn't drink often, or a large amount when she did, mainly because of her kidney problem but it didn't take much alcohol for Betty to get tipsy.

"That's pretty good," I encouraged her, and it was. "It needs to be a little more up tempo though."

"Play your guitar and hush," she told me and went back to singing the same lines, smiling like she had just won songwriter of the year.

I started putting some chord patterns together. "Hold on a minute," I told her. "Let me think."

"I'll go pee while you think," she informed me.

I was getting serious. This was a good idea. While Betty was in the bathroom I got a melody going with the hook line.

"Money can't buy love, money can't buy love, it can buy a whole lot of..." and I didn't have a rhyme for *love*.

I was one word away from the chorus. I knew that would be the chorus and I was playing a D, back to a G, then a C to D again and back to G, which was the base chord the song would be in.

Betty came back into the room.

"Listen to this," I said and sang those lines again, minus that one word I was missing.

"it can buy a whole lot of stuff, but money can't buy love," she chimed in.

Well, I'll be doggone. She had the word, *stuff*.

I wrote the lyrics to the chorus down on the pad and together we sang that chorus over and over a few times.

Money can't buy love, money can't buy love, it can buy a whole lot of stuff, but money can't buy love

Betty was working on her second glass of rum and coke and I was on my third beer. It was nice writing a song together like this. I always wanted her to write but she always said she wasn't a songwriter, and she wasn't really, but she had some good ideas and came up with a few good lines too, and besides, I liked the closeness we shared trying to be creative together. We just naturally enjoyed doing about everything together.

"We work good together," I told her, leaning over to kiss her gently on the lips.

"We sure do. Dawn's living proof of that," she smiled warmly and put a hand behind my head and pulled us back into another kiss, this one more passionate.

We could finish the song later.

The next day Betty and I finished writing *Money Can't Buy Love*. Helping write that song gave Betty a little confidence to help me with a few other songs. She helped me finish an idea Jim Hayner had started and asked me to help him with. It was called *The Generation Gap* and Jeannie C Riley recorded it right after we wrote it and it would eventually be nominated for a Grammy.

Then, there was the day I had stopped and picked up some Kentucky Fried Chicken and brought it home for supper. While we were eating I brought up how I had helped Daddy dress out chickens and sell them when I was a kid, saying back then everybody had chicken for dinner about every Sunday.

Later that afternoon Betty and I wrote a song called *Chicken Every Sunday*.

We were on a roll.

During the time I was writing as a staff writer for Cedarwood, I got to know Sammi Smith. I used her to sing some of my female songs on demos and I paid her $10 to sing *One Hurt At A Time* on a Monday afternoon demo session. That same week she recorded *Help Me Make It Through The Night*. To my knowledge Sammi didn't sing any more demos after that.

Karen Wheeler, daughter of longtime Grand Ole Opry sideman, Onie Wheeler, recorded *One Hurt At A Time* on Chart Records, the same independent label Lynn Anderson started out on. *One Hurt At A Time* did well enough in the charts for Karen that it landed her a contract with RCA. Still, I had never had a song go higher than the thirties in Billboard's top 100.

I used to ask some of the successful writers if I was doing something wrong in my writing.

"You are a good songwriter Charlie. Your time will come." Carl Perkins said to me one day at Cedarwood Publishing. "Like they say, every dog has his day."

It still amazes me how could I go from listening to Carl Perkins on the radio and jukebox back in Watts Mill, South Carolina, to sitting there talking to him in the flesh. In my opinion Carl Perkins had one of the greatest styles and sounds in rock 'n roll history. You can hear his guitar influence in the early careers of stars like The Beatles, Eric Clapton and many others.

Of course Carl's biggest hit was *Blue Suede Shoes*, recorded first by himself and then Elvis. He was such a humble man and you would never have guessed that he had written that monster song, along with *Matchbox* and *Honey Don't*, my personal all time favorite Carl Perkins song. Carl used the term *cool cat* quite a lot, and he certainly was a cool cat himself.

Carl Perkins became a good friend of mine. He even played guitar on a couple of my demos just because I ask him to. He didn't normally work demo sessions but he did for me and I felt privileged. I never forgot that favor. It was during this period that Johnny Cash recorded Carl's *Daddy Sang Bass*. Every time I was around Carl Perkins I realized I was in the presence of a musical legend.

On day I was hanging out with Carl at Cedarwood, looking through the charts when I saw the title *Trying To Beat The Morning Home*, recorded by newcomer T.G. Shepherd. "Wow! What a title!" I said aloud and showed it to Carl.

"Man, I wish I had thought of that one," he laughed

"You know," I told him, "Sometimes I get upset with myself because I didn't think of certain titles before somebody else did, like that one."

"Yeah," Carl replied. "And sometimes several writers come up with the same good hook at the same time. That always amazes me, how writers sometime think exactly alike."

He was right too. That has happened so many times in Nashville. But when you really think about how many songwriters are in Music City, it's a wonder that more ideas aren't duplicated.

Carl was recording on Columbia Records at that time, with Bill Denny co-producing with Carl. He was still just as great as ever singing Rockabilly and playing his unique style on guitar, but times and music were changing, and Carl never had a huge hit again. Carl eventually started working and touring with Johnny Cash. Two legends on the stage together: Cash and Perkins.

By 1970 I have had come to know a small scrapbook full of famous people. If I had to name the most generous, most adorable, most likeable, most talented and the most down to earth person I had met since I had been in Nashville, it would have to be Dolly Parton. Hands down. With Dolly, what you see is what you get. She is the real deal. Dolly Parton never forgot where she came from. And she always knows where she is going.

I went to see her one day in 1970.

"Hey, Joan. Is Dolly in?" In the South we say *hey* a lot instead of *hello*.

I was talking to Porter Wagoner and Dolly Parton's secretary, Joan.

"No Charlie, she didn't come in today."

"I've got a song I wanted to pitch to Dolly," I told Joan.

"Is that you Charlie Craig?"

I could recognize that voice anywhere. It was Dolly Parton calling out with that trademark giggle from her office just down the hall.

"Yeah, it's me," I answered back with a smile.

Joan looked at me and shrugged, a little embarrassed. "She told me to tell everybody she wasn't here," Joan whispered with a slight giggle of her own.

"Come on back here," Dolly called out.

It turned out Dolly really hadn't planned on coming into her office that day and she was wearing the cut off jeans and T-shirt she had been working around her house in. And she didn't have on a wig. She was probably as pretty as I have ever seen her that day. I remember thinking, how many men would give good money to be sitting across from Dolly Parton wearing cut off jeans and a T-shirt. Probably millions.

Old Memories and Me

"Charlie Craig if you tell anybody you saw me like this I'll kill you," Dolly laughed and tried to rearrange her natural hair with her hands.

"Dolly, I'm gonna tell everybody I see I saw you like this," I kidded her. Dolly was easy to talk to and cut up with.

"And I'll choke you," she giggled, like only Dolly can.

Nobody's eyes sparkle with life any more than Dolly Parton's.

We finally got around to me playing her the song I wanted her to hear. It was one of the songs I co-wrote with Betty, *Chicken Every Sunday*. Dolly loved it and put it on hold to record. Not only did she record it once, not twice, but three times.

"I can't get it right," she told me later. "If the verses are in the right key, then the chorus is too high, and if the chorus is in the right key, then the darn verses are too low."

I have never had anybody cut one of my songs three times, I mean, the same song on three different sessions. Dolly did it trying to get it the way she thought it should sound. I thought it was great all three times. Finally, she released it and put it in her *Joshua* album in 1971. I still receive royalties on that song even today.

I have always loved to write ballads. I think most country songwriters do. I remember writing *Champagne Dreams*, using my and Betty's tough days in Nashville as a guideline for the song. We had champagne dreams on a beer income. In the song I used wine instead of beer. It was always one of Betty's favorite songs that I wrote. She called it *our song*. Later, Leon Everett recorded it on RCA Records.

I was still getting a few songs recorded but not anything that would climb high in the charts or make a lot of money. I was in debt to Cedarwood with my weekly advance. I really wasn't getting anywhere, except depressed. Bill Denny asked me to assign my BMI royalties to Cedarwood to help recoup the money I owed from advances. I agreed in order to stay on a weekly draw. That turned out to be a bad decision on my part. It would tie up my future performance money for several years, even after I left Cedarwood. I am not blaming or condemning Bill Denny. He did what he had to do as head of Cedarwood, making a practical financial decision he felt justified to keep me on as a staff writer. However, my advice to all songwriters just starting out; don't ever assign your performance royalties over to a publishing company or anybody else for that matter.

I started drinking beer heavily around 1970. This despicable habit would cause a lot of strife in my life. I had never been a drinker back in South Carolina, but I started drinking beer to throw myself into an artificial world, where things seemed better than they actually were for me in the music business.

For the first year or so I got on a natural high just from getting a song or two recorded in somebody's album. Even though they might not have sold a lot it was enough to inflate my belief in myself and keep my dreams alive. Later, with other songwriters around me getting songs recorded that became singles and went up the charts, I started getting depressed and turned to drinking. It's funny how people that drink excessive can always find an excuse for it.

I was altering reality every night. I wrote at home, after Betty and Dawn had gone to bed, popping tops on the cheapest beer I could afford. I would wake up with a headache every morning, take two Tylenol and go back to bed and sleep until noon, or later. I grew a full beard and my hair got longer. With a hangover, I looked like a bum, or a hippy, trying to sober up.

Betty didn't like me drinking like that at all. We started having arguments, something we rarely did. I got up in the mornings grouchy and in a bad mood. I was turning into a real jerk at home. Still, Betty stood by me with her love and patience.

By now, Betty was absolutely gorgeous. Her hair was long, black and strait, several inches below her shoulders, and she still had an outstanding figure. I was married to one of the best looking women in all of Nashville and I was so proud every time we would go out. I was jealous when men would gawk at her, but deep inside that made me even prouder. She left no doubt who she belonged to, and never hesitated to put her arms around me in public. Betty loved me and she let everybody know it. She still thought I hung the moon.

We continued to have a near perfect marriage, except for me drinking beer every night. She did have a temper when she got riled though. She threw an ashtray at me once because she said I had looked at another woman and we were having a little debate about that. It turned into a big and serious debate when she threw that ashtray. I ducked and luckily it missed. She wound up snatching up her purse, the car keys and Dawn, and getting into the car and leaving. We had had little spats before, with one of us walking out the door, getting in the car, driving around the block a couple of times to cool off, then come right back home.

We had needed money so I had sold the 1965 Mustang, leaving us with only one car, therefore I couldn't go look for her that particular night. I was mad because she had thrown the ashtray but after about fifteen minutes had gone by and she hadn't come back, I started getting concerned. I peeped out through the blinds several times to see if I could see a car coming down the street, hoping it would be her coming back. Thirty minutes went by. I started feeling a bit panicky. At first I had thought, the heck with her, let her go. Now I was thinking, what if she doesn't come back. I walked outside the duplex and stood in the yard, watching every car that turned the corner, hoping it was Betty and Dawn.

After about ten minutes in the yard, I went back inside, sat down on the sofa and started crying. I didn't think she was coming back. I prayed and asked God to bring her back to me. It's funny how

Old Memories and Me

tough you think you are until something really gets tough to handle. About thirty minutes later I heard the car pull up. I opened the door for her and Dawn to come in. Betty walked by me with an expression I didn't expect. She didn't look mad anymore. She didn't say anything when she walked in but I could tell she didn't want to fight anymore. Neither did I. I was just glad to see her.

Every time I hurt her feelings, or made her mad, twenty minutes later I was so sorry and hated myself for that, always apologizing to her. This had been one of our more serious spats.

"Honey," I said as I closed the door. "I'm sorry."

She tossed her purse onto the couch. "For what? I threw the ashtray," she said and gave me a little remorseful smile and shrug.

"But it was my fault that you did that," I told her and was so glad to see her I practically ran the few feet over to her and pulled her into my arms.

We kissed. We both said I'm sorry. We kissed again.

Dawn fell asleep.

I could have walked to the Dairy Queen.

I was too glad to see her to get mad again though.

"Charlie," Betty said.

"What honey?" I propped up on one elbow and looked into her pretty brown eyes.

"I don't like for us to fight like we did tonight," she told me, looking a bit sad.

"I don't either, sweetheart," I told her and meant it with all my heart.

We turned out the light and lay in the dark talking for a while longer, about our dreams, and how things were going to get better for us. She told me I was the best songwriter in Nashville. I know she believed that too.

"How much do you love me?" She asked.

"More than anything in the whole world," I told her and brushed a strand of dark hair from her forehead.

"I love you more than anything in the whole world too," she said and kissed me softly.

The last thing I remember before I fell asleep was Betty taking my hand in hers and snuggling up to me. We slept that way a lot, arms and legs draped over each other. She probably looked like a little puppy laying over a long skinny log.

CHAPTER NINE

One day I walked across 16th Avenue to Capitol Records, which was right across the street from Cedarwood Publishing. George Richey had taken over as the head of the label then. That day I played him the song I had written with Betty, *Money Can't Buy Love*. I was pitching it to George for Billie Jo Spears. He took a copy of it for her and placed it on hold. On *hold* means they don't want you playing the song for anyone else because they intend to record it. Unfortunately, they don't always record the song but that's what *on hold* means.

A short time later, Charlie McCoy called me. "Hey, I played on a session last night George Richey produced," he told me. "We cut one of your songs."

"You did?" I started getting excited. "Which One?"

"*Money Can't Buy Love*," Charlie informed me.

"Oh, on Billie Jo Spears?" I was ecstatic.

"No, Roy Rogers."

"Who?" I thought I had misunderstood him.

"Roy Rogers," Charlie told me again.

"Roy Rogers, the king of the cowboys?" I couldn't believe it.

"Yeah," Charlie chuckled. He knew I was really happy and he was happy for me.

Billie Jo Spears was doing really well as a recording artist and I would have loved for her to record my song, but this was *Roy Rogers*. I called everybody I knew in Nashville and back home too. I mean, as a kid and even as an adult, I saw about every movie Roy Rogers made. Like millions of other people he was one of my heroes.

It was 1970 and Capital Records released *Money Can't Buy Love* by Roy Rogers as the A side single. I visited Ralph Emery's late night radio show and he interviewed me about the song and Roy Rogers. Ralph debuted the record that night to the world. Later, during the course of the record, I would call Ralph's request line and tell John Riggs, "*this is Jack Simpson in Dayton, Ohio. I want to request Roy Roger's Money Can't Buy Love.*" John finally caught on after a couple of times, knowing it was me, but he never told Ralph. I would sit up, sometimes for two more hours, until Ralph played the request. That show got a lot of request and it took some time to get around to playing them. Ralph Emery's show kept me up late a lot of nights.

Old Memories and Me

My phone conversations with John Riggs on the request line led to a close friendship between he and I. Betty and I had John and his wife, Linda, over for Thanksgiving dinner one year and set up a card table in the den to have enough room since Betty had so much food sitting in bowls and dishes on the dinette table in the kitchen.

I visited Ralph Emery again during the time *Money Can't Buy Love* was still getting airplay on a lot of stations around the country. Just by coincidence another western movie hero, Lash Larue was visiting with Ralph that night, along with his manager. The console around which the guests were seated was like a half circle, across from where Ralph sat at the control board. There was room enough for several people at a time to sit across from Ralph.

Ralph had talked with Lash LaRue and then invited me to join them around the console. I sat down and Ralph told the listeners that I had written Roy Roger's current single.

"Lash, you probably know Roy very well, don't you?" Ralph asked Lash LaRue.

Naturally, he did know Roy and somehow the conversation turned to Roy being the King Of Cowboys and Lash LaRue said the only reason Roy Rogers was King Of The Cowboys was because Gene Autry had been drafted into the army, insinuating if that had not happened, Gene Autrey would have been King Of The Cowboys, and not Roy.

I had no earthly idea if that was true or not and let me point out I was also a huge Gene Autry fan. I also liked all the movies I had seen Lash Larue in. However, Roy Rogers had recorded my song and I had come to know Roy personally. Without knowing any of the facts about Lash Larue's comment, I disputed it.

"Now, that's not true, mister," I snapped.

Ralph Emery looked up at me as only Ralph Emery can, arching his eyebrows, like, *I can't believe you just said that on my show.*

I was immensely relieved when Ralph didn't get upset with me. He chuckled and said, "Looks like you ruffled ole Charlie's feathers, Lash."

I actually don't recall the rest of the conversation but Ralph kept everything under control, as he always did, and the conversation ended with no hard feelings. Betty had listened to the interview on the radio and had stayed up to meet me when I walked in the door.

"I can't believe you were arguing with Lash LaRue on the radio," she laughed.

I laughed too. "Well, I had to take up for Roy."

"I'm glad you did," she told me, then added, "I made some cornbread. You want some cornbread and milk?"

"Yeah," I told her. "I'm starving."

Betty sat with me at the kitchen table while I ate a bowl of milk with cornbread crumbled up in it. We talked about how well the record was doing, especially with radio stations west of the Mississippi. That was a funny thing too. Most of Roy Roger's airplay was coming from stations located in states west of the Mississippi River. It was getting decent airplay east of the Mississippi but there was a big difference though.

Money Can't Buy Love finally topped out at # 35 in Billboard but made it into the twenties in one trade magazine. It got a lot of airplay and stayed in the charts a lot of weeks. It was my first recognized hit and really did a lot for my career. At some radio stations around the country it went to #1 on their local chart. There were also a lot of stations where it made top ten. I was surprised it didn't go any higher in Billboard but if you don't get all, or most of the *reporting* stations you won't make it to the top of the charts.

But it was a radio and fan hit and even more important it bonded a friendship between Betty and me with Roy Rogers, Dale Evans and their longtime manager, Art Rush. After he recorded the song I started picking pick Roy and Art up at the airport every time they would come to Nashville. Art would call in advance and give me their schedule and I always made myself available while they were in town. It certainly was a rewarding experience for me. Roy Rogers was one of the nicest people I have ever met, a perfect gentleman always and not once did I ever hear him say anything bad about anybody. Art Rush was the same way. He had been managing Roy, Dale and Dale Robertson, an actor probably most famous for his starring role in the hit television series, *Wells Fargo*, for 35 years when I met them. The amazing thing about that is there had never been a contract signed between them. It was all on a handshake. All the movies, television, rodeos, fairs, recordings, and millions of dollars made were all done on a handshake. That is unbelievable. To this day I have never seen anything that remarkable in the entertainment business.

Roy Rogers' real name was Leonard Sly and he was a former lead singer for the *Sons Of The Pioneers*. He had a nice mellow voice that was recognized and loved around the world.

It would be eighteen years later but I wonder how many people remember that in 1968 Roy Rogers and Dale Evans hosted the second CMA Awards show ever held and it was the first to be filmed. NBC showed it on television a week later.

Dawn was around eight years old when Roy Rogers recorded *Money Can't Buy Love*, a little beautiful brown-eyed blonde that Art Rush had a fit over. He seriously thought Betty and I should consider bringing her to California and let him try and get her into commercials, and eventually perhaps movies. We talked about it but decided to decline. I needed to be in Nashville to continue my pursuit in the music business. Besides we wanted Dawn to live a normal child's life. She could make decisions like that when she was old enough to decide for herself.

Betty and I didn't go to many of the music functions, like the

Old Memories and Me

award shows and label parties. It just wasn't our cup of tea. However, A few times during DJ Week every year, which was also the week of the CMA Award Show, we went downtown to the shows the labels held at the auditorium on James Robinson Parkway. Most of the record labels rented hotel suites near the auditorium and set up hospitality suites for the disc jockeys and fans that came to town by the thousands that week. I guess DJ Week must have been the beginning of both Fan Fair and CMA Week.

We went to the Capital Records show in 1970 and Roy Rogers performed *Money Can't Buy Love*, acknowledging Betty and I as the writers of the song as we watched from the audience. Naturally, that was a great feeling in front of our friends and peers in the music business. Backstage Roy made a picture with Betty and I, then one with Dawn. Waylon Jennings was there that night, visiting with Roy and some of the other Capital artist. Waylon made over Dawn as well, saying he wanted to adopt her. She was a little sweetheart, pretty as her mama. Waylon had a picture made with Dawn that night as well.

During those days, Mel Tillis was recording on a small independent label and hadn't made it yet as an artist. He was doing well enough to have a band and work the road though, and he had become close friends with Waylon Jennings. One day Mel approached me at Cedarwood.

"Way... Waylon Jennings nee...needs a bass player," Mel stuttered. "Don't you p-p-play bass, Charlie?"

Mel Tillis was a character, with a great sense of humor. At first I was like a lot of people and wondered if the stuttering and hand gesturing was a gimmick or something. Of course it wasn't. Melvin Tillis actually does stutter when he speaks. What is so strange is how when he sings he doesn't do it. And the hand motion he does to express himself just seems to come so natural to him. He became so popular doing that; other people started mimicking him.

"Yeah," I answered. Mel was humble and down to earth, but I was always in awe of him. This was one talented man, perhaps my favorite songwriter in all of Nashville. I looked at him as my mentor.

"Well...you...you..ought to..to..talk to..to..him." He said and gestured with his hand in a little swooping motion.

"I don't want to work the road, Mel." I told him.

"H..how you gonna b.be uh..a record..recording artist then?" Mel asked and smacked his lips together and raised his eyebrows.

One reason why I decided not to pursue a recording contract after I got to Nashville is I didn't want to travel and leave Betty and Dawn, and too I didn't want to go on the road and use other people's bands. If I could have started out with my own band and traveled in a big customized bus, then it would have been different.

"I've decided not to try and record," I informed Mel.

He nodded and smacked his lips again. "Damn r..right you

a..ain't if' n y..you won't wor..work the r..road!"

Danny Davis was still a producer at RCA and had become a good friend. Danny told me he was putting together a band to record instrumentals and asked me to be on the lookout for some original songs with great melodies. He explained that most of the album probably would be cover songs like Hank William's *I Saw The Light* but he wanted to do a couple of originals too. I immediately thought of one of Mel Tillis' songs and took Danny a copy of it. He loved it and he and his new band, *The Nashville Brass* recorded it on their first album. Mel's song was *Ruby, Don't Take Your Love To Town*. The album eventually sold over one million copies.I knew I wouldn't make a penny off of it but I just love great songs, and besides, I did two friends of mine a favor that day.

Of course Kenny Rogers would record that song later and have a monster hit with it.

Roger Sovine, son of the great Red Sovine, was a songplugger at Cedarwood for a while. Roger also had made a few records as an artist at one time. He was a pretty good singer. I asked him to sing a few songs of mine on demo sessions. One of those songs was *The Man From Love*. Del Reeves wound up recording it but I kept Roger Sovine's demo of it for a keepsake. Later, Roger went to work for BMI and would go on to become an executive with them. I use to call him up at BMI and ask for an advance on my performance royalties. That was back before the *Buffalo Case* that did away with performance advances. The *Buffalo Case* was a lawsuit filed by a television station owner in Buffalo, N. Y. over blanket licensing to BMI and ASCAP for the music they played on that station.As I understood it, that station wanted to pay the publishers and songwriters directly, eliminating ASCAP and BMI altogether. There is no way a publisher and songwriters can keep up with who is playing our music around the country. The case tied up millions of dollars of ASAP and BMI money for a while, until the case was appealed and won by those two affiliations. It was a huge victory for all songwriters and music publishers. However, it did away with writer's advances on performance royalties.

Before the *Buffalo Case* though, if Roger hedged any on giving me an advance, I would threaten to play my demo of him singing *The Man From Love* to everybody on *music row*. Of course I was joking with him. We had fun with that one for a few years. Actually, he sang the demo really well.

Roger pitched my songs as a songplugger at Cedarwood, but even after he went to BMI, he still would mention a song or two of mine to a producer, or an artist. He had always liked my writing and had always promoted me when the opportunity presented itself.

During those days, BMI President Frances Preston had her office in the New York offices. Roger Sovine was the top executive in the Nashville office. Along with Del Bryant, and later, Harry Warner,

Old Memories and Me

those three guys helped a lot of songwriters achieve their dreams and goals, including me. Of course it was their job to help BMI songwriters, but they always went beyond their duty and put their personal caring into helping songwriters. I know they did in my case. Over the years the entire staff at BMI has been really good to me. To this day I don't know what I would do if I couldn't call Nancy Moore at BMI and converse with her. Same thing with Jody Williams.

Back in those days the business was pretty laid back. Most of the time you had to make an appointment with a record producer to pitch your songs, but on occasions you might just drop by and catch them in a good mood and could walk right in and play a few songs. I had done that with Kelton Norton, the head of one of the major record labels. I would just pop in at his office and catch him not too busy and play him a song or two. However, one time I tried that and it was a bad day for him I guess and he told me I needed to get an appointment. So I did, and on the day I went over to his office for my 11 a.m. appointment with him, while I was waiting in the lobby right outside his office, an attractive and shapely blonde showed up just before 11 am. When Kelton came out of his office with the person he had just been meeting with, escorting them out, he spotted the blonde in the lobby.

"Hello there," he beamed at her. "Come on in."

He took her in his office and closed the door. I looked at his receptionist and she glanced at me and shrugged, a little apologizing curl on her lips that agreed with my own thoughts of what had just happened.

"Guess I should have wore a wig," I smirked.

Oh well, I decided I would wait. Fifteen or twenty minutes went by and the blonde was still in Kelton's office.

"Would you go in there and tell him I want it back. I don't want him to record any of my songs now."

I know my face was flushed I was so upset.

Before she could respond, Kelton emerged from his office again. He had heard my loud voice.

"What's the problem?" he asked, as if he had no idea how he had just shunned me so rudely.

"You told me to get an appointment, so I did," I reminded him, my tone still expressing my displeasure with the situation. "I have been here since 11 o'clock and you took that blonde in front of me, then that other songwriter just now. I know I don't look as good as her and I ain't got the writing credentials that he does, not yet anyway, but I am just as good as either one of them when it comes to deserving some respect." I was fuming.

"Well, I will be through in a few minutes," he told me. "Just calm down."

"No, I'm leaving, and I want my song back you took last week," I shot back.

He was getting a little miffed at me now. "You can have your damn song. I told you I would be through in a few minutes and then I will get with you."

He stepped back into his office, returned and tossed me my tape. I caught it and stomped out of the offices of one Nashville's more successful record labels.

I want to point out right here that this was no fault of the blonde, nor of the other songwriter. Neither of them had any idea of what was going on. I didn't know who the blonde was at all, nor did I really know the other songwriter that well, but I knew his name and reputation and I am sure if he had known I was waiting for my appointment he would not have gone in Kelton's office ahead of me.

The next time Kelton Norton and I saw each other we never mentioned that incident. It passed, like most things do, and I went back to playing songs for him. However, it never was as comfortable being around him as it once was. I now had his total respect though. He went on to produce a number of my songs over the next few years.

In all my years in the music business that was the only time I ever had words and a misunderstanding with a record label head or a producer. I don't know what it was, but for some reason Kelton Norton and I just never did gee haw. Those things just happen I guess but there would be other issues between the two of us in years to come. We learned to tolerate each other but we never really learned to like each other that much.

On another occasion when Roy Rogers came to town to record, he asked me to come up to his motel room at the *King Of The Road* and help him learn some of the songs he was going to record. I took my guitar and arrived that morning. I knocked on his room door and Roy let me in. He was in his shorts. I know it sounds stupid but I just never imagined that Roy Rogers even wore underwear like the rest of us do. I mean, I never really thought about it, of course, but he wasn't a real person, was he? Of course he was but it just struck me as odd to see him in his boxer shorts. Isn't that crazy. He was King of the Cowboys. A living legend. An icon. Naturally, he was a real person and that is the sad part about getting to know your heroes personally. After a while, the glamour is lost and they become just another person, and sometime a good friend. The more I think about it though; I'd rather have the personal relationship, the friendship, more so than the star thing only. I wouldn't trade those times with Roy Rogers for all the stardom in the world. Besides, he will always be King Of The Cowboys to me.

On that occasion that he was in town I took Roy through the Country Music Hall Of Fame one day and got my first experience of being with a superstar in public. The fans in the Hall Of Fame all wanted to get his autograph, his picture, touch him, anything they could get from him. People loved this man. He was the king of western movies. A huge star known all over most of the world. They mobbed him in every room we went into. I tried my best to become a bodyguard and protect him. I must have looked and sounded awkward. I had never been in a situation like that.

"Ladies and gentleman please let Mister Rogers enjoy his visit here at the Hall Of Fame," I announced to the crowd and tried to sound as official as I could. "Step back please."

Doggone if it didn't work. They were reluctant, but the fans moved away from him and politely allowed him to view the exhibits in the Hall Of Fame. I felt like a *big shot*. I was escorting Roy Rogers and people were listening to what I said. I wanted to tell them I wrote *Money Can't Buy Love*, I was so proud. But of course I didn't do that. I am proud but I am also very modest. Well, most of the time.

On another trip to Nashville, Roy asked me to take him down to the Ryman Auditorium where Johnny Cash was rehearsing for his network TV show.

"You think we can get in down there?" Roy asked.

"Hey," I said, and couldn't help but laugh a little, "We can get in anywhere with your credentials."

I drove him down to the Ryman and naturally the guards let us in upon recognition of Roy. We entered the backstage area and immediately spotted Johnny Cash onstage mingling with musicians and the production crew. He was dressed casual, wearing a T-shirt and jeans. Roy and I started across the stage toward Cash. John happened to turn around and saw us approaching. Naturally he recognized Roy Rogers and moved to greet him. When the three of us came face to face I did what I thought at the time I was supposed to do.

"Johnny Cash," I said a bit nervously, "this is Roy Rogers." Then, I added, "Roy this is Johnny Cash."

Maybe it was just in my petrified mind but it seemed like big John looked at me like he was thinking, *I know who he is, but who in the hell are you?*

"And I'm Charlie Craig," I added meekly. "I wrote *Money Can't Buy Love* that Roy recorded."

As soon as I said it I wished I hadn't. It sounded like I was bragging. I was just trying to identify myself to Johnny Cash.

As huge as a star as he was, Cash was also a humble and polite man.

"I really like that song," he told me and shook Roy Rogers' hand, then mine.

If you have never seen Johnny Cash in person, up close, you can't imagine how impressive this man is. Broad shoulders, massive chest and that deep voice sounding like God might sound making it thunder. He has the ability to dominate your attention, even if the President of the United States was in the same room. I have never been so in awe of anybody, not before nor since.

Johnny took us into June Carter Cash's dressing room and

introduced us. She was in curlers and had a white cream on her face, laid back in a chair while being attended to by a makeup person with the show. Yet, you would have thought she was at home and welcoming us into her family room. She was so down to earth and nice. June Carter Cash impressed me that day too.

That was a time I won't soon forget. That day I was in the presence of two icons at the same time, Roy Rogers and Johnny Cash. No, let me correct that: 3 icons. June Carter Cash belongs right up there with the elite in the world of show business and as a lady.

Betty and I were still in a bowling league at Donelson Bowl on Sunday nights. It continued to be a league made up of people in the music business. There were four people on each team, two males and two females-- mostly husbands and wives. Roy Rogers loved to bowl and carried his own bowling ball around with him just in case he might get the opportunity to bowl. When he found out Betty and I bowled in a league, he wanted to join in one Sunday night. I sat out and let him take my place on our team that now consisted of Betty, Gene Ferguson and his wife, Delores, and of course me. Gene Ferguson was Columbia Records national promotional man.

There was a league before ours and when they saw Roy Rogers there, most of them stayed over to watch him bowl. It wasn't common knowledge, but Roy was really shy and got very nervous around strange people in close quarters. With all the attention and fuss being made over him, he only bowled 110 the first game. Again, like at the Hall Of Fame, I stepped up and, along with the manager of the bowling ally, asked the people to leave. They did, slowly, but finally they were gone. Roy settled down and bowled 218 his last game. He really was a good bowler. He took my place on our bowling team a few other times. My team members were always glad to see him because he bowled better than I did. I didn't bowl many 218 games.

Roy became close with Betty as well as with me. I remember once we were all sitting around talking at a Capital Records dinner party and Betty told Roy Rogers we had horses and asked him if he would come out and ride sometimes with us.

"That would be like asking the postman to go on a hike on his day off," Roy responded with a chuckle.

Another funny remark made at that same party was when Roy told us that when Trigger, Jr. died he was going to have him stuffed and placed into their museum at Apple Valley, California. His lovely wife, Dale Evans, spoke up and joked with a cute smile, "Yes, and when you die I am going to have you stuffed and placed on top of him."

I recall when Bill Anderson had his syndicated television show and asked Roy to appear as a guest. I drove him out to the studio where Bill was taping. A very young Barbara Mandrel was also appearing on the show that night. She played a bunch of different instruments and blew everybody's mind.

Old Memories and Me

Bill Anderson had told Roy the crowd wouldn't be very large. Like I said, Roy got nervous around a crowd in close quarters. About two hundred people jammed into the place, but to Roy it looked like 2,000 in such a small studio. He got all jittery.

"I can't do this live," he told Bill and me. "I need to lip sync the song."

The song he was going to perform was my and Betty's *Money Can't Buy Love*.

I had to get in my car and rush over to Cedarwood Publishing and meet John Denny there to make Roy an acetate of the song. Roy performed the song, as he called it, lip syncing. He did a great job. You couldn't tell he wasn't performing it live.

Later, when I drove him back to the King Of The Road motel he thanked me. "I really appreciate you going to get that acetate, Charlie. I would have been up a creek without that thing," he chuckled.

We talked about how amazingly talented the young Barbara Mandrell was.

"That little gal is something else," Roy said. "I think she will go far, don't you?"

"Yeah," I agreed. "I met her once before, when her daddy, Irby, brought her by Cedarwood Publishing one day. Tonight is the first time I have seen her perform though. She is quite amazing, as you said."

I thanked Roy for performing my and Betty's song on Bill Anderson's television show. Bill's show was quite popular and I knew a lot of people would see Roy singing our song.

"Oh, it was my pleasure. I love that song and I just appreciate you letting me record it," Roy told me sincerely.

This was one of the nicest human beings I had ever known.

Oh, by the way, did I mention that my name got left off of the record as a writer when they pressed the records. Only Betty's name was listed as writer. Isn't that something-- I came to Nashville to make it as a songwriter and Betty made it before me.

One of the most embarrassing instances, or could have been, that happened concerning Roy Rogers happened one night when I was sitting in on bass for a friend at a club on White Bridge Road. Roy and his manager Art Rush were in town and had said they would drop by the club to see me perform after they finished the engagement they were attending. Roy had never seen me onstage before. I made the mistake of announcing that Roy Rogers might drop by later on that night. I suppose I was just so proud and wanted to show Roy off a little.

Now, how dumb was that. I knew better and as soon as I had said it into the microphone I started regretting it. People started coming up to me all excited and saying they wanted to meet Roy, wanted his autograph, some telling me how he had meant this and that to them all their lives. They were going to mob the poor man. As shy as he was he would go nuts in that place. I started thinking about calling him and suggest he not even come by there.

The thing that made up my mind was this one woman that came up to me when I was on a break, throwing her arm around my neck, and very drunkenly proclaiming, "Huney, ..ya telp ..Roy Rogerts... I have loevth his moobies for ears... ..and I wanna takeem..tu bed..an..screw em on top of..trigur....otay??"

Oh, my Lord!

I made a quick phone call.

"Hello, Art, this is Charlie. Don't bring Roy by the club tonight..."

I had some fun times with Roy Rogers, moments I will never forget. Memories I will cherish forever. He was one of a kind, a rare breed, the likes of which will never pass this way again. I thank God he blessed me with the opportunity to know Roy Rogers. It is one of the highlights of my life.

I eventually left Cedarwood Publishing and signed with Dolly Patron's publishing company, Owepar Music. She named it after her uncles, whose last names were Owens, and of course Parton after herself, thus Owepar. One of those uncles, Louis Owens, ran the company for her and he was the one who actually signed me as a staff writer. My advance stayed the same, $150 a week, as it was at Cedarwood.

It was a joy being around Dolly Parton and Porter Wagoner. They both would come into the office several times a week and I had an opportunity to get to know them a little better.

It was during this time that Dolly wrote songs like, *Like A Butterfly*, and eventually, *I Will Always Love You* and Of course I didn't witness her actually writing the songs, but I remember her singing *Like A Butterfly* for me one day in the office right after she had written it. That is such a beautiful song. Some years later, a butterfly would become Dolly's logo on the entrance to Dollywood.

It always amazed me how Dolly could play her guitar so well with those long fingernails. Dolly just amazed me period. She is an extremely talented lady and very smart.

Porter built a recording studio and called it Fireside Studio. I was the first to record there, doing a demo for Owepar Publishing. Before that we did our Demos out at Bobby Dyson's studio, the Cabin, which was at his house in Antioch, about fifteen minutes from downtown Nashville. I liked doing 6 p.m. demo sessions back then and when he wasn't on the road Porter would go out to the studio with me. He would buy snacks for all the musicians and myself.

Porter was talented in the studio. He co-produced most of his own records with RCA's Bob Ferguson. He also co-produced Dolly, and his and Dolly's duets. I am sure Dolly had a lot of input into her recordings. She is very talented in the studio herself, as well as one of the greatest songwriters in any genre of music. When Porter was

Old Memories and Me

in the studio with me on my demo sessions, he would allow me to do my own thing. I always appreciated his respect for my judgment and productions.

I really enjoyed my days at Owepar Music. Louis Owens was easy to work with and it was always nice to be around Porter and Dolly.

Dolly was always telling me stories, about times when she was growing up poor in Sevierville, Tennessee, near Gatlinburg and Pigeon Forge, in the Smokey Mountains. She told me once that she had to sleep with a bunch of her sisters and brothers, and in the wintertime it was too cold to get up and go outside to the outhouse, so they just peed in bed. She said the steam warmed them up for a while but then as it cooled off it got even colder in bed. I nearly choked laughing at some of her stories. Sometime later she did an interview with Playboy magazine and told some of those same stories. But I got to hear some of them first hand. I loved being around Dolly, and I still think of those times I was fortunate to spend with her. I love Dolly Parton, the entertainer, the songwriter, the person. You can't know Dolly and not love her.

Porter had a sense of humor too but he never told me any *wetting the bed* stories.

I believe Porter has been the same size all of his life. I never knew him to gain a pound. I remember watching him so many times on the stage of the Grand Ole Opry and thinking what a great entertainer he was. He knew how to work an audience and hold them captive with his charming personality.

I was with Dolly and Porter and Owepar Publishing for a little over a year when Dolly called me at home one day.

"Charlie Craig, if you can tell me who this is I will give you an autographed 8x10 color photograph of Dolly Parton."

I knew it was either Dolly or her sister Stella. They sounded a lot alike, especially over the telephone. I was sure it was Dolly though and I told her so.

She laughed and then got into a real serious mood.

"I'm splitting up with Porter and going out on my own," she told me.

I really wasn't surprised because I knew Dolly wanted to expand her music and audience. "Really?" I said and tried to sound surprised anyway.

"Yes, and I want to give you back your song catalog, all except the ones that have been recorded," she told me.

"But I still owe you six or seven thousand dollars on advances," I reminded her. All songwriters were on advance if you were a staff writer. We call it a *draw*.

"I know," Dolly said and told me the exact figure it was, to the cents. "It will be my gift to you."

If I haven't already mentioned it, let me point out that Dolly Parton is also a very generous lady.

It was talked all over Nashville and country music that Dolly and Porter were having an affair. I was around them almost daily during the week and not once did I see any evidence of that. I'm not saying it did, or didn't happen. I am saying they were business like around the office. Oh, they would cut up and act like kids sometimes, like the rest of us. Fun stuff. But they are both highly successful business people too.

"Are they having an affair?"

My answer was always the same. "I never saw them swing together, just sing together."

Best answer I ever gave to a question.

I continued to see Porter Wagoner backstage at The Opry now and then but I haven't seen Dolly Parton in years. I miss that too. She was one of my favorite people in this business and I admire her for the move she made when most people said she was deserting country music by getting an LA producer and recording some on the west coast. Dolly wanted to broaden her talents and she felt the move would benefit her. And it did. Big time. As far as I'm concerned it benefited country music too. She brought more new fans to country music than anyone else at that time. She never deserted anybody. If anything, a lot of Nashville deserted her, until they saw it was working and country music was getting a big boost by Dolly's extended popularity. After she started using strings on some of her records and they were big hits, a lot of artist in Nashville started doing the same thing. She held out her hand and took us along with her to the next level.

Thanks Dolly.

It was during the early or mid-seventies that I met Charlie Louvin. Charlie had been a big hit with his brother Ira as the Louvin Brothers. The Louvin's had some of the finest harmonies and wrote some of the greatest songs ever recorded, some that went on to become classics. I never had the pleasure of meeting Ira Louvin, he was killed in a car accident in 1965. That was three years before I moved to Nashville.

However, I did meet Charlie Louvin and we became pretty good pals, talking on Record Row and backstage at The Opry. It wasn't long after I met Charlie that he had an accident on his motorcycle. He was on 16th Avenue, out in front of Capital Records, and his motorcycle wouldn't start, so he had to run and push it to get it started. With Charlie running along beside the cycle, with the throttle open, it started up. Charlie tripped when it fired up and took off, dragging him along beside it down *music row*. Charlie wouldn't turn loose. He was trying to cut the switch off. Louvin had on a pair of Bermuda shorts and it tore his legs up something awful, and his elbows looked terrible too. Later, after a few years, I would kid Charlie about that incident and he would laugh good naturedly about it. Of course it wasn't funny at the time that

Old Memories and Me

it happened.

The Louvin Brothers had a unique sound and no other duet act could touch their high harmonies and performance of a song. Today, Charlie performs alone, sometimes with his niece Cathy Louvin, but mostly as a solo act. I loved his record of *See The Big Man Cry Mama*, a great song written by my friend Ed Bruce. Charlie Louvin has that natural hoarseness in his vocals, with real country soul. I love to hear him sing.

Those days were the beginnings of some long term friendships I made with Opry stars like Del Reeves, Bill Anderson, Jim Ed Brown, Billy Walker, Ray Pillow, Loretta Lynn, Doyle Wilburn, Jack Green, Porter and Dolly, Jeannie Seeley, Jim Ed Brown, Stonewall Jackson, and the list goes on an on.

I used to go over to Linebaugh's restaurant on Broadway with some of the stars and eat between their sets on The Opry. Ernest Tubb would be in there sometimes with his son Skeeter. The place had booths with those miniature jukeboxes at the booths where you could make a selection and drop a coin in to play it. Ernest use to play his own songs. If I had the hits he had, I would play my own songs too.

On one occasion, I left the Ryman backdoor entrance with Del Reeves and Bob Luman on our way to Linebaugh's and as usual there was a gathering of fans waiting there. The fans swarmed around Del and Bob Luman to get their autographs. I politely stepped back out of their way. After a few minutes, a lady, with her Del Reeves and Bob Luman's autograph secured, looked over at me and asked, very seriously, "Are you somebody?"

I smiled sheepishly and replied, "My mama thinks so."

After leaving Owepar Music I wrote for Tuckahoe Music, which was owned by Jim Reeves widow, Mary Reeves. I never knew Jim since he was killed in a plane crash in 1964 and I didn't move to Nashville until 1968.

I stayed with Tuckahoe Music about a year and while I was there Bud Logan, who was a Blue Boy in Jim Reeve's band, asked me to take his place and play bass in the Blue Boy Band. Of course at that time, in the late seventies, the band didn't tour and only played a few local gigs. Some of the band members like Bunky Keel and Leo Jackson worked a lot of recording sessions. Bud Logan recorded a few duets with Wilma Burgess during this time on Mary Reeve's Shamrock Record label and ran the publishing company. He was the one that actually signed me as a writer to Tuckahoe. Later Bud Logan became John Connelly's record producer and together they cut a lot of hit records.

I recall one of the gigs I did play with the Blue Boys was down in Murfreesboro, Tennessee on the back of a flatbed truck. Pee Wee King was on the show as well as Doug Kershaw. The Blue Boys backed both of them in their performances. We all did that same show later in

Nashville at Centennial Park.

Mary Reeves and Bud Logan had signed a singer by the name of George Kent to Shamrock Records and Bud produced his records. George Kent recorded 5 of my songs on one of his albums. He was a great country singer and a heck of a nice guy, as was Bud Logan. Bud and I became friends and although I haven't seen him in years he became one of the fond memories in my career I will always cherish.

After leaving Tuckahoe Music I visited my old friend Tommy Hill. He had left Starday Records and had his own small label, Stop Records. On this particular visit with Tommy Hill, he told me to bring him a couple of good songs and he would advance me some money to tide me over until I could sign with another publisher. He said we could work on a song-to-song basis.

I went home and got out my guitar to try and come up with something good. I just couldn't get my imagination going.

"I am so frustrated with the whole music business," I told Betty and opened up a can of beer. It was only about 2 o'clock in the afternoon.

"That is your biggest problem, right there," she said, referring to the beer.

"Please, don't start," I sighed and wanted to avoid the issue.

She was ironing clothes. She sat the iron down and stared at me for a few seconds.

"Have you took a good look at yourself lately?" she asked me. "You look like crap. You don't eat, you don't sleep, all you do is drink beer."

"So, I'm a terrible person," I said and shrugged. I knew she was right but I wanted her pity, not her accusations.

Betty sighed and went back to ironing. "Whatever, Charlie."

I sat the can of beer down and walked over to her. I stepped behind her and slid both arms around her and kissed the top of her head.

"I know you're right, honey," I told her. "But I just get so frustrated. I think I write good songs but I can't get them recorded. I mean, yeah, I've had a few good cuts but we're not making any real money because my songs evidently aren't good enough for singles and that is where the real money is."

She stopped ironing again and turned to face me, my arms still around her.

"Your songs are good enough," she told me and laid her cheek against my chest. "I think this town is just too stupid to realize how great you really are."

"Don't stop loving me," I said and my voice broke a little, tears wetting my eyes.

She raised her face to look up at me. "I won't ever stop loving you," she said and bit her lower lip slightly. There were tears forming in

Old Memories and Me

her eyes as well now. "But I want the man back I married, the man that always found strength in our love, not in a can of beer."

Oh, God, please help me, I screamed inside my head. I was about to fall apart, mentally exhausted from the strain and pressure of trying to get over the hump in the music business, going from one publisher to the other, feeling like I was just spinning my musical wheels. I felt like a failure. I pulled Betty as tightly into my arms as I could without hurting her.

"I want to be that man again, darling," I told her. "I wish we were back home in our little house on Lee Street."

"I won't let you quit," she said sternly, looking up at me. "Dammit Charlie, I won't."

"But I don't know what else to do," I said helplessly."If I could just get that first top 10 hit, just that first one...."

"You will get it," Betty assured me. "You will."

She kissed me then, so sweetly I thought her lips were made of honey.

As I have said many times, Betty is where I got my strength. She wouldn't let me quit and she wouldn't allow me to fail.

That night, I got my guitar out after Betty and Dawn had gone to bed. Betty's encouragement had me in the mood to write. I sat down at the kitchen table and started strumming my guitar, allowing my mind to wander.

> *Walk right up to me, look into my eyes*
> *You can see the fire, building up inside*
> *I can't stand it no longer, the damage has been done*
> *You been teasing me to death, now I'm a hungry son-of-a-gun*

I never know where most of my lines come from. They just pop into my head, then out of my mouth. It was happening that way that night. I had just started out by playing a rhythm pattern on my guitar, G to A to D then back to G. It was mostly heavy down beats, a driving groove. I was drinking beer and thinking about how every time Betty looked into my eyes with hers, she turned me on like turning on a faucet. I was picturing in my mind how sometimes she would just walk right up to me, looking all beautiful and sexy, and I threw myself into a bit of a lovey mood thinking about that. I opened up another beer, then another.

> *Lay a little lovin' on me, lay a little lovin' on*
> *Throw your arms around me, and lay a little lovin' on*

Then, I started getting tipsy and began to over write, throwing in some corny lines I thought sounded good in my altered state of mind. After about six beers, and half of a good song, I went to bed around 2 am.

I got up the next morning about 11 am, had a cup of coffee and ate a pack of peanut butter and crackers, which was my usual breakfast. The hops in the beer had my sinuses stopped up and I had a heck of a headache. Looking in the bathroom mirror I saw that I looked like something a cat had drug in.

Betty was in the den watching television. Dawn was in school, in the 4th grade.

I went into the den and flopped down beside Betty on the couch.

"I feel like shit," I groaned.

"You look like shit, too." she informed me and took a sip of black coffee. She didn't say it hateful, or mean, just matter of factly.

I rubbed my forehead, which felt like it had a band around it.

"I'm gonna quit drinking that crap." I stated and took a deep breath, hoping it would relieve some of the misery I felt. It didn't.

I lit up a cigarette.

"If you don't you're gonna kill yourself," she told me. She looked at me without smiling, but with concern. "Why did you drink last night, after we had just had that talk about your drinking?"

"I don't know," I answered meekly.

I was so miserable. This wasn't me, I mean it was, but it wasn't. I had never been a drinker. I was raised up to be a good person, attended Lucas Avenue Baptist Church every Sunday. I had reached the point to where I would try and tell myself that just because I was drinking beer, it wasn't as bad as if I were drinking whiskey. A lame excuse, I know. I didn't want to talk about my drinking. I wanted to pretend it was something I could stop anytime I wanted to.

"I wrote a good song last night," I told Betty, breaking the silence.

"Charlie, you write a good song almost every night," she said sincerely. She sat down her coffee cup. "Come here." She held out her arms.

What in the world would I do without that woman in my life......

Old Memories and Me

CHAPTER TEN

After I demoed *Lay A Little Loving On Me* with Tommy Hill helping me produce the session we got Del Reeves to come by Tommy's office to listen to it. Del and I were already friends but we had hit it off really well when he recorded my song *Paper Covered Comb*. I played the paper and comb on that record. Del and I became friends for life after that.

Del loved *Lay A Little Loving On Me*.

"I want that song," he told me emphatically, as though he dared me to play it for anybody else. "I'm gonna record that sucker."

But he almost didn't. I was at the session and with about fifteen minutes left of recording time, Del's producer Kelso Herston, told the musicians they were through. I approached Del and inquired rather loudly, "You ain't gonna cut my song, Del?"

Del looked at Kelso Herston for help. Del has never been a pushy person and at that time his career wasn't booming so he didn't insist on anything.

Kelso Herston said, "We don't have time for another tracking."

Larry Butler was playing piano on the session and came to my rescue. "We've got fifteen minutes. We can at least get a track on Charlie's song, Kelso."

Larry Butler was one of the in demand session pickers back then, and he would later become one of the most successful record producers in the history of country music, producing all of Kenny Roger's biggest hits, as well as Dottie West, B.J. Thomas, and Billie Jo Spears. He would also wind up producing Del Reeves.

With Butler suggesting they cut the track on my song, Kelso immediately agreed. Before they even got to the chorus Larry Butler was expressing his true sentiments of the song. "This is the best song we've done all morning!"

It turned out he was right. *Lay A Little Loving On Me* was the first single off of Del Reeves' next album. It went up the charts to #15 and put Del back in the spotlight again. It did a heck of a lot for my career too.

Betty bought me a black Stetson cowboy hat because she knew I had always wanted one. It was a really nice hat and she had paid pretty good money for it. However, when I put it on it was a little too

Old Memories and Me

big. Betty had ordered it in the mail so rather than try and send it back I stuffed paper inside of it to make it fit but to tell the honest truth, I looked kind of stupid in it. I just never looked good in a cowboy hat. My friend Ray Pennington, who was a producer with RCA at that time, wore a cowboy hat sometimes and it was mostly always a black one. Ray looked good in a hat. With Betty's approval I gave my Stetson to Ray Pennington.

Betty and I both had met Ray and his wife through the Sunday night bowling league at Donelson Lanes. We became instant friends.

Before Ray came to Nashville he was in Cincinnati, Ohio where he produced Kenny Price on Boone Records, which was owned by Bobby Bobo. Two of the hits Ray produced on Kenny Price were *Walking On New Grass* and *Happy Tracks*. Of course Kenny Price would go on to become one of the stars on *Hee Haw*. Ray Pennington would also come to Nashville and continue his producing talents as well as his songwriting skills.

Ray wrote *Rambling Man* that became a hit for Waylon Jennings and other artist would also record that great song. Ray produced Dave Kirby on one of my songs called *The Innocence Of Beth* which was on Monument Records. Later Ray would become head of Step One Records and have several years success there with artist such as *Clinton Gregory, Jack Greene, Billy Walker* and several more great acts.

Ray had a nice farm in Hendersonville and raised cattle and had a few horses so he also had a large field of hay. We had the two horses so I bought a hundred bales of hay from Ray a few times. He always gave me a good price and I think maybe it was because of the cowboy hat I had given him. Ray still has his farm today and I need to drive out sometime and say hello to my old friend.

Tex Davis and his wife Betty also bowled in that Sunday night bowling league. Back then that league was like a Who's Who with all of the country music musicians, songwriters, record producers, engineers, promotion people and arrangers. We even had one recording star for a while in Jerry Reed and his wife Sissy.

Tex Davis worked for Monument Records as their national promotion man. Tex had written the Gene Vincent classic *Be-Bop-A-Lula*. Tex was also Gene Vincent's manager back in the fifties when the rock n roller was a star. There were a lot of people who believe Gene Vincent was very close to being what Elvis later became, the king of rock n roll. He was certainly popular and great on stage. As I mentioned earlier, several of Gene Vincent's band members at one time were from my area and I was offered a job as bass player for some gigs but wasn't able to accept. I will always regret not being able to be a Blue Cap in his band.

I used to go by Monument and visit with Tex and we would tell each other stories from the fifties era we had experienced or just talk about things in general. He was the person I had originally played my song *The Innocence Of Beth* for and Tex then played it for Ray

Pennington, who in turn played it for Dave Kirby and he recorded it.

I recall a sad occasion that happened in 1971 when Johnny Meeks called me. Johnny is my friend from Laurens, South Carolina that I had worked some club gigs with and he later became Gene Vincent's guitar player for a few years until Vincent had gone to Europe to try and extend his career over there. Meeks called to tell me Gene Vincent had died on October 12, 1971 at the age of 36 and wanted me to notify Tex Davis of his death. I called Tex and naturally he was very saddened. I never knew for sure but I always thought Tex sent a donation to help with the cost of Gene Vincent's funeral. That is just my own opinion and may not be a fact at all.

Tex Davis is just another in a long line of wonderful people I have met in my music career that I am proud to call friend.

Glenn Sutton was a staff producer at Columbia Records. He and I had become friends and I would go over to his office and hang out with him on occasions. Glenn had co-written, along with Billy Sherrill, David Houston's breakout hit, *Almost Persuaded*. Glenn was married to Lynn Anderson at that time.

Glenn was a happy kind of guy, always into something to have fun with. He had this life size mannequin he would carry around Columbia Records and talk to it like it was a person, saying all kind of funny things. As well as I remember it had a mustache and a little goatee. Its head kind of reminded me of a wolf. Glenn had a lot of fun with that dummy.

Glenn also was into trying to learn to play steel guitar.

"Lloyd Green is giving me some lessons," he told me once.

Lloyd Green was one of the greatest steel players in Nashville history and well sought after for recording sessions. He had played on my first record when I visited Nashville and recorded in 1967.

One day I visited Glenn and he was rehearsing on his steel guitar in his office.

"See what this sounds like," he said to me and played a few bars.

"It sounds like the intro and turn around on about five Conway Twitty records," I laughed.

"That's good and you know it," Glenn grinned and played it again.

I had been concentrating on my writing and hadn't tried too hard to get a record deal, although it kind of lay in the back of my mind and would surface on occasions. That day I talked to Glenn Sutton about it.

"You want me to play steel on your records don't you?" he snickered.

"I'm serious, man," I told him. "I'd like to try and record."

"Well, I like your singing," he told me seriously. "Let me see if I can get Clive Davis to give me a budget to take you in the studio."

Old Memories and Me

He went back to playing around on his steel guitar so I thought that would be the last of it. However, a few weeks later Glenn told me that Clive Davis had approved a budget for him to cut four sides on me to see how it turned out. Naturally, I got excited and we started listening to songs, some of my own, some of Glenn's and some from other writers.

About as quickly as the excitement started it ended. Glenn called me one day and told me the session had been axed. He said he didn't know why and I believed him. I had my own opinion when I found out that Lynn Anderson was leaving Columbia. It was just my own personal opinion but I think all of Glen's projects might have been scarped for the time being because his star wife was leaving the label.

So much for launching my recording career.

Larry Butler always liked my writing and once he found a song he really liked he would record it over and over on somebody until he found the right artist for it. If not for Larry Butler recording so many of my songs in the seventies and early eighties, I don't guess I would have survived back then.

I have to tell you though, I worked hard for most of those cuts Larry Butler gave me. His office was on the 7th floor of the United Artist Tower. Back in Watts Mill, South Carolina, some 15 years earlier, I had gotten stuck in a stalled freight elevator one night in the cotton mill. I was alone in that thing for nearly four hours. It made me claustrophobic, especially being enclosed in elevators. I stopped riding elevators for many years. I walked those seven flights of stairs up to Larry Butler's office many times. Can you imagine a smoker with a hangover doing that? I would be gasping for breath by the time I got up to the seventh floor.

I came up with what I thought was a good idea. I would use somebody's office phone on the ground floor and call Larry's secretary, Michelle.

"I'm sending up a tape on the elevator, Michelle," I would tell her.

Then, I would rush over to the elevator, open the elevator door and lay a tape on the floor. Michelle would press the button to bring the elevator up to the top floor so she could get my tape. The only problem was, sometimes somebody else had pressed the button on another floor and the elevator would stop on its way up. I lost a few tapes like that.

Bad idea. Back to huffing and puffing the seven flights of stairs to Larry Butler's office.

Finally, I had to start riding elevators because they had started building taller office buildings on the row. But I wouldn't ride them alone. I use to call my friend John Riggs, who used to answer the request line for Ralph Emery on his late night WSM radio show. John would meet me and ride the elevators with me. If I got stuck, I wasn't going crazy by myself again.

Back then, where the Best Western Motel is today on Division Street, it was called the Hall Of Fame Motor Inn and there was a restaurant and lounge downstairs where the Hall Of Fame Lounge is now. I would take John there a lot and buy his lunch for riding elevators with me.

John shaves his head, completely bald. Once, Marty Robbins paid him $500 to paint an advertisement on his head to promote Marty's current record. John used to send out Christmas cards with *Merry Christmas* painted on his bald head. John is a songwriter and produces some independent sessions for singers wanting to make albums to sell back in their hometowns at the gigs they work. He and I have always talked on the phone and discussed the ups and downs of the music business. He is pure traditional country and gets upset with artists that record what he calls pop music and country radio plays it.

"That ain't country, Charlie," he says. "I'm just gonna stop listening to the radio."

"John, I agree that it's not country," I would tell him. "But if we are going to survive as songwriters we have to write what they are recording."

One of the big highlights in my career had nothing to do with somebody recording one of my songs. It was an opportunity I had to meet and work for Burt Reynolds.

Burt had starred in a movie filmed in Nashville called *WW And The Dixie Dance Kings*. Jerry Reed was in the movie and had become friends with Burt Reynolds. Burt threw a big party after the conclusion of the filming and wanted a band to play at the party. I was friends with Jerry Reed's manager, Harry Warner, and Harry hired me and my band to play at the party.

Burt Reynolds had rented a place called *Pee Wee's* out on 52nd Avenue. It was a huge place and seated a lot of people. A dinner was served and a lot of stars were there, including Don Williams, Merle Kilgore, Ned Beatty, Art Carney, and of course Burt Reynolds. Burt flew Adrienne Barbeau in from New York as his special guest. Adrienne Barbeau played the daughter on the TV sitcom *Maude*.

Burt met Betty and me in the parking lot when we arrived, not that he was out there waiting especially for us, he just happened to be there when we pulled up and parked. He came over to the car and introduced himself to us.

"Let me give you a hand with that," he said and promptly lifted my Baseman amplifier from the car trunk by himself. The three of us made a little small talk, then Burt helped me carry my bass and amp into the building. I went to the stage and set up my equipment. Betty sat at a table reserved for the band member's wives and guests.

Before we starting playing, Burt came back over to me and said, "Okay, this is your gig. There are a lot of entertainers here, probably too many to let them all entertain tonight, so I will let you

Old Memories and Me

be the judge of who gets on the stage and who doesn't. I trust you to handle that and if anybody gives you a problem, come and get me."

Well, he was right about that. The place was packed with musicians and singers.

There were Hollywood people there as well as Nashville people. The movie's producer and director were there, and a few actresses and actors from Hollywood. You could tell the Hollywood crowd from the Nashville folk, especially the men. It was suits and ties verses shirts and jeans. Our country ladies have as much uptown attire as anybody. They were dressed to kill in a vast array of multi-colored gowns, dresses and pants outfits, on par with the Hollywood ladies.

It turned out to be an easy gig for me that night. I sang my songs *Lay A Little Loving On Me* and *Money Can't Buy Love*. Jerry Reed got onstage and sang harmony with me on *Lay A Little Loving On Me*. Paul Yandell was out on the road working with Chet Adkins and Dale Sellers was playing lead guitar that night. Dale is left handed so when Jerry Reed, who is right handed, joined us onstage he played my bass on some songs. When he did *Alabama Wild Man* and *When You're Hot You're Hot* I sat with Betty and watched. Reed did his usual great performance, even without his trademark guitar. He played pretty good bass and Del Sellers did a darn good Jerry Reed impression on guitar when they did Jerry's songs.

Most of the performers that got on stage that night sang a couple of songs and got off. Don Williams performed, as did Merle Kilgore. My band backed most of the singers that performed. There was one performer though that didn't want the band to play along and did her thing by herself. She went on and on, and was very loud.

Finally, Burt Reynolds came over to me and draped an arm around my shoulder, leaning over, trying to whisper above the noise into my ear. "Get her off the stage now, please. I don't care how you do it but get her down from there. Everybody is going to leave."

I got my band members together and we went to the edge of the stage and as soon as she finished the song she was doing, I hastened out to the microphone and announced, "Let's give her a big hand!" I started applauding and the audience joined in. She bowed and left the stage smiling, so it worked out alright.

During one song we were playing, an up-tempo, the dance floor was packed, and I noticed this guy making his way through the crowded dancers. His expression was that of anger, at least it appeared that way to me. I also noticed a guy dancing with an extremely attractive young lady. This guy was on the short side and the girl was tall. She had on a very low cut dress and her half exposed breast struck the man she was dancing with directly in his face, and he kept burying his nose in her cleavage. All of a sudden I recognized the guy making his way through the crowd as Art Carney, and he was heading for that couple. I was thinking, *Oh, crap, that is his wife or daughter the guy is rubbing his face into.* When Art Carney reached them, he tapped the guy on the back of his shoulder, and when the guy turned around I thought Carney was going to punch him. Nope. They started dancing together. The other guy turned out to be an executive with the movie production. It was a hoot.

Betty had American Indian and French in her bloodline. It was the Indian that came out when she had a couple of drinks. That night she had a couple of drinks. Ned Beatty came over to the table where she was sitting and asked her to dance. She was tipsy and grinned at him, saying, "I will if you will go oink oink for me."

I was onstage playing at the time and I am told Ned Beatty didn't take that kindly and walked off. When they told me about it I nearly choked. Of course Betty was referring to the movie *Deliverance* that Ned Beatty had been in, along with Burt Reynolds. Normally, she wouldn't have said that, but the rum and coke gave her the brass to say it I guess. Later, sobered up, Betty felt badly about it.

"Did I really say that?" she asked me.

"Yep," I told her.

Anyway, it was a great night. I made a copy of the check Burt Reynolds gave me for the gig. It was for $500. Pretty good money back then. Pretty good money now too.

Betty, Dawn and I were enjoying life together, putting up volleyball net and playing volleyball in the field between the duplexes almost every afternoon after supper until dark and on weekends. A lot of the neighbors joined in and sometimes we would all grill out afterwards.

It was about this time that Betty and I bought Dawn a Honda CB 100 motorcycle. I was against it but I let them talk me into it. Dawn was a pretty responsible child but still, she was only about 12 or 13 years old at that time. We bought her a CB 100 because it was on the small side, but still, I was reluctant to buy it at first.

Dawn learned to ride the Honda really well and she was cute as a button on it. The Honda was white with blue stripes and she wore a helmet to match. Dawn has always been extremely athletic and could do about anything she set her mind to do.

She kept the Honda for well over a year and I think I held my breath most of that time and prayed she wouldn't have an accident. Of course she did, not with another vehicle though. She slid and fell down on the cycle a couple of rimes, one of the worst being when she tried to do a donut, spin in a circle, and slipped on the gravel. She skinned her legs and knees up something awful.

"That's it," I said firmly. "We're gettin' rid of that thing."

"I'll be alright, Daddy," Dawn told me. "I won't do another donut."

We didn't get rid of the Honda but I'll bet you anything she did donuts again.

Old Memories and Me

My band had moved into the new American Legion they had built between Madison and Rivergate Mall. The band still consists of Paul Yandell on lead guitar, Mike Copas on drums, Willie Rainsford on piano and myself on electric bass. I had added Jim Hoback to our group as a singer on certain songs. Jim wasn't in the music business and didn't play an instrument but he loved to get up and sing so I added him on. Sometimes I just do things simply because I feel it is a good thing and allows somebody to get to do something they might not otherwise get a chance to do. The few songs Jim performed the crowd seemed to really like, especially when he did *Elvira*. I sang mostly all country but did a few of the popular pop/rock songs such as *Kung Fu Fighting* and *Lying Eyes*. I did a few of my own compositions such as *Lay A Little Loving On Me, Sweeter Than The Day Before and Money Can't Buy Love*. Mike Copas and Willie Rainsford did both country and rock and all three of us did harmony backing each other. We had a great sound and covered about all of the current hits in country, rock and pop. Mike even did a couple of Stevie Wonder songs. One of my favorites for Mike Copas to sing was the Doobie Brother's *Long Train Running*. I loved doing the harmony on that song.

I was still drinking beer every night. It was a bad habit I couldn't break, but to be honest, I didn't try very hard either. I had to have that artificial world to make up for the real one where I felt like I was just dragging through the music business and not getting to the level where I wanted to be. It was starting to affect me emotionally, leaving my nerves bad after a night of drinking. I knew I had to stop and I kept promising God, Betty, Dawn and myself that I was going to. However, rather than count all the reasons I should stop drinking I kept looking for excuses not to. Most of my friends didn't know I was drinking the way I was.

I signed on as a writer with Gee Whiz Music in 1977, which was owned by Kelso Herston and Del Reeves. Del had just brought in his hometown friend Larry Atwood into the partnership about the time I signed. Betty had gotten a job a printing company off of Elm Hill Pike and I continued to work clubs on weekends to help out financially. Betty and I were slowly building up a small savings account and we tried to send a little money back home to help my daddy pay Mama's medical bills.

Not long after signing with Gee Whiz Music I wrote the best song I had written to that point in my career. It was called *I Would Like To See You Again*. Producer Larry Butler loved it the first time he heard it and immediately recorded it on Del Reeves.

"I don't think it came off on Del for a single, Charlie," Larry told me. "But I am going to keep cutting that song on somebody until I get a single. This is a hit song."

Larry Butler had also loved my song *Lay A Little Loving On Me* and would eventually produce it on B. J. Thomas, Bill Medley and then

Wayne Newton.

    Larry Butler hit me with a pleasant surprise one day.

    "Do you want to come out to the House Of Cash Studio tomorrow tonight?" Larry asked me one day in 1978. "I'm cutting Johnny Cash on *I Would Like To See You Again.*"

    Holy Cow. Johnny Cash was going to record one of my songs.

    The next night I drove out to The House Of Cash, the recording studio Johnny Cash owned in Hendersonville. June was there with their son, John Carter Cash. He was just a little fellow then. June only stayed a while and took him home. Before the recording actually got started, Johnny gave his secretary a fifty-dollar bill and sent her to a nearby market. She brought back a large bag of goodies for everybody to snack on. I stayed out of everybody's way. Johnny Cash said he remembered me from the Roy Rogers meeting and that made me feel good.

    I stayed in the control room with Larry Butler and the engineer. Larry had the engineer play Del Reeve's version of the song so the Tennessee Three, Earl Ball and Jimmy Capps could chart it and get the right feel. Cash had only heard my demo version of the song and spoke into his microphone in that booming voice. "Hold on. That's not the version I want to hear. I want to do this song like Charlie Craig does it."

    Butler pressed the talkback button so he could talk back and forth with Cash. He told John, "I don't have Charlie's demo with me."

    "Come in here and show us how this sucker's suppose to be done, Charlie. I like the way you sing it." Again, he sounded like God might sound making it thunder.

    I nearly fell over. "Yes sir," I said and wished my voice would stop quivering. Somehow I managed to keep my knees from buckling and made it into the recording room. I knew Larry Butler was watching me through the glass panel from the control room and probably laughing his fanny off at me. Knowing him the way I did, I also knew he was proud for me and this moment. He was that kind of man.

    Johnny Cash had pulled up a stool alongside his and told me to sit down. He handed me his guitar. *Oh Lord, don't let me drop it or scratch it up.* I started to turn my belt buckle around to keep from doing just that. John chuckled. "Look at the back of that thing. It's been through so many wars you can't hurt it with that little belt buckle."

    I started singing my song but about four lines into it I dropped my pick and had to dig another one out of my pocket. My mouth was dry and my fingers couldn't seem to find the right frets on his guitar.

    Johnny Cash saw how nervous I was and tried to relax me. "You need to calm down, boy," he laughed and put a hand on my shoulder. "You gonna bust a gut."

    I managed to grin at the icon sitting beside me and then somehow I got through singing the entire song without messing up again. When I had finished Johnny Cash complimented me on how I

Old Memories and Me

had performed it and told his band he wanted to keep that same real, *down to earth feeling* to it, as he called it.

That night Johnny Cash recorded my song, *I Would Like To See You Again* exactly the way I wrote it. Awesome falls short in trying to describe the way that made me feel.

Over the years since then, I have tried to rate the highlights in my career. There have been so many, but I do believe that night when I taught Johnny Cash my song, at his request, sitting beside him on that stool, playing his guitar, without a doubt, that is the ultimate privilege God has granted me in the music business.

That song didn't stop there though.

"May I speak to Charlie Craig," a deep, rich voice asked when I answered the phone at my home one day.

"This is he," I answered.

There was no mistaking that voice. I knew who it was.

"Charlie, this is Don Williams," he said. "I was in Denver last week and me and Waylon Jennings got on the bus to ride over to do the show there and I heard Johnny Cash singing *I Would Like To See You Again* on the radio. I told Waylon, John has recorded my song. I have had that song for almost a year."

"I gave it to your manager two years ago, Don," I told him.

"Well, I didn't know I had it that long," he sighed. Then he said, "but I recorded it yesterday. It was the first song I cut on the session."

"Well, thank you so much," I said. "I am a big fan of yours."

"I appreciate that," Don told me, then added, "I'm not going to try and cover Johnny Cash, but I love the song and it will be in my next album. I just wanted to tell you that I cut it yesterday."

"Well, thank you very much. You made my day, Don." And I really meant that.

Not only did Don Williams put *I Would Like To See You Again* in his next album, he also made it the B side of his next single.

Johnny Cash's single of *I Would Like To See You Again* gave me my first top 10 song. It was also my first BMI Award. I had finally arrived. Now I was officially a hit songwriter.

Yeehaw....

"Times are changing, John," I said to John Riggs one day while we were having a beer at the Hall Of Fame Motor Inn Lounge.

"I know," he sighed. "Pop singers are coming to town every day by the busloads. They're gonna to take over country music." He just shook his shaved head in disbelief.

He was referring to singers like Kenny Rogers and B. J. Thomas who were planning on recording in Nashville after great careers in the pop field. He didn't have anything against the singers themselves, he just thought they weren't country and should stay in the pop field. John Riggs wasn't the only one that felt like country music was trying to go pop and didn't like it any more than he did. I admit that I too was skeptical about it but songwriting is how I make my living so I try to change with the times. I would soon get songs recorded by both of the former pop artist I just mentioned. It wouldn't take long for everybody to start accepting the universal sound of Kenny Rogers and the great songs he would record. With Larry Butler producing him, *Lucille* and *The Gambler* would become two all time country classics. When Butler cut him on my song, *I Would Like To See You Again*, naturally I was thrilled.

Larry Butler also produced B. J. Thomas. One of B. J.'s hits was a Butler co-written song, *Another Somebody Done Me Wrong Song*. B. J. also recorded my song *Lay A Little Lovin On Me* with Butler producing.

Things went well with Gee Whiz Music, especially in the beginning, with *I Would Like To See You Again* doing so well. As usual, I had a lot of good times with Del Reeves. I would get him to do impersonations of Roy Acuff, Jimmy Dickens and Johnny Cash around the office. His ability was astonishing at impersonating other artist. He also did the actor Walter Brennen to perfection. I always thought the CMA should have presented Del Reeves with an *Entertainer Of The Decade Award*.

Del was also a little witty and prankish at times, like me.

I recall on one occasion that Del came into the office carrying a briefcase. The briefcase was closed and money was partially sticking out everywhere. It looked like he was carrying a wad of cash around in that briefcase.

Very seriously Del told me, "I have been around to all the record labels that owe me money, collecting royalties. I told them all I wanted my frigging royalties right now and I wanted it in cash, and I don't mean Johnny."

For a few seconds I just looked at him, puzzled and wondering what the heck he was doing. Then, simultaneously, we both started laughing.

Del opened up the briefcase. It was empty, except for a few fives and tens, and a bunch of ones. Closed, with all those bills sticking out, the briefcase had appeared to be stuffed full of money.

I recall another time when Del Reeves got a package in the mail. It was just a big brown paper bag, like you bag groceries in, and it had a few stamps on it, Del's picture pasted on, Nashville, Tennessee hand printed, and that's all. The thing arrived at Gee Whiz Music, just like that.

"What the hell is this?" Del laughed, then frowned and looked at me suspiciously. "You up to some crazy bull, Charlie Craig?"

"I didn't send that," I assured him truthfully.

"How the heck did it get here with no address?" Del wondered

Old Memories and Me

out loud.

I just shrugged being as puzzled as he was. Knowing Del, I was thinking he probably sent it to himself just to be funny.

As it turned out, somebody, somewhere, had unrolled recording tape from the reel, wadded it up in a big tangled mess and stuffed it into the bag. There was an envelope inside, with a note inside that. It read, "Mr. Del Reeves, please listen to my song and let me know if you think it is a hit or not."

Del and I laughed and accused each other again of mailing the bag. Finally, we believed each other didn't send it but never did find out who did send it. The real puzzle was how it arrived in the mail with just Del Reeve's picture and Nashville, Tennessee printed on it. Of course there was no way to untangle that wad of tape and play it.

Charlie McCoy used to have a bunch of music people over to his house every Memorial Day and Labor Day. We would play volleyball, softball, card games, shoot pool, play a little music, and watch slides from the bowling league Charlie had taken. He and his wife Susan had an indoor swimming pool as well, so we usually wound up going swimming late afternoon after most people had left..

Throughout the day on those occasions, perhaps a hundred or so people in the music business would drop by. A few of us, mostly the couples that bowled together in the bowling league on Sunday nights at Donelson Bowl usually got there around 11am and stayed until that night. We had nine or ten couples that were a pretty close-knit group and we did a lot of things together. In that group were Buddy and Marsha Harmon, Kenneth and Delores Buttrey, Wayne and Jerry Moss, Willie and Jeannie Ackerman, Cam and Delores Mullins, Barbara and Curly Chalker, Hal and Vickie Rugg, Jim and Laura Colvard, Charlie and Susan McCoy, and of course Betty and I. Out of those people were some of the greatest session musicians that ever recorded in Nashville's studios, coming up with signature licks on such classic hits as Waylon Jennings's *Only Daddy That'll Walk The Line* and Roy Orbison's *Candy Man*. A couple of them played on a lot of Elvis's records. Cam Mullins was an arranger of such classics as *For The Good Times*. A lot of those guys became members of the group Barefoot Jerry as well. It was an elite group of people.

When we played softball, whoever was choosing the players on each team would choose Dawn as one of the first players because she was so good. It was kind of funny with a bunch of us grown men waiting to be chosen and 14-year-old Dawn being picked ahead of us. She was that good though. Betty and I always tried to wind up on the same team playing volleyball. I hated playing against her because I would be reluctant to try and spike it for fear of hitting her with the ball, which I did on a few occasions.

"You did that on purpose," she would say, pointing at me with one hand and rubbing wherever the volleyball had hit her with the other. "Aw, honey," I'm sorry, "I would apologize. "I didn't mean to."

"I'll remember that tonight," she would assure me with a teasing smile and everybody would laugh.

Those were some fun times at Charlie and Susan McCoy's house on Memorial and Labor Days.

I became a writer for Charlie McCoy and Wayne Moss' publishing company for a while in the seventies. The company was Wormwood Music. It was during that time that Charlie approached me one Sunday night during our bowling league about needing a song.

"Charlie, I am doing a new album on Monument Records and this one will be me doing vocals," Charlie told me. "I need a good song so could you write me one?"

"When do you need it?" I asked him.

"I start tracking tomorrow at Cinderella Studio," he informed me.

"Tomorrow?" I laughed.

"Well, I will be recording for a few days," Charlie said.

That night I stayed up till the wee hours of the morning and write Charlie McCoy a song called *Drifting Lovers*. It had strong lyrics and a great melody. I went over to Charlie's house early the next morning and sang it for him.

"I love it," he told me with a broad grin. "I can stack some good harmonies on this little jewel.

He did just that too. He recorded the song and stacked an endless amount of harmony parts on the chorus himself. He is a great talent. His cut on *Drifting Lovers* turned out great.

Radio had always played Charlie's records of his harmonica instrumentals really well but for some reason they wouldn't play him as a vocalist. That was ridiculous too because he is an excellent singer. I still listen to his version of *Drifting Lovers* to this day and he I talked about the song recently and how it could fit in today's market still. I plan on pitching the song to all of the record labels. I don't believe anybody can beat his version of that song though, especially the way he performs the chorus.

Sometime later, Billy Jo Spears recorded my song *Rainy Days And Stormy Nights*, published by *Wormwood* and produced by Larry Butler. For a few years in the eighties Larry Butler really kept my songwriting career going for me.

Betty and I still played scrabble a lot and she was always making words I had never heard of before.

"*Adze* ? That is not a word," I told her. She had the *z* on a double space for extra points.

"Challenge it," she grinned with confidence.

If I challenged and it was a word, I would lose my turn.

Old Memories and Me

"It ain't a word," I said again. "Take it off the board."

"Either challenge it or make a word and let's move on," she said, crossing her arms and staring at me with that *you're afraid it's a word aren't you* look.

"I challenge," I said and pointed a finger at her. "That is not a word."

Betty handed me the scrabble dictionary. I turned the pages to the *a* section. "I know it's not a word," I mumbled as I searched the page.

Adze, a tool for trimming wood.

I slammed the dictionary closed. That woman knew more words than Webster.

After my band left the American Legion, we started playing a Friday and Saturday night gig at a joint on Lebanon Road. It was a rough place. Somebody was always fighting and kept the bouncers, brothers George and Bug Felts, busy breaking up brawls. It got pretty scary sometimes, and especially one Saturday night it got *real scary*.

Betty had gone with me and this guy sat down at her table uninvited. Naturally, he had been drinking too much and naturally he flirted with Betty. From the stage I kept glancing over to her table and keeping my eyes on this character. Betty told me later that the guy had asked her to dance and the more sternly she declined the angrier he got. She thought it might deter him to tell him she was married to the guy in the band, the tall one playing bass and singing.

It didn't deter him.

The guy told her he had a gun and wasn't afraid of me, or anybody else. He pulled his jacket open enough so she could see he really did have a gun tucked in his belt. Upon seeing the gun, and hearing the guy's threat, two ladies sitting at Betty's table excused themselves to go to the restroom. However, one of them went to look for George Felts, one of the bouncers and co-owner, while the other lady came down to the stage and informed me what was going on. Betty talked with the guy to keep him occupied, telling him he was going to get into a lot of trouble if he didn't leave. That's when he told her he had just gotten out of prison and wasn't afraid pf trouble either. This was shaping up to be a real bad situation.

When the lady told me the guy had a gun, my guitar player, a guy who was filling in for Paul Yandell, pulled a pistol out of his guitar case and tried to hand it to me. "Here, Charlie," he said. "Take my 38 to protect yourself."

Oh man, just what I needed, one guy after me with a gun and one of my band members trying to give me one to shoot it out with the nut.

"Put that gun up," I told him and took the strap of my bass

from around my neck. I didn't know what I was going to do but I sure wasn't going to try and be Wyatt Earp. I glanced at Betty and she was looking at me and shaking her head, her lips forming a silent, *nooo, don't come over here.*

James Hoback was on stage and had heard what was going on.

"Stay here on the stage, Charlie," he told me. "Me, and George and Bug will handle him." Hoback left the stage.

Naturally, I was very uneasy about the situation and my biggest concern was that this crazy guy with the gun was still sitting with Betty. At the moment I was more afraid for her than for myself. You don't always think rationally at a time like that and I didn't then. I stepped off the stage to go over to where Betty was, my instincts just drove me to do that.

By this time the guy with the gun knew we all were aware of his presence and he looked over to see me approaching him. That was bad for him and good for me. When he turned his head in my direction he didn't see George Felts coming at him from the other direction. George's brother Bug was two steps behind him. When the guy stood up to face me, George came up behind him and threw his huge right arm around the guy's neck and his huge left arm around his midsection, pinning both of his arms. George was so strong the guy's furious struggle was useless. Within seconds Bug had pulled the gun from the guy's belt. James Hoback helped hold the guy as they shoved and escorted him to the front door.

Betty put an arm around my waist and laid her head against me.

"Are you alright" I asked her and kissed her forehead.

"Yes," she told me, and then added, "That's one crazy bastard. He just got out of a psychiatric hospital." The only time Betty used profanity was when she was either mad or scared. At the moment she was a little bit of both.

Later, it dawned on me that when the guy stood up as I approached him, he never reached for the gun. I wonder why. Maybe it was like when I used to drive from Spartanburg to Watts Mill at 2am and fall asleep behind the wheel but somehow always got home safely.

I think God must watch over me no matter where I am, even in honky tonks.

George and Juanita Felts bought another place on Dickerson Road, and the band and I moved there with them. It wasn't as rough as the last place but the name didn't indicate that. It was called The Doghouse Lounge.

We had a big following and drew several hundred people every Friday and Saturday night. We also started playing Sunday nights from 8pm till midnight.

Paul Yandell was a perfectionist. No bad notes were allowed. Hit a bad note and he would tell you about it, right onstage and give

Old Memories and Me

you a sour look. It was my band and my gigs, but I have to give Paul Yandell credit for us being as good as we were. He pushed us to the ultimate best. It wasn't a fault of his, it was his strength and the reason he was a great guitarist, the reason I was a better bass player, and the reason I never wanted to go onstage or in the studio without him.

It did cause problems sometime though.

"Come on, Charlie," Paul said to me with a frown. "Play the damn song right."

We were in the middle of a Stevie Wonder song, Mike Copas singing the lead, and I was attempting to play all of those difficult bass riffs and sing harmony at the same time. I had evidently hit a couple of sour notes and Paul was letting me know about it, right on stage, with the dance floor full.

"Go to hell." I shot back at him over my shoulder. I have a quick temper, especially when I have had a few beers, and especially when I know I am wrong but don't want to be told I am.

Paul Yandell looked back at me with a stare that could have knocked Mohammed Ali down. He played his solo part a lot louder than usual and kept giving me that mean look. I kept looking back at him with the same kind of ugly stare. We were acting like two kids but at the moment we didn't care.

A couple of songs later I was singing *The End Is Not In Sight* and Paul hit one teeny little wrong note. I stopped singing and pulled away from the microphone just long enough to glance at Paul and say, "Play the damn thing right."

Paul didn't look up at me but I could see a slight grin on his face.

I loved that guy.

CHAPTER ELEVEN

I was about to go to court for the first time in my life. There was some question about who had pitched *I Would Like To See You Again* to Johnny Cash and because of an agreement made between Kelso Herston and Bob Moore, a session Bass player that owned an independent publishing company, that agreement would wind up putting us all in a courtroom.

I was present when Kelso and Bob made an agreement that Bob would get 50% publishing on any song he personally, or his company, got recorded. In the case of my song and Johnny Cash, there was a big dispute over who had taken Cash the song originally. It actually didn't involve or affect me, just the two publishing companies.

However Johnny Cash had heard the song, he liked it and agreed to record it. Larry Butler recalled playing my demo for him. When Del Reeves performed the song on the Grand Ole Opry, he always told the audience how he sang it to Cash backstage one night in a dressing room at the Opry. Bob Moore claimed his secretary sent it to John. That's how we wound up with a publishing lawsuit in court. It was a mess. Bob Moore sued Kelso and Del for half the publishing, saying his company got Johnny Cash to record the song. I was subpoenaed and had to testify. Larry Butler and I were just caught in the middle.

"You swear to tell the truth, the whole truth and nothing but the truth?"

"I do," I answered, with my left hand on the bible and my right raised.

I sat down at the witness stand, a bit nervous, just because I was in a court of law for the first time.

"Would you state your name for the court, please," Bob Moore's lawyer told me.

"Charlie Craig," I replied.

"Charlie, you are the writer of the song in question, isn't that correct?"

"Yes sir."

"I believe you were present when a meeting took place between Bob Moore and Kelso Herston concerning a co-publishing agreement."

Old Memories and Me

"Yes sir, I was."

"Would you tell the court, of your own personal knowledge, what was said at that meeting and your understanding of the agreement that was made that day between Bob Moore and Kelso Herston," the lawyer instructed me.

"Well," I began, and cleared my throat, glancing at the judge, who was looking at me very intently. I looked back at the lawyer. "Uh, I heard Kelso tell Bob that he would give him fifty percent publishing on any song that Bob was responsible for getting recorded out of the Gee Whiz Music catalog."

"And wasn't it understood that if any employee working for Bob Moore's publishing company was responsible for getting a Gee Whiz song recorded, that same agreement would be in effect?"

"Objection, your honor," Kelso Herston's attorney stood and stated from his seat. "Council is leading the witness."

I felt like I was in the middle of a Perry Mason trial.

"Over ruled," the judge said. "You can answer the question, Mr. Craig."

"Well, yes, I mean, from what was said, it was my understanding that if Michelle got a song recorded it would be the same as if Bob had. I mean, Michelle is Bob's secretary and she pitches songs for his company as well."

Kelso's lawyer objected to that too, saying I was speculating. I wasn't speculating though because I knew Michelle, and I knew she pitched songs for Bob Moore's publishing company. I knew everybody involved very well and it strange having to testify for one and against the other. It was very uncomfortable.

Later, during a recess, Kelso Herston told me I didn't have to volunteer that part about Michelle pitching songs as part of the agreement and he wished I hadn't done that. I said it because it was the truth as I knew it to be. If it hurt one party and helped the other, so be it. I just told the truth.

After recess, a strange thing happened, well at least I wasn't expecting it.

"Do you know Johnny Cash personally?" the judge asked me, right after I took the witness stand again.

"Yes sir," I told him.

"So, you wrote the song in dispute here today that Johnny Cash recorded?" he continued, as though he were in awe of what this was all about.

Again, I told him, "yes sir."

The judge then asked me if I could get him an autograph by Johnny Cash on the record of my song the lawsuit was about. We had the perfect script for a soap opera and didn't realize it. Later, I got the autograph from Johnny Cash for the judge and took it to his office and gave it to his secretary.

The court awarded Bob Moore 50% of the publishing on the Johnny Cash version of *I Would Like To See You Again* but not on the other versions recorded by Don Williams and Kenny Rogers because they were not in dispute.

I was glad when it was all over. I don't like courtrooms.

We tried to get back to South Carolina as often as we could. My daddy and mama had retired from Watts Mill and Betty's mother had moved back to Fort Mill, South Carolina, where Betty's brother Clarence Huntington, and her sister Juanita McGuirt, lived. Her twin, Bobbie Bolt, still lived in the Laurens area. My brother Bill was still in Charlotte, N.C. Dot was still in Laurens, and Ruby still lived in Columbia. With our families so scattered out we had a lot of traveling to do.

Daddy continued to have a big garden every year. So did Betty's mother. We always brought back fresh and frozen vegetables every time we went home. It was an eight-hour drive and we had to ice down the frozen stuff.

On one return trip back home to Nashville, we had so much food in the car from both our parents, it was hard climbing over the steep mountains without having to keep changing to low gear. We were driving Betty's 4-cylinder Chevette.

We usually came up Interstate 26 from the Laurens exit and got on Interstate 40 West at Asheville, N.C., but on this particular trip back home we went from Betty's mother's house in Marshville, N. C. and took another interstate when we got to Charlotte that went toward Winston Salem, N. C. We got on Interstate 40 West much farther east than usual, so we had to cross over Grandfather Mountain. That is a big sucker. I didn't think we were going to get over it loaded down with all our luggage and so much food we were taking back. Every fifty yards or so we had to stop and gear down to low gear and start again. They were working on the interstate to widen it going over that mountain and that mess didn't help any. If you have ever driven over Grandfather Mountain, you know how big and steep it is, especially before they worked on the highway that crosses it.

We finally got over the mountain and arrived safely home in Nashville, where we were still trying to climb the mountains the music business can put in your path.

Jack Greene and I met in 1968 and became friends immediately. We hung out backstage at the Grand Ole Opry over the years whenever I visited the show and he wasn't out on the road. I remember very well when he recorded both *There Goes My Everything* and *Statue Of A fool*, the latter being written by Jan Crutchfield 8 or 9 years before Jack recorded it. How could a song that powerful lay around that long without being recorded.

These were the days when Jack and I both drank a lot and one day I went out to his house and we decided to write a song while we were popping tops. I don't even remember how I got home that day but

Old Memories and Me

a few weeks later Jeannie Seeley called me.

"Charlie, I need your social security number," she told me.

"For what?" I asked her.

"Jack is going to record that song you and he wrote a few weeks ago."

"What song?"

"*Cheating River*," Jeannie informed me.

To this day I can't tell you a line in that song.

My drinking all the time was a bad habit I couldn't break but to be honest I didn't try very hard either. I had to have that artificial world to make up for the real one where I felt like I was just dragging through the music business and not getting to the level where I wanted to be. It was starting to affect me emotionally, leaving my nerves bad after a night of drinking. It also started having an effect on my performance as a man being intimate with my wife. This caused Betty to start doubting herself, thinking the problem was her. Naturally it wasn't her. She was still a beautiful and very desirable woman. It was me damaging and slowly destroying myself with booze. In all my years I have never taken drugs, never smoked pot, my only vice being the ten years that I drank beer heavily every night. I knew I had to stop and I kept promising God, Betty, Dawn and myself that I was going to. Most of my friends didn't know I was drinking the way I was.

I had developed a serious problem though. Never before had I had a problem performing as a man.

"What's wrong?" Betty asked me one night, looking at me a little confused.

"I don't know," I told her and I honestly didn't know.

This was the second time this had happened in a short period of time.

Betty turned on a lamp and sat up. She looked at me. "Are you alright?"

"I don't know...I can't..." I was embarrassed. I couldn't look at her.

"What is wrong?" she asked again. This time she looked sad, like her feelings were hurt. "Tell me. Is it me?"

"Oh Lord no," I assured her and this time I looked at her. I couldn't have her thinking that. "It isn't you, honey. I just can't."

"Why can't you?"

"I don't know," I reached out to touch her. I wanted to cry.

She pulled back from me and just looked at me, about to cry herself.

I was aching with desire for my beautiful wife but I couldn't perform.

"I'm sorry," I told her and I really meant it. I felt useless, spent, yet I hadn't done anything. "I'm going to see Doctor Friddell tomorrow."

The next day I went in to see our family doctor, Thomas Friddell. He had been our doctor since 1969 and had also become a friend.

"You need to stop drinking beer and get on a better diet with less cholesterol and start getting more exercise. Your sugar level is also high," Doctor Friddell told me. "Alcohol is a depressant and the high cholesterol, along with no exercise causes circulation problems. Poor circulation and alcohol is causing your dysfunctional problem."

"I've reached the point to where I'm afraid to even try with Betty," I told him, almost in tears. "I am afraid I will fail again."

"You reach a point to where you start thinking about it," Doctor Friddell said, "and that's increasing the problem. It becomes mental as well as physical."

Doctor Friddell suggested a diet that would lessen my cholesterol intake, told me to start walking every morning and afternoon, and to stop drinking.

I didn't do anything he told me to. I meant to, I just found excuses not to.

Dawn had been playing slow pitch softball at the Civitan Club in Donelson since she was 8 years old. The summer of 1977, that she turned 15, Betty and I decided to allow her to move up to open ball and play in a more competitive league. She had progressed into an outstanding little player that could run like a deer and hit and throw a softball better than most boys her age. She was around 5' 2" and weighed about 115 pounds. Dawn was a tomboy in a lot of ways but she was an extremely attractive girl that could catch the boys' eyes as well as she could catch a softball.

There were open leagues all over Nashville, most of them sanctioned by ASA (Amateur Softball Association) and you had to be at least 14 years old to play. There was no age limit as far as being too old. A lot of coaches had seen Dawn play in the Civitan league and was trying to get Betty and me to let her play for their team. The closest park, with a league that we liked, was at Cedar Hill Complex in Madison, about twenty minutes from where we lived in Hermitage. Dawn signed to play for a lady named Rosie Weyhmeyer, who coached the Sam Whitaker team in a 7 pm Monday night league at Cedar Hill. The first time she batted she hit a home run over the left fielders head and was crossing home plate by the time the cutoff got the ball. She was fast as lightening.

By year's end Rosie Weyhmeyer had asked me to help her coach and after the regular season ended, playing in a fall tournament over in Lebanon, Tennessee, I took over as head coach at the request of Rosie and the sponsor, Sam Whitaker.

For the next fifteen years I would coach a women's slow pitch

Old Memories and Me

softball team. Betty would assist me for ten of those fifteen years. We went from being called Sam Whitaker, to The Bandits, then finally, C.C. Riders. Softball would introduce Betty, Dawn and me to some people that would become lifelong friends, such as Jimmy and Mickey Burton, Harvey Mayors, Randy and Joanne Smith, Ray McClanahan and Will and Juanita Grandstaff would be among those friendships I will always cherish. There were others too, and a lot of softball players that are too numerous to name. However, I do have to mention two. Marion Bender, who played on the first team Betty and I actually assembled ourselves, and played for us 8-10 years, and Debbie Rowan, who played the last few years that I coached. Both were outstanding and dedicated players that became very close to our family and our personal lives.

Betty helped me with the softball coaching, but she always stayed in the background of my musical career. She was never awed by most of the stars, and she hated the politics in the music business. She had even stopped co-writing with me. She still supported me but she was just tired of all the good songs I was writing not getting recorded and hearing songs on the radio that were not nearly as good, in her opinion.

She didn't want in the music business personally but it wanted her.

Hee Haw was in its heyday and Charlie McCoy was music director for the show. He wanted to try and get Betty on *Hee Haw*. By now her hair had grown real long, down past her shoulders, and she matched the beauty of the *Hee Haw* girls, figure included. Charlie wanted her to consider joining the show and he thought he could get the producer's approval.

Nope. Betty declined the offer. She told me we came to Nashville to make me a star, not her. She had no desire to be anything but a loving wife and a good mother. As outspoken as she was, she was shy when it came to cameras and getting up in front of a lot of people. Betty said she was doing just fine bowling in three leagues, raising daughter Dawn, loving and supporting her husband, thank you very much.

It was also around 1977 that I signed with Power Play Music, owned by Moe Lytle. My old friend Tommy Hill was house producer for Moe's Starday/Gusto Records. Moe Lytle had bought Starday Records and added the name Gusto. Tommy Hill had recently produced huge hits like *Teddy Bear* and *Phantom 309* on Red Sovine for Gusto. I was head staff writer and ran the publishing company for Moe. Actually, I was the only staff writer. Moe had other writers bringing songs into the catalog every now and then, but I was the only writer signed exclusively at that time.

In 1978 Moe Lytle started doing albums on artists no longer on major labels and re-cutting, or re-releasing their former hits on television. You could only buy them through the television ads he ran nationally on TNN. I brought in Del Reeves, David Houston and Kitty Wells for him and Tommy Hill put the albums together. Moe also brought in some former pop and rock n roll acts for the TV sales. Among them were the fabulous Coasters.

The Coasters had nine past hits for the album so Moe asked me to go upstairs and write them a song so they would have 10 songs on the album. About an hour later I had written a fifties sounding song called *One Foot Dragging* and The Coasters recorded it the next day. That was an extra big thrill for me because I got started in music in the fifties. The Coasters were one of my all time favorite rock n roll groups. I certainly remembered they were singing *Searching* on the jukebox the night I met Betty and to get to watch them record my song was something special. They were a lot of fun to be around and to watch work in the studio.

While I was at Power Play Music, Tommy Hill produced me on a couple of my own songs and Moe put them out on Gusto Records. Neither of them did anything in the charts. I just wasn't meant to be a recording artist I suppose.

Also while I was at Power Play I had an opportunity to work with Charlie Dick, the late Patsy Cline's husband. Charlie was Gusto's promotion man. Charlie was a character. We became good buddies. Later, I would see him portrayed in the movie *Sweet Dreams*, the story of Patsy Cline's life. He talked about Patsy Cline some when we worked together at Gusto but a lot of the things I later saw in the movie he had never mentioned.

At that time, Charlie Dick drank beer a lot, like I did, day and night. I remember once Moe Lytle had told me he wanted me to do some promo work on Red Sovine's current record. That meant getting on the telephone and calling radio stations, the same thing Charlie Dick was doing. Charlie gave me a list of stations to call, the program directors names and the phone numbers. I took the list and went off to my office to make the calls.

Charlie Dick and I both had already had a couple of beers that morning, so I was feeling pretty good, real loose and relaxed. Most of the radio people I talked to were real friendly, a few even knew who I was, mainly because of the Johnny Cash hit, *I Would Like To See You Again* and the Roy Rogers record, *Money Can't Buy Love*. There were a couple of radio stations that said they didn't add records to their play list until they were in the national charts, so when I called a particular station up in Illinois I was already a bit annoyed at hearing that.

"Call me back when it's in the top 40," the program director told me. He had a hint of sarcasm to his voice that I didn't like from the get go. "I don't play records till they get in the top 40."

This station was a Billboard reporting station but with the two beers in me and this guy's attitude, I didn't care how important his station was at that moment.

Old Memories and Me

"Well, mister music director," I told him, "I guess by now you have heard the latest news out of Nashville."

"What's that?"

"All of the record labels announced this morning they are not going to mail out free records to radio stations anymore until the record gets in the top 40."

I heard him snort, caught off guard, then he said, "How the hell we gonna get them in the top 40 if we don't have the damn records to play?"

"That's a good point, mister music director," I told him with some sarcasm of my own. "You think about that for a while."

I hung up the phone, grinning.

I walked to Charlie Dick's office and stuck my head in the door. "Hey, Charlie, you can scratch that Illinois station off the list. I don't think they'll be playing any of our records for a while."

Red Sovine recorded one of my songs, *The Days Of You And Me*. Kim Morrison sang the background vocals. Kim was a fantastic vocalist, background as well as a lead singer. So was Sherry Grooms. I used Kim and Sherry on about all of my sessions back then.

I wrote a lot of good songs while I was at Power Play but I just couldn't seem to get anything going with them. Moe Lytle and Tommy Hill were both good to me and made everything I needed available to me, including the studio. It was just a timing thing I guess. Wrong songs at the wrong time.

My dysfunctional problem was getting worse and I was having quite a time handling it. So was Betty. Intimate times with her were becoming less frequent and with that happening, for the first time in the twenty-one years we had been married, we stopped talking about our problems. We had always talked about things. This time it was different. I couldn't convince her that my problem had nothing to do with my desire for her and she couldn't convince me that she cared enough to try and help me with that problem anymore. It got to where I was really afraid to try, self-doubt adding to the already bad situation. Betty took this very personal and it was emotionally painful for her. It grew like a sore until we just didn't talk about it. That is when the chill between us started. The love was still there, we just didn't acknowledge it any more.

It was the worst time in my life. I was a man without a destiny anymore, a man without a shoulder to lean on. It was unjustified but it was easy to feel sorry for myself. I got off to myself and cried at times.

I became angry and started accusing Betty of not wanting me sexually. I had to blame it on her because I wouldn't face up to the fact that this was a problem I caused with my drinking and didn't have the guts to quit. I needed that crutch I got out of getting high and making things easier, pretending my career was going better than it was, living in a drunken dream for hours every night. I was like a zombie.

I still had my band and we continued playing The Doghouse

Lounge on Dickerson Road every Friday through Sunday night. Mike Copas was still playing drums for me and Paul Yandell was still on guitar. I was on bass and had added Dean Mathis, formerly of the *New Beats*, who had a huge hit in the early sixties with a song called *I Like Bread And Butter*. We had a Mexican, who ironically had never been to Mexico. He sounded just like Freddy Fender. He didn't play all the chords right on his guitar so we kept his volume turned down real low. He was a great Freddy Fender sound alike and could flat tear up *Before The Next Teardrop Falls*. I cannot recall his name. Jim Hoback sang a few songs and played some tambourine. That rounded out the band. Sometimes though, Greg Galbraith, another well-known guitarist, would play with us and we would utilize twin electric guitars on certain songs.

One Sunday night there were two girls I had never seen before that came into The Doghouse Lounge. They sat at a table near the bandstand. Sunday nights were not a full house most of the time and that night the place was less than half filled. One of the girls came down to the bandstand and asked me to sing *Handy Man*. The whole time I sang the song both of them were smiling towards me. When the band took a break one of them motioned for me to come over to the table where they were sitting.

"Hello," the one that had requested *Handy Man* smiled. "I like the way you sing."

"Thanks," I said and smiled back.

They were both blonde, and young, perhaps 19 or 20 years old. The taller one looked to be the oldest.

"Wanna sit down?" That one had done all the talking so far. She was the one that seemed to be the oldest by a couple of years.

I sat down in a chair next to her.

"Your name is Charlie, right?" she asked.

"How did you know that?"

"She asked the waitress," the other girl laughed. "She likes you."

"The waitress likes me?" I kidded her.

"No, my sister likes you silly." She replied seriously, as though she really thought I didn't understand.

I looked at the one beside me, the one that was supposed to like me.

"I'm Missy," she told me smiling, then immediately took a sip from her mug of draft beer.

I talked with them during the band break. I learned that they were sisters. Missy was the oldest, as I had suspected but a little younger than I thought. She was nineteen. Her sister's name was Kathy and she was eighteen. They were from Indiana and both of them dated truck drivers. Missy and her truck-driving boyfriend actually had a trailer in a mobile home park not far from the Doghouse Lounge.

Old Memories and Me

Sometimes she went out on the road with him, other times she stayed in Nashville, in the trailer, while he made a run somewhere in his 18 wheeler. Missy started coming to the lounge about every Friday, Saturday and Sunday night. I talked to her every time she came in and before long I had told her about my problems at home. I told her about my drinking problem and how I was having a difficult time performing as a man and that I thought maybe it had something to do with me about to turn forty as well. I told her my wife didn't understand and I am sure I made it sound like *the poor misunderstood husband*. She sympathized with me and that was exactly what I wanted her to do. Yes, I had turned into a jerk.

Then I did something terrible and stupid. I had an affair with Missy. At least I tried to. I had the same problem with her I was having at home in bed. However, she didn't take it personal, so she tried to help me and there were times I was able to feel like a man again. I also felt like a piece of scum afterward.

I would go off by myself and cry like a baby. I felt ashamed and I was hurting because I was doing something I never dreamed I would do in a million years. I had broken my vows to my wonderful and trusting wife. I prayed to God for forgiveness, yet I kept seeing Missy because she was helping me with something that I desperately needed to overcome, yet that very pain she was helping ease was killing me inside. After several weeks of seeing Missy I broke down and told Betty about her.

"You son-of-a-bitch," Betty said, tears starting to form in her brown eyes. "How could you?"

"I don't know, honey," I said, hanging my head and feeling like I wanted to throw up.

"Don't call me honey," she snapped. She was hurt, but she was also very angry.

For a few moments we both just sat there across from each other and cried.

"I'm sorry," I sobbed, breaking the silence. "I really am, but you wouldn't help me when I needed you to."

She flung a sofa cushion at me. "You piece of shit," she shrieked. "Don't you try to blame me for this!" She didn't curse much, unless she was really mad. She was really mad.

"I'm not blaming you," I told her. "I just needed..." I didn't finish it.

"Who is she?" Betty demanded to know.

I told her all about Missy, at least what I knew about her.

"Missy?" she mocked through her tears. "What is she, a little girl?"

"Almost." I must have sounded really stupid when I said that. "She's nineteen."

"Nineteen?" Betty said, almost choking on the word. "My God,

Charlie!"

"I know, I know," I mumbled. I had no defense. "She's about to turn twenty though." That must have really sounded ridiculous.

"You're twice her age," Betty reminded me, grimacing, her voice almost a whisper, like, *this is unbelievable*.

"You're not going to leave me, are you?" I broke into tears again, my lips trembling.

"I don't know what I'm going to do," she told me and looked away, crying, biting her lower lip.

I went over to her and tried to put my arms around her.

"Don't," she told me and pushed me away. "Don't touch me." She wouldn't even look at me.

I felt like my life was over. I couldn't lose Betty. I just couldn't bear that.

Betty couldn't decide what she wanted to do about me having an affair. The mood was so cold between us our apartment was like an icehouse instead of a home. We started fussing and saying hateful things to each other. Naturally, I kept drinking a lot.

Then, I did my second stupid thing. I moved out. I stayed at Jim Hoback's trailer with him and his wife. It wasn't in the same trailer park as Missy's trailer, but not far away. Missy stayed over there a few nights too. I was really in a mess and I was drinking even more, if that was possible. I hated myself. I couldn't believe this was me doing this, yet I couldn't stop. I was crawling along the bottom of my own weakness, disgusted with myself, but yet not strong enough to do anything about it.

In the daytime, Missy and I would just ride around for a while, talking, and then park somewhere, mostly near the back of the Gusto Records building. George and Juanita Felts, the owners the Doghouse Lounge would let me stay in the apartment upstairs sometimes. Wasn't that a fitting place for a dog like me, the Doghouse Lounge.

That's what I felt like, a lowdown dog, but finding courage in cans of beer I stayed gone from home about a week. I would call Betty every day and check on her. We would both cry. I took money by the apartment. We would cry again.

I went in to work every day at Gusto and I either wrote a song, or got on the telephone calling program directors at radio stations, helping Charlie Dick promote records. I didn't crack any more funny remarks to the program directors. I didn't feel like being funny anymore. I really just wanted to die.

I told Charlie Dick about the affair. He didn't know what to tell me to do but he did lend an ear. We talked a lot, about both our lives. Charlie told me stories about his late wife, Patsy Cline. There were some stories about him and Dooley, Loretta Lynn's husband. I think they used to drink and raise a little hell together. Charlie and Dooley, not Charlie and Loretta.

Old Memories and Me

I don't know how many people at Gusto Records knew I wasn't living at home all the time. My old friend, Tommy Hill knew. I had talked to him about what was going on with me.

"You just be careful, Charlie, and watch yourself," was his advice, then he added, "I wish you could go home and work things out with Betty." Tommy liked Betty.

I was missing Betty and Dawn. I felt guilty every morning when I woke up and my nerves were a total wreck, until I had a few beers, then I was back in my false illusioned world again.

Missy went out on a run with her boyfriend for a few days. He didn't know about us at the time and she had to go out with him some to keep him from getting suspicious. She would somehow get to a phone and call me from on the road.

I went back home. Betty would hardly talk to me and she slept with her back to me. When we did talk, it turned into an argument.

I left again.

The perfect marriage had gone to hell, and it was all my fault.

Excessive drinking and having an affair were taking its toll on me. I was always irritable and getting hard to get along with. The person that disliked me the most was myself.

I think the worst thirty minutes in my life happened the afternoon Dawn got someone to bring her over to Jim Hoback's trailer. She was 15 years old. Missy was there and Dawn wanted to whip her, and no doubt she probably could have. Dawn has always been a beautiful and shapely girl, but she is a tomboy and very athletic and strong, even at 5 feet two inches tall and 115 pounds.

"You stay away from my daddy," she yelled from outside the trailer. It was all I could do to keep her outside. It was also all I could do to keep from looking for a hole to crawl into.

I was so ashamed and I was hurting because I had broken Dawn's heart too. I was in tears as I tried to restrain my daughter. During that time of my life I was either always drunk or crying, or both.

I tried to convince Dawn how much I still loved her and asked her not to hate me. She had always been a daddy's girl but now she said she didn't have a daddy. That cut like a knife, but I understood her feelings and I deserved the remark.

I wanted to go back home, but I didn't know how to do that anymore. Betty would tell me she still loved me but couldn't live with me because of what I had done to her, and to Dawn. I told her I still loved her too.

Finally, a few days before Thanksgiving, Betty told me over the phone that she was taking Dawn and going back to South Carolina to live. I nearly panicked. I asked her not to go. No, I begged her not to go.

"Can I come home and let's talk?" I was pleading with her.

I could hear her crying softly over the phone. Finally, she answered me. "Ok." It was almost a whisper.

I told Missy I was going home.

"I knew you would never really leave her for good," Missy said. She was hurt and I was sorry I had ever involved her. I didn't want to hurt her but I couldn't lose Betty.

It had come down to hurting Missy or hurting Betty even more than I already had. The choice wasn't even close. I was going home to the woman I had loved since that first night I laid eyes on her twenty one years ago.

I guess most people would have no sympathy for Missy, knowing I was married, but I take full blame for what happened. I had hurt Betty and Dawn, now I was hurting Missy. It was time to put an end to the wrong that was causing so many people pain.

"I'm sorry," I told her. "I love Betty and I need to go home."

She looked at me with tears in her eyes and didn't say anything for a few moments. Then she said, "I'm going home too, back to Indiana."

I just nodded. I didn't know what to say to her.

"Rob has asked me to marry him again," she told me. Robert was her boyfriend, the truck driver.

"You going to marry him?" I asked her.

She bit her lip and wiped a tear from her cheek. Yes, yes I am."

"That will probably be a good thing for you." I told her.

I turned to leave but looked back at her. "You know," I told her. "I do wish you happiness and if I could undo all of this hurt I have caused everybody, I would change things back. But I can't."

She smiled for a moment, wiped away a tear and said, "I know."

"Goodbye, Missy," I said.

"Yeah," she said and forced another smile. "You better get going."

"Yeah," I agreed. "I need to go home."

I left Missy standing outside a restaurant near the mobile home park where she had lived. I never saw or heard from her again.

It was going to take some time for the things to get back to normal at our house but we would make it because Betty and I wanted things to be the way they once were. I was the guilty one but Betty did everything she could to try and make me not feel guilty any more. Once she decided to forgive me she wanted to put it all behind us and move forward. I had fallen and she would pick me up again, the way she always had. Still, not many days went by the first couple of months after my affair that I didn't say how sorry I was over and over again. I would look into her eyes and start bawling from guilt, throw my arms around her and squeeze her so hard it's a wonder I hadn't took her breath away. I was so glad to be home I didn't want to let her out of my sight for fear she would change her mind and leave me.

I was surprised that Betty responded to being intimate with me

Old Memories and Me

as soon as she did. I still had my problem but with her helping me now it began to get better. We started having wonderful moments together again.

I hadn't stopped drinking beer completely but I had cut down quite a lot. I had also started watching my diet and took walks with Betty in the afternoons. I made sure I took my cholesterol medication as well.

I was still carrying a heavy guilt in my heart and conscience, so I started going to church again at Hermitage Hill Baptist Church. One Sunday morning during the invitation hymn I went down and got on my knees and rededicated my life to Jesus. I had a forgiving wife and daughter, and a forgiving Savior. I was truly a fortunate man.

I had put us through hell but now we were back in our Heaven again. I didn't deserve it but I would never leave it again.

CHAPTER TWELVE

I met Keith Stegall the latter part of 1979. Keith was recording for Epic Records back then and his manager, Charlie Monk, asked me to write with him to *keep him country*, as Charlie Monk put it.

Keith had written a couple of big pop hits, *Sexy Eyes* and *We're In This Love Together* but as a recording artist he was cutting country records. He was about as talented as anybody I had ever known. An excellent singer that could do either pop or country, a talented songwriter with hits written in country music as well as the pop field. He was good enough on acoustic guitar to work sessions for other artists had he chosen to do so, and an accomplished keyboard player. He also had an enormous amount of knowledge in the electronic field. I actually believe he could take a "studio board" apart and put it back together again, but maybe his most gifted talent of all might be his creative production abilities in the studio.

The first song Keith and I wrote together was called *I Think I'm In Love*, an up tempo honky tonker that Keith recorded on Epic and released it as a single. Later it would be recorded by Conway Twitty, Ed Bruce, Rodney Lay and Curtis Wright. The second song we penned turned out to be so R&B I couldn't even play it. I was supposed to keep him country, but I just used paper and pencil that day. Songs like that are why I call myself a writer. I don't even pick up my guitar with those kind of chords in the song, I just write.

Another one the songs Keith Stegall and I wrote right after we started co-writing was *Every Time It Rains*. George Strait recorded that one in 1982 and included it on his Right Or Wrong album. I had played the song for Strait's record producer, Ray Baker and Ray played it for George. There was a line in the chorus that said, *there's a monkey on my back with a family of four*, which George asked us to change. I came up with, *my mother-in-law says she's staying three weeks more*, and George loved that line and that is what he sang on the record.

> *Every time it rains I just washed my car*
> *The whole neighborhood goes swimming in my front yard*
> *My mother-in-law says she's staying for three weeks more*
> *Lord, every time it rains now don't it pour*

Old Memories and Me

By the time Keith and I had started writing together I had left Power Play and Gusto Records and signed with Screen Gems, a division of EMI. Charlie Feldman was running the company. The writer's contract with Screen Gems was a little more complex than any of the other contracts I had signed so I needed a lawyer to read it over. That is when I met attorney David Maddox and he not only has been my attorney for the past thirty years but also a dear friend.

Not long after I had signed with Screen Gems Charlie Feldman told me he was going to be music director for a new Robert Duvall movie called *Tender Mercies*. I thought he was kidding me when he told me they were going to use five of my songs in the movie. I got really excited until he told me three of them would be my demos of me singing. Most everybody else that performed songs in that movie cut master tracks but they used my demos. I didn't think the demo tracks sounded good enough but evidently the powers that be thought they were. The other two songs of mine were performed by Robert Duvall's co-star Betty Buckley and *the band* in the movie.

I knew nothing about songs in a movie so once again I called on David Maddox to handle the contract and negotiate the deal as to how much money I would receive up front for the five songs they would use in the movie. The songs in the movie I wrote were, *Off On Wednesdays, Midnight Tennessee Woman, Making Love And Making Out*, all performed by me in the movie and on the soundtrack album released by Liberty Records, and *The Best Bedroom In Town*, performed by Betty Buckley, and *Champagne Ladies And Barroom Babies*, performed by a band in the movie. Later, John Anderson recorded *Making Love And Making Out*, Ed Bruce recorded *Off On Wednesdays*, Judy Bailey recorded *The Best Bedroom In Town*, and Jack Greene recorded *Midnight Tennessee Woman*. So, I got a pretty good ride out of those songs.

When *Tender Mercies* was finished they sent us an advance copy in Nashville. Charlie Feldman took all the writers that had songs in the movie over to a theater at Vanderbilt University and we all watched it together. The first time I saw the movie I couldn't follow the dialog because I kept listening for my songs. You never get tired of hearing your own songs and they were my first songs in a movie. I felt like George Gershwin. Seriously though, it was kind of cool to see my name on the big screen when they rolled the credits. Like I said, I had never experienced that before. Robert Duval won Actor Of The Year for his role in the movie. He is a great actor and I was certainly proud to be a small musical part of the film. My music career was the best it had ever been.

I had written *The Best Bedroom In Town* in honor of how well things in that section of our house were going. I was down to drinking just a few beers at night and not any in the daytime at all. I was still aching in my soul for hurting Betty and having the affair. Over and over I would tell her how sorry I was.

"You have got to stop punishing yourself," she told me. "That is over with so let's put it behind us. I love you and you love me and that is all that matters."

I decided to quit playing at The Doghouse Lounge and told my loyal band members goodbye and gave up working clubs for good.

Twenty-one years of working the bars was enough. I was a recognized songwriter now and I wanted to concentrate on expanding that career. Besides, I wanted out of the environment where I made one of the biggest mistakes of my life.

Keith Stegall and I were on good roll writing. One morning while I was driving to meet him for a writing session at CBS Songs where he was a staff writer, I got an idea and when I arrived I got out my guitar and showed Keith what I had come up with in my head while driving.

> *Let's get over them together, and bury two old memories*
> *Let's get over them together, I'll help you and you help me*

Keith jumped right on what I had. "That's great, Charlie," he told me and started messing around on his keyboard with the melody I had and he made it even better. In minutes we had the chorus.

"What about this for the opening lines," Keith suggested, and sang them with a melody he created.

> *I don't know if we can make it, but baby let's give it a good try*

Then, I chimed in.

> *We're both coming off of losing, it ain't easy telling love goodbye.*

Keith Stegall and I always played off of each other really well when we wrote together. By lunchtime we pretty much had the song finished. Later, after we demoed it, I played it for Ray Baker and he placed it on hold for Moe Bandy and Becky Hobbs as a duet. A year before, Ray had produced Moe Bandy and Judy Bailey on my song *Following The Feeling* and it was my second top 10 record in Billboard.

When *Let's Get Over Them Together* came out by Moe Bandy and Becky Hobbs it also made it to top 10 in the national charts. It was a big radio hit and would keep getting strong airplay for years.

Keith Stegall and I clicked right from the start as co-writers, but even more as friends. Over the next ten years we would probably write 75-100 songs together and confide in each other about our personal lives. We shared both laughter and tears, knowing one could always count on the other, always be there. Keith became my best friend in Nashville.

After I had been with Screen Gems for a couple of years,

Old Memories and Me

Charlie Feldman had decided to take a position with BMI in their New York office. I had become close friends with Charlie Feldman and hated to see him leave but I was glad for him to get a job he really wanted and I knew he also loved New York. Charlie Monk was still running CBS song and had asked me to sign there when my contract was up with Screen Gems. Keith was still a staff writer at CBS songs and that played a big part in my decision to move over to CBS when Feldman left Screen Gems.

Jim McBride signed with CBS Songs about the same time I did. I hadn't known him before but we soon became lifetime friends and started writing together. Jim had already had a hit with Johnny Lee on *Bet Your Heart on Me* and a few other songs that had done well for him.

Things just seemed to be moving really fast about that time and CBS Songs purchased United Artist Music and that writing staff merged in with our writing staff at CBS. Charlie Monk had already left and Judy Harris had taken over as head of CBS. Not too long after purchasing the United Artist Catalog, CBS moved its offices into two houses owned by my old friend Harry Warner, who had booked me and my band for the Burt Reynolds movie party.

With the United Artist merger, we now had a group of great songwriters that would go on to even greater heights, not only as songwriters, but some as producers, and even a few as recording stars. Staff writers for CBS Songs now included, besides Keith Stegall and myself, but Jim McBride, T Graham Brown, Richard Leigh, Waylon Holyfield, Stewart Harris, Guy Clark, Mark Wright, Roger Murrah, Holly Dunn, Verlon Thompson, and Peter McCann, among others. This group of writers would turn out some of the biggest hits in country music during the 1980s and on into the 1990s.

One of the staff survivors through all of these mergers and purchases was Bob Mather. Bob was Director of Administration when I first signed with CBS and would remain in that capacity for many years to come, eventually earning the distinguished title of Associate Vice President of Administration. Bob Mather became a loyal and lifelong friend of mine that would assist me in royalty and other matters that are too numerous to mention here. Bob also became the chief chef when CBS Songs first started the now famous and ongoing *Hot Dog Day*. This is an annual event that still takes place today where all of the music business people gather to have lunch, free of charge, under a large tent dining on hot dogs, roast beef, drinks, and other goodies.

CBS Songs didn't have enough writer rooms with so many staff writers after the United Artist purchase, so Keith Stegall rented the downstairs of a house owned by Lib Hatcher for him and me, and his other co-writers, to write in. Lib Hatcher had recently moved to Nashville from North Carolina, bringing with her a young singer named Randy Traywick, soon to be called Randy Ray.

While Keith and I would write downstairs in the house, Lib

and Randy lived upstairs. Randy was working at Nashville Palace as a cook and singing on the Palace stage when he had the opportunity. Keith had already known Randy and told me what a great singer he was. We used him on a demo session to sing a couple of our songs once and I was blown away by Randy Ray's voice. I believe those first demos were some of Randy's first recordings in a Nashville studio.

"What part of North Carolina are you from," I asked Randy one day when we were about to write a song together.

"Marshville," he told me in that deep voice.

"You're kidding me," I laughed. "My mother-in-law lives in Marshville."

"Really?" Randy said and grinned that little curl on his mouth smile. That's what I called it anyway. He was very polite and a nice guy. I liked him right from the beginning.

That day we wrote a song called *Midnight Misery*. I kept looking around as he sang, looking for a reverb system. He just had a natural built in sound that was as rich as any voice I had ever heard.

When we finished the song, Randy sang it on a little jam box so we would remember it.

Keith Stegall co-produced Randy's first album with Kyle Lehning. Ironically, it took two releases of the song, but eventually *On The Other Hand* became a smash hit and launched the career of the newly named Randy *Travis*.

Randy and I became friends during that time and he still remains one of my favorite people, though I don't get to see him very often any more. In my rolodex I still have a phone number listed under Randy Ray. It's kind of like a souvenir.

Betty and I loved to go fishing. We would get up a lot of mornings before sun up and drive out to Old Hickory Lake. We had this one spot we really liked because we usually caught fish there. It was a big rock right at the water's edge. We both had a rod and reel and a cane pole each. We would use a cork on the cane poles, baited with a worm and leave it laying on the rock with the hook and worm in the water, while we cast our reels out for bass or catfish off the bottom.

The only problem was, this particular spot drew snakes a lot.

"Ch-ar-leee!!" Betty shrieked.

I saw it too, a snake swirling around near the rock, looking at us. I was ready for him. I kept a big stick on the rock and I grabbed it. I had to wait for him to get close enough for me to reach him. Betty had ran off the rock and onto the grass, making gasping noises, "ohm.. owww." I glanced at her to see her doing some kind of rapid Indian dance, like stomping would help the situation.

The snake finally got close enough to the rock for me to reach. I swung the stick and caught him just below his head. My follow through

Old Memories and Me

with the stick caused me to flip the snake onto the bank, not far from where Betty was.

"Char-leee," she yelled again and took off running.

"Oops," I said. "Sorry about that honey."

I guess the water kept me from getting a good lick on that snake. He didn't appear to be hurt and crawled quickly through the grass and back into the water.

"He's gone," I called out to Betty.

"You nearly threw him on me," she gasped. "And I'm not getting back on that rock."

You know it's funny that whenever we would get a little mouse in the house back in South Carolina I would jump up on the bed and try and hit it with a broom. I wasn't about to get on the floor with that little mouse, scared to death of him, but I would stand my ground and swing at a snake. Well, as long as he was in the water and I was on a rock I would.

Keith Stegall approached me one day and told me about a guitar player he had heard.

"I heard him at The Plantation Club over on Murfreesboro Road," Keith told me.

"He is awesome, Charlie. I would like to use him on some of our demo sessions."

Since I had worked the Nashville club circuit for a long time I wondered if I knew him. "What's his name?"

"Brent Mason," Keith told me.

I had never heard of him but I trusted Keith's instincts and agreed to use him on our sessions to see how he did. Well, how he did was simply amazing. Once he worked that first session, we never did another one without Brent Mason on guitar.

I became friends with Brent and we started writing songs together. We wound up writing a total of 34 songs together. I soon learned that Brent was also an excellent singer. This guy is multi talented.

Brent told me how Chet Atkins used to come out to the Plantation Club to hear him play and once Chet even brought George Benson with him. Now, you know you're good when those two come out to sit and watch you pick.

Brent Mason would go on to become one of Nashville's all time greatest session players and I feel good that Keith and I were probably one of the first to use him in the studio. Of course Keith gets the credit for that. He is the one that told me about him.

Another change was about to take place at CBS Songs. Jimmy Gilmer was brought in to head up the company and Judy Harris was moved to Creative Director.

This was about the time I met Peter McCann. He was a staff writer for CBS Songs out of the LA office and was moving to Nashville, so the main purpose of his visit was to look for a house here. Peter had had success in the pop field as both a songwriter and singer. He had an idea for a song but wanted a country songwriter to help him write it. Judy Harris introduced me to Peter after he had told her about his idea and asked her who she thought he should get to help him write it.

"Charlie Craig," Judy told him. "Without a doubt, Charlie Craig."

Peter showed me what he had started on the song, which wasn't much more than the hook at that point. We discussed how the song probably should be written then when Peter returned to Los Angeles, we talked on the phone and worked on it. A short time later he moved to Nashville and we finished the song. It was *She's Single Again*.

After we demoed the song, with Tara Hensley doing a marvelous job on the demo vocal, and producer Barry Beckett playing piano on the session, Judy Harris immediately started pitching it.

Then a publisher's nightmare happened.

Two different artists wanted to record the same song and there became a question of who should get the license to record and release it. The two artists in question were Reba McEntire and Janie Fricke. This was taking place around 1983 or '84.

Trying to remember back that far, and talking to a few other people about this, there seems to be a couple of different versions as to what exactly took place. The one fact remains clear is that both Bob Montgomery, Janie Fricke's producer, and Don Lanier, who worked in A&R for MCA Records, the label Reba McEntire recorded for, both had heard the song in separate meetings with Judy Harris at CBS Songs. It is also clear that both Bob and Don wanted the song for their respective artist.

Judy Harris recently told me that she recalls when Don Lanier had heard the song he placed it on hold for Reba but Reba was on the road and Don had tried unsuccessfully to get in touch with her about the song. In the meantime, Bob Montgomery was calling Judy, wanting the license to record the song and release it on Janie Fricke. Judy says Don Lanier finally took the song off hold, since he hadn't confirmed anything with Reba, and Bob Montgomery was then given permission to record it on Janie Fricke.

Judy Harris certainly should know better than I, since she was the one pitching the song, but here is my own recollection of what happened back then.

When Judy played the song initially for Bob Montgomery, he liked the song and asked for a copy, but didn't put it on hold. The same thing happened with Don Lanier. He liked it for Reba and wanted a copy to play for her, but didn't place the song on hold at that time either. A few days later Bob Montgomery called Judy and placed the song on hold to record on Janie Fricke. Then, right after that, Don Lanier called to put the song on hold for Reba but Judy had to tell him it was

Old Memories and Me

already on hold.

I could be wrong but that is the way I remember it.

I do know a lot of drama took place in the recording of that song. First, the day Janie Fricke was to record, she had a cold and sore throat. Bob Montgomery called and got the demo singer's telephone number. So, our demo singer, Tara Hensley, sang the scratch vocal on Janie's tracking session. They recorded Janie's tracks in the same key as our demo session and the arrangement was almost identical. Peter McCann and I did cut a heck of a demo on that song.

Shortly thereafter, Reba goes into the studio to record and she plays my and Peter McCann's demo of *She's Single Again*.

Later, Reba recounted this to me. "My session leader, who was the guitar player, said he had just cut that song with Janie Fricke. I asked him how did you guys record it. He told me just like that demo. I then took him and my producer, Jimmy Bowen, into another room and said, okay, let's come up with a different arrangement."

Reba cut the song entirely different than our demo or Janie's version, which as I have said, was exactly like our demo. Reba started the song out with just an acoustic guitar and steel guitar, then kicks in the entire band at the beginning of the second verse. It is a different tempo entirely but it is also a real cool version of the song.

This story doesn't end there.

CBS had a meeting in Hawaii for staff members of the New York, Nashville and Las Angeles offices. Jimmy Gilmer, the head of the Nashville publishing division, and Rick Blackburn, CEO of Columbia records, Nashville, which was owned by CBS, are seated together on the flight to Hawaii. The subject came up about *She's Single Again*.

"That's going to be Janie Fricke's second single off her new album," Blackburn informed Gilmer. "*Somebody Else's Fire* is going to be the first single off the album."

Now Jimmy Gilmer was in a pickle. He didn't want to make Janie Fricke nor Reba McEntire mad, yet he was employed by CBS and felt obligated to tell Rick Blackburn that Reba had recorded the song as well and once Columbia Records released Janie's album, Reba would probably release *She's Single Again* as her single. So, that is what he did. He told Rick Blackburn that Reba had recorded the song.

The moment the plane set down in Hawaii, Rick Blackburn made a call and changed Janie Fricke's first release off of her new album. It would now be, *She's Single Again*.

One other little tidbit concerning this episode: during Fan Fair that year, I was watching the local news and saw where Reba was doing a show and Janie was in the audience. Reba told the fans a little about *She's Single Again*, and how both she and Janie had recorded the song, then Reba called Janie up on stage to perform it with her.

"Whose version did you do? I asked Reba a few days later.

"Who's do you think?" Reba answered candidly. "Mine, of

course."

Well, after all, it was Reba's show.

She's Single Again went to #1 in billboard by Janie Fricke and was nominated as Contemporary Country Song Of The Year by the TNN/Music City News Awards in 1985. Peter McCann and I are forever grateful to both Janie Fricke and Reba McEntire for liking our song and thank both of them for recording it. I think it shows the true class of both ladies that no ill feelings were ever expressed between them over that situation.

I do love Peter McCann's perspective of all of this though.

It's like two women showing up at a party wearing the same dress.

When Dawn turned eighteen she got married. My new son-in-law was Richard Smith. Betty had stopped coaching softball, mostly because she started having some stomach and chest pains. She said she thought it was from smoking. I was still smoking at that time too. Dawn was still playing on the team and Betty continued to go to all the league games and most of the tournaments with us.

I said she had stopped coaching, but she would sit in a lawn chair behind the backstop and yell, "Keep your eyes on the ball, Dawn," or "Hit your cutoff, Marion."

The girls on the softball team all loved Betty. She had somewhat of a temper, and she would speak her mind, telling it like it was, but she was adorable yelling out from behind the backstop in that little high-pitched southern drawl of hers.

And she would yell at the umpires. "Are you blind mister ump?"

"Keep 'em straight Mama," I would call out to her from the dugout, or from the third base coach's box if we were on offense.

"Don't call me mama," she would shout back. "I'm not your mama."

I would call her that a lot just to rile her, good naturedly of course. It always worked too.

We had some great times with those softball teams. I recall when Janie Fricke was climbing the charts to #1 with *She's Single Again*, the girls had a lot of fun with it. When one of our players batted and got a base hit, the rest of the girls in the dugout would sing the line, *she got a single again.*

We had a few scary times too. I remember one league game at the Cedar Hill complex, Dawn was playing shortstop, and a ball took a bad hop and hit her in the face. By that time we had started playing USSSA ball as well as ASA, and USSSA was the first to use the smaller 11-inch softball. It was harder and traveled faster. It popped Dawn a hard lick that night, right in her eye.

I ran out on the field to see about her. She was down on both

Old Memories and Me

knees, clutching her eye with her hand. Dawn was tough and didn't want anybody to see her cry. At this moment she was struggling to keep from crying but her main concern was trying to get a contact lens out before her eye was swollen shut. Carol Stromatt had run in from the outfield to see about her as well and was trying to help her get the lens out.

"Ohhh," Dawn snapped. "Get your finger out of my eye, Carol. It hurts bad enough without you poking it!"

"I gotta get your contact lens out, Dawn" Carol apologized.

Later we would all laugh about that but at the moment things weren't too funny.

I told you Dawn was tough. She already had a bad burn and bruise on her upper leg from sliding into second base that night, and now her right eye was swollen shut. No way could she play shortstop like that.

"I can play catcher," she said.

I put her behind the plate, moved my catcher to the outfield and brought Marion Bender in to play shortstop. Dawn finished the game like that and wound up getting the hit that drove in our winning run.

Carol Wiley played left field for our team for several years. Carol had an arm like a cannon. We were playing in the City Tournament once and we were on defense, the bases were loaded, and the girl at bat hit a deep fly ball to left field. Carol Wiley caught the ball about 275 feet deep, near the fence. The runner on third base tagged up and took off for home plate. Carol threw the ball home like a rocket, trying to throw the runner out at the plate. She threw the ball clear over the backstop and over the bleachers behind it. She cleared out a whole row of spectators sitting in lawn chairs near the trees.

"Carol, home plate is over here," I yelled out to her and pointed to the plate.

Wiley shook her head and yelled back, "The sun got in my eyes!"

We finished second in the City Tournament that year. Carol Wiley threw out two runners trying to take extra bases in the championship game. Dawn and Marion Bender kept hitting the fence about every time they batted. I got kicked out of the championship game for questioning an umpire's call a little too strongly. In 15 years of coaching softball that was the only time I was ejected.

Harvey Major's was helping me coach during that time. Harvey and I had become really close friends and the times I spent with him were some wonderful times, on and off the softball fields.

We had won Randy Smith's USSSA NIT Tournament earlier that year, beating a solid Cincinnati team for the title and a World Series berth. We always had a good team and we had a special team that year.

Softball was a big part of my life and the last year I coached we were ranked 3rd in the nation in USSSA most of the year and finished 8th in the ASA Class A Nationals in Montgomery, Alabama.

Dr. Friddell told Betty she had to have gall bladder surgery. Her chest pains weren't coming from smoking after all. She would hurt clear through her chest to her back. The gall bladder surgery she had was before they started laser surgery. They had to make a big incision so she was in Donelson Hospital for several days. She was sick as a dog. It was a tough surgery and recovery. I got the hospital staff to put a cot in her room and I spent the night there with her the entire time she was there. I didn't want to be at home without her, especially at night. We still acted like newlyweds even though we were in our forties and had been married nearly 22 years.

We didn't have any health insurance on her because we couldn't get it with so many limitations due to her kidney disease and being a smoker. We were fortunate we were doing well enough financially to pay for it.

Keith Stegall and I were continuing to write together several times a week. We just had a natural feel that worked together and we penned some of the best songs coming out of Nashville in the eighties. I say that modestly but songs like, *Between An Old Memory And Me, Let's Get Over Them Together, I Think I'm In Love,* and *I'll Take The Memories* would all become songs that would live for a long time on the radio and become very popular with country music fans all over the country and in some cases, all over the world. Great ideas and hooks just came naturally and God given to Keith and I back then.

Other songs of mine and Keith's recorded in the eighties were, *Your Memory Always Finds Its Way Back Home* by Moe Bandy, *Every time It Rains* by George Strait, *My Heart Is In The Right Place This Time,* co-written with Roger Murrah, and recorded by Barbara Mandrell. There was also *Burning Love* by Johnny Tiillotson, *All American Country Boy* by both Jerry Reed and Con Hunley and then later by Alan Jackson. After Keith had recorded *I Think I'm In Love,* both Conway Twitty and Ed Bruce recorded it. Mel McDaniel recorded mine, Keith's and Roger Murrah's *I'll Keep Your Memory Around* and Marty Stuart recorded mine and Keith's *Matches.*

I remember the day we wrote *Matches*. Keith had supposedly quit smoking but he had hid a pack of cigarettes and a big box of stove matches in the room where we usually wrote at CBS Songs. I got to looking at those matches and said, "You know, you can't burn very many things without a match. You can't burn a bridge, a memory, love, or anything without a match." A few minutes later we were writing *Matches.*

A lot of songs are born from something as simple as that incident. I remember another occasion when Keith and I were writing a song about an old flame and we needed an *e* rhyme. We came up with *between an old memory and me* for that rhyme. We instantly knew that

Old Memories and Me

line was a killer hook for a song, so we stopped writing the one we were working on and that's when we wrote one of our classics, *Between An Old Memory And Me*. You don't write songs like that one very often.

Keith and I continued writing together, working in the studio and demoing our songs. Keith produced his own records on Epic and we usually tried to come up with something for him to record.

One day I was trying to come up with an idea with Jim McBride and Keith came into the office where we were.

"You guys got anything going?" he asked us.

"Not a thing," Jim told him.

"Wee's brain dead today," I joked.

"Well, I've got two lines that keep going over and over in my head," Keith told us.

"What are they?" Jim asked him. "I'm sure they're better than anything Charlie and I have."

Keith told us the two lines.

California sun, Puerto Rican rum

Even though there were just two lines, we all liked the way they had a nice sound about them. The three of us went upstairs to where Keith had his keyboard and a few hours later we had written a song called *California*. Keith recorded it on his next album and made it a single. It went to #11 in Billboard but made it inside the top 10 in a couple of other national charts. It would turn out to be a pretty good record for Keith as an artist and for the three of us as writers as well. Keith did a really nice video of the song. That song would get airplay for many years to come.

I was still having guilty moments about the affair and I would sometimes tell Betty so. I still hurt for what I had done to her.

"Charlie, stop it," she told me one day. "There is no need to keep punishing yourself." She held my face between her hands and looked straight into the eyes. "I love you, and I know you love me, and that is all that matters. That is behind us, not even important anymore." Then she kissed me softly.

"I love you more than anything in this world," I told her and wiped a tear from my eye.

I know, I cry a lot.

Betty and I had finally gotten into a pretty decent financial shape and we had signed papers on a house a contractor was building. It was in Mt. Juliet, in Wilson County, about fifteen minutes from where we now lived in a pretty nice duplex in Hermitage.

My music career was going good again but personally things were heartbreaking. My brother Bill died of lung cancer in May of 1982. That really hit me hard, even though we all had known he was dying for months. Still, when he passed away it was tough losing my hero, my only brother. Mama was always saying she had cancer whenever something was hurting her physically or she would get real sick. "I got Mama's cancer," Bill said, showing a sense of humor in his final months of life.

Just a few months before he died, Betty's mother, Miss Jessie had passed away. That ripped out Betty's heart and I felt helpless trying to ease her hurt. It pained me as well. I was close to my mother-in-law. Miss Jessie was really good to me and treated me like her own son. Betty and I were with her the night she passed away at her home in Marshville, N. C.

Daddy had had a stroke in April of 1981 and died of a massive heart attack six months after Bill passed away. He never even knew Bill had died. We never told him, thinking it was best because of the shape he was in. Mama was staying an extended time with Betty and I in Nashville and I had to wake her up about 7:30 one morning and tell her. It was one of the hardest things I had ever had to do.

"Mama, I have to tell you something," I said as I sat on the bed beside her. "Daddy died about an hour ago."

"No, no," she moaned so pitifully and sat up in bed. "Not my man, nooo."

I held my mama in my arms and cried with her. My mama and daddy had been married for over sixty years.

Mama died of a heart attack in 1985. It had really hurt when Bill had died but losing Mama and Daddy was even worse. You never think your mama and daddy will die. They are like Superman and Wonder Woman.

It was a terrible time in our lives in such a short period. It didn't end there.

In 1986 we found out that Betty had lymphoma in the walls of her stomach, cancer of the lymph nodes. I wondered if God was mad at me about what I had done but of course I knew better than that. I prayed and asked God to give me the cancer. I didn't want my precious Betty to have it.

They wanted to do a few more x-rays on Betty's stomach to check some things. I went with her to the x-ray room at Donelson Hospital one day and while I was sitting in the waiting room I looked over and saw someone I thought I recognized.

"Aren't you Keith Whitley?" I asked.

He looked up from the magazine he was reading. "Yes," he answered.

"I'm Charlie Craig," I told him and leaned over, extending my hand to shake his.

"Hello, Charlie," Keith Whitley said politely. "Your name sounds familiar."

I told him I was a songwriter. He asked what were some of the songs I had written and I named off a few.

Old Memories and Me

"Yes, *I Would Like To See You Again*," he said. "That is how I know your name. I really like that song."

"Thank you," I smiled. "Johnny Cash gave me a great record on that song."

"I love John's version but I love Don Williams' version too," Keith informed me.

As it turned out, Keith Whitley was waiting for his wife while she also had x-rays made. We exchanged small talk for a few minutes until his wife came into the room, finished with her appointment, and they left.

"Nice to meet you," I told Keith.

"Send me some songs sometime," he told me.

They did surgery on Betty and removed 2/3 of her stomach. Her doctors thought they got all the cancer but to be safe, they wanted her to take radiation treatments. I was scared to death she would die. I prayed in my car, I prayed in the shower, in the closet, everywhere, asking God to spare her and not take her from me.

Since we didn't have any health insurance on Betty we were especially grateful that the royalties were presently coming in with a pretty good sum on both the Janie Fricke single, *She's Single Again,* and Moe Bandy and Becky Hobbs duet single of *Let's Get Over Them Together.* Without those performance royalties I don't know what we would have done. We did have to get out of the contract to build the house that was already in progress. We just couldn't afford it now. Under the circumstances they took mercy on our situation and let us out of it.

A cancer specialist told us there were several types of lymphoma and they were not sure which one she had at the time. Several pathologists had different opinions. A Vanderbilt University doctor, considered the leading expert at that time, returned from a European trip and gave his opinion on which type lymphoma she had. It was definitely malignant and radiation was recommended by the experts as well.

Then, we witnessed a miracle. When the radiation doctors learned that Betty had a kidney problem they told her they couldn't give her radiation in that part of her body for fear of damaging her kidney. They ran a test and found her kidney disease no longer existed. It had been there since she was six years old, now it was gone. There is no doubt God healed her kidney so she could take the radiation. There is no other explanation.

She took the 21 treatments at Baptist Hospital in Nashville. We went there Monday through Friday every week for four weeks and one day.

Of course I was worried sick about the cancer still being there but it was in God's hands and I continued to look to him. I must have prayed about every hour or so during those treatments. He answered my prayers. I told you Betty was a strong person and she not only got herself through that ordeal, but she helped me find the strength too. We both gave God the credit though. The cancer was in remission and after five years she would be declared cured. The radiation took its toll though. She had a lot of problems with her stomach after that and she never was the same physically.

"If I had it to go over again I wouldn't take the radiation," Betty said. "I feel like my intestines have been cooked in a microwave oven."

I felt so sorry for her. The cancer was gone but the effects of the radiation treatments would stay with her the rest of her life. I just wanted to hold her all the time and take care of her.

It was in May of 1986 that I quit smoking. Betty didn't quit. She continued smoking two and three packs a day. She loved her black coffee and cigarettes. Betty also read a lot, especially Agatha Christie and gothic novels. She was already well educated, with two years of Business College, but all that reading and keeping up with world events through television and newspapers, she became very intelligent.

The only way I could quit smoking was to keep the pack of cigarettes I had at the time in my shirt pocket during the day and on the nightstand by the bed at night. It was a pack of Salem Menthol, half empty, and I would panic if I didn't have them near. I cannot count the times I reached and pulled one from the pack, sometimes actually lighting it before realizing what I was doing and forcing myself to put it out.

I went into nicotine withdrawals. My doctor gave me an antidepressant. I wound up in bed for two or three days. I thought I was dying. Well, not really dying but I was in a mess with my nerves. I finally made it though and I haven't smoked a cigarette since. I still have that half pack of Salem. They are so hard after all these years that if I dropped one on the floor it would probably bounce two feet.

It wasn't long after Betty's bout with cancer that I met Alan Jackson. It would be one of the most important meetings of my career.

Old Memories and Me

CHAPTER THIRTEEN

It was 1987 and I was watching *Nashville Now* one night with Betty and we saw this tall guy, with long blonde hair, wearing a cowboy hat, on the show. Ralph Emery was the host of *Nashville Now* and he told everybody how this young man worked in the mailroom at TNN. He brought him on the show and let him sing a couple of songs and interviewed him. I was really impressed. Betty and I agreed we were looking at a future super star.

"Are you thinking what I'm thinking," I asked Betty.

"Yes," she assured me. "You need to write with this guy. He is great, Charlie."

I can't describe the feeling I had, like I already knew this young man, yet I had never laid eyes on him before. I know it is easy to say now, after he has become a mega star, but I knew that night I saw him on *Nashville Now* he was going to be something special.

The next morning Betty said, "Call that Jackson boy."

I called Alan Jackson's publisher.

"But he doesn't have a record deal, Charlie," Marty Gamblin informed me on the telephone. Marty ran Glen Campbell's publishing company, Seventh Son Music. "We signed him as a writer but he is really green. He's never written with anybody like you. He doesn't have a record deal or nothing"

"Well, I don't care if I have to write every line in the song," I told Marty. "This guy's gonna be a star and I want to be with him when he gets there. I want to write with him."

Marty Gamblin set up a writing appointment between Alan and me. We hit if off immediately. I liked his down home mannerism and humble smile. He usually wore a baseball cap and jeans, a plain long sleeve denim shirt, but he still looked like a star. He just had a natural charisma about him. A lot of songwriters write well together, and become pals, but not only did Alan and I become very good writers together, we also developed a close friendship. Alan's wife, Denise was still working as an airline stewardess and Alan and I would talk some on the telephone at night. Denise would be gone several days at a time on flights and Alan would usually go home at night and watch TV. He liked old western movies a lot.

Sometimes we would write at CBS Songs and sometimes

Old Memories and Me

over at Barry Coburn's office. Alan had recently signed a management contract with Coburn. We had a lot of fun on those writing sessions. We were very serious about our songwriting but we both knew how to cut up and laugh until we could get a serious idea working.

When Alan didn't like a particular line or something, he would always say *naw*. It was hardly ever no, just *naw*. I use to kid him about saying that. He can be a little hardheaded sometimes but Alan usually made the right decisions when it came to his music. I have always said he could have marketed himself. I have never seen anybody more focused in this business than Alan Jackson.

I knew right away Alan was an excellent songwriter. It was very rare to run into somebody as new to the business as he was, yet have as much advanced talent as Alan had. Alan knew exactly what he wanted to say in a song once he started writing it, whether it was with me, somebody else, or by himself. Like I said, he is very focused on everything he does. When he gets his mind set on something not many people can change it, except perhaps Denise.

There are a lot of things I admire about Alan, but perhaps the thing that stands out the most to me is the fact that he will look outside his own songwriting skills for songs to record. He is an excellent songwriter, and without a doubt could write his entire album, but he looks at everybody's material and not just his own.

I could never tell which one he loved the most, writing a song or singing it. After we would get a verse, and maybe a chorus wrote, he would sing what we had and I would sing harmony with him. We use to laugh and say we sounded like Lonzo and Oscar, a comedian duet on the Grand Ole Opry for years. I still have one work tape of us on one writing session, with all the talking, mistakes, stopping and starting all over again, laughing and just hamming it up while the cassette was recording. It was a song called *I'll Still Be Loving You*. Later on, when Alan was out on the road, doing a sound check before a show, he taped that song with his band. He would do that sometime on sound check, record a new song just to see how it would come off, or feel.

Usually, when Alan and I were writing, after a verse and chorus it was about time for lunch. That was another thing we hit it off on, we both liked to go to lunch. On one occasion Alan wanted to go to a popular greasy hamburger joint. We arrived and sat down in a booth and the waitress came over to take our order. I am a picky guy when it comes to my food and I always notice a waiter or waitress's hands. This gal had dirt under all of her fingernails and she looked like she had been working on a construction job all morning. Alan ordered a cheeseburger and a beer. I told the waitress to let me look over the menu for a minute. When she had left our booth, I told Alan, "I ain't eatin' in here."

"Why?" he asked.

"Did you see all the dirt under her fingernails?"

"Aw, you eat more dirt than that when you were a kid," he

told me with that grin that would later become so recognizable all over the country.

"Yeah," I said. "But it was my dirt. I ain't eatin' hers."

I told him to go ahead and eat and we could stop by one of the fast food drive-through on the way back to the office and get me something to go.

"Well, they probably got more dirty fingernails, runny noses and stuff at those places than anywhere," Alan laughed.

"Well, when I pass the drive-through I turn my head and just stick my hand out the car window," I told him laughing. "That way I don't have to see and I won't know what they look like, if they got dirty hands or not."

Alan thought my logic was funny, perhaps even a bit ridiculous, but he cancelled his order and took me to a place on West End Avenue called *Fuddruckers*. They cook the meat, give you a bun with it and you go over to a self service bar that includes lettuce, tomato, pickles, relish, hot cheese, etc.

"Now, make your own burger," Alan told me.

It was during this time that CBS Songs was purchased by SKB Entertainment. Judy Harris, who has always been one of the best songpluggers in Nashville, left and started her own publishing company with partner Debra Richardson. Appropriately they named the company Harris-Richardson.

SBK not only had purchased the huge CBS/United Artist song catalogs, but they had a production company. More space was needed so SBK moved into the Combine Music Building, which was located right across the street from Columbia Records. It was also next door to where my old publisher, Cedarwood Publishing once was.

One day Alan Jackson and I were writing in what I called one of the two *crows nest* on the third floor of the SBK/Combine Building. Guy Clark used one and I usually wrote in the other one. It was a very small room. Alan and I were fishing for an idea, running lines by each other. Nothing was happening.

"I got this idea I been working on," he said. "I was watching an old John Wayne movie the other night and saw this wanted poster in the sheriff's office."

He showed me a little of what he had started.

Excuse me, ma'am can you help me, I'd like to place an ad with you today

"I like the fire out of that" I told him.

After he sang a little more he told me he had shown it to a couple of other writers but nobody got interested in helping him write it.

"Well, I will," I said. "But heck, Alan, you got this already

Old Memories and Me

started."

"Naw, we can write it if you want to," he said. "Besides, I ain't figured out how to end it."

We wrote *Wanted* that day.

Alan Jackson didn't sit idly around waiting for a record deal and music to come to him. He put together a three-piece band, got an old used white van, and hit the road working wherever he could on weekends. I recall that van had 3 doors; the driver's side, the passenger's side and one in the rear. There wasn't a door on the side. Later, when Alan would get his first tour bus, it had a door on the side. It was unusual for a tour bus to have a side door. Looking back, for some reason, I have always thought that first van he had really needed a door on the side to have an easier access for the band and their instruments, and he finally got a side door with that first bus. I haven't stayed awake nights thinking about it, but I do remember thinking that.

I don't think Alan made a whole lot of money on those first weekend gigs in that van but he was surely already building up a following of fans.

"How'd you do this weekend, Alan," I asked him once.

"It cost me $26 to go play in Birmingham, Alabama," he said.

Boy, wouldn't that change.

Alan had just come back from playing another gig down in Alabama and he told me about going out to this old country store down there. He said there was an old wooden Indian standing out front and the elderly storeowner told him it was the original wooden Indian that Hank Williams had wrote Kawliga about many years ago. Alan said, "Kawliga's still standing there." So, we wrote that song, *Kawliga's Still Standing There*.

There's another song we wrote called *Broken Heart Rendezvous* that Alan already had the first two lines to when we got together to write one day. He loved those lines and grinned when he sang them to me that first time.

She had two blue eyes, and I had two blue ribbon beers

We wrote the song and it is as country as a mule eating briars. Sometimes, when we would get together after that to write, or just run into each other somewhere, we would sing those opening lines, *she had two blue eyes, and I had two blue ribbon beers*, and we would always laugh, not really because it was funny, but because we liked those lines so much.

I believe if Alan Jackson ever goes into the studio and just records songs that he personally likes, regardless of marketing value, or whatever, just songs he loves, and enjoys singing, I believe he will record *Broken Heart Rendezvous* and *Kawliga's Still Standing There*. They are probably too country for today's market, but in the world of *real* country music, then these two songs are classics.

Keith Stegall decided to give up his recording career right in the middle of a chart record. It was the first song he and I had co-written together, *I Think I'm In Love*, and it was climbing the charts but Keith said he wanted to concentrate on writing and spend more time in the studio with other people. He sold his tour bus to Randy Travis and stopped working the road.

Knowing firsthand how good Keith was in the studio, and Alan Jackson being such a great country singer, I thought what a natural fit they would be. I told Keith about Alan, and Alan about Keith. I think they had probably met in passing but they didn't really know each other well at that point.

The next time Keith and I scheduled a writing session he suggested that I bring Alan along. Alan agreed and we went out to Keith's house in Brentwood. While I was driving out there I came up with an idea and had the opening lines by the time I arrived. I showed them to Keith and Alan.

> *It's twilight and the streetlights are coming on*
> *I'm in a stream of cars on this boulevard headed home....*

That's all I had but it was enough for the three of us to lock onto.

That day we wrote a great ballad called *Bring On The Night*.

Alan has said I was the first person to pay him to sing a demo. Right after I met him I paid him $30 to sing a song I had written. He was good in the studio, a natural, with a great presence to his voice on the microphone.

After he and I had written several songs together, including *Wanted*, we did demos on them. Actually, they were what we call work tapes, just an acoustic guitar, a bass and a drum machine. EMI only had an eight-track machine back then and I remember the day we first laid *Wanted* down. Besides using a drum machine, Verlon Thompson played acoustic guitar, I played bass and Alan sang both the lead vocal and harmony. I still have that work demo as a keepsake, as well as the work demos on all of the songs Alan and I wrote together.

I played some of those work demos for Margie Hunt at Columbia Records right after Alan and I did them. She had a fit over Alan. "Who in the world is this guy?"

Margie played Alan for her boss, Bob Montgomery at Columbia, but in the beginning he seemed more interested in getting *Wanted* for Ricky Van Shelton to record. Ricky was just coming off of his hit, *Somebody Lied*, and it would have been a perfect follow up song for him. Alan, myself and our publishers talked it over and decided to hold on to the song because we believed it would help land Alan a record deal. I never stopped believing in him and as much as I would have

Old Memories and Me

loved to have a Ricky Van Shelton cut, I felt in my heart Alan Jackson was the one that should record *Wanted*.

Not long after that Keith Stegall produced a full band demo session on Alan at Studio 19. They started pitching Alan to record labels using that demo.

Alan did his final showcase at the Hall Of Fame Lounge. I sat at a table with Bob Montgomery, from Columbia Records. I think he had begun talks with Alan about possibly signing with that label, but another record label head was also in the audience that night. His name was Tim Dubois and he had just opened a division of Arista Records in Nashville. Tim Dubois signed Alan Jackson to Arista just days after that showcase.

Among the songs recorded on that first album, co-produced by Keith Stegall and Scott Hendrix, was *Wanted*. The label thought it was the song that would break Alan as an artist. Before they recorded it though, they wanted to cut out the last verse, reason being it made the song too long for a brand new artist to get played on the radio. This is a verse nobody has ever heard. At first, Alan and I were hesitant about dropping the verse, not that it made any difference because we didn't have much say so in the matter. It was Alan's first album and he was just happy to have the opportunity to record. We finally agreed, again not that it really mattered. Record labels generally do what they want to, especially with a new artist. Today, Alan Jackson records what he wants to, the way he wants to.

I had hoped that Alan would record *Bring On The Night* on that first album but it didn't make it.

I left SBK and joined Judy Harris at her new publishing company in a pink house on 17th Avenue, South. After Alan Jackson's first album was completed and Keith Stegall had mixed it, he dropped by my office at Harris-Richardson Publishing and played it for me. Keith told me they were planning on releasing an up-tempo first, to get Alan some exposure, then put out *Wanted*. They believed it would be Alan's breakout hit. Keith played me the entire album that day. I had already heard most of the songs, but he played me one song I had never heard before, *Here In The Real World*.

"Hey," I told Keith, "that song is competition for *Wanted*. Who wrote that?"

"Alan Jackson and Mark Erwin," he told me.

"Man, that is a great little song," I said and really believed that.

Here In The Real World became the title of the album and the first hit single off the album. They followed that with *Wanted* and the sales was well over a million after those two singles. Alan Jackson was on his way to becoming a mega star. Both *Here In The Real World* and *Wanted* went to #1. Right behind those two ballads came *Chasing That Neon Rainbow*, a song Alan wrote with my friend Jim McBride. That first album initially sold over 3 million. It has surpassed that figure today.

During CMA Week that first year Alan's album was released, Betty, Alan, Denise and I went down on music row and hung out the night of the Country Music Awards Show. A lot of the publishing companies and record labels had televisions set up for anybody that wanted to watch the awards. The four of us stopped by Arista Records, Alan's record label, and they had his album playing continuously before the awards show came on. We all thought that was really cool.

"Next year you will be up for an award and you and Denise will be down at the award show in person," Betty told Alan.

We all four laughed about that but I think we all actually believed that was a good possibility because *Here In The Real World* was climbing up the national charts, both the single and the album.

The four of us visited a couple of other parties going on that night and then went back to Arista to watch the Awards Show on their big screen TV.

It had been four years since I had stopped smoking. Without cigarettes, my appetite had increased and I was gaining weight. For the first time in my life I weighed more than 160 pounds. I was around 190 at that point, so I had gained 30 pounds. I stayed on Betty constantly to stop smoking too but it was to no avail. She said she liked smoking and didn't want to quit.

"I'm not quittin' smoking," she stated emphatically, a cigarette hanging kind of loosely from her lips as she handled the controls on a Super Mario Nintendo game. "I like smoking."

"You look like a gangster's doll with that cigarette hanging from your mouth like that," I kidded her.

"Go buy yourself a Tommy gun then," she shot back as she twisted and turned trying to make Mario leap over a fireball coming at him.

"We gonna rob a bank?" I laughed.

"They been robbing us, we might as well rob them a while," she said and then added, "Doggone it," as Mario got killed.

Betty and I had been able to pay off all of the large medical bills accumulated from her bout with lymphoma, thanks to the royalties from *She's Single Again* and *Let's Get Over Them Together*. However, we still owed the Internal Revenue money on taxes, so when Alan Jackson called me one night and told me that *Wanted* was going to be his next single, naturally I was very pleased and excited.

"That's great, Alan," I told him over the phone.

I also told him that Betty and Dawn wanted one of his *Here In The Real World* t-shirts.

"Go by the office and tell Josephine and Jewel to give you a couple of them," he told me.

The next morning I went by Barry Coburn's office, Ten Ten

Old Memories and Me

Management, to pick up the t-shirts. Barry was Alan's manager now. Jewel Coburn, Barry's lovely wife, was excited for me that *Wanted* was set to be the next single. Josephine, a girl that worked in the office, was elated as well. We kind of all hugged, high-fived and celebrated a little.

I thanked the ladies for the *Here In The Real World* t-shirts and left.

Ten Ten Management was set up on a knoll on 16th Avenue, South, and as I was coming down the steps toward the street Barry Coburn was walking up.

"Hey," I exclaimed, still beaming with excitement. "Alan called me last night and told me *Wanted* was going to be his next single."

"Not if EMI doesn't give Arista the control composition they are asking for, then it won't be," Barry told me in his Australian accent. I could tell he was upset.

EMI had bought SBK Entertainment, which had purchased CBS Songs earlier. So EMI now owned my CBS catalog and *Wanted* was in that catalog.

"What?" I asked puzzled.

"I just left Arista," Barry said. "And they informed me that EMI is refusing to give up the control comp on the songs they published of yours and Jim McBride's that are on the album."

I had no earthly idea what he was talking about.

"What are you talking about?" I was bewildered. I was also very quickly getting depressed. Whatever it was, I was afraid it was about to cost me a single that could very well be one of the biggest records of my career.

"Well, if EMI doesn't agree to take a cut in the rate, those songs won't be released on the album," Barry told me with concern in both his voice and his expression.

"They are already on the album," I reminded him. "How they gonna take them off now?"

"I meant they probably won't be considered as singles," he answered.

I didn't need to hear this, especially something I didn't even understand. Barry told me he didn't know what was going to happen and we would just have to wait and see. Barry left and walked up the steps and went into his office.

I used my cell phone and immediately called Alan. I didn't reach him. I called Celia Froehlig at EMI, my publisher on *Wanted*.

"Hi, Charlie," Celia said as she came on the line.

"Celia, I just had a conversation with Barry Coburn," I told her. "He says if EMI doesn't give Arista control comp on *Wanted* that it won't be the next single. What the heck is going on? What is control comp anyway?"

Celia could tell I was upset. "Just calm down," she said soothingly. "Control Composition is a clause in every recording artist contract that allows the record label to recoup a percentage of that artist's share of any songs they write, or co-write, that is included on an album. They do that to help recoup some of the recording cost of the album. It is something that is in every recording artist contract now, not just Alan Jackson's, and not just at Arista. All the labels are including it in their artist contracts. It doesn't include the artist's co-writers but sometimes the labels ask for the co-writers' publisher to also concede a portion of their royalties too. EMI won't agree to do that though and that is what Barry Coburn was talking about."

"I need that single, Celia," I told her.

"I know you do, Charlie," she said caringly. "But let me tell you something. Alan Jackson has probably the hottest album on the market right now and if Arista Records thinks *Wanted* is the next song that will keep that momentum going, they will release it as the next single whether EMI agrees to the control composition or not. Trust me. "

I felt a little better after talking to Celia. I still wanted to talk to Alan though. I wondered if he knew what was going on. He hadn't mentioned it last night. I doubted that he did know.

I called Alan that night and told him about the conversation I had had with Barry Coburn and the one with Celia at EMI.

"Charlie, I don't understand about how all that stuff works," Alan said. "But don't worry about it. Let me see what's going on."

As it turned out, Celia Froehlig was right. EMI didn't give Arista the reduced rate and they released *Wanted* as Alan Jackson's next single just like she predicted.

Celia was right about another thing too. Every other record label in town did have the control composition in their artist contract. To my own personal knowledge it never came up again on any of Alan Jackson's other albums that I had songs on but it would come up again on a few other artist that I had co-written with.

I knew when the control composition thing first came up and they also wanted his co-writers to take a reduced rate, Alan didn't know anything like that was going on. He would never want his co-writers to have to sacrifice anything. I know him well enough to know that and I believe that sincerely.

Not long after all of that happened Betty and I attended a baby shower for Denise Jackson at Marty and Sherry Gamblin's home one Saturday night. Denise was pregnant with her first child, Mattie, and they invited both husbands and wives to the shower. That night Alan told me he was leaving on Monday for the desert in California to shoot the video on *Wanted*.

"The desert?" I asked him. "Why the desert?"

He didn't know he said. "They just told me to go out there. I guess they don't want to come to Nashville."

Today, Alan Jackson would tell them to come to Nashville… and bring the desert with them.

Old Memories and Me

Wanted shot up the charts to #1 and in 1991 it was nominated song of the year by TNN/Music City News. They had me as a quest on *Video Morning* to talk about that song and a few of my other songs. They also asked me to tell the story about hiring Charlie Daniels to work the American Legion back in the seventies.

The TNN/Music City News Awards was televised on TNN and everybody involved with the show had to go to the Opry House at Opryland and rehearse the day of the show. I think rehearsals started about 2 pm that day. I sat right behind Garth Brooks, whom I had met a little earlier that year on the *Nashville Now* set. I got to know Vince Gill at that rehearsal as well. Garth was nominated as a songwriter for co-writing *If Tomorrow Never Comes* with Kent Blazey and Vince for *Nobody Answers When I Call Your Name,* a song he co-wrote with Tim Dubois. We had to go through everything just like we would do it that night for the live television performance.

Alan Jackson was on tour in Canada so I represented us by myself. Jimmy Dean, Ray Stevens and Kathy Bailey (of Bailey and The Boys) were co-hosting the show. During rehearsals Jimmy Dean called me to the stage by introducing me as Charley Pride. The producer made him introduce me again to get it right. Everything that was said, performed or played, had to be done exactly the way it would be done later that night for the live television show. I, like every other award winner, had to go up on stage and mimic an acceptance speech. Mickey Gilley sang *Wanted* in Alan Jackson's absence. He went right through the rehearsal performing it without a hitch.

I joked around with Garth Brooks a lot during rehearsals. "I think you ought to go up and accept my award for me," I told him. "I'm not used to this limelight thing."

He laughed. "You can do it Charley Pride," he joked, referring to Jimmy Dean's error of calling me the super star by accident.

Garth and I talked about doing some co-writing in the future. He told me on several occasions he thought *Wanted* was a great song. I certainly told him how much I liked his song, *If Tomorrow Never Comes.*

I talked with Vince Gill some that day as well. Like Garth, he was easy to talk to and get to know. Vince and I also talked about writing a song together.

The rehearsals were fun for the most part, but we had to start over quite often, especially the dialogs. Jimmy Dean and Ray Stevens hammed it up a lot too and started laughing at their own humor a few times. That delayed things a little. They did a great job though, along with Kathy Bailey. It was kind of cool going through the whole thing, the songs being performed, either by the artist that recorded the hit, or in a couple of cases, the songwriter singing the song themselves, with the full orchestra playing, and everybody making their acceptance speech. The producer and directors were timing everything, including the commercials.`

After rehearsals they fed us a catered dinner in an area backstage of the Grand Ole Opry house. After dinner we went to our respective dressing rooms and put on the attire we were wearing for the show. I put on a rented black tuxedo. Denise Jackson and Barry Coburn came backstage to congratulate me. All ten nominated songs were already winners and would receive an award. We had made it to that point by receiving enough votes. *Here In The Real World*, co-written by Alan and Mark Irwin, was nominated for song of the year as well.

I had been pretty relaxed during rehearsals all afternoon, but now it was getting close to the real deal, the live show, and I was getting a little nervous about going up on stage by myself. An idea struck me.

"Why don't you go on stage with me Denise," I told her. "We'll accept the award together."

"Can I do that?" she asked, beaming somewhat, the excitement at the thought showing.

"Sure you can," I told her.

Barry Coburn spoke up. "She can't do that, Charlie. They only want the songwriters and performers onstage."

"Aw," I assured him. "I have been with the producer of the show all afternoon, he's a cool guy. He will let us do that."

Barry seemed a little perturbed with me. "Charlie, can I see you over here for a moment?"

I sighed. I kind of knew what was coming. I moved away from Denise and over to where Barry had walked to.

"Listen," he began in a low voice. "I had rather Denise not go onstage. Alan and I want to keep her private so whenever she goes out in public she won't have to worry about people recognizing her and mobbing her."

I didn't understand that. I also knew Denise wanted to do this. This was all new to her as well and I am sure exciting. It would be fun for her. However, I didn't know what Alan's stance would be in this matter so I backed off. "Ok," I said to Barry. "But I don't think I'm going to get mobbed at Kroger's tomorrow after I go on television for a few minutes tonight." Kroger is a grocery store chain.

I probably shouldn't have said that to him. It couldn't be easy managing the hottest new act in all of country music. Barry Coburn is a good guy and I am sure he was trying to do what he felt was best for both Alan and Denise.

I turned to speak to Denise again but she had already gone to her seat out front. I felt bad but there was nothing I could do. I never mentioned the incident to Alan so I don't know what his thoughts would have been.

Betty was watching the show at home. So were my sisters and everybody back in Watts Mill, South Carolina. Dawn had joined the Marines and was in Paris Island, South Carolina. When it came time for me to go onstage and accept the award for *Wanted*, I was trembling.

Old Memories and Me

Those things are kind of funny though. Once I got up and started moving, I wasn't as nervous. No, that's not true. I am just trying to make myself sound braver than I was. I was still shaking when I arrived at the microphone. Somehow I did get through my little acceptance speech. Thank goodness I did remember to acknowledge Mickey Gilley's performance of *Wanted*.

"Great job, Mickey," I told him, as he stood beside me onstage.

I couldn't remember anything I had rehearsed to say, so I just ad-libbed it. I did thank Alan for allowing me to write *Wanted* with him, telling the audience that he was up in Canada on tour, probably placing want ads. I realized immediately how stupid that must have sounded. I wasn't used to being in the limelight on national television. I was more in my natural element sitting in a chair in a writer's room with a guitar in my hand.

That was quite a night for me though. Having one of the top 10 songs for the entire year of 1990 was really something to be proud of. That song would be one of several that Alan Jackson would record of mine in the years to come. That song would also come to be referred to by both the music industry and a lot of fans as one of the best country ballads ever written. I have been told that *Wanted* is now listed in the top 30 country songs of all time. I have not personally documented that as being true though.

I remember the first time I saw Alan Jackson perform *Wanted* in concert. He called me and told me he was opening for Eddie Rabbit in Hopkinsville, Kentucky on a Friday night. He got tickets and backstage passes for Betty, Dawn and me. It was really strange sitting in the audience, with all the people screaming when he sang *Wanted*. It was his current single at the time and climbing the charts on its way to #1. Actually, the crowd went crazy over every song he performed that night.

During intermission, between Alan's show and Eddie Rabbit's, there were two long lines going into the Men's Room and I was standing right behind two guys in that line as they were talking about how great Alan's show had been. Then they started singing the chorus to *Wanted* and high-fived each other as they sang.

Wanted, one good hearted woman...

I wanted to tell them, "*hey I helped him write that song,*" but I restrained myself.

Alan and I did a television interview about *Wanted* for the Crook & Chase TV Show. I recall we were seated on a couch and on camera as I was telling how I had seen Alan on *Nashville Now* and how I had called his publisher the next morning. I went on to explain how I was told he was green and inexperienced. I said he wasn't as green as they thought and I said he was a great songwriter and a great singer, really bragging on him. Then, I turned to Alan and said, "Now, say something good about me."

Alan just sat there silent for a few seconds, with the TV cameras rolling, then he looked over at me with a sly grin and said, "You tell the truth, Charlie."

Alan Jackson has a great sense of humor and is very quick witted.

Not long after that he did a show at the new Opry House and Alan had told me he had added something new to his show but he wouldn't tell me what it was. I didn't know what to expect. Hardly anybody did until he did the show that night. After he finished a song, all the stage lights went out for perhaps 15-20 seconds. The lights came back on in perfect timing with the music and Alan singing *Don't Rock The Jukebox*. A huge inflatable multi-colored jukebox was rocking in the background on stage. It was an incredible sight. I never thought to ask but I would bet that thing was Alan's own idea. It was really awesome.

Alan Jackson would go on to record more of my songs over the years. The song that he, Keith Stegall and I wrote back in 1987 would wind up on his very popular album, *Drive*. For 13 years I sent that song out to his house every time he was about to record until he finally cut it.

Both the Tennessean Newspaper and Billboard Magazine picked *Bring On The Night* as one of the better cuts on the *Drive* album. Alan told them, "If Charlie Craig hadn't been so persistent and sent me that song for 13 years I might not have cut it."

Alan actually had played the song for Denise and she loved it and told him he should record it. I have been sending my songs to Denise ever since. ….I'm just kidding.

I'm not waving a flag here and saying I told you so, but I am so proud of Alan Jackson. I predicted his success back in 1986. I just didn't know he was going to get ridiculous with it and be the mega star he has become. He surely is one of country music's all time greats and will be labeled a legend one day. Personally, I think he already is a legend.

I don't get to see Alan much anymore and that's the sad part of seeing one of your friends make it big in this music business. They are just snatched away into another world it seems. That is no fault of their own, just the nature of success and nobody is more happy for Alan and his success than I am. I do miss those writing sessions we had. Not only did we write some good songs together, we had a lot of fun doing it.

Thank you Alan, not only for the songs you have recorded of mine, but for the friendship and putting up with me always asking for autographed pictures and CDs for relatives and friends. *They made me do it.*

Old Memories and Me

CHAPTER FOURTEEN

I had written several songs with Roger Murrah, one of Nashville's most successful songwriters. I had met Roger when we both were writing for CBS Songs. He had since signed with Tom Collins Music. Roger, Keith Stegall and I had written a song together called *My Heart Is In The Right Place This Time* and Tom Collins produced it on Barbara Mandrell. Roger and I went to the studio the day Barbara recorded it. Until that session, I don't think I had seen her since that night back in the early 70s when she was on Bill Anderson's TV show and I drove Roy Rogers out to the studio to be on the same show. I think she was around 18 years old then, maybe younger. I really enjoyed watching Barbara Mandrell record our song that day. She was a natural pro and so talented.

I hung out around Tom Collins Music a lot back then. I was friends with Roger Murrah and a couple of other writers that wrote for Tom's company. I also was friends with Tom. I had first met Tom Collins in the early seventies when he was running a publishing company for Charley Pride and Jack Johnson. I respected Tom's opinion on songs and when he first heard my song *I Would Like To See You Again*, even before Johnny Cash had recorded it, Tom told me it was one of the best songs he had heard in quite some time. That gave me added hope for the song.

One day while I was at Tom Collins music I showed Roger Murrah an idea I had. I also had a pretty good melody going too that had a Waylon Jennings feel to it.

"Yeah man," Roger beamed. "I like it, Charlie. It does have a Waylon feel. You want me to see if Waylon wants to write it with us?"

I had met Waylon on numerous occasions over the years but I didn't really know him that well and I had never written a song with him. I have always been a huge Waylon Jennings fan though. Roger Murrah had written quite a bit with Waylon and knew him pretty well.

"Are you kidding," I exclaimed. "I would love to write with Waylon."

Roger set the writing appointment up for Tuesday, May 9th. It was 1989. I remember that date so well because something terrible happened on that date. They found Keith Whitley dead in his home in Goodlettsville that day. The coroner said later he had died of an

Old Memories and Me

overdose of alcohol. Keith Whitley was only 33 years old.

Waylon Jennings, Roger Murrah and I cancelled our writing appointment because of the sad news and rescheduled it for a later date.

I had only met Keith Whitley that once, in the waiting room at Donelson Hospital, when our wives were having x-rays. Keith Whitley had divorced since that day and was married to Lorrie Morgan when he died. I had known Lorrie since she was a little girl, and her daddy, George Morgan, used to bring her by Cedarwood Publishing. Lorrie had recently recorded my and Keith Stegall's song, *I'll Take The Memories*, on her first BNA album. I went to the funeral home for visitation the day before Keith Whitley's funeral to pay my condolences to Lorrie. She had been married to Keith for about 2 ½ years.

Naturally, Lorrie Morgan was devastated. I didn't know what to say to her, so I just gave her a warm hug and told her I was sorry. She forced a smile through tear-swollen eyes and thanked me for coming. After a few minutes Lorrie led me down to Keith Whitley's casket. We stood there silent for a moment with our arms around each other.

Finally, Lorrie said, "You know Charlie, Keith loved *Between And Old Memory An Me* so much."

"I know," I told her.

Then I told her, "Country Music has lost one of the greatest singers we ever had."

Of course she already knew that.

Then I told her something she didn't know.

"Keith called Keith Stegall Sunday night," I began. "He told Keith Stegall that he had been listening to the cuts on his new album and *Between An Old Memory And Me* was one of his favorite songs on the album."

Lorrie looked at me, surprised. "Really, "she asked. "This was this past Sunday night?" That would have been two nights before they found him dead on Tuesday.

"Yes," I confirmed. "Keith Stegall told me himself that he had called him."

"Charlie," Lorrie said, her voice very low and her expression still showing surprise of learning this. "Keith Stegall might have been the last person to talk to Keith before he died."

"I know," I said. I had already thought about that.

All of country music was saddened from the news of Keith Whitley's death. Although I had only met him once, I too was saddened, especially for Lorrie Morgan. She was suffering the greatest loss of us all.

Waylon Jennings, Roger Murrah and I finally got together one morning at Tom Collin's office and wrote the song I had started weeks earlier.

"I really like this idea, hoss," Waylon told me.

Waylon called a lot of people hoss. He was *the hoss* though.

"Well, I'm glad you like it," I told him. "Thanks for taking the time to come and help Roger and I write it."

It was really neat writing with Waylon Jennings. Along with Willie Nelson, he was one of the original outlaws, and that is part of country music history. Once again I was privileged to be sitting right beside a country music legend.

The song we wrote that day was called *Waking Up With You*. Waylon recorded it on one of his last albums for Columbia Records. I will always cherish the day I wrote that song with Waylon Jennings, and of course along with my dear friend, Roger Murrah.

A few days later Jessie Colter surprised me and called to tell me how much she liked the song and she actually thanked us for using a line from one of her songs in our chorus.

Whenever I do a writers night now I sometimes perform *Waking Up With You* in memory of Waylon Jennings.

I am so glad I was at the ceremony dinner when Waylon was inducted into the Nashville Songwriters Hall Of Fame in the performer/songwriter category.

There was a new singer/songwriter in town. He was about as country and down to earth as anybody I have known in this music business.

One day Charley Monk called and asked me to write with that new songwriter he had signed at Acuff-Rose Publishing. Charlie Monk had teamed me up with Keith Stegall, so I thought, why not.

"He is from South Carolina like you are," Charley Monk informed me. "You two should hit it off well."

Hello, Aaron Tippin.

What you see is what you get with Aaron Tippin, nothing more, nothing less, a lot like I found Dolly Parton to be in that respect. It didn't take me long to know that Aaron and I would be friends for life. Charley Monk was right. Aaron Tippin and I hit it off well, right from the start.

"What part of South Carolina are you from?" I asked Aaron.

We were in the small office I occupied on the second floor of Harris-Richardson Music, about to give it a go with writing a song, along with Mark Collie, who also wrote for Harris-Richardson. Mark was already signed as an artist with MCA. We were going to try and write Mark a hit that day for his debut album.

"Travelers Rest," Aaron told me. 'You from Laurens, ain't cha?"

"Watts Mill," I corrected him.

"Where in hell is Watts Mill," Aaron laughed.

"Where in hell is Travelers Rest?" I ribbed back at him. I actually knew where Travelers Rest was.

Old Memories and Me

Aaron Tippin looked more like a mechanic, which he was, or a bulldozer operator, which he was, or a hunter, which he was, but not like an airplane pilot and country music singer, which he was. He was, as they say, a jack-of-all-trades. I have never known anybody quite like him. When the going gets tough, he just gets tougher. When you need a friend to step up, there he is with those broad shoulders to lean on.

I knew Acuff-Rose and Charley Monk were trying to get Aaron Tippin a record deal. I remember thinking, with him having that crew cut, sounding as country as Vernon Oxford, and dipping snuff, man, ain't no way they're gonna pull this off.

By the way, if you don't know who Vernon Oxford is, well think of Hank Williams, and consider Hank pop compared to Vernon Oxford. So, Aaron Tippin was country to the bone.

I had two songs recorded by Vernon Oxford in the seventies and loved both of them. One actually did very well in Europe.

"I have a hook," I told Aaron and Mark Collie.

A hook is a line that the song is built around, usually the title as well.

I strummed my guitar a few seconds, just looking from Aaron to Mark.

"Well, you gonna tell us what it is?" Aaron asked.

"Naw, I thought I'd let you guess." I said.

Mark Collie laughed. "You boys are crazy."

He might have a point there.

I told them the line, *I miss misbehaving*.

It was Aaron's and Mark's turn to look at each other for a few seconds now.

"That's good, Charlie." Aaron told me. "I like that. That's why you make the big bucks, ain't it?"

Yeah, right Aaron.

To this day, Aaron and I rib and joke around with each other like that. We can be serious, when we have to, but even then it is hard.

That day Mark Collie, Aaron Tippin and I wrote a really good song. We called it *I Miss Misbehavin'*.

Later on, Aaron signed with RCA Records and he recorded *I Miss Misbehaving*. It made the album and probably should have been a single but back then RCA only put nine songs on the cassette and that particular cassette sold, I believe, over 300,000, without *I Miss Misbehaving* on it. The CD sold enough for the total sales to exceed a million. They couldn't release *I Miss Misbehaving* as a single because over 300,000 people didn't have it on the cassette they had already bought. This was no fault of Aaron's. He didn't make those decisions, and too, this is just my personal opinion of what happened. *You Gotta Stand For Something* was the biggest hit off the album. Aaron Tippin has always stood for something-- family, friends, and what's right. Aaron's co-writer on *You Gotta Stand For Something* was another South Carolina boy, Buddy Brock.

    Aaron signed with Reba McIntyre's Starstruck Entertainment and they handled his management and bookings.

    A few months after Aaron had started touring, he came over to my house to write. I don't even remember the name of the song we wrote now, but we had a good time that night. Betty fixed supper for us-- beef stroganoff, French style green beans, and a fruit salad. We sat at the dining room table and talked.

    "I'm thinking about buying a tour bus," Aaron told us.

    "You're kidding?" I said.

    "No," Aaron said. "I'm serious. My tour dates are picking up really good and my merchandise is out selling most of the acts I'm opening for."

    I personally thought it was a little early for him to be considering buying a tour bus. That was a lot of money. I thought he should continue leasing one for a while.

    Now, I know you're thinking I should have minded my own business, but you have to understand about Aaron and me. We could talk to each other, offer unasked for advice, meddle if you want to call it that.

    We talked about the bus thing a while longer.

    "I think Aaron knows what he's doing," Betty chimed in.

    Betty had come to love Aaron Tippin as I had. Dawn had too.

    "Thank ya, Betty," Aaron told her and smirked at me.

    So, Aaron was going to buy a bus. Smart move. I knew it would be. Aaron knew what he was doing.

    Later, when we finished writing whatever song it was we wrote that night, Aaron and I clowned around for my video camera. Billy Craven, Aaron's tour manager at the time, and would go on to become his business manager, had come back over to our house to pick Aaron up and was acting as cameraman.

    Aaron sat in a chair, playing my guitar and singing the lines we had written. I got behind him, and without his knowledge pretended to pour liquor from an empty brandy container I had picked up from a shelf. We just hammered it up, I sang harmony with him while Aaron continued to pick my guitar and sing.

    It just occurred to me. Aaron never brought a guitar when we wrote. He always used mine. How could he afford a bus. He didn't even have a guitar.

    It was while I was writing for Harris-Richardson that I co-wrote *Tropical Depression* with Alan Jackson and Jim McBride. That song would wind up in what I believe is still Alan's biggest selling album, *A Lot About Living, A Little About Love*. I think the sells on that album are in excess of eight million. Even though it was never a single, *Tropical Depression* actually charted in the singles chart, which means it was getting airplay off the album because of its popularity.

Old Memories and Me

I always thought *Tropical Depression* should have been a single and Tim Dubois, the man who ran Arista Records, and had signed Alan to his record contract, told me once that had they pulled another single from that album it would have been *Tropical Depression*. I jokingly told Tim, "Gee thanks, Tim. You just told me I probably lost a hundred thousand dollars or more."

Judy Harris started another publishing company with three former high school friends. They called it Four Of A Kind Music. I followed Judy and signed to write for her new company. Judy Harris and I are close friends. Besides, she is one of Nashville's best songpluggers.

I had met brothers Mike McGuire and Bud McGuire, and had written a couple of songs with them. Mike played drums with the group Shenandoah and sang one of the harmony parts behind lead singer Marty Raybon.

One day Mike McGuire, Stowe Dailey, who also was a writer for Four Of A Kind Music, and myself, were writing together. We were upstairs on the second floor at Four Of A Kind Music. Mike had come up with a great hook line, *her leaving's been a long time coming,* and the three of us were trying to come up with a line to complete that statement, then write a song around it. I went downstairs to potty.

The stairs were a narrow, spiral staircase, and I was making my way down when two things hit me. One, my urge to pee was getting worse, and two, I thought of the line we are searching for. I stopped mid-way down the stairs. What to do? Man, I might forget the line if I don't get back up there and tell Mike and Stowe, and write it down. On the other hand, if I didn't get to the bathroom real quick I wasn't going to make it.

Oh well, grunt and hold it. I ran back upstairs.

"I got it!" I announced, talking fast as I re-entered the room.

"Got what?" Mike asked.

"The line," I told him, and was already backing out the door, legs crossed in an effort to hold *the urge*. Man I had to get to the bathroom. "*Her leaving's been a long time coming, and I guess I had it coming all along*...write that down"

I barely made it back down those narrow stairs to the bathroom.

That day Mike McGuire, Stowe Dailey and I wrote *Leavin's Been A Long Time Coming*. Shenandoah would later record it and have a top 5 single with it. It would be the title of the album as well. Also, later own Troy Aikman, the Dallas Cowboys quarterback, would auction off the lyrics at a fundraiser. Aikman appeared in the video of *Leavin's Been A Long Time Coming*, along with the legendary Eddy Arnold.

Later, when Mike told me what Troy Aikman had told him how much money the lyrics went for at the benefit auction, I laughed and kidded him. "Heck, Mike, that's more than we made off of writer's royalties."

Mike McGuire and I become close friends. We used to kid each other a lot, him calling me *old man*, and me referring to him as *fat boy*. He really wasn't fat but I was in my mid-fifties so I guess he had a point about the age thing, although he swears he was just ribbing me. Mike was bad about discovering he had left his wallet at home sometimes when we would go to lunch, right when it came time to pay. I kidded him about that too. He must still owe me about $50 for lunches.

Not only did I become friends with Mike and Bud McGuire, but I also got to know Shenandoah's lead singer, Marty Raybon pretty well too. Marty has always been one of my favorite singers. I still stay in touch and call all three of them from time to time and chat.

During this time I had started writing a few songs with Buddy Brock, the writer Aaron Tippin had brought to Nashville. Buddy wrote for Acuff-Rose and one day I was over writing with him. We had written a pretty good song and were singing it together as we laid it down on a small tape recorder. Nashville songwriters do that so we won't forget our melodies.

"We ought to get us a record deal as a duet," Buddy laughed, in mock of how badly we sounded together. "We can call ourselves the Fat and the Ugly."

I arched my eyebrows and tried not to crack a smile. "What do you need me for?"

Arista Records was on fire with Alan Jackson, Diamond Rio, and Brooks and Dunn, burning up the charts and selling a ton of records. Pam Tillis and Steve Warner were also doing well on that label, as was Michelle Wright with her big hit, *Take It Like A Man*.

Tim Dubois had the hottest label going in town. He had actually teamed up Brooks and Dunn. He had also signed another artist that had had two top 10 records on Arista, Rob Crosby. Rob's two hits on Arista as an artist, which he also penned, were *She's A Natural* and *Love Will Bring Her Around*. Rob had also written Lee Greenwood's hit *Holding A Good Hand*.

I met Rob Crosby right after I had left Four Of A Kind Music and signed with Erv Woolsey at Muy Bueno. Erv also managed George Strait.

"Where are you from Rob?" I asked Rob Crosby one day when we were about to write a song together over at Muy Bueno.

"Sumter, South Carolina," he told me.

When I first came to Nashville in 1968 there wasn't hardly anybody from South Carolina. Aaron Tippin gives me credit for being the Carolina pioneer for himself and others that followed years later.

I told Rob I was from Watts Mill, right outside of Laurens. He knew where Laurens was, but not Watts Mill.

Old Memories and Me

Rob Crosby and I would go on to write a bunch of songs together over the next twenty or so years. He is a one of the best singers in Nashville and Betty loved to hear him perform. She used to sit and listen to our demos with Rob singing.

"This town is just plain stupid," she told me. "Rob Crosby sings better than most artists on the radio." She was indeed a plainspoken woman that spoke her mind.

I don't think many people would disagree with Betty's opinion about Rob. I didn't understand it myself but after he was dropped by Arista he just never could land another record deal.

I have met a lot of wonderful and great people in this music business, but none more remarkable than Billy Lawson. Billy is a fantastic songwriter and sings well enough to be a recording artist himself. I admire him for all of that, I admire him as a person even more.

Billy was 26 years old when I met him during my stay with Muy Bueno. We wrote a bunch of songs together over a period of time and I got to know Billy really well. It was sad to hear him tell me about the death of his parents and how his father had taken his mother's life, then his father had taken his own life. Billy was only about 18 years old at the time and was left to take care of himself and three younger brothers.

It was after I met Billy Lawson that tragedy struck a couple of more times in his young life. One of his brothers was killed in an accident and the other was shot to death. I recall when his brother was murdered how Billy's anger ran as deep as his hurt. It was certainly understandable how he would be furious with the person that had shot his brother and I called him and talked with him for probably an hour right after it happened. Billy was so upset he was telling me he was going after the man and take things into his own hands. Naturally, it wasn't the rationally Billy Lawson that I had come to know that was talking like that but at the time it was understandable the way he felt under the circumstances.

I prayed with Billy over the phone that night and after we talked with Jesus about everything, Billy had calmed down to the point that he was able to promise me he would let the law handle everything, and thank goodness he did.

I can't even imagine what it would be like to lose my parents in the manner in which he did, then lose two of his younger brothers, one of which was murdered. Billy Lawson, even at that young age, was able to endure and overcome all of that tragedy and somehow move on with his life.

In between those sad and difficult times, Billy and I had a lot fun writing songs and sometimes just hanging out together. He would drive up from his home near the Alabama line and we would write every Wednesday. We ate lunch almost every time he was in Nashville at a Thai food place called The International Market.

Billy was getting a few songs recorded and was in hopes of landing a record deal himself. He was watching his weight and would arrive on those Wednesdays and say to me, "Charlie, I've lost five pounds since last week. Can't you tell?"

I would kid him and say, "Billy, it looks like you've gained 5 pounds since last week to me."

I saw Billy recently and he looks wonderfully fit and trim.

Billy Lawson would go on to write such #1 hits as Trace Atkin's *I Left Something Turned On At Home* and Rick Trevino's *I'm Learning As You Go*.

Billy has told me that Billy Bob Thornton has shown some interest in his life story as a possible movie.

I was at Muy Bueno writing one day when Betty called. I knew as soon as I got on the phone something was terribly wrong.

"Charlie," she sobbed. "Mark was killed this morning."

Mark was Betty's twin sister Bobbie Bolt's son.

"Oh no," I gasped. What she said put an instant sick feeling in the pit of my stomach. "What happened, honey?"

Betty went on to tell me that Mark Bolt had been driving one of his daddy's flatbed 18-wheeler logging trucks, loaded down with 80 ton of logs. I would get more details later about how Mark had started to cross an intersection on the Laurens By Pass, as the traffic light had turned green going in his direction, and a pickup truck ran through the red light coming from the other direction. Mark evidently saw the pickup and swerved to his right to try and avoid a collision and had gone over the low concrete wall and dropped some 20-30 feet into shallow Little River below. There was a large metal plate behind the truck cab, separating it from the logs behind it, but the force of the impact drove the logs right through the back of the truck cab into Mark.

It was a horrible time. Naturally, Bobbie and Jack were devastated. Betty, Dawn and I went to Laurens the next day. Mark Bolt was laid to rest in the little country church cemetery across the gravel road from Bobbie and Jack's house, where they attend church. You can see his headstone from their screened in back porch.

Mark Bolt was just a few months shy of his 27th birthday.

We returned home with heavy hearts but trying to get back to some kind existence. I didn't even try to write for the next few days. I did go in to the office at Muy Bueno and hang out for a while one morning. George Strait happened to be in town.

Since Erv Woolsey manages George, the superstar had a suite on the third floor of the office building and that is where he stays whenever he is in town. George never moved to Nashville. To my knowledge he lived in Texas when he had his first hit, *Unwound*, and still does today.

Old Memories and Me

On this particular day George Strait had stopped on the second floor to visit with some of the staff writers for Muy Bueno, as he did quite often when he was in town and at the office. We had coffee and donuts with George that morning.

"Isn't that a new bus outside, George?" I asked him.

"Yeah," he said. "I've only had it a little while. Have you not seen it yet?"

"No," I told him. "It looks really nice though."

He told his bus driver, "Hey, take Charlie out and let him see the bus."

Man, you should've seen that bus. It was a Prevost, top of the line, loaded with everything you could possibly think of. The driver had his on stereo system up front. There was a television monitor up front as well, for the driver to view everything behind, no rearview mirror for this baby. George had a plush stateroom in the back. I never asked what it cost but it looked like a million dollar ride to me.

When George Strait starred in the movie *Pure Country*, I was invited to the premiere. It was held at one of the large theatres in Metro Center. A lot of the invited guests arrived early and mingled in the lobby. I remember talking with Garth and Sandy Brooks. Randy Travis and his wife Lib were there. I sat with Randy and Lib during the premiere. I enjoyed the movie and thought George did a great job. After the showing of the film, I attended an invitation only reception and had a chance to speak with George and his wife Norma. I told George I thought he had done a great job in *Pure Country*. George Strait is really a nice guy-- easy to talk to.

He also has a sense of humor too. I kidded him once about a song I had written with Billy Lawson called *I Missed The Boat*. George really liked that song and had put it on hold a couple of years in a row when he was getting ready to record. However, he hadn't recorded it.

"I'm gonna tick you off this year when you get ready to record, George," I told him one night, seated at a table with him at the BMI Awards dinner.

"Yeah, how's that?" he asked. He was sort of already grinning. He figured I was up to something I guess.

"I ain't gonna pitch you *I Missed The Boat* this year," I told him, just picking at him.

"And I'm not going to cut it again this year either," he laughed.

Good comeback George.

Man, I love this business and the people in it, people like George Strait.

CHAPTER FIFTEEN

Dawn gave birth to Kyle Christopher Smith on April 9, 1992. His middle name was in memory of Mark Christopher Bolt, Betty's twin sister's son that had been killed driving the logging truck. Betty and I were finally grandparents and needless to say, we were tickled pink.
"He looks just like me," I said proudly.
"No, he don't," Betty shot back just as proudly. "He looks like me. He's got brown eyes like mine."
Well, that was true.
I knew Kyle was going to be special from day one. He had a brown birthmark on the left side of his chin. It made me think of the *Star of David*. I knew Betty and I would spoil him too. We spoiled his mama, so why stop now. It was a good spoiling though. Betty made sure we all kept our feet on the ground.
"Daddy, I want a new bicycle." That would be Dawn.
"No, it's not but three months until Christmas." That would be me.
"But Daddy, please." Dawn again.
"Alright." Me again.
"No, absolutely not." That would be Betty. "It's ridiculous to buy her a bicycle a few months before Christmas."
I told you Betty kept our feet on the ground. On the other hand, there were times Betty would give in as well as me. We all have our weakness. As Kyle got a little older, when he was 3 years old, Betty had him playing Nintendo. We bought him a Super Mario player and game at age 4. Before he was 5 years old he was actually pretty good at playing *Mario*.
At that age Kyle had platinum blonde hair, just like his mama did when she was little. He was a doll and I took videos of him all the time, as well as photographs. When I would video him playing Nintendo he would look right at the camera and grin.
"Can you see me, papa?"
"I see you, Kyle."
Betty and I would push Kyle in his stroller and walk around the neighborhood. Evidently I wasn't walking enough. I had gotten overweight and weighed 215 pounds. I was 55 years old when Kyle was born but my hair was still dark. Parts of my goatee were gray though. I

Old Memories and Me

had all but stopped drinking beer completely and felt the best I had in a few years. Betty's hair had turned about gray all over, with some dark highlights. Sometimes I wondered if the 21 radiation treatments didn't cause her to turn gray a few years early. Of course she was now 56 years old. She was still a beautiful woman and I thought her salt and pepper hair added to her appeal.

We both wondered how we got to be in our mid-fifties so fast. It seemed not that long ago we were in our early twenties and just starting out our lives together. It seemed sometimes like our lives were speeding by on roller skates while everybody around us was walking.

EMI was getting a few of my older songs recorded. Ed Bruce had recorded *Off On Wednesday* and my and Keith Stegall's *I think I'm In Love*. Conway Twitty had also recorded *I Think I'm In Love*. Con Hunley had recorded a super version of my and Keith's *All American Country Boy*. However, I wasn't getting a lot of songs recorded out of my Muy Bueno catalog. It was no fault of the company though. Bobby Cottle, the songplugger there, was pitching my material regularly and believed in my songs. Sometimes it just isn't happening. So when Chuck Howard called me one day with an offer I responded.

"Charlie, this is Chuck Howard," Chuck said over the phone.

"How ya doing Chuck," I asked him.

"Great," he responded. Then, "Hey man, I got a good deal for you."

"Yeah?"

"Yeah," Chuck told me. "Me and Bowen are starting up a new publishing company. Your buddy Keith Stegall has already signed and I want to get you over here with us."

The Bowen he was referring to was the record producer Jimmy Bowen, and at that time the CEO of Capital Records, Nashville division. I had heard that Jimmy Bowen and Chuck Howard had sold their Great Cumberland Music and were starting up a new company.

"I'm gonna double the money you made last year," Chuck boasted, laughing a little. Chuck had had some success and could be a little cocky sometimes, but in a good naturedly way. He was a likeable guy.

"You are?" I tried to sound like I believed him but I was rolling my eyes.

"Yeah, how much did you make last year?" He asked.

I didn't hesitate. "$600,000," I told him. Of course that wasn't true. I just said that high figure because Chuck had said he was going to double what I had made.

Chuck skipped right over the subject.

"We got some good writers already signed and we have good funding," Chuck informed me. "EMI, your old publisher is funding the company."

Erv's wife, Connie Woolsey was good enough to release me from my contract at Muy Bueno and I signed with Chuck Howard and

Jimmy Bowen's newly formed Tower Street Music. However, it was a really long and complicated contract and by the time my attorney, David Maddox, and the EMI lawyers came to terms on everything, I had already been with Tower Street nearly two months, actually unofficially until we singed the papers. I got a generous weekly advance, probably more than most writers in Nashville were getting at that time, but I had a good track record and was still writing commercial songs.

Alan Jackson had bought a large home in Brentwood, Nashville's version of Beverly Hills. A lot of stars live in Brentwood and it is very upscale for the most part. Chuck Howard lived around the corner from Alan.

"Alan Jackson is selling a ton of records," Chuck said one day. We had been to lunch and were on our way back to the office at Tower Street. "That means Keith Stegall's making a lot of money as his producer."

"Yeah," I agreed. "They are doing pretty good."

"Pretty good?" Chuck laughed. "Alan has sold over three million on this current album, and a producer will get around $300,000-$400,000 per million. That means Keith will make a million bucks, man." I personally had no idea what producers made and I certainly didn't know what Keith was making.

"That is where the big money is right now," Chuck Howard stated. "Producing records, that's where it's at."

Not long after that Chuck Howard was producing John Berry, a new artist from Georgia. John Berry started having hit singles, so I guess he was selling albums and based on what Chuck had told me about producers he was probably making a lot of money.

Me, I was still bringing up the rear at the bottom of the money pole in this business with several hundred other Nashville songwriters at 6 cents an album.

Tower Street never really got off the ground. I left after a year and went back to EMI. Celia Froehlig was still running the company and songplugger Robin Palmer had asked me to talk to Celia about re-signing with EMI. Celia and I talked and I went back to the company I had already spent 12 years with as a writer. Those 12 years included all of my catalogs at Screen Gems, CBS Songs and SBK that had been bought by EMI. All but one of the songs I had co-written with Alan Jackson was in my CBS/EMI catalog, along with perhaps 75-100 songs I had written with Keith Stegall.

It was the mid-90's and I needed to get more songs recorded like I had done in the eighties. I was getting album cuts but I needed singles.

I continued to write with Rob Crosby. I also had written with David Ball, Tim Nichols, Jim McBride, and a few others songwriters.

I called Vince Gill and asked him to write. He agreed and we set up a writing appointment. I am a sentimental and tender hearted

Old Memories and Me

guy and so is Vince Gill. Both of us can be very emotional.

"Should I take a box of Kleenex with me," I joked with Betty the morning I was leaving to meet Vince to write.

On that first writing session with Vince we never came up with a killer hook but we had a lot of fun trying to. He is a blast to be around, great sense of humor and a very humble guy. We did write a song that day but I have forgotten the title because as I said, we never came up with a good idea.

We would do better on another day though.

When I said Aaron Tippin was a jack-of-all-trades I wasn't exaggerating.

"What do you want with this piece of junk?" I asked Aaron.

I was sitting in the seat of a half-rusted front-end loader, in a drizzle of rain, pressing down on the brakes whenever Aaron told me too. He was down under the thing, flat on his back, bleeding the brakes. Two of the tires were flat.

"I'm gonna use it," he informed me.

"How," I wanted to know. "It won't run."

Aaron grunted, trying to turn a wet nut with a wet wrench. "It will when I get through with it," he said. Then he asked me, "What was that last line you said?"

In the rain, fooling around with a broken down, rusted, front-end loader, we were trying to write a song.

"I don't remember," I laughed and wiped the rain from my face.

"Well, think, Charlie" he said and laughed too.

The rain was soaking my head and running down my face. "Gimme your baseball cap, Aaron," I told him. "You don't need it down there."

He pulled off his cap and tossed it up to me. "Sissy."

I pulled his camouflage hunting cap down on my head.

"Hit the brakes again," Aaron told me.

I hit the brake and it went flat to the floor. "Still ain't working, pal," I informed him.

Aaron peered up from under the front-end loader. "You look like shit, Charlie."

"So do you," I told him.

We both laughed.

We were both soaking wet. Aaron was laying in wet grass and some mud, flat on his back. We looked like two drowned ducks.

"You got another line in your head? I asked him, getting back to the song we were trying to write.

"Nope," he said. "I come up with the last line. It's your time."

That rainy day, somehow, we managed to get a verse and chorus written to a pretty good song. We finished it later and Aaron recorded it. It's called *She's Got A Way Of Making Me Forget*.

Songs are written in a lot of different places around Nashville every day but not many are written in the rain and mud, in a junkyard full of broken down dump trucks and front-end loaders.

Aaron used the front-end loader and other heavy equipment he had bought and fixed up to build a road up to the top of a mountain he had bought about two hours East of Nashville. He also dug out the basement for the log house he and his wife Thea were about to build, right on the top of that mountain. It is an absolutely beautiful place. It is difficult to get Aaron to come down from his mountain of paradise unless he just has to go into Nashville on business or when he goes out on the road.

Aaron Tippin owns several small planes and a helicopter these days. He has done very well since that first day I met him, way back yonder, as we would say in South Carolina.

He also owns a guitar now.

Dawn and Richard had been divorced for a while and Dawn and Kyle were living with Betty and I. Dawn still played softball and traveled a lot of weekends to tournaments. There was a team out of Chicago that flew her to all of their tournaments. She played left center field for them. She usually made All Tournament regardless of what team she played for.

One weekend when she was playing softball in Chicago, I had to take Kyle to the emergency room at Summit Medical Center in Hermitage. He was about 4 years old. He had been crying and complaining about his stomach hurting. Kyle's dad, Richard, was visiting with him that Saturday, and Kyle's pains got so intense we took him to the emergency room. I didn't call Dawn at first. I wanted to see what was wrong before I alarmed her with her being so far away.

I knew Kyle had not been able to have a bowel movement for a couple of days and that turned out to be the problem. He wouldn't let anybody hold him but me. Whenever he was sick or in pain he always wanted his papa to hold him. I used to walk the floor about all night sometimes, holding him when he had earaches. He had to have tubes about three different times.

At the emergency room they tried enemas but that didn't work. The doctors said they were going to try using a tube to unblock him and if that didn't work they would have to do surgery.

I decided I needed to call Dawn and tell her. I finally reached her on her cell at the ball field where they were playing in Chicago. She nearly panicked. I was trying to calm her down but inside I was about to panic myself with the fear he may have to have surgery. He was only 5 years old. Dawn was going to call about the next flight out of O'Hare Airport and call me back. I called Betty and told her what was going on. She had stayed home with Richard's twins, Seagie and Skylar. They were children from another marriage.

"Charlie, call me as soon as you know anything," Betty told me, fighting back tears.

I got off in a room and got down on my knees and prayed. I know I wasn't his father, but I couldn't have loved him any more than if I had been. I pray every day of my life and talk to Jesus and I pray every night. I have always turned to Jesus when I am afraid or in need too. I was afraid and in need that afternoon. I asked Jesus to help my grandson and spare him from having to have surgery. I cried.

Richard was worried too. Although he was divorced from Dawn, he loved Kyle with every ounce of love a father could possibly have and he was a good dad. Dawn had called back to tell me she couldn't get a flight for another two hours but she was already on her way to the airport. She was crying.

"Please God, let my baby be alright." She was on her cell with me but she was reaching out to God, just like I was.

When they took Kyle into the room to do the tube procedure, Richard and I went in there with him. It was against hospital policy but the doctors allowed us to anyway. Kyle was still in pain and now he was scared as well. He didn't know anything about the possibility of surgery but he saw those tubes they were going to use and wanted to leave. It was breaking my heart to see him like that, especially when he called out my name, "Papa!" He stretched out his arms towards me and Richard. We couldn't pick him up or hold him though.

I had to leave the room, tears streaming down my face.

God answered our prayers once again and through his mercy the doctors were able to unblock Kyle's intestines with the tubes and fluid. I cried again, this time from joy and I was also able to wrap my arms around Kyle. So did Richard. Then Richard and I hugged each other.

We took Kyle home a little later. I picked Dawn up at the airport and even though she knew by then that Kyle was fine, she made me break the speed limit to get home.

"I'm not ever going out of town and leave him again." She was crying.

I went to church that Sunday and went down to the front of the altar, knelt down and thanked God for helping my grandson. I also told Him I was sorry for not always holding up my end of things when he was always holding up His end.

Betty and I had been talking about building a new house. We had looked in several new subdivisions, especially in the Mt. Juliet area, which was just across the Davidson County line from where we lived in Hermitage. We had saved up some money from royalties but it was going to cost a good bit to get into the kind of house we wanted and besides putting enough money down to contract a builder, we would need new drapes, some new furniture and we wanted to build a fence around the back yard for privacy, maybe even put in a pool. As in the past, God just seemed to look out for us.

"Hello," I answered when my cell phone rang one December morning, about two weeks before Christmas, 1993.

"Charlie, this is Greg Brown."

Greg Brown was a record producer.

"Hello, Greg."

"How would you like a Travis Tritt cut?" Greg asked me.

"That would be great," I said and felt I was about to get some good news.

"Well, you got one last night," Greg informed me cheerfully.

"Wow," I laughed. "What a Christmas present."

I looked over at Betty sitting on the couch drinking coffee. I nodded and smiled at her but she had no idea what I was trying to tell her.

"Guess what song Travis cut of yours," Greg prodded me.

A few weeks before, Greg had called me and asked me to bring him a copy of my song *I Would Like To See You Again*, the song Johnny Cash had had a hit with back in 1978. Greg had said he wanted to run it past Travis to consider recording.

"*I Would Like To See You Again?*" That was a good guess.

"No, *Between An Old Memory And Me*," Greg Brown told me and chuckled. "It turned out great too."

I would learn that Keith Stegall's dad, Bob, had taken Greg the song, so he gets the credit for that Travis Tritt cut, not I.

I looked at Betty again. "Travis Tritt cut *Between An Old Memory And Me* last night," I told her.

Betty arched her eyebrows and grinned. That was one of her favorite songs of mine.

Greg Brown went on to tell me that he wanted me to come in and hear the raw cut, no mix at that point, of course, but he wanted to warn me that they hadn't recorded the song quite as country as Keith Stegall and I had written it. He said they did it real edgy.

I recall when I went to Greg Brown's office and he played the Travis Tritt cut, I thought, "*this is what it would sound like if Bob Segar had recorded it.*" I loved it and felt like it would be a hit. Greg told me it would be on Tritt's next album, *Ten Feet Tall And Bullet Proof*.

The night before Christmas Eve, perhaps 10 days after Greg Brown had called me, Keith Stegall called me. Betty and I were lying in bed watching a movie on TV.

"Charlie, Keith," Keith said. For 25 years he always said that when he called and I answered. *Charlie, Keith*, drawing out my name a bit. Just one of those little habits you pick up on from old friends.

Hey, Keith," I said and I thought I knew why he was calling because I knew he was down in Muscle Shoals, Alabama, co-producing an album on *Shenandoah*. Besides, I could hear voices in the background

Old Memories and Me

I recognized.

"Mike McGuire wants to talk to you," Keith told me.

A couple of seconds passed, then, "Hey old man, we cut our song," Mike laughed.

"Way to go fat boy," I said and laughed too.

"Man, it sounds good," Mike said, then, "Hey Keith, play a little of *Leavin's Been A Long Time Coming* for Charlie."

I couldn't tell a whole lot over the phone but I certainly recognized the song I had written with Mike and Stowe Dailey over at Judy Harris' office that day.

"Whaddya think?" Mike asked after Keith had played about a minute of the track.

"Sounds great man," I said.

I guess because I already knew the lyrics I could make some of them out over the phone. It had a great groove, I could tell that for sure.

"Here, Marty wants to talk to you."

Mike McGuire had handed the phone to Marty Raybon, *Shenandoah's* great lead singer.

"Hey, Charlie," Marty said in his usual well mannered tone that had a touch of soulful sound. "How ya doing buddy?"

"Doing good, Marty," I told him. "Thanks for cutting the song."

"Hey man, it's a great song. I think it turned out real good," Marty said. "Course we got to add harmony and I want to re-sing it. I've only done a scratch vocal."

I heard Keith's voice in the background. "Hey, that's my dime you guys are talking on."

"I better let you go," Marty told me. "Merry Christmas, Charlie."

"Merry Christmas to you Marty and tell everybody there I said thanks," I said sincerely.

Keith got back on the phone just long enough to say "I'll talk to you later. Just wanted you to know we cut your song."

"Thanks pal," I told him.

Afterward, Betty and I lay in bed and talked about that house we had been planning on building. We had a Travis Tritt and a Shenandoah cut now and it sounded like both of them were going to be singles.

"I want a big kitchen," Betty said, propped up on her pillow. She was pretty much gray haired now but still as beautiful as ever.

"You can have your big kitchen if I can have a pool table room," I bargained with a smile.

We would get both.

CHAPTER SIXTEEN

Shenandoah climbed the charts in 1994 with *Leavin's Been A Long Time Coming*. It peaked at #5 in Billboard but went a little higher in a couple of other charts. Travis Tritt came out later that year with *Between An Old Memory And Me* and by the first part of 1995 it had reached #3 in the charts. Travis appeared on the Jay Leno *Tonight Show* and performed that song. It went over extremely well with both Leno and his audience. I still have the video of the show.

"I really love to hear Travis sing that song," Betty told me, laying in bed that night, right after we had watched Travis on the *Tonight Show*. "You know that's one of my favorite songs that you've written."

"It has become one of my favorites too," I told her.

We lay there silent for a few moments. Finally, Betty rolled over onto her side to face me. "Do you remember the first time I told you I love you?"

"You mean the night I fell out of the car?" I chuckled.

She smiled and told me, "Yeah, and I was just thinking back to when we first met. All the times we went skating, or just rode around at night. Then after we married we didn't have hardly anything but each other. It never took much to make us happy." There were a few tears in her eyes.

"Honey," I said and half sat up. "Don't be sad."

She bit her lip to gain her composure and then smiled even more. "I'm not sad. I am happy. You know sometimes you cry because you are so happy, and I am so happy."

I leaned over and kissed her sweetly. Then I told her, "I am happy too, Betty. I don't deserve you but I do thank God every day that he gave you to me."

Now there were tears in my eyes.

Then she grinned broadly, "No, you probably don't deserve me but everybody gets lucky every now and then."

"I love you, Betty Craig," I smiled and kissed her again.

"How much do you love me?"

"More than anything in the whole world," I told her and never meant it more than I did right then.

Dawn has always lived with us a lot but she would get an

Old Memories and Me

apartment sometimes and she and Kyle would move into their own place. When she wasn't living with us, and Kyle was still 5 or 6 years old, about 9 o'clock at night Betty would tell me, "You might as well get your shoes on. Kyle will be calling in a few minutes."

In a matter of minutes the phone would ring. It would be Kyle.

"Can you come and get me papa?"

"I'll be right there."

I would go get him and he would sleep that night between his papa and his nanny.

Bob Stegall called me one day. Bob is Keith Stegall's dad.

"Charlie, Tanya Tucker is recording today and I think *I'll Take The Memories* would be perfect for her," he told me. "Jerry Crutchfield is producing her. Don't you know Crutchfield?"

I'll Take The Memories was my and Keith Stegall's song that Lorrie Morgan had recorded on her debut album with BNA.

"Yeah, but not really well," I replied to Keith's dad.

"They are recording at 2 o'clock today," Bob informed me. "Can't you take a copy of the song to the studio?"

"I'd rather not," I said. I don't like walking into a studio when somebody is recording. "Let me call Robin Palmer at EMI and get a copy made right quick and I will take it to Crutchfield's office." I glanced at my watch. "It's not quite 12:30, so maybe I can catch him before he goes into the studio."

I called Robin Palmer and she happened to be in her office. She made me a copy of *I'll Take The Memories* and I drove to EMI and picked it up. I then drove to Jerry Crutchfield's office. I got lucky and saw him about to enter his front door carrying a bag. He was about to eat his lunch.

"Excuse me, Jerry," I said as I approached him. "I'm Charlie Craig."

I held out my hand and he shook it politely. "Yeah, how are you doing, Charlie," he said.

"I'm doing fine," I told him. "I hate to bother you but I have a song that Keith Stegall and I wrote that we think would be good for Tanya Tucker."

"Well, give me a copy and I will take to the studio in a little while and Tanya and I will listen to it," Jerry told me.

I handed him the tape and thanked him. Later that night Keith called me.

"Charlie, Keith" he said, drawing out my name in a slow drawl.

"Hey, Keith," I said. "I gave Crutchfield our song for Tanya Tucker today."

"I know," Keith responded. "I was mixing earlier this afternoon in another room at the same studio where they are recording. They cut it on the first session."

"Well, that was fast," I told him. "Tanya must have liked it."
"I guess so," Keith laughed. "She cut it."
I wish they were all that easy.
Betty and I finally decided to build our new house in a new subdivision in Mt. Juliet. There were already a lot of houses built in the subdivision but there were also a lot of empty lots to choose from. We picked a lot at the back of a cul-de-sac. We chose that particular lot because it would have a bigger back yard than the other lots we looked at.
We visited with the builder numerous times, picking out carpet, tiles for the bathrooms, light fixtures, and having several upgrades made in the floor plans. We upgraded from 2 ½ baths to 3 full baths. We changed a ledge that separated the family room from the kitchen to a bar. We wanted a solid top stove rather than the conventional eyelet burners. The kitchen was 15x33, including the dining area, so Betty would have her large kitchen. The family room on the other side of the bar was 21x20, so there was a huge open space look to that area of the house. There was a gas fireplace bordered by marble and a marble hearth. A study, dining room, front living room, and a full bath completed the downstairs.
Upstairs there would be three bedrooms and my pool room, which was 17x15. My and Betty's master bedroom was on the opposite end of the upstairs from my pool room and was the exact same measurements, 17x15. Our bathroom was large, with his and hers vanities, a row of 4 lights above each mirror. The bathtub had a 6-jet whirlpool and a separate glass shower at one end of the tub. The walk-in closet was very spacious, with shelves above the clothes area. There was a separate toilet room.
Two other bedrooms completed the upstairs.
There was a long railing where you could look down into the open area over the hanging chandelier in the front foyer. There were two storage rooms upstairs on each side of the pool room, each 10x20. We would have a two-car garage.
This was our floor plan and we loved it.
We paid a good bit down for the upgrades and to start the construction of our new home. The only time we had ever spent that much money at one time was for medical bills for Betty's surgeries and radiation.
It wasn't going to be a mansion by any stretch of the imagination, but it was going to be over 3,000 square feet and our dream home. We had lived in apartments and duplexes for so long, this might seem like a mansion after all.
I had pretty much stopped drinking beer completely by now. I just needed to watch what I was eating and get some of the weight off. I was trying but *The Cooker's* fried chicken tenders and the *Hermitage House Smorgasbord's* home cooking was too good to back away from

Old Memories and Me

too often. Those were my and Betty's two favorite places to eat out. My favorite meal for Betty to cook was beef stroganoff. She had a great recipe for that. She usually had French style green beans, fruit salad and croissant rolls with that meal.

Since Betty's bout with cancer when the radiation treatments had made her so sick, I had learned to cook pretty well myself. To be honest, I cooked a lot of stuff I just made up.

One day I baked some chicken in the oven, then put it in a big pan on top of the stove, dumped in several cans of chicken and rice soup, a can of cheddar cheese, and added some diced onions and a little garlic.

"What is that?" Dawn asked when she saw it.

"I don't know," I laughed. "It has more chicken than anything so I guess it's chicken goulash."

It was really good. Betty and Dawn asked me to make it again some time later but I had forgotten what amounts of everything I had used. It wasn't as good the second time.

I learned that cooking is a lot like songwriting. You better write it down.

I called Vince Gill one day about writing again. The only day he had open for a while was that Sunday afternoon. I met him at EMI and we tossed a couple of ideas around. Vince was starting to record his next album the following morning and we were trying to come up with something different from anything he already had to record.

"I have a song I wrote by myself back in 1980," I told Vince. I think the reason it has never been recorded is because it needs some work. Let me show you a little of it and see what you think."

"Sure," Vince said.

Just as I started to sing him the song I had an idea. "Let me run upstairs right quick and run off a couple sets of lyrics and you can see what I have already. Besides, I don't remember the whole song anyway."

Vince waited patiently while I ran upstairs, pulled the lyric sheet from the Screen Gems file cabinet, made two copies and returned downstairs. I gave Vince a copy of the lyrics and read one myself as I sang him the song I had written a few years earlier.

"It's pretty good the way it is," Vince told me when I had finished showing him what I had. "I really love the hook. We probably can tighten the verses and chorus up in a few places and come up with another melody. There are some keeper lines in there though."

We rewrote most all of the song, especially the chorus, and Vince came up with a great melody for the chorus, which he is so famous for anyway. He gave the song what I call that *high lonesome* sound. We did keep basically the melody I had originally written for the verses.

In minutes Vince had a real cool feel working and his voice just fit the mood of what he was getting into. Of course Vince Gill's voice can fit any song and mood.

The funny part of this little story is what happened when we finished writing the song and were ready to lay it down on a little portable recorder. I put my guitar down to let Vince record the work tape by himself. He is such a great guitar player and an awesome singer. I didn't want to mess him up.

"What are you doing?" Vince asked me.

"You lay it down," I told him. "You don't need me messing you up."

"You're gonna play too," Vince informed me. "I'm not playing if you don't. Pick up your guitar." He was grinning.

I picked up my guitar. Vince hit record on the little jam box.

We started playing the song and Vince came in on the first verse singing. On the second line he messed up.

"Damn it," he frowned.

The tape was still running. We started over.

Vince messed up again.

"Shit."

The tape was still recording everything.

"Uh Vince," I asked and tried to look real serious. "You want me to do this?"

I still have that work tape and you couldn't buy it from me.

Betty and I would drive out to see how the new house was coming along several times a week. It's funny how rooms don't look nearly as big as they are supposed to be when there is only the framed in 2x4s and flooring. It all starts shaping up once the walls are put in, especially the dry walls.

It is a good thing we kept a regular check on things though. There were several things that were wrong and had to be redone once we pointed it out to the builders. They had framed in the downstairs bath a half bath when it was suppose to be a full bath. The bar separating the family room and kitchen was a ledge. These were part of the upgrades Betty and I had paid extra for. The builders were going by the original floor plans.

Betty kept them straight though. "We want this done right or you'll have to build the entire house all over."

New Year's came and 1996 rolled in. I was 59 years old, trimmed back down a little to around 185 pounds. I needed to get down to about 180 though. Betty, now 60, continued to have some problems, both from where they had removed 2/3 of her stomach and from the radiation. She hardly complained and just toughed it out. Her long hair was silvery and peppered now. She still had those beautiful brown eyes and was still pretty even though she had been through so much illness. She got tired pretty easy but that didn't keep her from getting outside and pitching Kyle a plastic ball to hit with his plastic bat, or sit in a chair

Old Memories and Me

with him for hours playing *Nintendo*.
   The new house was coming along slower than planned, mostly because of bad weather. It didn't look like they would meet the March closing date.
   I went in to EMI about every day. Gary Overton was now running the company. I was co-writing some with a couple of EMI's great staff writers, Richard Leigh and Wayland Holyfield. Richard had written Crystal Gayle's breakout hit, *Don't It Make My Brown Eyes Blue* and Wayland had penned Ann Murray's *Could I Have This Dance*. Guy Clark and Verlon Thompson were still staff writers as well, along with myself and Peter McCann from the *old school* and CBS Song days.
   I had recouped all of the advance I had been paid by CBS and SBK, which had been well over a hundred thousand dollars, and made the company more money beyond that, especially with the Alan Jackson cuts I had gotten over the past six years. However, I was on a very large advance with EMI now and the royalties from my old catalogs were coming to me directly and hardly no royalties were recouping the big advance balance I was building up in the new deal because most all of my cuts were from my old catalogs. When I had signed my new contract with EMI I had made sure they couldn't recoup from my old catalogs they owned. That is a common thing writers do that have been around for a long time and resign with a publisher after being away for a while.
   Gary O (that is what about everybody in the business calls Gary Overton) called me into his office one day and we went over the figures of my new deal, which was now approaching 5 years.
   "It's a pretty large amount in the red, pal," Gary said to me. He called me pal because we were close friends.
   "I know," I agreed.
   "You're still getting songs recorded, they're just not coming out of this new catalog," he pointed out.
   "Yeah, I have been thinking about this same thing," I told him. "I don't want it to take forever to recoup this catalog because there are some great songs in here and when they do get recorded I would like for it not take so long to get out of the red."
   "You know I would like to keep you here, Charlie," Gary said. "You have been with this company a long time, nearly 17 years total now."
   I knew Gary was leading up to something he wasn't looking forward to doing. My contract still had a few more months left on it and Gary and I agreed if we didn't get a couple of good cuts by the time it was up, I would leave EMI. It would be kind of sad leaving the company I had been with for so long, but there was a kind of solace there too, knowing if I ever needed them they would be there for me. I felt that in my heart.
   My old catalogs would continue to be pitched and naturally I would continue to draw my royalties from that catalog. The songs I had

written in the eighties, and especially those co-written with both Keith Stegall and Alan Jackson, were still bringing in good royalties. Betty and I had a pretty good bank account, so we would be fine financially.

I had been thinking about starting my own publishing company so now was the time to do it. I registered *Song Machine Music* with BMI and launched my own publishing company.

For the first time since Betty and I had arrived in Nashville back in 1968, we were back on our own. It wasn't quite as scary this time though. We had a little more than $900 now and they were playing my songs all over the world.

They finally finished our new house and on April 25, 1996, Betty and I signed the closing papers. On the way back home we stopped to celebrate at O'Charley's Restaurant. Betty got prime rib and I had a steak. We had a glass of wine, something I never drink, nor did Betty, but it was a special occasion.

We already had everything packed at our old place. The movers arrived the next morning and we moved into our new home in Mt. Juliet.

I carried Betty over the threshold and nearly dropped her again, like I did on our honeymoon some 39 years earlier.

"It's going to be a lot of work," Betty said as we stood in the big family room looking at all of the boxes we had packed. "Let's just take our time and not try to do everything in one or two days."

"When are the people coming about the curtains?" I asked her.

"Not until the first of the week," she answered, then smiled and added, "Not curtains though, drapes. These won't come from Wal-Mart's."

Man, was she ever right. The people came about the drapes from Brentwood the next week. Betty was having custom made drapes for every room downstairs. After measuring all of the windows downstairs we were informed the cost would be just over $10,000.

I had to sit down when the guy told us the amount.

On June 28, 1996, Dawn married Frank Primm. It was her second marriage. They moved into a duplex in Mt. Juliet that was only about 10-12 minutes from our house.

Sometime in the spring of 1996, I met five people that would eventually become as close as family to me. Three members of that family would also set this town back on its musical ears for a while.

"Charlie, you have just got to hear these two kids and their dad sing," Lee Bach told me on the phone. "They're over here in my office right now. Can I bring them over?"

EMI had continued to allow me to use their writer rooms. I was in one of those rooms writing a song with another writer. It was a Friday afternoon.

Old Memories and Me

"I am in the middle of a writing session, Lee," I told him. "How about Monday?"

"They are from Canada and have to go back this Sunday," Lee informed me. There was both an excitement in his tone and a deep concern for me to hear these people sing before they had to leave town.

As a favor to my friend, Lee Bach, I asked the writer I was writing with to take a thirty-minute break so I could listen to this father and his kids sing. Lee brought them over to EMI.

The girl was 13, the boy 11 and the dad was probably in his late thirties. The mother was with them, a very pretty blonde lady, and another sibling, a pretty 9-year-old girl. The 9 year old didn't sing, just the dad and the other two kids.

After Lee Bach introduced everybody, the dad played an acoustic guitar and the three of them sang, the 13-year-old little cutie doing the lead and her brother and dad doing perfect harmony with her.

Holy Cow......

Hello, *The Wilkinsons*.

"Wow," I exclaimed. "You guys are absolutely incredible. I love that song, too."

It was *26 Cents*.

They all three thanked me. They weren't a bit shy. Amanda and Tyler both were pretty doggone sharp for a 13 and 11 year old, standing in an office at EMI, kind of auditioning I guess, but you would have thought they were home in their own living room.

"Did you guys write that yourself?" I asked.

"I wrote it with a writer up in Canada," Steve told me.

"Sing another one," I said and I couldn't hide my excitement.

The Wilkinsons sang two more songs for me. I cancelled my writing appointment and got on the telephone. I wanted some of my friends at the record labels to hear this group. They were fabulous. Amanda and Tyler sounded a lot older than 13 and 11.

"Hey, this is Charlie Craig. Is Keith Stegall in?" Keith was an executive with Mercury Records then.

"Charlie, Keith is on vacation down in the Cayman's."

Yeah, I knew that. I had forgotten.

"Hi, this is Charlie Craig. Is Tim Dubois in?" Tim was still the head of Arista.

"He isn't, Charlie. Sorry," Tim's secretary told me. "Have you tried his cell?"

I tried Tim Dubois' cell phone but didn't get him. I called Doug Johnson over at Epic and he was visiting his parents in Marietta, Georgia. I tried Jim Ed Norman at Warner Brothers but couldn't locate him either.

Friday afternoon is a bad time to try and get hold of a record executive. I wanted somebody to hear these people though. I got Glen Middleworth, Pat Finch and Robin Palmer into a room. They were all on the creative staff there at EMI. The Wilkinsons sang *26 Cents* and another song for them. Glenn, Pat and Robin loved them as well as I did but, unfortunately those three guys didn't work for a record label and I was looking for a record deal for the Wilkinsons.

I thought The Wilkinsons should be recording and I thought *26 Cents* was a hit song. There was nothing I could do that day so I told the Wilkinsons to stay in touch with me and I would talk to the record labels the following week and try and set something up.

I loved this family from the start. There was just something special about them. Not only were they extremely talented, they had an appeal about them that made me just want to be around them, whether they were singing or not. I had to tell Steve, Chris, Amanda, Tyler and Kiaya goodbye that Friday afternoon but I had a feeling I would be seeing them again.

The following Monday I was on the phone to all of the labels. I was being told by a lot of people they had heard them a year before when they were in town. Everybody agreed they were great but they were just too young to sell records.

"But they don't sound like kids," was my response to that. "They can be huge in country music. Come on, listen to me."

Nobody did.

Remember Alan Jackson? I get the same kind of excitement with these people as I did him.

"Yeah, but he wasn't 13 years old, Charlie," somebody remarked.

"Well, David was a kid too, but he slew Goliath," I replied.

The Wilkinsons wrote me a nice letter and thanked me for what I had tried to do for them that Friday I had heard them sing. I called them up in Canada and told Steve I would continue to try and convince somebody to take a chance on them. They appreciated that as well.

Steve Wilkinson was a carpenter up in Canada, mostly building houses. He would continue using a hammer but it was eating away at his heart to bring his family to Nashville and record country music. It was now eating away at mine too. I knew The Wilkinsons were a star act. I just had to convince the powers that be in Nashville and sometimes that's like trying to mow grass with a rubber bladed lawn mower.

I have had reflux problems for years but one day I had a pain in my upper stomach and chest a little different than I had ever had before. My left arm was hurting as well. Dawn drove me to the emergency room at Summit Medical Center in Hermitage.

"So you wrote *Wanted*?" the guy taking my blood pressure asked me.

"Well, I wrote it with Alan Jackson," I told him.

I was laying on a table in a room at the emergency room.

"My wife sings," he informed me.

"Yeah?" I grunted and wondered why he was talking about music to me while I was possibly having a heart attack.

"We just live across the street from the hospital, right off of Central Pike," he said and started hooking up an EKG machine to my chest.

His name was Randy Farrow. I would later become close friends with him and his wife, Jill. I also would later rib him about trying to get me to help his wife get a record deal while I was having a heart attack.

They ran a urine test and the enzyme level indicated a possible heart attack. The cardiologist on duty suggested I be moved to the intensive care unit for the weekend, until they could do a cardiac catheterization test on Monday.

In intensive care they put liquid nitro into the IV as a precaution but at one point the nurse on duty had increased it to level higher than it should have been.

Betty and Kyle's father, Richard, were there with me. All of a sudden I started feeling week, then it got worse and I felt like I was drifting off and leaving my body.

"I think I'm dying," I told them.

"You're white as a sheet, Charlie," Betty said with deep concern and rushed over to take my hand.

Richard ran out into the hall looking for help.

"I feel so weak, honey," I told Betty and I really thought I was dying. I didn't hurt anywhere; I just felt really weak and had no control over my body at all, like I was drifting away.

Betty held my hand and turned toward the door and yelled "Somebody get in here!"

At that instance Richard arrived with a doctor and two nurses, one of whom was the intensive care nurse.

The doctor moved to beside me and started asking me things I don't recall. The nurse was checking the IV stand. Everything became a blur to me for the next few minutes.

After perhaps another 10-15 minutes I started feeling a little better. What had happened was the on duty intensive care nurse had mistakenly given me too much nitroglycerin and my blood pressure dropped to way below normal. I came close to losing consciousness. There was no physical damage done but it was a frightening experience, for me, Betty and Richard.

I stayed in intensive care all weekend and on Monday I met Dr. Hal Roseman, a cardiologist. He performed the cardiac catheterization procedure, where they enter the artery in your groin area by inserting a tiny tube and go up into the heart area to look around with a micro camera. It was really weird to be sedated, yet awake and aware of what was going on. I looked up at the TV monitor for a few minutes and could see my heart and what looked to me like a little wire moving around. My heart didn't look anything like I would have imagined. It was sort of round. I didn't really expect it to be heart shaped, like in valentines, but not round like that either.

Dr. Roseman had his head and upper body under a little tent, along with a nurse. He peeked out at me at one point.

"Charlie, I meant to get in bed early last night but I was out later than I had planned, so my hands are a little shaky," he said as he grinned at me.

I liked Hal Roseman from that moment on. We would later become close friends.

After conducting the catheterization, Dr. Roseman explained things to me.

"Charlie, you have a blockage that will require a couple of stints to be inserted into that artery," he told me.

He explained to me that he was going to leave the tube inserted into my artery and I was going to be transported by ambulance to Centennial Medical Center for the stint procedure.

"After that," Roseman told me, "We will bring you back here to Summit for the night. You should be able to go home sometime tomorrow."

Betty, Dawn and Kyle met me at Centennial. While they stayed in the waiting room until Dr. Roseman arrived and performed the stints implant. Afterward, the ambulance returned me to Summit Medical Center.

I couldn't believe how easy the procedure had gone. The hardest part was having to lay for about six hours with my right leg stretched straight out and not being able to bend it. I was told not to raise my head and upper body for those six hours as well.

It isn't easy lying flat on your back while trying to urinate in a jar.

"Nurse..."

Old Memories and Me

CHAPTER SEVENTEEN

Betty and I loved our new home. Once the drapes were all up, both downstairs and upstairs, it looked really nice. Blinds had been made for all of the windows and a western cedar fence was up and in place around the large back yard. The builder had put in the shrubbery in front of the house and one tree had been planted. We wanted a weeping willow in the back yard.

"I've hit rock again," I panted, sweat running down my face as I leaned on the post hole diggers I was using to dig down into the earth to plant the weeping willow we had bought. "I think our entire property must be sitting on a giant slab of rock."

It was September but it was still hot. Betty handed me the plastic Pepsi bottle she had been drinking from. I took a couple of sips.

"Maybe you should start digging in a different place," she suggested, her gray hair glistening in the bright sun.

I gave her a *you can't be serious* stare. "I'm not startin' another hole."

Betty giggled at me. "You want me to dig a while?" she offered.

"No, it's too hard to do," I assured her.

I went back to plunging the post diggers into the hole. I had already widened the hole somewhat with a shovel.

Clink. Another doggone rock. I got the shovel and used my foot to drive it down beside the rock and pried on all sides until I got it loose enough to dig it the rest of the way out with my gloved hands. I was sweating like a horse and my back was aching.

"This is the last thing I am going to try and plant out here," I gasped deeply, down on my knees and using my arm to wipe the perspiration from my forehead. I was 59 years old and about to turn 60 in a few more weeks. At that moment I felt 80.

We had run into the same problem on the other side of the backyard. There was a large rock underground over on that side that must have been at least 20x20. I had gotten two dump trucks full of dirt to build a mound there and we had planted gladiolas all over it. They grew so tall we had to stake them. They were absolutely gorgeous. There were purple ones, red, and white ones. They became Betty's favorite.

Old Memories and Me

We learned that Wilson County is full of underground rocks. The in ground swimming pool idea was scrapped. We would have had to have the yard dynamited to get through the rocks and that would have unsettled the foundation of the house.

I finally got the weeping willow tree planted. Sitting on rocks, it would take that thing twelve years just to get 30 feet high, but it is beautiful.

Keith Stegall recorded a new album on Mercury Records. It had been over twelve years since he had recorded himself, mostly producing others, especially Alan Jackson. Alan was still one of the hottest acts in country music and his albums were all multi-platinum. Keith had established himself as one of the best producers in the industry, something that came as no surprise to me. Keith included his and my song *Every Time It Rains* on his Mercury album.

Keith and I still saw each other a lot back then. We weren't writing together much any more but I would go by his office at Mercury or we would have lunch sometimes. He used to call me late at night after he got home and things kind of settled down in his busy world. We would just chat and catch up, talk about old times, things like that.

I recall Keith calling me about 9 o'clock one night.

"Charlie, Keith." He always did that and I had come to expect to hear him address me like that when I answered his phone calls. I think I would miss that if he hadn't done it.

"Hello, Keith," I said. "What's going on?"

"Well, I'm a little lost," he laughed.

"Whaddya mean, you're lost," I laughed also. "Where are you?"

That was kind of dumb of me to ask when he had just told me he was lost.

"I am in Canada somewhere, man," he told me.

"What are you doing in Canada?" I asked him.

"I came up here to see Terry Clark perform live," Keith said.

"Who's Terry Clark?"

"She's a singer Mercury is interested in signing," he informed me. "I flew up here and rented a car but I am having a time finding this town I am looking for."

"Well, you surely don't expect me to tell you how to find it," I laughed.

"No," he chuckled. "I just thought I would call you. I am by myself and just thought I would call while I am trying to find this place."

Keith Stegall and I were really close. We shared a lot of things, not only in our profession, but in our personal lives. If one of us had something that was upsetting to us we would tell the other about it. If we had some good news, we would share that as well. Keith and I have written sad songs together, happy songs, funny songs, been in the studio together, laughed together, and even cried together. I love him like my own brother.

I guess Keith finally found where he was going that night and got to hear Terry Clark as well. Mercury later signed her to a recording contract.

I continued to write and was writing some great songs, especially with James Dean Hicks, Rob Crosby and also with Mel Besher and Lee Bach. I had been thinking about producing for a while but I had just never really pursued it. I had produced about all of my own demos over the years and had plenty of experience in the studio. I had a good working relationship with a lot of great session musicians, so I finally thought I would give it a try.

I called Jim Ed Norman, the CEO at Warner Brother Records, and ask him to go to lunch, saying I wanted to talk to him about something. Jim Ed gave me an appointment date and I picked him up at Warner Brothers that day of the luncheon.

We had a nice lunch at *Amerigo's* and talked about the industry, among other things. I had known Jim Ed Norman for quite a while. However, for some reason I couldn't get up the nerve to ask him about producing an act for Warner Bothers. With all of my many years of experience in Nashville, record producing was uncharted waters for me.

After we finished lunch I drove him back to Warner Brothers. Just as he started to get out of my car, he looked over at me and asked, "By the way, what did you want to talk to me about?"

I just spit it out. "Well, I have been wanting to do some producing Jim Ed. I was wondering what you might think about that?"

"Do you have anybody already in mind you want to produce?" he inquired.

"No, but in this talented town I am sure I can find somebody," I smiled.

Jim smiled back, then told me seriously, "When you find that somebody, call me and I will give you a budget to take them into the studio."

Well, I'll be doggone, just like that he had agreed to allow me to give it a try.

On February 5th, 1997, Dawn gave birth to Franklin Delano Primm, my and Betty's second grandson. Dawn and Frank Primm had divorced and she had moved back home. Kyle was 5 years old but would be turning 6 in April. Good thing we had built a big house because we now were a family of five living there. Betty and I didn't mind though. We were a very close family and we had plenty of room now.

Del was an average size baby when he was born but soon after he gained weight pretty quickly. He was cute as he could be, looking like an infant wrestler. Kyle was born skinny and he was still thin. His

Old Memories and Me

hair wasn't exactly platinum any more but still blonde.

In the beginning I had wanted three children. Even though I was only the grandfather of two of them I felt like I had all three now.

I had been writing some with a young singer/songwriter in town who's name was Tracey Hagans. He was really good and a nice looking young man to boot. Tracey had also been working with Brad Allen, who I met while I was writing that one year at Tower Street Music. I knew several other great singers, both female and male, but after writing a couple of more times with Tracey and going into the studio with him singing the demos, I decided he was the singer I wanted to present to Jim Ed Norman at Warner Brothers. Since he was already involved with Brad Allen I didn't want to cut Brad out of anything so I told him we would produce Tracey together.

I wanted to make sure we had a few great songs together before I called Jim Ed so we started looking for songs. I called all of the big publishers in Nashville and some of the smaller ones I knew had good catalogs. I threw a couple of my own songs into the stack and after Tracey, Brad and I agreed on four songs we felt strongly about, I called Jim Ed Norman.

"Jim Ed, I have found the act I would like to produce," I told him over the phone. "His name is Tracey Hagen."

"Do you really believe in him, Charlie?" Jim Ed asked me.

"Yes, I do, very strongly," I assured him.

"Alright then, give me until tomorrow to speak with Danny Kee and then you give him a call to come in and meet with him for the budget. "

"Don't you want to hear Tracey first?" I asked, a bit surprised.

"You said you believe in him and that is good enough for me," Jim Ed Norman told me.

I had been in Nashville 28 years at that time and I had never had anybody show that much confidence in me before. I mean, there were people that believed in me, but Jim Ed Norman was willing to allow me to spend several thousand dollars in the studio on an artist he never heard or even laid eyes on before, strictly based on my personal opinion. That was quite a compliment to me.

I met with Danny Kee at Warner Brother Records a few days later and we went over a budget to record three songs and a production contract that gave Warner Brothers the first option to sign Tracey Hagen and they would have 60 days to decide that once I had turned the project in. If they should decide to pass I would have the option to take the master and pitch Tracey elsewhere.

I co-produced Tracey with Brad Allen as planned and we decided on using Masterphonic Studio. We had a great session with some of the best session players in Nashville, or the world for that matter. After we finished the session and mixed it, I turned it in to Danny Kee at Warner. Then we waited.

The contract gave Warner Brothers a lot longer time to make a decision, but after only a few weeks Jim Ed Norman called me and told me he was very pleased with the job I had done on producing Tracey Hagans but they had decided to sign Michael Peterson. Warner was only going to sign one more male act for the time being and they thought Peterson offered more of what they were looking for at the moment.

I was naturally disappointed but I certainly didn't question the decision. As it turned out Michael Peterson did very well on Warner Brothers for a while.

This left me open to pitch the master of Tracy to other labels. The first person I called was Doug Johnson. Doug had recently left Epic and taken over as head of Giant Records.

"I like him," Doug told me after listening to the session. "When can you bring him in and let me meet him?"

"Whenever you like," I said.

Doug gave me a date and I took Tracey in to meet him. Talks take a while, then negotiations, then a contract. Doug finally offered to take Tracey in on a trial basis to see how everything would turn out before signing him to a full recording contract. Doug Johnson told me as much as he would like for me to produce him, he felt he should work with Tracey and do the session himself. I didn't want to knock Tracey out of an opportunity to get a record deal so I stepped aside, along with Brad Allen.

Not that I was upset with Doug Johnson, but I stayed away from the sessions when they went in to record. Tracey called me later and told me he wasn't happy with the direction Doug was trying to take him. That happens a lot in this business. A producer sees things one way and the artist another. It is not a knock on either the artist or the producer. It is just the nature of the beast, so to speak.

Eventually Tracey Hagans and Giant Records parted ways. I remained friends with Doug Johnson. It was just a business thing that didn't work out. I pitched Tracey Hagans to a couple more labels but nothing happened. I really felt bad for Tracey. He was a talented young man, as both a songwriter and singer.

Several months later Jim Ed Norman would allow me to take another new act into the studio and produce for Warner Brothers.

Betty and I loved to sit on our front porch steps late in the afternoon and talk. The deck out back of the house is 10x20 and a lot larger than our small front porch but we just enjoyed sitting on those steps and looking out into the cul-de-sac in the evenings. Sometimes one of the neighbors would walk over and talk with us for a while. We had great neighbors. On one side were Brian and Michelle Sharp, with their two little girls, Emily and Emma. Brian is a doctor at Summit Medical Center emergency room. On the other side were The Young's, A.A. and Roberta, and their three teenage children, Angelia, Robert and Ashley.

Old Memories and Me

A.A. was a railroad detective for years until he retired from that job and went to work in security at Opryland Hotel. He had also been my *mister fix it* when something broke around my house. He prefers to be called Double A.

Up on one corner of the cul-de-sac were Rick and Becky Fultz, and their daughter Amanda, who was close to Kyle's age. Rick was with the Corp Of Engineers. On the other corner were Malcolm and Peggy Sloan, with their two daughters, Annie and Allison. Malcolm is a computer analyst and Peggy worked for Purity Dairies for years.

On holidays such as 4th of July and New Years everybody in our cul-de-sac would get together and shoot fireworks. Brian Sharp and I would always buy a couple of grand finale *bad mothers* to finish off the night with.

Sometimes, before dark on the 4th of July, Double A would set up his gas grill at the end of his driveway and we would have a cookout. Double A was our chief cook and a good one too. Later, well after dark, we would shoot off the fireworks.

Those were some wonderful days I won't ever forget. Good neighbors, good friends, just doing the simple things in life that are so much fun. About everybody has moved now, except for the Young's and my family. Time marches on but memories hang around forever.

The Wilkinsons finally took the plunge and moved to Nashville. Two weeks after they arrived they went out to the Broken Spoke on Trinity Lane to see songwriter Reese Mason perform at a writers' night. Reese convinced Lee Rascone, who was in charge of the writers' night at the Spoke for years, to let The Wilkinsons get onstage and perform a couple of songs. According to Steve Wilkinson, an independent promotion guy by the name of Keith Stansill heard them that Friday night and started phoning people he knew in the music business, I suppose much like I did a year or so before. Steve says his cell phone started ringing Monday morning from record labels and other music business people.

Steve Wilkinson called me.

"Charlie, man about every record label in town is calling me wanting to talk to us about signing a record deal," he told me. "All of a sudden things are getting crazy."

"Wow," I responded. "What are you going to do, I mean, have you decided on any label or anything?"

"No," Steve said. "I was hoping I could talk with you and get some advice on this, Charlie."

"Sure, I will be glad to talk with you," I told him. "I don't know how much I can help but I will sure try."

"We don't really know a lot of folks here, you know," Steve said. "You are about the only person I know that has a lot of experience in the business that I would listen to and trust to give me an unbiased opinion."

That really flattered me. "I appreciate that, Steve," I told him sincerely. "When would you like to get together?"

"The sooner the better," he said. "I have labels calling me every day now."

I think the thing that made a difference in all of the labels being interested now, where as they were not before, was that Mike Curb had taken a chance on 14 year old LeeAnn Rimes and signed her to Curb and released *Blue*. The results of that great move are history and it proved a teenager could sell records.

Over the next ten days I met with Steve Wilkinson at least five times. On two of those meetings Amanda and Tyler were with us and on another Chris and Kiaya joined in for a family meeting.

MCA, Giant and Lyric Street were all heavily involved with trying to sign The Wilkinsons at this point. Arista was showing interest as well. The heads of MCA, Giant and Lyric Street, along with staff members, had already taken The Wilkinsons to dinner. A large management firm was also trying to sign them and they had their preference of which record label The Wilkinsons should sign with.

My good friend Vince Gill had invited them backstage at the Grand Ole Opry one Saturday night and surprised them by allowing them to come on stage and perform in one of his slots. Vince was signed to MCA as an artist and I am sure that label had asked Vince for a little help in the matter. I called Vince and told him The Wilkinsons had been consulting me for my opinion on what to do and I wanted him to know I didn't want any of this to interfere with our relationship. Vince assured me that it wouldn't and I believed him. I really already knew that. Vince is a great guy and just as I was, trying to help out wherever he could. His main focus was his belief in this talented singing family.

I met Steve and family at one of our favorite eating places, The International Market, a Thai food place. It was time for them to make a decision and they wanted to get it over with.

"Well, you can't go wrong with any of these labels," I told them. "They are all great opportunities."

They all agreed. For over a week we had talked about the pros and cons of each label and what they had to offer. MCA had the largest roster, with super stars such as Vince, George Strait, Reba McEntire and a host of others. With Disney owning Lyric Street I think a movie had been mentioned.

"Do you wanna make movies or records?" I ribbed The Wilkinsons.

"You know," Amanda said, "I think the hardest part for me is that all of the people at each of the labels have been so nice and you hate to tell any of them no."

Tyler and Steve agreed with that. "It's a tough decision, man,"

Old Memories and Me

Steve sighed.

For the next thirty minutes or so I listened to Steve, Amanda, Tyler, and Chris as they openly discussed their individual viewpoints on the matter. It was quite a decision to make but it had to be made.

Steve looked at me, eyebrows raised, and grinned. "What do you think Charlie?"

"Well," I sighed. "It's a decision you guys have to make, but…"

Steve raised his brows even more. "But what?"

"Well, I have been going over everything in my mind, I mean everything that has taken place in the past couple of weeks. I keep coming back to the same thing," I told them.

"What?"

"You told me when the labels took you to dinner that the heads of the labels and a few staff members were there," I said. "But with Giant Records, Doug Johnson brought along his wife."

"Yes, he did." Steve said.

"It may not be a big deal," I continued, "but you guys have stressed a family relationship and atmosphere, and when I think about that aspect of it, and how many artist are already ahead of you on the other two labels, I keep coming up with Giant Records. Giant really only has Clay Walker over there that has had hit records before." I shrugged, almost apologetic, wondering if what I said was reason enough for them to pick Giant Records.

"That does make sense," Steve said and glanced at his family members.

We talked a while longer and left. I went home. About two hours later Steve called me.

"I have been thinking about what you said about a family atmosphere," he said. "I just have a gut feeling we should sign with Giant."

"Then do it," I said. "If that is how you feel." Then I added, "but make sure it is something you really want and not something I might have influenced. As I have said, you really can't go wrong with any of the other labels."

My opinions had been difficult all along because I was well acquainted with Tony Brown at MCA and had great respect for his abilities. His success and reputation certainly spoke volumes for him. I didn't really know anybody that well at Lyric Street but Randy Goodrum had an excellent track record in the business.

I had known Doug Johnson, the head of Giant Records, the longest and had dealt with him in the business more frequently. I also knew him pretty well personally. Doug had talked to me about perhaps coming to work for him at Giant after the first of the year to do some A&R work there. I honestly didn't allow that part to enter into any of my opinions or suggestions to The Wilkinsons. I tried to be as biased as I could, as Steve Wilkinson had expected me to be. I can honestly say that

I was. "Well, our lawyer is advising us differently and the management firm we will probably sign with is too," Steve told me. "I just have this feeling about Giant though, and what you have said makes a lot of sense. There is definitely a family atmosphere every time we visit with Giant Records."

"It's your decision, Steve." I reminded him. "Your lawyer and manger aren't the ones signing the contracts and doing the recording. Of course, neither am I."

Steve was silent for a few seconds. Then, just like that he said, "I am going to call Doug Johnson and tell him we are signing with Giant Records."

Steve Wilkinson called Doug Johnson. Doug Johnson called me. "Come on down here, Charlie," he said jubilantly. "We're going to have a party and celebrate."

The Wilkinsons first single on Giant Records was *26 Cents*, the same song they had sang to me at EMI nearly three years before when Amanda was 13 and Tyler 11. I had practically begged this town to sign them to a record deal. Now, Amanda was 16 years old and singing the lead on the #1 record in America.

I couldn't help but smile.

The only Tornado I had ever seen was when I was a kid back on my daddy's small farm in Watts Mill. The day it hit near our house we had been picking cotton and were trying to tie the burlap sheets where we had emptied our sacks full of cotton. All of a sudden the wind got so strong it nearly snatched the sheets from our hands. The one I was tying was stretched out on the other end where nobody was holding it as though somebody was, flapping wildly in the air, cotton blowing away in every direction. Fortunately, none of us were injured and no property was damaged badly, but that was a scary day.

Then, one afternoon in 1998, I witnessed my second Tornado.

Dawn, Del and I had just finished buying a few groceries at Kroger Grocery in Hermitage and had carried our grocery bags out to put them in my van. The wind started blowing furiously. The sky overhead was as dark as night.

"Turn on the radio, Daddy," Dawn said. "See if there is a Tornado in the area."

While Dawn hurriedly put the groceries in the back of the van I jumped into the front seat and turned on the radio. Instantly I heard the report.

"A tornado has hit East Nashville, leaving extensive damage and is now approaching the Hermitage area. Everybody in that area should take cover immediately," the announcer on the radio warned.

I looked out through the window shield and saw the huge

Old Memories and Me

funnel coming across the land across from Kroger where President Andrew Jackson's historical home is. I jumped back out of the van. Dawn had seen the funnel as well and had grabbed Del and was already headed back into Kroger.

"Run, Daddy," she yelled.

I was right behind her and as we approached the electronic doors at the front of the store, they were opening and closing rapidly, as though invisible people were passing through. We ran inside and the Kroger employees were instructing everybody to go to the back of the store, away from the glass front.

I thought about Betty and Kyle alone at home and worried about their safety. Once Dawn, Del and I were at the rear of the store I tried calling home on my cell.

All circuits are busy.

A young black man came running to where we were, out of breath and looking like he had seen hell itself. He was holding his chest. I thought he was having a heart attack. We got him to sit down and lean against the wall.

"Are you alright?" I asked him with concern.

"Oh man," he said, his voice quivering as he shook his head. "I have been in a hurricane down in Florida, but it was nothing like this."

The man calmed down enough to explain to us that he was a truck driver and was passing by up on Lebanon Road when the Tornado hit. He said the wind lifted his eighteen-wheeler up off the ground and set it back down just long enough for him to jump out and run. He had run down across the parking lot and into the store.

The Kroger building shook somewhat but stayed intact. We could hear what sounded like a giant freight train roaring by outside. I feared for Betty and Kyle. My cell still wouldn't work. I headed toward the front of the store to use a land phone.

"Daddy," Dawn called out. "Don't go up there yet."

By the time I reached the service counter at the front of the store the storm had subsided some. I reached over the counter and grabbed a telephone and dialed my house number. It took several rings but Betty finally answered.

"Betty, are you and Kyle alright?" I gasped into the phone.

"Yes," she answered. "We got in the closet under the stairs. Where are you?"

"We are in Kroger's," I told her, so relieved she and Kyle were alright.

Dawn and Del joined me.

"They're both alright," I told Dawn.

She let out a sigh of relief and hugged Del.

"I think it has passed," I told Betty. "We're coming home."

"Be careful," she warned. "It's still raining hard here but the wind has let up."

Once outside in the parking lot we saw the truck drivers' eighteen-wheeler laying on its side in the parking lot. The wind had blown it some 150 yards from Lebanon Road to where it lay in a bent and twisted heap.

The wind had ripped one of those grocery cart holders from the asphalt and had thrown it into the back of my van, making a large dent in the rear door.Other than that the van seemed alright. Dawn, Del and I drove home, seeing trees that had been ripped from the ground and lay around like big broken toothpicks. Some buildings had windows blown out and shingles ripped from roofs. A couple of houses on down Lebanon road had been damaged more severely but for the most part the storm appeared to have lifted back up after touching down briefly in the Hermitage and Mt Juliet areas.

At my house we found only a few slats in the wooden fence were broken but that was all the damage we had. We were very fortunate that day and I thank God for keeping my family safe through that frantic ordeal.

Betty had developed a deep cough. I finally talked her into going to see Dr. Friddell. After listening to Betty's lungs with a stethoscope he decided to take a chest x-ray. I waited with Betty in the examining room after the x-ray. When Dr. Friddell came back into the room I knew, before he ever said a word, I just knew with a deep fear what he was going to say. There were tears in the corners of his eyes.

"It's the cancer," he told us in a low and caring voice. He had been our family doctor and friend for the past twenty-six years and it wasn't easy for him to tell us such bad news.

I think I swallowed my heart when he said those words, *it's the cancer*. Betty didn't say a word. I knelt down beside the chair she was seated in and took her hand in mine. "Are you sure," I asked Dr. Friddell.

"Yes," he said. "It's pretty large."

I wanted to scream. Instead I choked back my tears and squeezed Betty's hand and looked at her.

"Well," she sighed. "I guess we can go home now, Charlie."

Her eyes were moist but she wasn't crying. She was one of the strongest persons I have ever known.

We went home and talked about it.

"I'm not taking radiation again," Betty informed me. "I am tired of being sick. I hated radiation before and I will hate it this time."

"Oh, honey," I said, my voice pleading. "You may have to take it."

"You don't know how bad that stuff is on your system and your entire body," she said.

Of course I didn't know because I hadn't had to experience it first hand, just seeing her go through it nine years earlier.

Dr. Friddell scheduled Betty an appointment with Dr.

Old Memories and Me

Espenshade, a lung specialist. At his office they did another x-ray and determined the malignant growth was the size of a baseball. They then gave Betty a breathing test to see if she had enough breathing capacity to perform surgery to remove the cancer. They would have to remove a good portion of her lung. She didn't pass the breathing test.

"We will have to try and treat it with radiation," Dr. Espenshade told us.

Betty and I talked it over again, about the radiation treatments. Dawn also talked to her. She decided to take the treatments, I believe more for Dawn and I than for herself.

An appointment was set up at Baptist hospital to see Dr. Burton Grant, an oncologist.

Betty and I immediately found him to be a caring man, not just a doctor always talking in medical terms. He was also a Christian. I felt good that Betty was in his care.

"So, you are in the music business?" Dr. Grant asked me. I assume he had seen my occupation in Betty's files.

"Yes," I replied. I am a songwriter."

"My daughter is in the music business," he told me.

"Oh, what does she do?" I asked.

"She sings and she writes as well," he answered.

"What is her name?" I inquired.

"Amy Grant," he smiled.

I smiled back. "Really? " Then added, "She is a talented young lady."

"Thank you," Dr. Grant said. "I think so." He smiled again.

He told us Betty would need to take thirty radiation treatments.

"Thirty?" Betty asked with some apprehension.

"Because of the size of the tumor you will need that many treatments," Dr. Grant informed her.

"What are her chances?" I asked and was afraid of the answer.

"Well, that is actually in God's hands," he sighed.

Betty would have to take the radiation five days a week for six weeks. She would start the following Monday.

As we left Baptist Hospital that day Betty seemed a bit angry. "I had to beat cancer once," she stated without looking at me. "I don't see why I have to beat it again."

I was in a deep depression over Betty having cancer again. I was afraid before, this time I was petrified. This time it was more serious. This time she was out on a limb with no safety net. No surgery. No doctors telling us they thought they had gotten all of the cancer and felt she would make it.

I just couldn't lose her. I have always talked to God all

during the day, driving down the road, in a restaurant, anywhere and everywhere, and at night before going to sleep. Now I was praying every hour or so, begging God to spare Betty and to heal her from the cancer. I asked my church to pray for her, and all my friends.

That Sunday at church I went down during the invitation and re-dedicated my life to Jesus. I held my pastor Dean Haun's hands and he prayed with me as I wept. I told him I wanted to be baptized again. I felt a need deep in my heart and soul to be washed clean again. Two Sunday's later I was baptized for the second time in my life. The first time I was 14 years old. This time I was 60.

I felt clean again but I was still afraid.

Betty completed the 30 radiation treatments. Dr. Grant x-rayed her and told us there was no sign of the tumor. Before we could get too excited about that he warned us it could now just be microscopic. He wanted Betty to come back in thirty days for another x-ray.

Betty had already lost some weight and didn't feel good at all. She hardly felt like going out anywhere. I didn't work a lot so I could stay home with her. I wanted to be with her every minute I possibly could. I kept trying to make myself believe God was going to answer my prayers and spare her again, just like he had before, but in the pit of my stomach I had this constant sick feeling I was going to lose the love of my life. I would get off by myself and pray and I would cry. I would sometimes hold Betty's hand and pray. I think she had already accepted the fact she was dying.

"If something happens to me," she told me just before we went back to see Dr. Grant to see if the tumor had returned, "I want you to be strong so you can take care of Dawn, Kyle and Del. They will really need you."

"Don't talk like that," I said, with teary eyes and I kissed her cheek. "You are going to be alright. The cancer isn't back."

They did the x-ray. It was back. I can't describe how much my heart broke at that moment and how everything in my world just seemed to collapse.

Dr. Burton Grant told us he was sorry and recommended Betty see a doctor about chemotherapy. He couldn't give her any more radiation. Betty didn't want to go see the chemo doctor but at my pleading request she finally gave in and went.

"I can give you a couple of treatments a week for a while and extend your life for perhaps a few months, but I can't cure you," the doctor told her. "I'm sorry."

I had just thought I couldn't feel any more down and depressed but my spirit and life sank a little more when he said that.

"I know the chemo will make me even more sicker than I already am," Betty told the doctor. "I had rather enjoy what time I have left the best I can without all of that."

Betty never ceased to amaze me with her strength and

Old Memories and Me

willingness to accept even the worst of news. During the conversation with the chemotherapist she never showed any signs of fear or depression. She had already accepted her faith some time ago.

"I understand your decision," the doctor told her. "I wish all of my terminal patients had the strength and understanding you have. Some of them plead for one more treatment, just one more to see if it can help."

He told us Betty might have six to eight months left to live.

I left the doctor's office with tears in my eyes, biting my lip to keep from breaking down and bawling like a baby. I squeezed Betty's hand as we walked to the car. I couldn't think of anything to say. I'm not sure I could have even talked at that moment anyway.

"It will be alright, Charlie," Betty told me and squeezed our hands together tighter. She even managed to smile at me.

"No it won't," I whispered and lost it completely. I threw both arms around my darling, my whole world, and cried so hard I trembled all over.

There in that parking lot my dying wife was trying to console me, when it should have been the other way around. Of course it had always been that way. Betty had always picked me up and gave me strength.

Oh Lord, what would I ever do without her.

That Christmas we tried to treat it as a normal Christmas, putting up a tree and decorating it together, having a big meal and exchanging gifts on Christmas Eve night as we had done for forty years. It was different though and we all knew it. This would most likely be Betty's last Christmas with us.

CHAPTER EIGHTEEN

New Years didn't bring any cheer to the Craig household. Time was slipping away and I was losing grip on trying to hold on to everything I lived and breathed for. I would still have Dawn, Kyle and Del, and I loved them dearly, but at the time all I could think about was how could I possibly live without Betty once she was gone.

Kyle would only be six years old in April but he would come to me and put his arms around me, knowing I was sad. He was too young to really comprehend what was happening to his nanny but he knew something bad was wrong.

"I love you, papa," he would say and give me a kiss on the cheek. "I will take care of you."

Kyle had lived with Betty and I a big part of his young life and was almost like a son. Of course we knew he wasn't and his dad, Richard Smith, knew how close Betty and I were with Kyle but never resented it.

Betty stayed in bed a lot but she would come downstairs and sit at the dinette table and drink a cup of coffee and smoke a cigarette while we talked. Yes, she still smoked. She had said there was no reason to quit now. I didn't bother her about it anymore.

On some days we would sit out on the front steps and talk, just like we had done since we first moved into our new house. That was still her favorite place to sit and talk.

I think by this time I was just numb and living every day in a haze. I was hurting and I was afraid but in some strange way I was like somebody else and this wasn't me and not happening in my life.

I had to do some work and a couple of days a week I would go down to music row for a few hours. I would call Betty about every thirty minutes to check on her. Dawn was at work, Kyle was at school in first grade and Del was in day care. Michelle Sharp would also keep check on her for me.

Keith Stegall had put a song of mine on hold called *Love Is Alive* for Terry Clark, a song I had co-written with Shane Teeters and Bruce Boutin. As it turned out Mark Wills recorded the song. Carson Chamberlain had produced Mark's album and had all of the writers and publishers over to Mercury to hear our cuts. There were some great ballads on the album.

Old Memories and Me

After the listening party Carson called me off to the side and told me they were going to release one of the ballads as the first single but he felt like *Love Is Alive* would eventually be a single.

They kept having number one records with the ballads and never got around to releasing an up-tempo from that album. I couldn't blame them. You don't stop riding a winning horse and the ballads were doing great. Besides, it was a platinum album so my co-writers and I did alright on sales.

Betty loved the baked squash from *The Cooker* in Hermitage and since she was too sick to eat out any more I would bring her home squash and a cornbread muffin. I liked their chicken tenders and I also loved their squash. We would sometimes eat up in the bedroom and talk. She wasn't eating a lot. She kept her Pepsi beside the bed though. For years she had kept a Pepsi, with the twist off top, by our bed or on a table beside a chair where she might read or watch television. That and her black coffee, and of course her cigarettes. The pain had set in some but she refused to take morphine or any other heavy pain medication.

Betty had cut her long hair short and even though I loved it long I wasn't about to say anything. She was completely gray now and very thin. It broke my heart more to see her deteriorating right before my eyes. Except for her kidney problem, she had always looked like the perfect picture of health, so beautiful and extremely well figured.

My two sisters, Ruby and Dot, along with my brothers-in-law, Bob and Jerry, came over from South Carolina to visit. Betty came downstairs a lot while they were here and sat on the couch to talk with them. She was weak, but still strong enough not to remain completely bedridden. Soon after they had left, Betty's twin, Bobbie Bolt, their other sister, Juanita McGuirt, came up to spend a week with her. The three of them had always been very close.

While Bobbie and Juanita were here with Betty I spent some time pitching songs to the record labels. My heart wasn't into it but I had to keep trying to move forward even though the future wouldn't include Betty. I tried not to think about that as much as my mind and heart would allow me to. There are no words I can say that can describe what I was going through. I was even praying and asking God to take me instead. I knew now He wasn't going to heal her and I had started asking Him to ease her pain and not let her suffer.

I drove out to Percy Priest Lake one afternoon and parked. I sat there looking out across the water, thinking about my life with Betty, how we first met, the things we did back in South Carolina after we first married, like leaving each other love notes, just remembering all of the wonderful times. I wept.

Betty had always loved Rob Crosby's singing and while Bobbie and Juanita were here she wanted them to hear him. Rob was kind enough to come over late one afternoon and sing several songs for them, and especially for Betty.

Knowing that Betty was dying I knew I wanted to keep as many memories of my life with her that I could. I had a few videotapes but there were hundreds of pictures in one of the storage rooms, some dating back to our honeymoon. I started going through those photographs, a lot of them black and white from the 50s and early 60s, making sure they were still there. They were becoming like precious jewels to me now. Looking at those pictures gave me both a wonderful feeling and a sad one. Naturally, I cried as I went through them.

I don't know what made me think of them, I suppose those old wonderful pictures did it, but three lines started going through my head.

If forever should end today
And there's no tomorrow for us
What a day yesterday was.

As difficult as it was, I got my guitar out and started singing those lines, coming up with a melody as I went along. I knew those three lines would be the chorus. I started writing a verse.

Looking through these old photographs
Don't they bring some good memories back
Some of them make us laugh, some make us cry
I'm glad we kept all of these souvenirs, to prove that our love was here
Look at how happy we were, pictures don't lie

Then, that chorus....

If forever should end today
And there's no tomorrow for us
What a day yesterday was

There was one old black and white picture made right after my and Betty's honeymoon, in 1957. She had my old Silvertone guitar in her hands, pretending to play it. She had on a pair of shorts and looked like a million bucks. I was cutting up in the picture, caught in a pose while dancing. I knew that had to be the first line of the second verse.

Here's one of us with you calm and cool
Look at me acting a fool....

It was beautiful, one of the prettiest songs I had ever written. It was going to be my farewell song to Betty. I took my guitar and went into the bedroom and sang what I had started for her. I couldn't get through it without crying as I sang it.

"That is so beautiful, honey," she told me, tears in her eyes as

Old Memories and Me

well. "Thank you."

We held each other for a long while, like we didn't want to ever let go. I was crying so much my lips were quivering.

That afternoon I tried to finish the song but I just couldn't. It was getting to me and was way to painful to write now.

A few days later my friend Mel Besher came by to see how I was holding up and to visit Betty. While he was there I showed him what I had of the song and asked him to help me finish it. I couldn't do it by myself without breaking down.

Mel helped me finish *What A Day Yesterday Was* and I went into the studio to demo it. I asked Mel to sing the demo. Again it was just too much for me to handle right then.

After we had demoed the song I sent it out to Alan Jackson's house. The next day he called me.

"Charlie, I really like that song *What A Day Yesterday Was*," he told me. "Don't let anybody else have it. I want to record it on my next album."

As he had always done, when he personally would tell me he was going to cut one of my songs, Alan recorded *What A Day Yesterday Was*. He did a wonderful job with the song, even using a mandolin as I had on the demo. It was beautiful. He sent me an advance copy and I played it for Betty. She loved it. We both cried while we listened to it but it was a mixture of both sadness of the inevitable to come and the happy memories of the past.

Dawn wanted to spend as much time with her mother as she could before she died, so she got a 4-month leave from her work so she could stay home. Doug Johnson had asked me to do some A&R work for him at Giant Records. A&R stands for Artist & Repertoire, a person that looks for songs for the artist to record. Since it was only about ten hours a week he wanted me to work, and with Dawn home with Betty, I accepted the job. I gave what I made to Dawn since she didn't have any income now that she was on leave.

Working for Doug gave me an opportunity to try and get my mind off of things a little. It didn't help a lot but at least I was occupied enough that I wasn't crying twenty-four hours a day. I am sure I was keeping Betty from getting some rest by always going into our bedroom and talking, seeing if she needed anything, just wanting to be near her and fearing every conversation with her might be our last one.

One morning I got a call from a man named David Godbold. He informed me that he was the Chairman of the Board for the South Carolina Entertainment Hall Of Fame.

"Charlie, the state of South Carolina wants to honor you by inducting you into the South Carolina Entertainment Hall Of Fame this year," David Godbold told me.

I thought I had misunderstood him.

"They want to induct me?" I asked surprised.

"Yes," he told me. "It is something that is long overdue."

Naturally, I was flattered. "Wow," I replied. "That is quite an honor and I do appreciate that."

Godbold told me the induction ceremony was to be held in Myrtle Beach, South Carolina and told me the date. I explained to him that my wife was dying and that I didn't want to leave her, in fear that she would pass away while I was gone. I suggested that I have one of my sisters attend the ceremony and accept the award for me. David gave me his sympathy and told me that would fine for my sister to accept my induction on my behalf.

I decided to tape an acceptation speech and send it to David Godbold. I felt if my home state was going to bestow such a high honor on me at least I could send my gratitude in a video in my absence.

Alan Jackson had a video crew he used on his shows and volunteered their services to video me. We taped my acceptance speech but it turned out we didn't need it.

"Charlie, David Godbold here," he said in a phone call to me. "We want to come to Nashville, if it is agreeable with you, and induct you into the Hall Of Fame on the *Crook And Chase* television show."

I didn't know what to say. That really touched me.

"I hate for you to go to that trouble," I told him.

"Charlie, you are one of our state's legendary songwriters and we want to honor you in person," David Godbold told me. "We are so sorry about Betty's illness and this will give her an opportunity to watch the ceremony on television. I know she is as proud of you as the state of South Carolina is."

I couldn't believe they were going to this much extreme on my behalf. I was, and still am, just a plain and simple man from Watts Mill, South Carolina. We didn't even have a traffic light back there when I was growing up. Now they were going to put me into a hall of fame.

"We're going to induct a couple of other songwriting South Carolina boys along with you," Godbold told me. "Rob Crosby and Buddy Brock."

Of course, I knew both of them well. We were friends and had written a number of songs together, especially Rob Crosby and I.

Betty and Dawn were so excited for me. So were my sisters and Betty's sisters. Both my and Betty's nieces and nephews were all informed and everybody was going to be watching the show on *Crook And Chase*.

On the day of the show and induction, I wore a black suit with a blue shirt, collar unbuttoned. Rob Crosby, Buddy Brock and myself were taken to a room backstage in the building where Lorraine Crook and Charlie Chase taped their television show. Lorraine's husband, Jim Owen was the show's producer. He was also a native of South Carolina

Old Memories and Me

and already a member of the Entertainment Hall Of Fame there. Jim met with us back stage and went over the procedure we would go through once we went onto the set with Loraine and Charlie. We were each asked to perform a portion of one of our hit songs. I had thought about singing *Wanted* but that song is in ¾ timing and very difficult for me personally to perform with just my guitar without jumping timing. I do fine as long as a band is backing me but just me and myself, it scares me to death. Therefore, I decided to perform *Between An Old Memory And Me*.

While we were lounging around in that room, one of the show's staff members suggested we write a funny song about Lorraine Crook. They wanted it to be a total surprise to her. So, Buddy, Rob and I came up with a little humorous ditty for our lovely co-hostess.

Shortly thereafter, the three of us were escorted to a place just out of sight of the shows set, where it was already in progress. While standing there, waiting to be inducted into the South Carolina Entertainment Hall Of Fame, a funny thought crossed my mind. I recalled my 12th grade homeroom high school teacher telling me, "*Charles Craig, if you don't change your attitude, you won't ever amount to anything.*"

To that teacher's credit, she was absolutely right at the time. I suppose somewhere along the way I must have changed my attitude.

Then, Lorraine and Charlie were introducing us to the audience, both there in attendance and on television. Rob Crosby, Buddy Brock and I strolled onto the set carrying our guitars. We sat down on the three stools provided for us and Lorraine Crook explained what we were there for. Charlie Chase joined in to help name some of the hits the three of us had written in our careers and told the audience we each were going to perform one of those hits. They started with me.

I sang the first verse of *Between An Old Memory And Me*. When I had finished Charlie Chase pointed out how he liked the low note I hit when singing the line, *pouring whiskey down*, and he attempted to mimic me on that line.

Rob Crosby performed a little of his *She's A Natural* and Buddy Brock did a portion of *Ain't Nothing Wrong With The Radio*.

Charlie Chase mentioned that some songs are written in all kind of places. He asked where the strangest place was any of us had written a song and what had we written it down on. Rob Crosby pointed to me to answer that question.

"Toilet paper," I said. "I guess I should have given Charmin co writer."

"You don't have to tell us where you wrote it," Charlie Chase laughed, "but is it a song we would recognize?"

"I hope not," I said and grinned.

That little segment got a good laugh from everybody, including the audience.

Then, Lorraine said, "Look at the monitor, Charlie. There's a young gentleman that wants to say something to you."

They showed a video Alan Jackson had taped on his tour bus out on the road, to congratulate me on my induction, and as he put it, *whatever they're doing to you over there*. Alan said, "You are a good ole boy that writes hits songs and you wrote with me when I first came to Nashville, when nobody else would. You paid me to sing demos when I didn't have much to do back then. I appreciate that and I'll always remember it." Then he added, "I've cut a lot of your songs, and in fact, I've got one of your songs on my new album." He was referring to *What A Day Yesterday Was*. It was really nice what he had said about me and I was both grateful and humbled by his remarks on that video.

Next they showed a video Aaron Tippin had sent in to congratulate the three of us. Aaron and Buddy Brock had come to Nashville together and had known each other a long time. Of course I had become best of friends with Aaron myself. They had edited out the part where Aaron had talked to and about me, I suppose because Alan had already done that and they wanted to keep things even. That was understandable. Later, they sent me the video of Aaron and I was able to see and hear his tribute to me.

"We understand the three of you wrote a song backstage," Lorraine said. "Is this your first time to write together, the three of you?"

"I have written with both Rob and Buddy," I told her. "But this is the first song the three of us have written together."

"One of the crew members of the show asked us to write a song about our host and hostess," Rob explained to her.

The three of us sang the song.

> *She might be good-looking, but Lorraine's cooking*
> *Ain't nothing to brag about*
> *She says you can't beat it, but Charlie won't eat it*
> *And even the dog spits it out*

It was a hoot and the audience loved it, and you know Charlie Chase did.

Then, David Godbold and Jim Owen came onto the set and Rob Crosby, Buddy Brock and I were officially inducted into the South Carolina Entertainment Hall Of Fame. They gave each of us a gold-framed certificate that had been signed by Governor Hodges. It was really nice.

That will always be one of the highlights of my career.

Betty was getting weaker and losing weight rapidly. The end was near and I knew it. I woke up every morning afraid she would be already gone. There were things that had to be done that I dreaded doing. They couldn't be avoided though, and needed to be taken care of soon.

Old Memories and Me

We didn't own any burial plots, so I had to go out to Mt. Juliet Funeral Home to talk to them about buying a plot in the Mt. Juliet Cemetery. That is where Betty had said she wanted to be buried after we had talked it over and I had agreed that would be a place I would like as well. The owners had taken me to the cemetery and showed me the plots that were available. That was really tough, knowing I was about to buy a place to bury the love of my life.

They didn't have many plots left where you could put up headstones. Land was getting scarce, plus the upkeep was easier with the flat markers. I wanted a headstone.

Near the back of the country cemetery was a plot that had room for three burials. It was near a fence and some trees. I could see cows grazing in a pasture in the distance. I knew Betty would like that. Before I bought them I wanted her to see them. I drove home and got Betty in our van and drove her out to the cemetery. It was August and a very hot day. She didn't have the strength to walk down to the plots. She sat in the van and I walked down to them and stood so she could see where they were. I walked back to the van.

"That is a nice place," she said. "I like it."

It was like she was talking about a place to build a house or something. Oh, how I wished that was what we were doing.

The cemetery thing was rough enough, but not nearly as hard as when I had to go to the funeral home and pick out pictures of caskets to take home and let Betty see them. I had rather been shot in the head, walked through fire, than to have to do that. Neither would have been as painful as what I felt looking at those caskets.

"Just buy something cheap to bury me in," she told me. "We have spent so much money on medical bills. We don't have insurance. I don't need anything real fancy."

"Honey, I can't do that," I told her. "I want it to be something nice for you."

I wanted to scream but I didn't want to put any more pressure on her. She already knew how hard this was for me. If I had broken down during those discussions she would have wanted me to just let the funeral director pick everything out. I didn't want anybody doing it but us. As much as it hurt, as hard as it was, this was for my wife, my sweetheart, and I wanted it to be the best, and I wanted to do it myself. That may sound crazy, or even morbid, but that was how I felt.

From the pictures I had brought home she picked out a blue casket. It was one that I want to be buried in as well when it is my time. I want it to match hers.

Betty and I talked every day about when the time did come what would happen.

"I will be in heaven with Jesus," she told me. "I will have a new body, be young again, and I will be able to run and laugh again."

"I know," I told her. I didn't want to talk about it but I had to.

"Charlie, it's alright to cry when I'm gone," she told me and held my hand. "But promise me, when you leave the cemetery you won't cry anymore."

"I can't promise you that," I told her and was already crying.

"Life is for the living, honey," she said softly.

How could she be so calm. I was going crazy in my mind, my heart was being ripped apart, and I was so scared I couldn't sleep at night for fear she would die while I was asleep. I have said it before, Betty is one of the strongest persons I had ever known. Here she was at the door of death and she was trying to prepare me. She was already prepared. She had made her peace with God.

"I want you to meet somebody some day," she told me. "You will need somebody in your life. I want you to meet somebody that will be good to you. I don't want you to be alone."

"Oh, Betty, sweetheart, there's no way I can ever love anybody but you," I sobbed.

"Honey, don't cry," she told me. "You will see me again. When it comes your time to go, I will come with Jesus to get you." She smiled as sweetly as an angel when she said that.

"Dawn, you need to come home," I said. "I think you mother is dying."

"Oh no Daddy," Dawn said and started crying over the phone. "I will be right there."

It was Sunday, two days after Thanksgiving, November 29th. Our wedding anniversary is on the 29th. I had had a feeling all day this was the end. Somehow I just knew. For one thing she asked me for half of a pain pill and she had somehow avoided taking them until that day. I had given it to her and she kept drifting on and off to sleep.

I called Bobbie. "Bobbie, she's dying," I told her and tried not to cry but I couldn't help it.

"Can she talk to me," Bobbie asked me and I could tell she was now crying too.

"I don't know," I said. "Let me see." I turned to Betty. "Honey, wake up."

Betty opened her eyes. She was so weak. She weighed less than sixty pounds.

"Bobbie wants to speak to you," I told her.

She held out her hand weakly. It was amazing how alert she was. She took the phone and spoke with Bobbie, her voice very soft and low. She didn't mention dying. I'm not sure she knew she was that close to dying. She told Bobbie she loved her and handed me the phone.

"Call me when it's over," Bobbie said as she cried and told me she loved me too.

I called Betty's best friend Marsha Harman and she came over. I also called my preacher at Hermitage Hills Baptist Church, Dean Haun. He also came over after Sunday night's services.

I was sitting on Betty's right side, holding her right hand. Dawn was on her left side, holding her left hand. Marsha Harman was

Old Memories and Me

sitting at the foot of the bed, her hand on Betty through the covers. Dean Haun was standing next to me, his hand on my shoulder.

"Betty," I said softly. "Can you hear me?"

She opened her brown eyes and looked at me, a faint smile on her face.

"Do you know who I am, honey?" I asked, biting my lip. She was about to leave me forever.

"Of course I do," she told me. "You are my husband, Charlie Craig."

I gently squeezed her hand. "I love you more than anything in this world."

"I love you more than anything in this world too," she smiled. "But honey, I am tired and need to sleep for a little while."

"Alright," I replied. I lifted her hand and kissed it. It felt so cold.

Betty closed her eyes. I looked over at Dawn and through tears we gave each other a helpless smile.

Two of our neighbors, Michelle Sharp and Roberta Young were with Kyle and Del downstairs.

I had to tell Betty goodbye and that I loved her one more time. I wouldn't get the chance ever again.

"Honey, can you hear me," I whispered as I leaned closer to her face that was still beautiful despite all she had been through. Her hair had grown back long again. I had to call her name again but she finally opened her eyes.

"Honey, I don't mean to be hateful," she told me. "But I am so tired and you keep waking me up."

I kissed her on her forehead. "I won't wake you up again my darling. Go back to sleep. I love you." I could barely talk through my grief.

"I love you too," she smiled weakly but it was so sweet.

"I love you too, Mama," Dawn told her, nearly choking on her own tears.

"I love you too, Dawn," Betty answered and smiled at our only child.

Those were the last words we would ever hear my beloved Betty say.

Three minutes later, we watched her take her last breath. I squeezed her hand.

It was 9:05 pm, November 29, 1998. Betty Joyce Craig was 62 years old and she was gone forever.

"She just stepped into glory," Preacher Dean Haun said and patted me on my shoulder.

"Oh, Jesus, please take care of her." I bowed my head and cried so hard I trembled all over.

It was the darkest time of my life.

CHAPTER NINETEEN

Betty had told me her wishes and given me instructions on how she wanted her funeral to be handled. I followed her desires without question. There was to be no services with a preacher and she didn't want her body viewed by anyone but family members and close friends. At first she didn't want me to have an open visitation but she finally agreed to allow that after I pointed out to her that there would be a lot of people wanting to come by and see Dawn and I, to show their love and sympathy.

The day after she had passed away I took Kyle to the funeral home to see his nanny. He was only six years old and Dawn and I felt he was too young to attend the funeral. He did want to see her and I wanted him to. He was Betty's pride and joy.

Del was only a year old so we didn't take him to the funeral home.

I held Kyle's hand and led him into the chapel. At Betty's casket I picked him up and held him in my arms so he could see her. I didn't know what his reaction would be. I fought to hold my own tears for his benefit. It was tough but I somehow managed not fall to pieces, at least until Kyle did something that touched me so deeply I cannot put it into words.

Unknowing to me, Kyle had brought a little rock to the funeral home with him. He took it from his pocket and showed it to me.

"What's that?" I asked him.

"A rock to help build nanny's mansion in Heaven, papa," he told me.

If I live to be 200 years old I know I will never feel again what I felt at that moment. It touched me so deeply I felt chills all over my body and needless to say, I couldn't hold back the tears after that.

I leaned forward, with my wonderful grandson in my arms, so he could place his little rock under her hands. I helped him place it beside the small locket with a picture of Betty and I together that I had placed in her hands earlier that morning.

The next night we held visitation in a room completely separate from the chapel where Betty's body was. At least a couple hundred people came by to pay their respects to Dawn and me. I had a picture of Betty that I enlarged and placed it in a floral arrangement

Old Memories and Me

in the middle of all of the flowers people had sent. There were a lot of beautiful flowers. Alan and Denise Jackson sent a tree type plant that was set in a gorgeous and large ceramic pot. Most all of the record labels sent flowers or reefs. BMI sent a large potted plant.

    Vince Gill was on tour and called me from out on the road somewhere. He gave me his heartfelt sympathy and told me I was going to need somebody to spend some time with in the coming weeks and he wanted to be one of those people. He told me we would have a few breakfast and lunches and take in a few Vanderbilt basketball games. He kept his word during some dark and dismal times ahead.

    I stayed on tranquilizers constantly from the night Betty passed away until sometime after the funeral. Dawn and I both were in somewhat of a shock, not yet feeling the reality that Betty was gone from our lives forever, at least on this earth. We were both hurting now but it would really hit hard later.

    It would have been so easy for me to turn back to drinking again but I would reach into my heart where Betty was and she would give me strength not to do that.

    I felt so sorry for Dawn. As grieving as I was myself, I knew she was in pain too and I didn't know how to ease it for her. I knew I couldn't but still, I wished I could. She had always been so close to Betty, sometimes talking things over like sisters. Dawn had inherited a lot of her mother's genes; her good looks, her figure, and her strength, which she was clinging to now.

    My sisters Ruby and Dot came as did their husbands, and Betty's sisters, Bobbie and Juanita. Several of my and Betty's nieces and nephews were there as well. The active pallbearers included Aaron Tippin, Keith Stegall, Jim McBride, Rob Crosby, Double A Young and one of Betty's nephews, Daryl Huntington.

    Aaron Tippin and his wife Thea had came by during visitation but didn't view Betty's body. Aaron said he just couldn't do it. However, the next day, just before the services, Aaron went down to see her. I went with him. Aaron put his around me and I could feel him trembling. Then, bless his heart, he lost it and his knees buckled somewhat and I had to help him to a seat. He sat there for a few minutes until he was able to regain control of his emotions again. Aaron loved Betty and she loved him. He has always been like family to us and always will be.

    Since Betty didn't want a preacher led service, it was up to me to do it. I have always been a talker but that day it didn't come easy at all. I asked Betty's best friend of some thirty years, Marsha Harman, to say a few words. Marsha made one of the most beautiful and moving testimonials about her friend, and my beloved wife, that I have ever heard. Double A Young made a talk, and his wife, Roberta read a scripture from the Bible.

    Dawn then told how Del, who was less than 2 years old, had

been upstairs when Betty was so weak and calling for help one day, and we couldn't hear her from downstairs, how that little grandson, who didn't know hardly more than four or five words, came to the top of the stairs and called out, "*help.*" As Dawn pointed out, we all know that God did that. Then she told the people gathered in the chapel about Kyle giving his nanny the rock to help build her Heavenly mansion.

Then, somehow Dawn was able to get through reciting a poem she had written for her mother. I want to share that poem with you.

> *One of my little princes gave me a stone*
> *Because he knew one day soon I would be gone*
> *I met Saint Peter at the Pearly Gate*
> *He said your mansion's not ready yet, and I would have to wait*
> *I told Saint Peter that would be fine*
> *That I need not wait for that mansion of mine*
> *Because for my journey I brought my own little stone*
> *That would be a good foundation for my Heavenly home*
> *I told Saint Peter once my journey was done*
> *I need to get settled and guard more than one*
> *I left behind one Prince that cried for help*
> *And my other Prince gave me this rock that I've kept*
> *I also left behind my husband and child*
> *And without me there*
> *They find it hard to smile*
> *I want them to remember my battle with cancer is won*
> *And please find peace cause another angel is home*
> *But I know it will be hard for them to wait*
> *But they need to remember, I'll be waiting at the gate*

When I stepped back to the podium I reminded our friends gathered there how outspoken Betty was and told them how I always showed her every song I had written. I always wanted her opinion. If it was a bad song, she would say, "that's not a good song, honey." If she thought it was a good song and nobody would record it, she would say, "they're stupid."

Then, I told them about going through some old pictures of Betty and me and how those photographs inspired me to come up with the beginning lines to *What A Day Yesterday Was*. I closed the service by having the funeral home director play *What A Day Yesterday Was*. We all sat there in silence as we listened to Alan Jackson sing that song from his CD, each of us remembering Betty in our on way. I remembered a lifetime in those three and a half minutes.

Just before we closed the casket, I had them play Vince Gill singing *Go Rest High On That Mountain*.

At the gravesite, my dear friend Rob Crosby sang for Betty one last time as he somehow got through *Come Home It's Supper Time*.

Old Memories and Me

Then we laid my darling to rest. A few days later the headstone would be put in place with the words engraved, *What A Day Yesterday Was*.

I have heard all of my life how some people say they have seen loves one again, after they have died, maybe for just a few minutes, one last final time.

For the next few weeks I prayed and begged God to let me see Betty again. He never answered those prayers. As time passed I came to realize that it is true, some of God's greatest gifts are unanswered prayers. For if He had allowed me to see her again, as I was asking of Him, how would I have ever began to heal and try to get on with my life.

I went the cemetery every day, sometimes twice a day, for a long time. I would take a lounge chair sometimes and sit there talking to her. Sometimes I would sit in the grass and talk to her. I would cry but sometimes through those tears I would smile and remember so many good times. Those were the times God gave to us. Then, I would cry again when I remembered the few bad times. Those were the times I gave to us.

One day when I was by her grave I was so depressed I didn't think I could go on. I was talking to God and asking him to help me. "Lord, I can't do this by myself," I told Him. "You've got to help me get through this."

I was down on my knees, pleading. I didn't care about tomorrow, there was no tomorrow. I couldn't go on anymore without Betty. I was so devastated I wanted to crawl into the grave beside her. My name was already carved there on the headstone beside hers. It just needed the dates filled in.

"Please Jesus," I wept. "Let me know you are here. Let me know you will help me get through this darkness that is smothering and choking me."

It was a cloudy day but just then the sun came out. At first I didn't notice but then I realized the sun was only shinning in a path that covered mostly only where I was kneeling by Betty's grave. I looked around to see it was still cloudy and there was no sunshine anywhere else.

"God? Is that you?"

One of the three trees near the grave started moving its cedar limbs, like in a soft breeze, but there was no breeze blowing. I wiped the tears from my eyes to see more clearly. "God, if that's you, do that again." The branches on the tree moved again.

"Oh, Jesus," I cried again but this time I was smiling too.

I know some of you reading this will say I was hallucinating, that I was so depressed over Betty's death I was looking for anything to help relieve the pain and suffering I was going through. Some of you will actually think I made this up about God. I wasn't quite sure what to think or believe myself. What happened next though left no doubt that God was telling me He was there.

There is a railroad track right beside the cemetery. You have to cross it to get into the cemetery. I have seen trains a couple of times a day, for years, run that track. Freight trains carrying steel beams, new cars, all kinds of cargo. But that day, just moments after the sun had come out, just after the tree had blown in the breeze that wasn't there, a train went by on those tracks carrying passengers. I couldn't make out their faces, only their silhouettes. I had never seen a passenger train on that track before.

"God, is that the train to glory?" I asked, my mouth wide open. The train blew it's horn.

I knew then, without a doubt, I was in the presence of our God Almighty.

Kyle lived with me most of the time after Betty's death. I tried not to break down and cry in front of him but one day I just lost it. Kyle was sitting on the couch in the family room and I was standing.

"Sit down, Papa," he said as he stood. "I want to talk to you."

I sat down on the couch and was already trying to gain my composure. I was like a little puppy, lost and helpless.

"Papa," Kyle began as he knelt his lean little frame in front of me. "You know Nanny doesn't want you to be sad and crying like this."

I managed to nod my agreement to that.

"Now, you've got to think about nanny being in Heaven and being well again," Kyle told me. "She's watching us right now and she wants you to smile."

"I know Kyle," I said to my 6-year-old grandson. I tried to smile.

"You will see her again someday, Papa," he reminded me. "You know that, don't you, Papa?"

I put my arms around him and pulled him close to me. "Yes, my dear little Kyle. I know that, I said to him, my eyes still wet with tears but through him I was gaining control of my emotions again.

Over the next few months Kyle would be a strength that would help me get through some dark times I may not have made it through without him. It is amazing how God can use a six year old to show us older folks the light and the way. It was almost like Betty was sending her strength to me through Kyle now, for he was her pride and joy, just as he was mine.

Dawn was there for me as well but she was hurting badly too. After all, she had lost her mother. Somebody had to be strong so I suppose Kyle decided it would have to be him.

For a long while after Betty's death, at precisely 9:05 pm every Sunday night I would light a candle and place it on the night stand on Betty's side of the bed. I felt I needed to do that in her memory. I would say a prayer and then blow the candle out. I would find a kind of peace

Old Memories and Me

in doing that.

I went out to the cemetery sometimes twice a day but always several times a week. I would always kneel down and kiss the grass over where Betty's head is. You may think that to be morbid but until you have walked in my shoes, you don't know. It was my way of saying hello when I arrived and then goodbye when I left. I usually talked to her about things that were going on in my daily life, my career, any new songs I had written, just like I always did. Of course I knew she wasn't really there but that was the last place I saw her. I would always say a prayer just before I left.

I was going to hurt for a long time. I missed Betty so much. However, ever since that experience with the sun, the tree and the passenger train, that day God told me he would help me get through my grief, it got a little better, at least enough that I wanted to live again. I would still have times I would just start crying and sit down somewhere and let it all out again, but I wasn't in a total darkness anymore and I knew Betty was in a much better place. She had told me herself, *I will be with Jesus, free of pain, smiling and young again.*

There was one other thing I needed to do in order to move on with my life. I needed to take her clothes and things from our closet. I had been putting off doing that for several months but I finally did, giving some things to the Salvation Army and Goodwill the way I thought she would want me to do. I kept some things she wore a lot and packed them away in boxes. I wanted to always keep those.

It had been 20 years since I had the affair and now I couldn't hold her in my arms and tell her I'm sorry anymore. But I still held her in my heart and told her. She had forgiven me. God had forgiven me. I just can't forgive myself.

I tried writing again but I was writing songs about Betty and how much I missed her, sad songs, depressing songs, songs like *Another Day Without You*. After more talks with Jesus, and some of them long ones, I knew I had to start my life over, but I wouldn't be alone. I had Dawn, Kyle, Del, and of course Jesus. I also had Betty's sweet memory of 41 years and not many people have all of that. Some marriages don't last nearly as long as ours did. Some people were homeless, with nobody in their life. Some people didn't even know Jesus. As bad as I was still hurting over my loss, I also realized I was pretty doggone lucky.

I had a high mountain to climb and I decided I needed to get started. I called Rob Crosby and Steve Wilkinson and the three of us started writing together on a regular basis. The three of us wrote well together. Both Rob and Steve played excellent acoustic guitar so we came up with some great melodies as well. I play acoustic guitar pretty well myself but not as good as they did. My strength has always been with lyrics.

We wrote two songs that would be on The Wilkinsons' second

album on Giant Records, *Me, Myself And I* and *Don't Look At Me Like That*. Tyler sang the lead on both of those songs and did a super job.

Vince Gill took me to breakfast at The Pancake Pantry one morning. I don't recall what all he ordered but I do remember he got sausage and told the waitress he wanted them burnt.

"Why do you want them burnt?" I asked him.

"So they will be done," he replied with a slight grin.

Well, that made sense.

Vince has a great sense of humor. He would put some funny messages on his cell phone. I remember once when he had gone to England he left a message on his cell making his voice sound very English, saying he was visiting with the Queen Mother.

I recall Vince and I going to lunch at another of his favorite eateries, The Sportsman's Bar And Grill. We had parked across the street and were walking to the restaurant when a girl spotted us. She was pumping gas in her car at a gas station on the corner. She alerted her girlfriend waiting in the car, then together they ran over to head off Vince. She left the gas line in her car and still pumping. Vince was kind enough to give them his autograph.

The two smiling girls returned to their car and Vince and I went into The Sportsman.

"You know, Vince," I said, dead serious. "I guess I need to apologize to you for me drawing so much attention when we go out somewhere like this."

Vince said, "No problem pal," and smiled. Then, he ordered red beans and corn fritters.

"You want those corn fritters burnt?"

Dawn was still playing softball with a team and they were going to a tournament in Rock Hill, South Carolina. It was a chance to take my grandsons to watch her play and also we could see a lot of both my and Betty's family while we were there. Betty's sister, Juanita McGuirt, actually lived in Rock Hill, along with a couple of Betty's nieces and nephews. My sisters didn't live that far away either.

Kyle and Del wanted to play Nintendo on the 8-hour trip. I had traded my New Yorker for a Chrysler minivan a couple of years earlier. I don't know why they call them mini vans, they are seven passenger vehicles.

I went to Sears and bought a small screen television with an adapter to plug it into a cigarette lighter for power. I also purchased the plugs I needed to hook up the Nintendo. I went home and hooked everything up. It worked perfectly. The only problem was, where to sit the TV so it wouldn't fall over in the van. We tried the floor but the boys couldn't see the screen without laying flat in the floor too. It just wasn't working out so I took it all back to Sears.

Old Memories and Me

I had bought my New Yorker and minivan from Bob Frensley Chrysler, which was just down the street from Sears at Rivergate Mall. I drove down there and went inside to talk to Bob Frensley. Bob had gone to high school with Bobby Wright, Johnny Wright and Kitty Well's son, with whom I was good friends with.

"Bob, do you have any vans with televisions in them?" I asked.

"No," he informed me. "Chrysler doesn't make a conversion van."

"I need a van with a television," I told him.

"Well, just down the street is Tom Bannen Chevrolet," Bob told me. "They have conversion vans and conversion vans have televisions."

I chatted with Bob Frensley for a few minutes, then drove down to Tom Bannen's Chevrolet. I pulled onto the car lot and immediately saw several big vans. One white one with gold trim in particular caught my eye. I parked and walked over to it. It was really big with a raised roof in the middle. From the outside it was beautiful.

"Good afternoon," a salesman said as he approached me. "You interested in a conversion van?"

"I'm not sure," I told him. "I need a van with a television in it."

"Well, this one has that and more," he told me.

"Could I see inside of it?" I asked.

"Sure. Let me get the key," the salesman said.

In a few minutes he returned and unlocked the van. I climbed inside and sat in the drivers seat. Oh my goodness. I had never seen a vehicle this fantastic.

There were 4 leather captain chairs and a leather seat in the back that let down into a nice size bed. The entire seating area was paneled with plenty of storage cabinets. There was a 13-inch television, with a VCR, and a Nintendo hookup in a separate side panel. Each seat had it's own earphones, overhead reading light and drink holder. There were two radios and two CD players. All of the widows had blinds. There was a built in radar detector. The back of all four of the captain seats let down to nearly a flat position for sleeping, if so desired. The entire passenger section had lights that reminded me of lights in the passenger section of an airplane. It was like a small bus. It was called a Southern Comfort Express.It was certainly that and more.

Well, my grandsons had their television for Nintendo. I traded my mini van and drove that beauty home.

"Papa," Kyle gulped when he saw the big van. "We just wanted a little TV."

"I love it, Papa," Del said with excitement and immediately started pulling the blinds up and down at one window.

When Dawn came home and saw it she gasped. "Daddy, I don't believe you. You bought this so the boys can play Nintendo on the road?"

I smiled and shrugged. "I spoiled you. I might as well spoil them too."

David Godbold, the chairman of the South Carolina Entertainment Hall Of Fame called me and asked me to become a board member and be responsible for inducting a South Carolina native songwriter into the hall of fame each year. He also informed me that the board had voted to induct Betty in to the hall of fame that year, 1999. Godbold said they wanted to honor her for being so supportive of my career and for helping me write a few of my early songs that Dolly Parton, Roy Rogers and Jeannie C. Riley had recorded.

As a new board member in direct charge of country songwriters to be inducted, after serious consideration I decided that Stewart Harris should be inducted for that year. Stewart is from Edisto, S. C. and had written somewhere around 8 or 9 number one hits, among those being several by Travis Tritt and *No One Else On Earth* by Wynona.

The Crook And Chase TV Show had been moved to Myrtle Beach and that year's hall of fame inductions would be the entire show that day. Kyle rode down with me, along with Mel Besher. We drove the conversion van for the 11-hour trip. They put us into a very nice motel not far from where the Crook and Chase studio was. Besides Stewart Harris, they were inducting Maurice Williams, who had written and recorded the huge hit, *Stay*, Lloyd Price, of *You Got Personality, Stagger Lee* and *Lawdy Miss Clawdy* fame, Arthur Smith, who wrote *Guitar Boogie* and *Dueling Banjos*, and Mickey Spillane, the author of all of the Mike Hammer private detective novels. There was an older black gentleman by the name of Drink Small, a blues and gospel pioneer who was also inducted.

Vanna White, from *Wheel Of Fortune*, and Chubby Checker, mister *The Twist*, were former inductees that were guest on the show. Seeing Chubby Checker caused me to recall how he got his name and I told Kyle and Mel Besher the story of how Dick Clark had come up with the idea for a dance to go with the song *The Twist*. Hank Ballad and The Midnighters had already had a hit with the song, minus the dance.

Dick Clark was looking for a heavy set black singer to re-record the song and do the twist while performing it. He found the guy he wanted and Dick Clark's wife, as I have been told, played off of Fats Domino's name and came up with Chubby Checker. The rest is history.

It was a great show and watching Maurice Williams and Lloyd Price perform was a treat. Stewart Harris performed as well and I was really proud of him. I went onstage and accepted Betty's induction into the hall of fame and it was a bit emotional but I held up pretty well.

After the show we went to dinner. I was able to spend a little time talking with Vanna White. She gave me a phone number to call and say hi sometime. I also talked quite a bit with Lloyd Price and Maurice Williams. They were both rock n roll legends to me. I couldn't believe I was inducted into the South Carolina Hall Of Fame a year

Old Memories and Me

before they were.

I had to be in the studio on Monday so we drove back on Sunday. I drove over to the beach to let Kyle see the ocean before we left. We would be coming back in a couple of months. The hall of fame had a board meeting planned and they wanted me to attend.

I wanted to really get my publishing company going and that meant doing several more demos and buying a few more pieces of equipment for making copies at my office at home. I didn't want to dip any further into my savings since I had spent so much already. I went to see Brian Williams at SunTrust Bank and because of my track record and success in the music business he set me up a business account that made a certain amount of cash available to me just by writing checks as I needed it, up to an agreed amount.

I continued to write songs with Rob Crosby and Steve Wilkinsons, along with Mel Besher and Lee Bach. Sometimes Steve and I would write alone, or maybe Amanda would join us. I became really close with The Wilkinsons and would go out to eat a lot with them or just hang out somewhere.

One day Steve asked me to meet them at EMI. When I arrived there was Steve, Amanda and Tyler. They gave me a miniature *Tachamine* acoustic guitar in a beautiful felt lined case.

"What's this for," I asked, quite surprised.

"You have been so great to us, being the first to try and help us get a record deal, and for all of the other wonderful things you do," Steve told me.

"And because we love you," Amanda added.

I was so moved I almost cried.

"You guys didn't have to do this," I told them.

"We know," Tyler grinned. "But we wanted to anyway."

I stretched out my arms as far as I could and hugged all three of them at the same time.

You can have money, and you may have fame, but if you don't have loving friends, you don't have anything.

I called my old friend from Watts Mill, Pete Estes, one day just to see how he and Anne were doing. Pete and Anne had known Betty well and we talked about her for a little while and that brought Pete to tell me of another friend that had died.

"You knew Brad Simmons died, didn't you Charles?" Pete asked me. He still called me Charles.

"No, I didn't know that," I told him. 'When? What happened to him?"

"It was last year, along about the same time Betty passed away as I recall," Pete said. "He died of cancer."

Brad Simmons had married my high school sweetheart, Polly Powers.

"Was he still working with the FBI?" I asked.

"No, he had retired from the FBI and was working for SLED, down in Columbia," Pete informed me. SLED was the South Carolina Law Enforcement Department.

"They live in Columbia?" I asked. "The last I heard they were in Ohio somewhere."

"Yeah, they moved to Columbia," Pete said. "Polly was up here in Laurens not along ago visiting her sisters."

I hadn't seen or talked to Polly since 1957 when she came by my and Betty's house on Smythe Street to tell me she and Brad were moving to Washington, DC so Brad could go to FBI training. We were all very young then and Betty hadn't liked Polly coming by to tell me bye. She still believed I had umpired a softball game between Watts Mill and Clinton and had cheated for Watts Mill. Polly played on that team.

I had been good friends with Brad and I wondered if Betty would mind me calling Polly and give her my condolences. Surely she wouldn't. Not now, she was an angel.

"Do you have Polly's telephone number?"

Pete gave me Polly's number. After I hung up I thought about if I should call her. I was still hurting over losing Betty and I didn't want to do anything that would tarnish my love for her. This was my old sweetheart but that was 45 years ago. My love for Betty was still deep in my heart and would always be. I admitted to myself it would be nice to speak to Polly after all these years and to especially ask her about Brad. She must be hurting as well. I decided it was alright to call.

"Hello," a voice answered and I knew it was Polly's voice. It really hadn't changed much.

Hello," I said back. 'This is an old friend of yours."

"An old friend? Who?" she asked, her voice pleasant but curious.

"You have to guess," I told her and smiled on my end. "We went to Ford High School together."

"Ummmm," she said. "I know your voice."

"Well, you should," I laughed.

"Charles? Yes, that is you, isn't it?" she said and I could detect a bit of excitement.

"Yes, it's me," I confessed. "How are you, Polly."

"Doing pretty good," she told me. "Where are you?"

"I am in Nashville," I told her.

"Yes, I heard you had moved there, when, back in the sixties?"

"Nineteen sixty eight."

"I have asked about you when I would go home, if anybody knew where you were. Somebody told me you were in Nashville and doing real good," she said.

"I have done alright," I told her. "I told you back when we were dating I was going to go to Nashville one day, remember?"

"Yes, I remember," she laughed. "And you did it."

Old Memories and Me

I was silent for a few seconds, then I said, "Polly, I heard Brad had passed away."

"Yes, Brad died last September," she told me.

"I am so sorry to hear that," I said sincerely.

"Thank you," she said. "It's been rough but I have hung in there."

"Betty died last November," I told her.

"Oh, I didn't know that," she told me. "What happened?"

"She had lung cancer," I said.

Polly and I talked for another forty-five minutes or so, bringing each other up to date on our families and our lives. I told her a little about my music.

"I will let you go," I told her. "I just wanted to call and say hello and tell you I am sorry to hear about Brad."

"Well, I am glad you called," she said. "I'm sorry to hear about Betty too. Y'all were married a long time too, like Brad and I were."

"When I come back home to visit, I will come to Columbia to see Ruby," I told her. "Maybe you can go to lunch with us, Ruby, Bob and I."

"That would be nice," she replied. "I haven't seen you in over forty years."

"I know," I laughed. "We're both old now."

We talked a few more minutes and hung up. I was glad I had called her. I didn't feel bad about it. I felt Betty probably already knew I had called Polly but just in case she didn't know, I would tell her next time I went to the cemetery.

CHAPTER TWENTY

New Years came and 2000 rolled in without much flare for me. Betty had been gone a little over a year. I had framed pictures all over the house of her, some of us together, some of Betty, Dawn and I together, and others. I had taken those old photographs downtown to a place called Chromatics and they were able to restore most of them and even enlarged some of them to 15x20s. Dawn had given me a 12-frame picture stand for Christmas and I had it filled with pictures of Betty in my bedroom.

David Godbold called for me to attend a S. C. Hall of Fame board meeting in April. I called Betty's twin sister, Bobbie, and we agreed to rent a condo at Myrtle Beach together. Dawn and my grandsons were going, Betty and Bobbie's nephew Daryl Huntington were coming down, and Bobbie's two grandchildren.

Since my phone call to Polly Powers Simmons, I had flown to Columbia once to visit Ruby. Polly had gone to dinner with us and it was really nice to see her again after all those years. We even rode up to Watts Mill and had lunch one day with several of our other friends we had known all of our lives, including Pete and Anne Estes, Carol Hardin and his wife, Billy Fulbright, Bruce Cook and the former Jackie Burgess and her husband. Polly and I visited Ford High School and it was amazing how much it still was the same as it was in the mid fifties when we were there. The auditorium still had the same projection booth, the same seats, and even the stage floor was the same. In the gym one of the original time clocks was still on the wall. It didn't appear that the classrooms had changed at all. It was like going back in time.

We had enjoyed seeing each other again and there was a good feeling between us.

Polly did say, "Now that we have found each other again, let's don't lose touch."

Both Dawn and Bobbie thought it would be nice to invite Polly to the beach with us. She brought one of her grandsons, Tanner, who was Kyle's age, which was 8. Del was 3 years old now. We had a condo full of people but we had three rooms and a big balcony. Most of the kids slept on pallets.In case you don't know what a pallet is, that's a bed on the floor made out of a couple of blankets and pillows. I had one of the bedrooms to myself.

Old Memories and Me

We were on the 7th floor of a high-rise motel. The view was beautiful.

I attended the Hall of Fame board meeting. Somebody brought up James Brown being in the South Carolina Entertainment Hall Of Fame and this person suggested that perhaps he should be removed since he had been in jail for assault. That didn't set well with me. I asked to be heard and was granted permission to speak.

"Ladies and gentleman, it is my understanding that a person is inducted into the South Carolina Entertainment Hall Of Fame based on what they have achieved in the entertainment world, and not based on their morals or personal lives," I began, then added, "If we are going to remove James Brown from that honor because he did something wrong, then I will have to return my plaque and induction as well. I haven't spent time in jail, but I too have done some things that are wrong, some things I am ashamed of, actually. So, if you remove James Brown from the hall of fame, then remove me as well."

I received a very nice applause and both James Brown and I remain in the South Carolina Entertainment Hall Of Fame today.

Randy and Jill Farrow and I became close friends after Betty's death, going out to dinner, spending time with me and just being there for me. If you recall, Randy is head of the emergency room at Summit Medical Center and was the one telling me about his wife being a singer while I was in the ER on a table having a heart attack. I still kid him about that.

One of our favorite places to eat was the Hermitage Cooker. Randy and I would usually change our meals up but Jill always got a grill chicken sandwich.

"You're gonna turn into a chicken," I kidded her.

"And you're going to turn into squash," she joked back because I did love the Cookers baked squash.

They had a son, Taylor, who was Kyle's age and they would sleep over with each other a lot. Randy had a pool table, as I did, and we both loved to shoot pool. That is where the comparison ends.

Randy Farrow is a pool shark. He makes easy shots, he makes impossible shots, he makes all shots. Me, I make some hard shots sometimes and miss most of the ones that are straight in the pocket. I have seen Randy Farrow run the table a couple of times before I ever got off the stool to chalk my cue stick.

"You missed that on purpose," I would say. "Just so I could get one shot this game."

"No I didn't," he would laugh.

This couple was so good to me. They knew I was still hurting and lonely after losing Betty. They were a lot younger than me. In fact, when me met, Jill was either twenty-eight or twenty-nine. For years though, she refused to turn thirty. She will tell you that herself.

Jill is a beautiful young woman, blonde hair and hazel eyes.

What is so weird is Taylor is her son and Randy's stepson. However, Taylor has dark hair and brown eyes just like Randy. He actually looks like Randy and nothing like Jill. You would think Taylor is Randy's son and Jill's stepson.

Jill had aspirations to become a singer. We decided to find some songs that fit her style and go into the studio and do a demo on her, with me producing. I do a lot of independent producing and then pitch the singers to the record labels, all for a fee. Since Randy and Jill had done so much for me emotionally, I refused to charge Jill anything to produce the session.

We recorded four songs at County Q Studio and they turned out really good. I pitched the session to a few record labels but unfortunately nothing happened. That is certainly the norm in this town. It is probably easier to tame a tiger with a toothpick than to get a record deal in Nashville. That is just the way it is.

Randy and Jill are originally from Louisiana and Jill really missed her family, as I am sure Randy missed his. Jill would go out to Betty's grave sometimes and just sit there because she said it was peaceful there and it made her feel close to her family for some reason. After her father died and her sister was killed in an accident, she would visit there even more. She bought flowers for Betty's grave without telling me. Jill Farrow is a loving and caring person and I felt so bad for her when she lost her father and sister in such a short time frame.

I will always be grateful for both Randy and Jill's friendship. They helped me get through some tough and lonely times in my life when I often wondered if I even wanted to survive. Then, I would look at Dawn, Kyle and Del and knew I had to go on.

Bobbie Bolt had been telling me I needed to get involved doing something with myself other than writing songs during the day and going to dinner occasionally with somebody. I wasn't doing anything with myself but watching TV at night and just wasting away I suppose. Dawn had her own place and wasn't living with me but Kyle stayed with me most of the time. He was 8 years old and wanted to take care of his papa. He had done a wonderful job of that to.

"I know you love to play spades," Bobbie told me one day when she called me from South Carolina. "You need to get on the Internet and play spades. It's a lot of fun, Charlie."

I had no idea what she was talking about. "How can you play spades on a computer?"

"MSN has a game site and one of the games they offer is spades," Bobbie informed me. "You can play spades, hearts, backgammon, all kind of games."

I didn't even know how to turn a computer on. We had bought Kyle a computer but I had never been on it. I used a word processor to store my lyrics and royalty statements. It was simple and easy.

"I have never been on a computer," I told Bobbie.

Old Memories and Me

"I can show you how," she said. "I can walk you through it. It's easy, really."

Dawn came over and showed me how to use the computer and over the phone Bobbie showed me how to get onto the MSN spades site. It took a little doing, but with Bobbie's help, I finally got the hang of it and before long I was playing spades on the thing. It really amazed me in the beginning.

You logged on and then went into this site where there were several levels of spades play to choose from. Once you did that you had different rooms to choose from to play in. You just clicked the mouse on one of those and go into that particular room. Once in there you saw 75 different tables you could then choose from to play at. All of the players at each of those tables were little drawn characters sitting in chairs at the tables and each player had their name, or nickname as they called it, above their seat. If a seat was empty there would be a picture of a little computer there, called a bot.

After I played a few games and got the hang of how it all worked, I started playing in the rated rooms. That is where you got 1600 points to begin with and if you won a game, your rating would go up. If you lost, it would go down. You played with a partner that you could see sitting across the table from you. Well, you could see that little figure in a seat with their name above it. Of course you couldn't see what anybody really looked like. They were all just images at the table.

You could chat with everybody at the table by typing in a space just below the playing area. It was pretty neat really. There was also a thing called *zone friends*. That is where you could add anybody's name to your friends list and when they were online you could click on his or her name on your *friends list* and a little insert would come up on your screen. You could type them a brief message and hit send and it would get to them in an instant. A lot of people would zone each other to chat, even if one was in one game room and the other in another room. Two partners playing spades could also zone each other and talk in order to cheat. You always suspected that when players were taking too long to bid or play a card.

I was a good spade player and did pretty well. I started playing every night. It was as much fun as Bobbie had said it would be. Bobbie and I played together as partners some nights, which felt kind of weird at first since Jack and I were always partners playing against Betty and her.

When you play often, as I started doing, you learn who some of the better players are and you add them to your zone friends and zone them to ask them to come to a certain table to be your partner. It wasn't long until I had a couple of players I always tried to pair up with.

I was glad Bobbie had talked me into learning how to play spades on the Internet. Now I had something to do with myself at night.

I had been writing with Teresa Wade and we were writing

some pretty good songs together. Teresa was a good singer as well as a good writer. She was writing for Charlie Daniel's publishing company at that time. Keith Stegall had remarried and was having a wedding reception at the Brentwood Country Club. He had invited me and told me it was alright if I wanted to bring somebody with me. I was telling Teresa about it and she said she would like to go. I told her sure, she could go with me. It wasn't a date or anything. We were just friends and writing partners.

It was a nice wedding reception and a lot of invited people attended. Alan and Denise Jackson were there and Alan and I had a few pictures made together. I had a couple made with Keith and Alan and I together. Tony Brown and his lovely wife Anastasia were in attendance. Keith had hired a small orchestra and the dance floor stayed full. I danced with Teresa all night long. We slow danced some but we rock n rolled a lot too. Teresa was only thirty years old but I did my best to keep up with her. Keith's 80-year-old grandmother was there and she was dancing as much as anybody. I danced with her a couple of times myself. I had never seen that long legged Jackson guy dance but he did that night and looked pretty smooth at it too.

Later that night, after I was home and in bed, I woke up about 3am with a terrible cramp in my right calf. It hurt like hell. I jumped out of bed to get some relief. Finally it subsided and I lay back down. "Ohhh." It was my right thigh cramping now. I jumped back up, hobbling around and moaning.

For the rest of the night I cramped in places I hadn't used in years from all that dancing at Keith's wedding reception.

"Hello, Keith."
"Yeah, Charlie."
"If you have another wedding reception, please don't invite me."
Ohhh………..

I was really enjoying playing spades on the Internet and I had met a few people I played with regularly, both male and female. I was even emailing a few of the females and talking on instant messenger with them. I admit there were a few flirting conversations at times but nothing serious, not until I met this particular girl from Illinois.

She and I not only played spades together but we started emailing each other several times a day, talking every night on instant messenger and eventually on the telephone. We sent each other a picture of ourselves. She was very pretty, with pale blue eyes and long blonde hair.

I was developing feelings for this girl and felt a little guilty about that, like I might be disloyal to Betty's memory. I talked to Bobbie about it and she made me feel less guilty about meeting someone and talking with her. Bobbie knew my heart would always belong to Betty

Old Memories and Me

but she also knew Betty had told me she wanted me to meet someone and be happy again. Bobbie did caution me about meeting women on the Internet.

"Just be careful, Charlie," Bobbie warned me. "You're lonely and very vulnerable right now and there are women who will take advantage of you."

The girl's name was Brenda Shireman. She was 34 years old and she had a 14-year-old teenage daughter and a baby girl that was only a few weeks old. I had only known her for a short time but I was already caught between letting myself really get involved with her or just walking away, especially after learning about a new baby. My mind and better judgment were screaming, run away from this situation, but my lonely heart was saying ride it out a little longer and then decide.

Brenda and I had a lot of fun playing spades together and just talking to each other in general. However, I learned early on that she liked to flirt on the Internet with guys that would blitz the table where we were playing spades. She told me she would stop the flirting if we got really serious with each other. Well, we got really serious with each other but the flirting continued. By this time I felt like I was falling in love with her and wanted to believe anything she told me.

"It's just all in fun and doesn't mean anything," she would tell me, referring to the flirting. "They're not real people."

They were real to me. One of them even knew her children's names and said he was planning on stopping in Galesburg the next time he was passing that way. He said he would come to Rail City, her mom's bar, and have lunch with Brenda. It sounded like she knew him pretty well.

I continued talking with Brenda even though it was a situation I was leery of. There was just something about her that I couldn't break away from though. I had said I would ride it out a while and I rode it out too long because between emailing each other several times a day, playing spades every night together and talking on the phone several times a week, I fell in love with Brenda Shireman and she said she had fallen in love with me too. With the love for Betty still in my heart nearly two years after her death I never would have dreamed this could happen, especially over a computer.

Brenda's life wasn't going very well at that time. She was operating the kitchen in her mom's bar serving lunches all week and not making enough money to really live on. A finance company had repossessed her car and having a baby just a few weeks old and a 14-year-old teenage daughter made things really tough for her. She needed a miracle and I raised my hand. I was still living in a deep depression from losing Betty, lonely and needing someone to fill that big void in my life and Brenda raised her hand. So there we were, two desperate misfits reaching out for one another.

I had to be out of my mind but I was thinking with my heart

and not my mind. I was twenty-nine years older than she was and I had found her to be a big flirt on the computer and I didn't like it. That in itself should have been enough of a warning sign but I made myself want to believe she would stop that as she promised she would.

She was accustomed to having her space because she had been divorced for a while and even when she was married her husband was a truck driver and was gone on the road a lot. On the other hand, Betty and I did everything together and I was used to being with someone and sharing everything about my life.

How could this possibly work with us being so different? When the heart is blinded by love, or for the need for love, it can't see a thing better judgment is telling it, so I jumped right in.

Brenda didn't like flying so I paid for a rental car and she drove down to Mt. Juliet with her two children. A couple of weeks later I flew to Galesburg, Illinois to meet Brenda's mother, Karen Villarreal, her grandmother Pauline, who everybody called Big G, and her two brothers Billy and Brett Villarreal. I got along very well with her family.

After about a month we started planning on getting married and Brenda informed me that she had to bring her dog, Bubba, with her to Tennessee. He was huge, a mastiff, and reminded me of Cujo. I finally agreed but I told her Bubba had to stay outside.

"He can't stay outside," she told me. "He is an inside dog and he will die living outdoors."

"He's too big to stay in the house," I protested. "He will ruin my carpets just like he has ruined yours."

"I'm not moving without him and I'm not putting him in your yard," she said firmly.

"That horse of a dog is not living inside my house," I shot back. "Come on, Bren, this is ridiculous."

"Then, we've got a problem," she said.

I thought for a few minutes, and then told her, "Alright, alright, I will build him a large doghouse."

"He will die outside, Charlie," she whined.

"Ok, I will build him a large doghouse inside my garage," I announced. "And I will put a heater and an air conditioner in it."

"He is used to a TV too," Brenda pouted with a grin. "He has to have a TV and a couch."

Oh my Lord.

"Alright," I sighed. "I will get him a little TV and we can take this old couch of yours down there.

He's already used to it."

When I got back home I walked next door to my good neighbor Double A Young's house.

"I need your help building a dog house," I told him.

"For Con?" he asked.

Con was my chow.

Old Memories and Me

"No, Brenda's dog," I informed him. "I have to build it inside my garage."

"Do what?" Double A asked, looking at me like I had lost my mind.

No doubt I had, indeed.

Aaron Tippin had opened a little restaurant on the main highway near his home. It had a gun shop in the back and Aaron Tippin paraphernalia for sale. The menu was mainly beans, cornbread, hotdogs and sandwiches. I would go down to Aaron's house and sometimes we would write a song and other times we would just ride around in his truck while he ran errands and did his thing in the community where just about everybody knows him and honks their horn and waves when they pass on the highway. We would always have lunch at his and Thea's restaurant.

I can't count the times Aaron would do an interview with a radio station, talk over a business situation with an associate, and discuss something with Thea, all on his cell phone while we drove around doing different things here and there. The man never stops.

"Why don't you slow down and catch your breath sometimes," I told him on one such occasion.

"I ain't got time, pal," he answered. "I got too much stuff to do."

After just a few hours with him I felt like I had done a day's work when all I had really done was sit in the passenger seat of his truck and hold on while he darted down one winding road and up another hilly one.

I told Aaron about Brenda and me planning on marrying her.

"She's 34 and has a three month old baby," I informed him.

Aaron lowered his head and looked at me over the top of his sunglasses. He never said a word.

He didn't have to. His look said enough.

Just four months after we had met, on Monday, September 25, 2000, in a magistrate's office at the Courthouse in Lebanon, Tennessee, Brenda Shireman and I were married at 11 am. The first thing we did was go to Burger King for lunch. That was our honeymoon because she and her kids had to catch a plane back to Galesburg later that afternoon. It took some doing but I had finally talked her into flying.

I turned 65 years old that Saturday and celebrated it by eating breakfast at Shoney's with Kyle. The next day I flew to Galesburg to drive the U-Haul with Brenda and her children's belongings back to Mt. Juliet. I had already gotten Brenda a new PT Cruiser and she drove it down.

Tionna, Brenda's 14 year old daughter, would be moving into Dawn's old bedroom. I had bought her 4-month-old baby, Callie, a new crib and had it set up in my bedroom, which would of course be my and Brenda's room now. Bubba had his built-in doghouse in the garage. Woody, Brenda's cat, had the run of the house. I had a brand new HP2000 computer I had bought for Brenda, complete with a printer, sitting on a desk in the study. I had tried to have everything ready and make them as comfortable and happy as possible.

However, I would soon learn that some things are just naturally impossible.

Old Memories and Me

CHAPTER TWENTY-ONE

Brenda wanted to get involved with helping me in the music business. I thought that would be nice and I started teaching her things and even called and set up a couple of appointments at record labels for her to pitch songs after I took her with me a few times to get the hang of it. She came back home upset and saying she wasn't going back there again. Both of the A&R people she had played songs for were females and she came back all upset with them because they hadn't taken any of the songs she had played for them. She even called them a few unflattering names. I recalled her brother Billy telling me how Brenda didn't get along with other females very well.

I explained to Brenda that nobody gets every song recorded they play for the record labels, not even I did. I tried to make her understand being turned down wasn't anything personal but she still said she wasn't going to pitch songs anymore.

Those first few months together had its ups and downs but we had some good times together. As far as her working with me in my music career, some things went well but others frustrated her. I think it was all like a new toy for her but it wore off quickly and she would become bored.

Brenda set me up a music website on the Internet and did some other things concerning my music on the computer. On my new website we posted four letters of recommendation from Alan Jackson, Jim Ed Norman, who was president of Warner Brother Records, Nashville Division, Doug Johnson, president of Giant Records, and Steve Wilkinson of The Wilkinsons. I was really proud of those letters and the high honor each of those people paid me in the things they said about me. I have copied them from my website and posted them below.

To Whom It May Concern:

This letter serves to signify my friendship with Charlie Craig. Charlie and I were introduced back in 1986. I have always felt that Charlie possesses a very good ear for songs and for recognizing real talent.

Charlie's songwriting success confirms his ability and aggressiveness in getting his music heard and having number one songs recorded.

Sincerely,

[signature]

Alan Jackson

To Whom It May Concern:

    I have had the distinction of working with Charlie Craig as well as enjoying his friendship. Charlie is a man with passion, determination, and integrity. Not only is he a prolific award winning songwriter, I believe he has a gift for spotting potential star quality. He has a vision for seeing where an artist is, what they are capable of becoming and what is needed to complete that evolution; true artist development.
    Most recently Charlie helped Giant Records secure a deal with The Wilkinsons. In such a competitive market I don't believe we could have made the deal without Charlie's involvement.
    I believe Charlie would be a valuable asset to any music company, especially in a creative/management aspect.

Sincerely,

[signature]

Doug Johnson
President
Giant Records

Whom It May Concern:

    I've had the distinct pleasure of working with Charlie Craig. I have found him to be an honest and dependable man of integrity. Warner Bros. was sufficiently impressed with not only those personal traits, but his professional abilities as well and this led to his doing record production for our company.
    His success as a songwriter is well documented. He was also involved with the early careers of artists like Randy Travis and Alan

Jackson, and he played a significant role in the more recent signing of The Wilkinsons to Giant Records Nashville.

I would extend to Charlie the highest compliment by saying that I would gladly hire him for any position, or for work on any project for which he was qualified.

Sincerely,

Jim Ed Norman
President
Warner Bros. Records, Nashville

To Whom It May Concern:

The Wilkinsons have been associated with Charlie Craig for the past 8 years and have known Mr. Craig to be a man of honesty and integrity. His 30 odd years in the music business as writer/producer have been both successful and have given Mr. Craig a standing of respect among not only the writing community but also with recording artists, such as Alan Jackson, Vince Gill, and Aaron Tippin, many of whom Mr. Craig has worked with at the very start of their careers. His talents as a writer/producer are well known of Nashville's Music Row. I recommend him without hesitation.

Steve Wilkinson
Member of Giant/Warner Bros. recording act, The Wilkinsons

Sometime later, right after a bad argument between Brenda and I occurred, she ripped the originals of those letters of recommendation in half just to spite me. I did the best I could to put them back together with scotch tape. I had to copy them from my website to post them above. Of all the hateful things she did to me, ripping those letters in half was probably the most spiteful. I can't begin to tell you how that hurt and upset me. I was furious.

There soon came a time when she would get on her computer as soon as she got up in the mornings, playing spades and backgammon and instant messaging people. She had pretty much lost all interest in working with me in my music. When I was on my computer in the next room I could hear the plunking sound every time somebody would send her an instant message. A lot of times it would be a man and sometimes I would see the message on her computer screen saying things like, hello beautiful, and come to table 34 and let's play a game together. A few times I recognized the name of the guy that flirted with her a lot before we married, the one that had said he was coming to her mom's bar to have lunch with her. He was still flirting with her and she allowed him to. Naturally, I didn't like that. She had promised to stop the flirting after we were married. She didn't stop.

"You're so frigging jealous," she would tell me when I would question her about all the flirting on her computer, except she used the real *f* word and I don't want to use that word in my book. That word was just naturally part of her vocabulary.

Brenda began telling me how she needed her space and that became a problem between us as well. When she would go back home to Galesburg for a visit she never wanted me to go with her. I couldn't understand why she never wanted me to visit her family with her. She would want me to stay at home and keep Callie while she went up to Galesburg. I'm sorry but I didn't marry her to become a babysitter while she would go back to Galesburg for four or five days at a time. I learned to love Callie like my own child and I helped tend to her a lot. I probably changed as many, if not more, diapers than Brenda did. I would get up in the middle of the night and get Callie a bottle. I was good to both of Brenda's children but I wouldn't agree to keep Callie whenever she wanted to go to Galesburg without me. Christmas was the only time she wanted me to go back home with her.

Her family didn't like it that she didn't want me to go with her on visits.

"Just get in the car and come with her anyway," her mom told me several times.

I couldn't help but feel like perhaps she was ashamed of me being so much older than her and didn't want her friends to know that. I kept remembering her not introducing me to anyone in her mom's bar that first time I was there.

Her youngest brother Billy came down to take a masonry job in Nashville and he stayed with us. He needed $600 to get some tools and I gave it to him. Billy was a hard worker and I didn't mind helping him out.

Billy loved his sister but he knew how she was and he didn't like the way she was treating me, staying on the computer all day and flirting with men.

"Take that computer away from her, Charlie," he told me one day, speaking loud enough for Brenda to hear him in the next room. "That will put a stop to that flirting."

"You shut up, Billy," Brenda yelled back, halfway laughing. "Charlie and I are doing just fine without you interfering."

"Yeah, as long as you're getting your way everything is fine, right Brenda?" He replied and winked at me, but he was serious and Brenda knew it. Then he added, "I'd put your fat butt to work if it was me."

She didn't really have a fat rear but Billy was trying to get under her skin.

"Shut up Billy," Brenda said and she didn't laugh that time.

Brenda had her good sides and could be sweet as pie at times. She would go with me to the Broken Spoke while I did a writers' night with a few other songwriters. She would hold my hand while we sat at a table waiting for time for me to go onstage, even giving me a little kiss and smiling. We would go visit with our friends Marshall and Barbara Moore and usually have a good time together there as well. Every time we were around other people Brenda was usually nice to me and even showed affection for me. However, it seemed once we were in the car alone and headed home she would turn back into a cold and indifferent person. She wouldn't even want me to hold her hand in the car. She changed moods like the weather.

Things just went from bad to worse between Brenda and me. We argued about everything. I didn't get a lot of writing or song pitching done during the latter days of our marriage because my nerves had gotten so bad. It got to the point that I dreaded getting up in the mornings. I knew as soon as I walked downstairs we would argue about something. Even sometimes when I would tell her I loved her she would ignore me as though I hadn't said a word.

"I said I love you, Brenda," I would tell her when she didn't respond.

"You've already told me that once this morning," she would reply coldly, never looking away from her computer. She could be so heartless at times.

With all of the arguing and problems we had you probably wonder if we had any kind of sex life. Well, of course we did but usually it would be Brenda's decision since she liked to be in control of all situations. Our intimate times mostly occurred on the nights Brenda would make herself vodka and Sprite drinks and soaked in the hot tub in our bathroom. Sometimes I would sit by the tub and talk with her and those were some of our most peaceful moments, no arguing or name calling, just talking.

Later, when Callie would fall asleep Brenda would get out of the tub and get into bed. I would join her and for the rest of the night all was well with our marriage...

A couple of days later we were back to arguing again.

It was during this time that Keith Stegall called and told me

Old Memories and Me

Alan Jackson had recorded *Bring On The Night*, the song that Keith, Alan and I had written back in 1987. This is the song Alan had told the media that I had sent him for 13 years in a row. I am told he said, if Charlie Craig hadn't been so persistent I might not have recorded it.

I suppose I really am a persistent person. Doug Johnson told somebody once, when he was heading up Epic Records, that I was one of the most persistent songwriters he had ever seen. He said if I played him a song and he passed on it, then the next time I played him songs I would play that same song again, and then again, every time I pitched him songs. I think he started taking certain songs of mine just to keep me from bringing them back to him.

Brenda's other brother Brett came down to visit and he and I went to a Vanderbilt basketball game. He, Brenda and I had fun doing other things like going to a laser gun place and doing battles and also go-cart racing.

Brett had his own business back in Galesburg and was doing well with that. Like Billy, Brett and I got along very well and he never sided with Brenda when we argued. Actually, he never took sides at all but he didn't approve of her staying on the computer all day and all the flirting she did. He also encouraged me to come to Galesburg with Brenda when she came to visit. He even told her she did wrong not wanting me to come home with her to visit.

I got along very well with all of Brenda's family, including Big G, her grandmother. I had a good relationship with her family but not with Brenda.

Her mom even joked and said I should have married her instead of Brenda.

I suppose I spoiled Brenda too much from the beginning. I had paid off her little house up in

Wataga because of the ridiculous high interest she was paying a loan company down in Texas she had found on the Internet when she had bought the house. After I paid it off she sold it to a woman in Wataga and we financed it ourselves. I rarely saw any of the payments myself though. I bought her a nice tanning bed for her birthday. I paid for airline tickets for some of her family members to fly down to visit. On one occasion I paid one of her friend's plane fare as well. Brenda wanted a rented limo to ride them from the airport to the house. We started spending money like it was growing on trees in the backyard.

We started arguing more and more, still mostly about her staying on the computer and all the flirting. Sometimes I think she deliberately tried to make me jealous with some of the things she did, like deleting all of the incoming and outgoing calls on our home phone while I was at work and going into another room and closing the door to talk when she would get a phone call. Whether she was guilty of doing anything wrong or not, she made it look like she was.

Brenda never hesitated to ask for money for her family members but if my daughter needed money Brenda would pitch a fit if I let Dawn have any. Most of the time Dawn only needed $25 or $50 for groceries.

When I think back on how I allowed myself to be manipulated I get so upset with myself. Nobody put a gun to my head and made me do that. I just allowed myself to be controlled like a gutless man. I would dislike myself for being so weak with Brenda for years to come. I neglected my daughter and grandsons too often during my time with Brenda. Only God will ever come between us again.

I wasn't perfect during our marriage and I admit I probably should have let some things go rather than insisting we talk about some issue when she didn't want to. I guess our age difference was more of a problem than either of us wanted to admit as well.

There were several times I went to the cemetery and got on my knees at Betty's grave and prayed, asking God to tell me what to do. I talked to Betty about my marriage and situation with Brenda but of course she couldn't answer me. I have no doubt she would have told me this was not the woman she meant when she had told me she wanted me to meet someone after she was gone, someone that would be good to me.

I hope angels can't look down from Heaven and see what is happening to their love ones here on this earth. Betty would be so sad to see how much I was hurting.

There were a lot of other things that happened during my marriage to Brenda that I won't go into. It would really serve no purpose to bring all of them up now. She thought I was insanely jealous, as she put it, and I thought she had no morals. Eventually I guess we finally reached a point to where we thought of each other as he's jealous and she's jaded.

I know now my marriage to Brenda is something that should have never happened but it did and I'm not blaming anyone but myself for getting involved with her. We never really had a chance though. Brenda had her way of living, her way of doing things, and I had mine. Neither one of us was perfect and I admit again that sometimes I might have been too pushy in wanting her to explain certain things she did rather than just let it go. The age difference could have been an issue, and no doubt her flirting and ever changing moods were, but the biggest problem Brenda and I had was we had no common ground between us. She wouldn't change and I couldn't change. It's really that simple.

In September 2000 we had married in a magistrate's office in Lebanon, Tennessee. In September 2002 in a courtroom in Lebanon, Tennessee we were divorced. It ended in the same building where it

Old Memories and Me

had all begun...

CHAPTER TWENTY-TWO

Keith Stegall called me to see how I was doing after the divorce.
"Charlie, Keith," he said.
"Hey, Keith," I replied.
"Just checking on you," he told me. "You doing alright with everything you've been through?"
"Yeah," I replied, with a chuckle. "I'll be ok with the help of tranquilizers and prayer."
Keith laughed. "That sounds like a song title."
Well, indeed it did become a song title when I was later writing with Steve Wilkinson. I told Steve about the conversation between me and Keith and Steve loved the idea. I called Keith to see if he wanted to write the song with us, since he was the first to think of it being a song when I said the line.
"Man, I'm in the studio with Jamie O'Neal," Keith told me. "You guys go ahead and write it."
That day Steve Wilkinson and I wrote Tranquilizers and Prayer. It is tongue in cheek but it's based on a lot of things that actually happened while I was going through the divorce with Brenda. It was pretty easy to write because I had lived most of it. I suppose it kind of wrote itself.

I got the litter and she took the cat
I wouldn't treat a dog like that

A young aspiring songwriter named Jami Grooms was a professional carpet cleaner in 2002 and he had already shampooed my carpets a couple of times when he arrived at my home one day to do them again.
"Did you know Travis Tritt and Ray Charles performed your song *Between An Old Memory And Me* on CMT's Crossroads last night?" he asked me as soon as he entered my foyer.
"Really?" I responded surprised. "No, I didn't know that."
Jami told me a little about the taping. "During a commercial break Ray Charles told Travis that *Between An Old Memory And Me* was

Old Memories and Me

one of his favorite country songs."

"Wow," I said and I know I was grinning with pride. "That is so cool that Ray Charles and Travis did the song and Ray made that kind of comment."

When the show aired in November I watched it and of course I taped it. I had called CMT to find out when the show would air and the person I talked to had told me that the highlight of the show was when Travis and Ray performed *Between An Old Memory And Me*.

Watching the show that night I got chills and I won't lie, there were a few tears in my eyes. I had been fortunate to have some big name stars record my songs but to hear and see Ray Charles sing one of my songs was beyond description. Naturally, it was another highlight in my career I will always cherish.

It would be nearly seven years later that my dear friend Margie Hunt would call me and during our conversation she reminded me how much Ray Charles loved *Between An Old Memory And Me*. I told her I had heard that. Then, she told me something that I didn't know.

"Not long after they taped Crossroads Ray Charles called me from LA," Margie told me. "He said he hadn't been feeling well the night of the taping and he wanted to come back and resing his part again on *Between An Old Memory And Me*."

"Really?" I said. "I had never heard about that."

"Well," Margie continued, "Ray loved that song and asked me to call CMT and tell them not to do the final edit of the show until he could resing his part. He flew into Nashville on his private plane at his own expense. I picked him and his manager up at the airport and drove them to a studio where he redid his parts on that song."

"You are kidding me," I said.

"No, he did that, because he loved that song and wanted his part to be right," Margie Hunt told me.

I had gotten chills the night I had watched Travis Tritt and Ray Charles perform *Between An Old Memory And Me* on that show and now I had chills again.

I had met Jilla Roberts in 2001 when she had lived in California and now she was coming to town as often as she could. She had moved to Las Vegas from California because her elderly father lived in Vegas, and too, she was working the casinos there as an entertainer. When Jilla would come to town we would write and sometimes go out to dinner. We became very close to each other. We were both recently divorced and had some things in common. Jilla was planning on eventually moving to Nashville, not because of me, but to pursue a recording career in country music.

I was also still writing a lot with Steve Wilkinson and on occasion Amanda Wilkinson would join us to write. Steve and I just naturally clicked as co-writers, about like Keith Stegall and I did when we were writing a lot in the eighties.

Steve and I were writing one day and he came up with a great hook about having big pockets. I loved the idea and after throwing some thoughts around about how to write the song, I actually reached back into my heart and mind to that first night I met Betty back in 1957, when we were at Mineral Springs park and I kissed her for the first time, right after drinking a Dr. Pepper, and I came up with the opening lines for the song.

> *I recall the first time that we kissed*
> *And the taste of Dr. Pepper on your lips*

Steve and I finished the song that day and later he would sing the lead vocals on it as The Wilkinsons would include it in one of their albums.

I got a call from a lady in Orlando, Florida one day. Her name was Rhonda Bulford and Jack Kapanka had recommended that she call me. Rhonda had a 17-year-old son, Johnny Bulford, who wrote songs and sang. I agreed to meet with them and they drove up to Nashville from Orlando. I met with them in one of the writer's rooms at EMI. The whole Bulford family came. There was Rhonda, her husband Johnny, 15-year-old daughter Ally, and 17-year-old little Johnny. He wasn't so little though. He wasn't fat, just a big boy at 6 feet 1 inch and about 285 pounds.

"We really appreciate you meeting with us," Rhonda Bulford told me. "We have heard so much about you and we love the songs you have written."

"Well, thank you," I replied.

Ally was looking at me with a nervous smile. "I can't believe we're sittin' here with you," she remarked.

I looked around the small writers room like I thought she must be talking about somebody else. I have never been a shy person but I had never gotten used to people treating me like I was special because of the songs I had written. I didn't see myself as anything but a simple person.

"We all feel honored that you agreed to meet with us," Rhonda told me.

"Well, I feel honored to meet with you too," I smiled from one Bulford family member to the other.

Young Johnny Bulford played excellent acoustic guitar and sang me several songs he had written. He was quite impressive, especially for a 17 year old. He was writing beyond his years and had a good voice. He reminded me of a young James Taylor. His pretty sister, Ally, sang excellent harmony with him, as did his mother.

Later we used the EMI Studio and laid down a few guitar

Old Memories and Me

vocals of Johnny singing his songs. Before the Bulford's left town we talked further about the possibilities of Johnny doing something with his talents in country music. I told them I would work with him and once we got a few good tracks recorded I would play him for the record labels. At seventeen he was still a bit young but I knew he wasn't far away from being ready to present to the industry. He just needed a little grooming.

The sales on Alan Jackson's *Drive* album had been really great, somewhere around 4 million, so I had made pretty well on *Bring On The Night* from that CD and *Wanted* was still getting an exceptional lot of airplay, especially for a song that was released back in 1990. *Between An Old Memory And Me, Leavin's Been A Long Time Coming, She's Single Again, Following The Feeling* and *Let's Get Over Them Together* were all still receiving good airplay and bringing in royalties from sales. Some of my other older songs were still earning royalties as well. I was slowly getting back on my feet financially after the costly marriage I had been in.

The pains were beginning to heal from that marriage but I was starting to feel lonely again. Jilla Roberts and I had some lunches together, a few more dinners, but she was out of town working a lot. She and I loved each other dearly but to say we were a romantic pair would be close, but not entirely correct. There had always been a spark there but never a real fire, for whatever reason.

About eight months after my divorce from Brenda I met a young lady who lived in Scottsdale, Arizona and she and I started talking on the phone and emailing each other. Her name was Cindy Desotta and she was originally from Canada. She didn't have any children and she didn't appear to be a big flirt. There was one thing though that nearly made me back away from her. She was only 36 years old. However, since I wasn't looking for a long-term relationship, especially getting married again, I didn't think it would matter about the age difference.

Yeah, I know. I should know better.

After knowing Cindy for about a month, I flew her here to Nashville for a weekend. She was as pretty in person as she had been in her pictures. I got her a motel room and she stayed there. We both had been in a bad relationship recently and wanted to take things slow. On that initial meeting in person neither of us made any commitments nor did we have any sexual experiences together. It was just a chance for two people to meet each other, get to know one another, then see what happened after that. I didn't intend to make the same mistake twice.

What happened after that was we continued to talk on the phone and a couple of weeks later I flew to Scottsdale. I had never been to Arizona but had always wanted to. I actually flew into Phoenix and Cindy picked me up and drove us to Scottsdale, which is a suburb of Phoenix. I found Scottsdale to be absolutely gorgeous, with palm trees, cactus, some beautiful desert flowers and mountains in the background for a scenic setting. One of those mountains had two humps and they called it Camel Back Mountain.

We had lunch at a Mexican restaurant and I would soon learn that Scottsdale had a Mexican restaurant about every three or four blocks, much like we have McDonalds in Nashville. Most all of the Mexican restaurants had elegant décor, as did most of the other restaurants there, regardless of the origin or menu.

Cindy had a nice apartment with a wonderful view from her balcony of a mountain in the distance. I stayed at her apartment the four days I was there. We became very close and started learning each other's little quirks as well as the good things.

Cindy was really into natural medicines, yoga and meditation. She had this thing about mind control, or whatever you call it.

"I can't sleep," she told me one night. "I can hear you thinking."

"You can hear me what?" I laughed. I thought she was joking with me.

She rolled over to face me. "Your mind is racing with thought waves and I can feel the energy," she swore. "It is keeping me awake, Charlie."

I rose up on one elbow. "Cindy, please tell me you are putting me on."

"Nooo, Charlie," she said seriously. "You have to shut your mind down when you go to bed to sleep."

"My mind never shuts down," I told her.

"You're going to have to close out all of your thoughts," she told me with a little frown that I could see in the dim light seeping in from outside through the curtains. "I need my sleep."

"You need your head examined," I said with a little sarcastic chuckle.

I promptly got up and stalked off into the front room and slept on her short love seat. There wasn't a whole lot of love in that seat that night and it wasn't long enough for my six foot two inch frame either.

I just lay there thinking how stupid it was to expect somebody not to think, especially a creative songwriter. I fell asleep thinking..............

I actually had a really good time while I was in Scottsdale. It was very hot though, hovering around 115 degrees during the day. Cindy and I went to some really nice restaurants and to some cool places, one being an old western town where they reenacted gunfights and everybody was dressed like Matt Dillon and Miss Kitty.

A few weeks later I flew back out to Scottsdale for the second time. Cindy and I were developing affectionate feelings for each other, despite our differences in some things. She made me spaghetti at home one night for dinner but it was all natural ingredients. The noodles

Old Memories and Me

were made from eggshells and the sauce was from hamburger with no hormones. I don't know what else was in it.

"You like it?" she asked, smiling as we sat at her high round table with high back bar chairs.

"I'm sorry," I told her. "I can't eat this."

"It's alright," she said with another sweet smile. "I can put it in the refrigerator and eat it later."

She really was a pretty young lady, blonde hair and brown eyes, and endowed somewhat like Dolly Parton is.

One thing I couldn't quite get used to in Scottsdale was all of those adobe homes with two and three car garages. In Clint Eastwood westerns, adobes don't have garages.

On Sunday afternoon I flew back home. I knew I would miss Cindy, even with her medicine-tasting natural foods and not thinking when trying to sleep.

Giant Records folded and The Wilkinsons were looking for a new label. Their first two albums on Giant had done really well, especially for a new act, selling around 700,000 total. Giant had been a branch of Warner Brothers and for whatever reason Warner didn't pick up their option. They did keep Blake Shelton, who was one of the last artists Giant had signed before closing its doors.

I had continued to write with Steve Wilkinson, staying closely united with the Wilkinson family. Steve and I hung out a lot together even when we weren't writing. He seemed more like a brother than just a close friend. I loved doing demo sessions of our songs. Amanda would usually sing the lead vocals on them and then Steve, Tyler and Amanda would stack harmonies that would sound out of this world. Amanda was without a doubt one of the top female singers in country music.

I had one of Nashville's top record executives tell me once he considered Amanda one of the best female vocalists he had ever worked with. This CEO was also a producer and had work with some of the biggest female names in the recording industry. That was quite a tribute to my little Canadian princess.

I had worked a few writers' nights with The Wilkinsons and since these were usually gigs I had booked, I normally sang the first song, then we would take turns until all four of us had performed a number, then start over again.

One night we were about to start a set at the Commodore Lounge and I told Amanda to sing first.

"You always sing first," she replied. "It's your gig."

"I want you to sing first tonight," I insisted.

Amanda shrugged good naturedly and said to her dad, "Let's do *26 Cents*."

After they had finished the song I said to the audience, "I want to thank The Wilkinsons for opening for me tonight."

Amanda looked at me and grinned. She reached over and

punched me playfully in my ribs.
That is the only time I ever had a name act open for me.

I got a call from Cindy one day.
"Charlie, I have been in an accident," she told me, her voice trembling.
"What kind of accident?" I asked her. "Are you alright?"
"An automobile accident," she informed me, her voice nearly breaking. "Somebody rear ended me."
"When?" I asked her.
"Just a few minutes ago," Cindy said. "I'm waiting for the police to get here now."
Cindy explained to me how she had been stopped at a traffic light in Scottsdale and a pickup truck rammed her from the rear. She said the force shoved her stopped vehicle forward and nearly sent her under a semi truck that was stopped in front of her.
She would find out the next day that her car was totaled. She only had collision insurance but nothing to cover her own car. The pickup truck owner didn't have any insurance.
I flew out to Scottsdale and rented Cindy a car. I also took her to a medical clinic for a MRI because she was complaining of pains in the back of her neck. She had no medical insurance. The MRI was $450 and I put it on my debit card. I stayed with Cindy for several days, driving around looking for a used car. She had nobody to turn to but me for financial help. Her mom and dad weren't able to help back in Canada.
I had to get back to Nashville so I paid for the rental car for another week. A few days later Cindy called me.
"I found a car, Charlie," she told me.
"What kind?" I asked her.
"A 1994 Mazda she replied. "It's going to cost $4500. Can you send that today or tomorrow?"
They won't hold the car but a couple of days."
You already know, don't you. I sent her the money.

I had recently noticed a change in my voice. It was getting more mellow and had a richer sound. I hadn't thought about recording as an artist in thirty years. I was 66 years old and it was certainly too late in life to try and become a recording star now. I chuckled at that thought.
However, with the encouragement of friends, and especially with Steve Wilkinson urging me onward, I decided to record a CD performing some of the hits I had been fortunate enough to write or co-write over the years. I booked studio time at EMI Studio, with

Old Memories and Me

Chris Latham as engineer, brought in six of the greatest musicians in the world, along with Monty Allen and Brittany Allyn for background vocals, and recorded 14 songs. Twelve of the songs had been previously recorded, which was the intended concept, but I also included two originals.

After I had produced the tracks myself and was ready to do my vocals I told Chris Latham, "I will sing each song three times and you can comp the best vocal from those. I won't get any better after the third try."

After my vocals were done, and Monty and Brittany had finished the harmony parts, I decided to have a few artists talk with me on the CD. My good friend Aaron Tippin did one conversation with me and the lovely Lorrie Morgan came into the studio and did another. Peter McCann came by and he and I talked on the CD about how we came to write *She's Single Again*.

Finally the album was finished and ready to be mixed and mastered. I had planned on Chris Latham mixing it but I had recently been asked to fly down to Orlando, Florida to do a benefit show, along with Tom Wompat and actor David Carradine. Johnny Bulford was also going to perform. It was perfect timing to showcase my new CD but Chris Latham already had a previous booking that would keep him busy for the next several weeks. I went to County Q and had it mixed it there so I could get it mastered and to a CD presser in time to take copies with me to Orlando.

The songs on that CD included, *Wanted, Matches, Between An Old Memory And Me, Midnight Tennessee Woman, Bring On The Night, I Would Like To See You Again, I'll Take The Memories, Let's Get Over Them Together, She's Single Again, Following The Feeling, She's Got A Way, Lay A Little Loving On Me* and the two original songs, *Everybody Falls* and *How Many Bridges*. Brittany Allyn did the two duets with me, *Let's Get Over Them Together* and *Following The Feeling*. Brittany also performed the two female songs, *She's Single Again* and *I'll Take The Memories*.

I was somewhat amazed at how well the CD turned out. However, I have always said, *if you want to be successful, surround yourself with successful people*. That is exactly what I did for my CD. The musicians I used were, Jeff King on lead guitar, Robert Arthur on acoustic guitar, Jim "Moose" Brown on keyboards, Dave Pomeroy on bass, Seth Rausch on drums and Wanda Vick played everything but the kitchen sink, but mostly dobra, fiddle, mandolin, banjo, and Weissenborn.

I titled the CD, *Old Memories And Me*. I never pitched it to any major record labels to pick up, instead I pressed CDs myself and sold them at writers' nights, a few gigs I worked, seminars, *CD Baby*, and on my website.

It didn't go platinum but it went over well in my neighborhood…

I flew back out to Scottsdale, Arizona to see Cindy. She wanted me to move to Scottsdale, for us to get married, get a condo there and me commute back and forth to Nashville.

"Cindy, it's a 3 ½ hour flight from Nashville to Scottsdale," I laughed. "That's 7 hours round trip. That is not a distance you commute."

On one visit with her she took me up to Sedona, Arizona. That is the most beautiful place I have ever seen. The mountains there just seem to spring up everywhere in various colors. We had lunch in a restaurant that was all glass on one side, facing some of the mountains. We went up into a chapel that was about ¾ ways up the side of one mountain, the glass A-frame sticking out into space. You could light a candle in the chapel and meditate, look out and see a cloud drift by, like God Himself was just outside that window. It was breathtaking.

I read somewhere while I was in Sedona that John Wayne had filmed 64 of his movies there. On the way up we had stopped in Cave Creek, at a stucco gift shop. I went out back and sat on an old wooden table, near the cactus, looking out across a desert and sagebrush. I kept expecting to see Clint Eastwood riding by any minute.

I loved Arizona and I wrote a song about Arizona and Cindy, along with Marty Brown, called *Arizona*.

> *I said where'd you get a name like that way out here in the desert*
> *She just smiled for a moment, then took another sip from her Corona*
> *That's the night I fell in love with Arizona*

About a month later Cindy had to go back home to Toronto, Ontario for a while to help her ailing grandmother. She would need her car so I flew out to Scottsdale to drive back with her. I didn't want her to have to drive that far alone. I remember just before we got to Interstate 40 to head east towards Albuquerque, New Mexico, we passed through Winslow, Arizona, the town named in the Eagles song *Take It Easy*. I thought that was so cool.

We actually took the long way because I needed to be in Nashville for a few days. After 4 days in Nashville we headed to the northern border. I had never been to Canada before. We crossed over at Detroit, where my friend Terrie Lea lived, the singer I had produced a few songs on in 2001.

Since Cindy had purchased the car in the Unified States she had to pay a tax as we crossed the border. I don't recall the exact amount I paid but I think it was a little over $500.

Women sure can get expensive. Well, at least the ones I kept getting involved with did.

The Canadian city just across the border where we crossed is Windsor and it has a big casino and I like to play the slot machines. When I went to the cashier window I gave the lady a hundred dollars in

Old Memories and Me

American currency. She gave me back $140 in Canadian money.

"I'm not fooling with the slot machines," I told Cindy. "I'm staying right here and keep giving this nice lady a hundred dollars. I win $40 every time I do that."

Terrie Lea came over and drove me back across the border when I left Cindy in Windsor after a two-day stay there. It was only a 1½-hour drive to Toronto from there so she would be alright. I flew back to Nashville from Detroit.

Cindy and I had practically driven from Mexico to Canada, with a stopover in Nashville. That is a far piece folks. Not bad for a 65 year old man. Most people guessed me to still be in my fifties.

CHAPTER TWENTY-THREE

Dawn had remarried and my new son-in-law was Dallas Matthews. I kidded her that she kept trying to live out my and Peter McCann's song, *She's Single Again*.

Is this number four, is this number five......

Dallas had a house in a cove over on Old Hickory Lake, about 15 or so minutes from me. Kyle was 12 years old now and Del 7. Kyle lived with Dawn and Dallas but he would stay with me some too. That bond has just always been there since Dawn moved back home when he was just a few months old. I love Del too but he has always been more of a mama's boy and stayed close to her when he wasn't at his dad's house every other weekend.

Dallas had a son, Cody, who was a year older than Kyle and when Cody came over to visit from his mom's house, Kyle would hang out with him a lot.

Now that it was warmer weather I flew up to Toronto to see Cindy. Toronto is a large city but didn't have as many skyscrapers as I had expected, like in New York. We drove around Lake Ontario to Niagara Falls one day and that was nice. I had never seen the falls.

Cindy was talking about going back to Arizona and Scottsdale. Even though she was a native of Canada she hated it there. She didn't like any part of the East coast. She didn't like Nashville either, nor any place with trees and grass and cold weather. She liked the desert sand and hot weather year round. She wanted me to move to Arizona with her, either to Scottsdale or Fountain Hills.

"I can't leave Nashville, Cindy," I told her. "That is where my work is, my career."

"If you love me you will come with me to Arizona," she pressed.

"You move to Nashville," I suggested.

"I can't live in Nashville," she told me. "You know that."

"And I can't live in Arizona," I reminded her.

"You can go back and forth," Cindy said.

I sighed. "We have been over that. It won't work."

I flew back home to Nashville, not angry, nor was Cindy, but there

Old Memories and Me

was just no middle ground in our situation.

2004 arrived with no particular fanfare. I wasn't dating anyone but Cindy and she was still up in Toronto. It was somewhere around 30 below zero there and I just don't like deep freeze weather, especially with 20 inches of snow on the ground to go with it. My friend Jami Grooms and his band were playing at a club not for from where I live so I went there New Years Eve and hung out with them for a couple of hours.

I was still writing songs but not a lot was going on. I was getting a few album cuts here and there and that's about all. Retiring was out of the question though. There is no way I can just stop writing completely. It is in my blood and flows constantly to my brain. There are some days after all these years that I have to put it on the back burner for a while and get back to it later but that creative drive is always there.

I was just in kind of a lag, bored actually, when David Godbold called me one day. David was still the guy heading up the South Carolina Entertainment Hall Of Fame and he was now doing the same in the state of North Carolina.

"Charlie, Andy Griffith is coming to Nashville to induct Earle Scruggs into the North Carolina Music and Entertainment Hall Of Fame," Godbold informed me. "He doesn't want a limo to ride around in. He wants a van and I told him about you and your conversion van. Andy said that would be perfect."

"Andy Griffith wants to ride around in my van?" I asked with a chuckle. "That should be a blast. I'd love to hang out with him."

"He and his wife will be there that Friday through Sunday afternoon," David Godbold told me. "The induction will be that Saturday night on the Grand Ole Opry show."

Of course I was delighted to be able to meet Andy Griffith and be with him for three days. It puzzled me though that they were just now inducting Earle Scruggs into the North Carolina Hall Of Fame and South Carolina had inducted me into theirs six years earlier. That made no sense at all. I mean, this was *Earle Scruggs*.

When the day arrived, David Godbold and I drove over in my van to Signature Airfield, the private airstrip adjoining Nashville International Airport. Andy Griffith and his wife flew in on a private twin-engine plane. When I first came eyeball to eyeball with Andy Griffith, I remember thinking, *why he looks just like himself*. I almost caught myself looking around for Barney.

David Godbold introduced everybody. Andy had that nice Mayberry smile he had on his television show. He also looked like Matlock.

"Nice to meet you, Charlie" Andy said and shook my hand.

"Nice to meet you too," I told him and certainly meant it.

Andy's wife was a lot younger than him. I learned later they had been married for ten years. She was an attractive, no nonsense, blonde lady that would prove to be very protective of Andy, in a professional and private way, not a jealous woman type thing.

After getting their luggage into my van, Andy told me, "I need to go out to Earle Scruggs house for a rehearsal. Do you know where he lives, Charlie?"

I glanced over my shoulder to where Andy and his wife were seated in the two captain chairs directly behind me and Godbold. "I'm not sure," I told Andy. "I know where his son, Randy lives, but I have never been to Earle's house."

David Godbold had the address to Earle Scruggs home on Franklin Road so we found it easily. It set back off of Franklin Road a bit, a long, white brick, ranch style home. The front lawn looked like a golf course it was so trimmed and cared for, a rich green. I parked at the end of the house where the garages were. I don't recall who came out to greet us but he led us in through the garage and Earle and his wife met us in the kitchen area.

Andy Griffith and Earle Scruggs appeared to have met before and exchanged handshakes like old friends. Mrs. Griffith and Mrs. Scruggs appeared not to have met before and exchanged pleasant hellos. Andy introduced David Godbold and me to the Scruggs.

Earle led everybody down a long hallway and I recall passing a room on our left with the door open. It was pure white. White carpet, white walls and ceiling, white drapes, with everything appearing to be a spotless white. I only had a glance as we passed and I didn't want to seem nosey and stare into the room, but that was the quick impression I got. It was beautiful, as was every room I saw in the Scruggs home.

Earle Scruggs led us to the far end of the house, and into what I suppose was a den, or family room. It was a very large room. Marty Stuart was there, and Glenn Duncan, along with Randy Scruggs and his brother, who's name I cannot recall. I already knew Glenn Duncan, Randy Scruggs and Marty Stuart. Marty had recorded my and Keith Stegall's song, *Matches*, back in the eighties.

Everybody was introduced and reintroduced. Marty Stuart said to me what he always says when I see him.

"I am gonna cut *Matches* again one of these days, Charlie. I still love that song."

It was a fascinating rehearsal to watch as Andy Griffith and Earle Scruggs went over with the other pickers what they would do on the Opry stage the next night, prior to the induction presentation. Andy was going to perform *Whoa Mule*, so they rehearsed that first.

I never really noticed when Andy played his guitar on The Andy Griffith show but I learned that day, along with everybody else, that he doesn't use a strap or a pick when he plays his guitar. He props his foot on something, then rest his guitar on his leg and strums the strings with his fingers. That day they tried to change that.

"I feel like I'm choking," Andy told everybody as he stood

there with a strap somebody had put on his guitar, then around his neck. They hadn't adjusted it very well and his guitar was setting too high up in front of him. "Get this thing off of me."

"Here," Marty Stuart said, reaching out a hand to assist Andy. "Let me adjust that thing for you."

"No, no," Andy insisted. "Just take it off. I can't use that thing. Never have been able to."

They took the strap off of Andy's guitar and he handed somebody the pick they had given him.

"Here, I can't use that thing either," he informed them. "I'm just a plain ole picker. I'm not a fancy musician like you fellows are." He was grinning but he meant it.

Now that they had left him alone to just be himself, Andy propped his right foot on a stool, rested his guitar on his leg and used the fingers on his right hand to strum out the rhythm and performed *Whoa Mule* to perfection.

After the rehearsal we left the Scruggs home and headed to Opryland Hotel where Andy and his wife would be staying in the Presidential Suite.

"Can we stop by the Grand Ole Opry House?" Andy asked. "I'd like to see the stage and where I will be performing tomorrow night."

The four of us went to the Opry House and a guard let us in. I don't think I had ever been at the Opry with nobody in the seats out front. It appeared to be even larger empty.

Andy found a spot on the stage he felt comfortable with.

"Okay," he said, more to himself than anybody. "First thing I'll do is tell my joke about the man in the barber shop, then I'll sing *Whoa Mule*." He then glanced first at his wife, then at me and Godbold, and said, "I'm gonna need a stool to prop my foot on to play my guitar."

I found a stool somewhere.

"How's this one?" I asked Andy.

"Let me see it," he said and I handed it to him. He sat it down on the stage and put his right foot up on it.

"Yeah, that will work just fine," he told me.

"I will hide it somewhere over there where you will come out onto the stage," I told him.

"No," Andy said, arching his brows. "Take it with you so we will be sure and have it tomorrow night."

"Ok," I replied. I couldn't help but smile. Andy smiled back at me.

"Now then," he said. "When David Godbold hands me the plaque to present to Earle Scruggs, Charlie, I want you to be out here on stage too, so I can hand you my guitar so I can hold the plaque with both hands. I don't want to drop the thing."

Andy Griffith had everything all planned out, right down to

that stool, and it was an honor for me to be in charge of that stool.

The next night, Saturday, I wore a black suit and tie. I was going to be on the Grand Ole Opry stage with Andy Griffith and Earle Scruggs, two icons, with the television cameras rolling, so I had to look as sharp as I could.

I picked David Godbold up at his motel and we drove to the Opryland Hotel and picked up Andy and his wife. Then, I drove the short distance to the Opry House.

I parked and as we got out of the van I asked Andy, "Isn't that the coat you wore on Matlock?"

Andy told me that it indeed was the coat he wore on that show.

After so many years of working and being around a lot of super stars, I am not easily impressed anymore, but walking alongside *Sherriff Andy Taylor* and *Matlock* himself, I felt at least two inches taller than I actually am.

Backstage was a mad house and the Opry was packed. I suppose it had been advertised that Andy and Earle would be there.

The first thing I did was find a stage hand and gave him Andy's stool, making him take an oath that he would guard it with his life and have it onstage for Andy when he needed it. Even then, I kept asking the guy, *where's the stool?*

That night, Earle Scruggs and the band that had rehearsed the day before, performed a song first, then Marty Stuart introduced Andy Griffith. As Andy walked out onto the stage the audience went absolutely berserk. Perhaps only the resurrection of Hank Williams could have equaled the response Andy Griffith got at the Grand Ole Opry that night.

Andy told his joke, then the stage hand placed the stool at his feet, as I breathed a sigh of relief. Andy then performed *Whoa Mule*.

After the song ended, Andy's wife, David Godbold and I went onstage. Andy immediately handed me his *Mayberry* guitar. I held it like the queen's jewels.

Godbold handed Andy the plaque.

"Earle," Andy began. "As a fellow North Carolinian, it is my honor, and a privilege, to induct you into the Country Music Hall Of Fame."

No, no, Andy. The North Carolina Entertainment Hall Of Fame. He's already in the Country Music Hall Of Fame.

The Country Music Hall Of Fame covers all of country music and is part of the CMA Awards every year. I don't think anybody caught that but me.

As Earle Scruggs started to reach to take the plaque from Andy, he took the strap from his shoulder, and I suppose seeing me standing there holding Andy's guitar, he handed me his banjo.

Oh, my goodness. There I stood holding Andy Griffith's

Old Memories and Me

Mayberry guitar and Earle Scruggs *Martha White/Beverley Hillbilly's* banjo. If my mama hadn't raised me better, I think I would have peed my pants right there on the Grand Ole Opry stage.

Sunday after lunch, I drove Andy Griffith and his wife back to board their private plane to return home to Mt. Airy, North Carolina. It had been both a joy and a pleasure to be with Andy and his wife that weekend. I hated to see them go.

I don't imagine many people have had the opportunity to talk with Andy Griffith about your first guitar and first tape recorder, to share those kinds of stories and experiences the way Andy and I did those few days. He is a man and an experience I will never forget.

Somebody pass me the mashed potatoes. I've already got lots of gravy in my life.

The benefit show in Orlando was set for September 20th and I flew down a couple of days early to spend some time with my friends, the Bulford's. Cindy Desotta wanted to come down too so I asked the people putting on the benefit if they would fly her down from Toronto as a favor. They were gracious enough to do so.

That Friday night Johnny Bulford and I appeared on a *Little Grand Ole Opry* show in a small town about ninety minutes outside of Orlando. Then, on Saturday we did the benefit show at a mall in Orlando. Tom Wompat and David Carradine were there to perform as well. It poured down rain so the crowd was off but I enjoyed myself, especially dinner at Cattleman's Steak House.

I didn't see Tom Wompat perform but I did watch David Carradine for a little while. It was just him and his guitar and he did songs he had written.

Johnny Bulford showed me a few new songs he had recently written. They were really good. He was getting better with every song he wrote and his vocals were getting stronger and he was sounding more mature.

"After the first of the year I want to come to Nashville and record a few of my songs with a full band," he told me.

"I will look forward to that," I assured him.

Before we caught our separate flights back to Nashville and Toronto, Cindy told me it was going to cost $2000 to get her car fixed to comply with the Canada regulations to qualify for her license plates. Here in the states we go through an emission test that cost $10, at least that's the cost in Nashville. In Canada they evidently check a lot more about the condition of your car.

"That's about half of what I paid for the car," I told Cindy. "That's ridiculous."

"I have to get my plates Charlie," Cindy said. "But I can't qualify until I get the carburetor and a few other things fixed."

"I am not going to pay $2000 to get a $4500 car repaired," I told her adamantly.

"But, Charlie," Cindy sighed. "I have to get it fixed to get my license plates."

You readers are smart. You already know what I did, don't you.

Yeah, I gave her the money.

After the first of the year Johnny Bulford came to Nashville, along with his mom and sister Ally. I produced 3 songs on him at County Q Studio. Johnny had written, or co-written, all three songs; *Now*, *Goodbye Cry* and a brand new song called *New Song*. I brought in Monty Allen and Brittany Allyn to add the harmonies.

Once the session was mixed I called several record labels and set up appointments to play it for them. At RCA Leslie Roberts loved Johnny.

"Who is this guy," she asked me after hearing the session.

"His name is Johnny Bulford," I told her. "He is from Orlando, Florida. He's about to turn eighteen Leslie, and I swear, this kid is amazing."

"When can I meet him? " she asked. "When can you bring him in?"

"I will check with him and see when would be a good time for him to come back to Nashville and I will call you," I told her.

Over at Curb Records Doug Johnson reacted pretty much the same way Leslie Roberts had at RCA.

"Who is this guy?"

The same thing happened with Cris Lacy at Warner Brothers. She loved what I played her of Johnny Bulford.

I coordinated the visits with RCA, Curb and Warner Brothers so Johnny could see them all in two days time. We took Robert Arthur along to play acoustic guitar with Johnny so it would sound fuller with two guitars.

Leslie Roberts, Doug Johnson and Cris Lacy all loved him even more in person. Doug loved his voice but seemed even more impressed with his songwriting.

"He writes well beyond his years," Doug said.

Cris Lacy mentioned flying down to Orlando to see Johnny perform live.

Leslie Roberts wanted him to stay in touch. She wanted to hear any new songs he wrote and at some point wanted him to come back to RCA and perhaps perform live for the other RCA staff members as well.

Everybody that heard him was impressed but nobody really made a move to sign him to a record contract. Sometimes I think Music Row is built on molasses ground because things sure do move slow most of the time.

Through my youngest grandson Del's stepmother, Lisa Primm,

Old Memories and Me

I was approached about helping to bring in talent for a benefit to aid The Mental Health Association Of Middle Tennessee, to be held at the Ryman Auditorium. The benefit was called, Jammin' To Beat the Blues.

We needed a headliner and Lee Ann Womack was gracious enough to do the show. I brought in my dear friends, The Wilkinsons, and I got Jilla Roberts in the lineup as well. Tyler Alexander was a young act I had produced and I was able to get him on the show too. Bruce Channel, of *Hey Baby* fame, was there and that was a special treat for me because as a teenager I would perform that song and play harmonica at the same time. Buddy Jewel, that year's Nashville Star winner did an acoustic set to round out the show. I chose not to perform so I could get my friends on the show instead.

That afternoon I met Ruth Landers, actress and mother/manager of actresses Audrey and Judy Landers. Audrey Landers is probably most remembered for her role on the mega sitcom hit, *Dallas*, as playing the character J.R. Ewing's mistress. Judy was the co-star of *BJ and the Bear*. The Lander sisters both had appeared, as well as starred, in many movies.

Joe Danna, from JD Jam Records, out of Florida, had brought Ruth Landers to town for the benefit to see Tyler Alexander perform. We had all gone to an early dinner prior to the show at the Ryman.

After the benefit we were invited to an invitation only party at producer Tony Brown's beautiful home that was hosted by Tony and his lovely wife, Anastasia.

At one point in the evening Tony Brown played some classical piano for everybody and that was a treat. Following Tony, Jilla Roberts performed a copula a song she and I had written with Monty Allen. That wasn't an easy thing to do, considering the company she was in, and standing in the middle of a room full of people, with no microphone. She did a magnificent job and I was really proud of her. During her performance Tony Brown smiled in my direction and gave me a thumbs up. It was all very informal but certainly entertaining.

The next day I spent a lot of time with Ruth Landers. She was a very interesting lady, very much a businesswoman, charming, and also very attractive. There was something about her that reminded me of Dolly Parton. That's as much a compliment to Dolly as it is to Ruth.

We had lunch together and later drove to the airport and sat in my car listening to some of my songs. Ruth was very familiar with country music but hadn't known I had written, or co-written some of the hits she recognized.

"I didn't know you wrote *Wanted*," she told me. "I love that song, Charlie."

"Actually, I wrote it with Alan Jackson," I replied. "The song was his idea and it has really been a big song for both of us."

I played Ruth Landers a couple of songs I had written about Betty and she cried, showing the tender side of such a charming lady.

She particularly liked *What A Day Yesterday Was*.

"That is such a beautiful song," she told me, not trying to hide the tears rolling down her cheek.

Ruth told me someone she had loved very much had also died from cancer. We must have talked for over an hour sitting in my car, listening to my songs, talking in between each one, getting to know each other.

Naturally, I knew who her two daughters were, Audrey and Judy Landers. She told me about her grandchildren and I could see her eyes light up with pride. This was a woman dedicated to, and filled with love for her family. I told her about Dawn and my two grandsons. She told me how her entire family had moved from Beverly Hills to Sarasota, Florida in 1999. She invited me to come down and visit.

Eventually, we went inside The Nashville Airport and after she checked in we sat in a coffee shop and talked until time for her to go through security and board her flight. I knew this was a lady I was going to like a lot.

I go out to Bob Stegall's office and visit with him quite a lot. Bob is Keith Stegall's dad. Bob played steel guitar in legendary Johnny Horton's band back in the early fifties. Later, Bob recorded as an artist himself and another legend, Jim Reeves, played rhythm guitar on his records. How many people can make that claim?

Bob and I can talk for hours exchanging stories from yesteryears. He is a little older than I am but he has never looked his age either. Keith Stegall looks a lot like his dad and I suppose he inherited his musical talents from him as well. When Keith bought a house for his offices in the Berry Hill section of Nashville, Bob moved his office into one of the rooms and operates his publishing company there. Keith has a studio in the back of the building where he does mostly overdubs and mixing.

Keith has done really well in the business, not only as a songwriter, and as an artist himself on Epic Records in the early eighties, but as a producer he has been Alan Jackson's producer from day one and he has also produced hits on Jamie O'Neal, Clay Walker, and several other big name acts.

I still call Bob Stegall or stop by and visit with him on a regular basis today. He has been a good friend over the years.

Ruth Landers had produced a movie that featured her granddaughters, Lindsey and Kristy Landers, with her grandson Daniel also in the movie, as were Audrey and Judy, her daughters. The movie was called *Fantasy Island* and Ruth called me and told me she really liked my song *Because Of You* that I had produced on Tyler Alexander

Old Memories and Me

and she had done some editing to include it in a scene in the movie. This was the same song I had produced on Chris Young a couple of years earlier. A good song just seems to find a way to hang around and get attention.

After telling me about putting my song in her movie Ruth talked to me about coming to Saratoga, Florida to visit her. She also wanted me to work with Lindsay and Kristy, Judy's daughters, to see how they would do singing country music. Lindsay was sixteen and Kristy fourteen at that time.

It is difficult to get a good flight connection into Sarasota, so I flew me into Tampa, where her son-in-law, Judy's husband, Tom Niedenfuer, picked me up and drove me the 45 minutes to Sarasota. Tom was a Las Angeles Dodger relief pitcher. He had retired at age thirty-two. He was a very likeable guy and told me a little about his baseball career during the drive. He also told me that he hung out a lot with *ESPN* basketball analyst Dick Vitale, traveling with him sometimes on his college broadcast games. Since I am a college basketball junkie I found that to be really cool.

Ruth Landers lives in a beautifully exclusive neighborhood, as do her daughters, Audrey and Judy. Ruth met and greeted me at the door and she looked even more ravishing than I remembered when she had visited Nashville. That day she had on a long black dress that had colorful flowers up one side. She is still a very shapely woman and it was easy to see where her daughters got their good looks from.

"Hello, Charlie," she smiled and gave me a warm hug.

"Hello, Ruth," I said and stepped back to look at her. "Wow, aren't you something else."

"Ohhh," she laughed pleasantly. "You are too nice."

As I entered the spacious entrance to her home I immediately knew I was walking into one of the most beautiful houses I had ever seen, and I have seen some beauties.

The floors in that area were marble and there was a white grand piano with lights beneath that reflected off the floor. There were two enormous chandeliers, one near the front entrance and the other over an elegant dining table. Later, I would inquire, and Ruth would tell me how she had moved each one of those huge hanging crystal chandeliers in individual 18-wheelers when she moved from Beverley Hills to Sarasota in 1999. Each one must have been 25-30 feet long, hanging from a ceiling that reached the top of the second story home on that end of the house.

The kitchen, dinette, and family room area was very spacious as well. It was one large open area with a billiard table in the family room section. I have a pool table, but that was a *billiard table*. Just off the kitchen and dinette area was a large patio and swimming pool that was completely enclosed in glass, including the ceiling.

Upstairs was a very unique theatre room just for watching

movies and she had hundreds of DVDs. All of the bedrooms were large with spacious bathrooms. The entire house was elegant and spotless with lovely décor.

By the way, at my own decision, I left my shoes at the front door.

For the first time since Betty had died I had met a female that didn't want or need something from me, other than just me for myself.

That afternoon I met Judy Landers and her two lovely teenage daughter's, Lindsay, 16, and Kristy 14. A little later Audrey Landers came over as well. It was easy to see the genes of Ruth Landers in her beautiful siblings.

Around sundown Ruth and I went for a walk along the streets of the plush neighborhood where she lived. She put her arm into mine and we had a marvelous time just strolling along walking her dog and talking.

On that first visit I stayed four days and worked with Lindsay and Kristy most afternoons after school, rehearsing different country songs and one in particular that I had written with Steve Wilkinson and Illya Toshinsky. It was called *Walk On Water*.

While I was there, Ruth, Judy, Lindsay, Kristy and I went on a boat ride that took us through the channel waterway leading out to the Gulf of Mexico. I remember a school of dolphins jumping through the water as they moved along with us for a brief spell. That was a beautiful sight.

Judy was piloting the boat and she pulled into a large cove, then headed slowly to the shore of a peninsula. We left the boat there and walked along a path that was lush with greenery, palm tress and colorful flowers. We walked through the edge of a yard near the end of the peninsula.

"That house belongs to Stephen King," Ruth informed me.

"It looks nice but it looks kind of like an airplane hanger with windows," I remarked. I wasn't making light of the house, for I am sure it was a very expensive place, but it didn't look like your normal house. Kind of like Stephen King's books, just different. In any event it would make my little 3100 square foot home look like a nanny's quarters.

It was only about another 50 yards farther to the other side of the peninsula and the blue waters of the gulf. The five of us walked barefooted in the white sand along the beach, looking for seashells and unusual little rocks and pebbles.

Eventually we came to a large beach house right on the waterfront. There had been a hurricane pass through the area a couple of months earlier and the house had been damaged badly. They had it roped off to keep people from going inside where it could be dangerous. It was sad to see such a beautiful place damaged like that. The force of the storm had actually moved the house from its foundation and the cement floor of the garage was still lifted from the ground and sitting

Old Memories and Me

at a tilted angle. I was told it belonged to a cancer research doctor and Ruth had shot a lot of the scenes from *Fantasy Island* in the home before the hurricane had hit. A little more inland, probably thirty yards from the damaged beachfront home, the doctor had a couple of smaller beach houses that were not hit by the hurricane winds.

Cindy called my cell a couple of times while I was there. She was jealous that I was staying at Ruth's home.

"I am in my own guest room, Cindy," I told her.

"Yeah, well I'll bet she is flirting with you and making passes at you," she said to me and I could tell she was really worried about it.

"She is not," I assured her.

Ruth Landers had not flirted with me, not in a way Cindy was thinking. Ruth and I became close while I was with her and there were a few moments that I would describe as a little romantic, but nothing that would make a gossip column. We were just friends.Perhaps more would develop between us but I won't speculate further on that.

To say I enjoyed my four-day stay with Ruth and the rest of the Landers would be an understatement. It was a marvelous time for me.

Before I left, Ruth and I made plans for me to come back for another visit.

I visit Betty's gravesite and keep a nice arrangement of artificial flowers in the two holders on each side of the headstone. I still kiss the ground where her head would be when I arrive and again when I leave. I always say a prayer while I am there because ever since God spoke to me there right after Betty's death, I feel especially close to Him there.

One Sunday afternoon when I went to the cemetery I was shocked to see a canvas on the ground covering a freshly dug grave, right beside where Betty was buried. I immediately used my cell phone to call the funeral home that took care of the cemetery. There was no answer so I drove by there. The door was locked and nobody came when I rang the doorbell. I tried calling again but still no answer.

Early the next morning I called them again. This time they answered.

"You have dug a new grave on my plot beside where my wife is buried," I told the lady.

"There is a burial there today at 11am, Mr. Craig," she replied.

"But the grave site is next to your plot, not on your plot."

"No ma'am," I informed her. "They dug the grave on the plot I own."

"I will run over and there and check," she told me.

Fifteen minutes later she called me back.

"Mr. Craig, you are absolutely right," she said in disbelief. "They did dig the grave on your plot and I do apologize."

The lady told me they would move the burial up until later that day, fill in the hole on my plot and dig another grave one plot over. I felt sorry for the family of the deceased that the service would have to be delayed.

I had an appointment with Dr. Friddell that morning to see about a sore throat and congestion I had. He x-rayed my chest.

"There is a spot on your lung that we need to check," he told me. "I want to send you to have a CT Scan." I could tell he was a little concerned.

"Well," I smiled and said with my sense of humor. "If it's cancer, they've already dug a hole to bury me in."

I had the CT Scan and when the report came back the next day to Dr. Friddell he told me everything was alright, so I booked a flight and flew home to South Carolina to visit my sisters and Bobbie, Betty's twin. As I always do when I go home, I spent some time with my high school sweetheart Polly Powers Simmons. Polly will always have a special place in my heart.

I always feel a bit guilty that I don't get up to Rock Hill to see Juanita McGuirt, Betty's other sister, but by the time I visit my sister Ruby in Columbia, then my sister Dot in Greenville, with Bobbie and my other family members in Laurens and Watts Mill, I just run out of time. I guess that is a lame excuse. I do love Juniata though and remember some good times with her and Dee. I need to visit her soon because time keeps slipping away, just as I wrote in a song Red Sovine recorded back in the late seventies called, *The Days Of Me And You*.

> Time keeps slipping away
> Minute by minute each day
> Some things that I wanted to do
> I just didn't get around to
> And I wasted the days of me and you

Dawn, Dallas and my two grandsons moved in with me. I was actually glad because I had a lot of room and I was also lonely at times. After my divorce from Brenda I had gone furniture shopping and replaced the furniture I had given her. Dawn had gone with me and we had picked out a nice bunk bed and matching chest of drawers for the boys. We had bought a really nice dinette table with a white tile top that had natural wood down the center and along the outside edges. There were six wooden high back chairs and the table would let out on rollers to a larger size if needed. There was good cabinet space beneath. It was really nice and it gave us plenty of dining space without using the dining room. Like most families we only use the dining room for special occasions like Thanksgiving and Christmas.

Dawn had helped me pick out a dark blue leather family room suite that consist of a large sofa with lazy boys on both ends, a matching

Old Memories and Me

love seat and a high back lazy boy chair that also matched. The two end lamps were blue with blue shades and the oak wood end tables matched the coffee table that had a top that lifted up. A large white floor lamp, a black marble top table and my 62-inch wide screen television completed the room. It was nice and it was comfortable. It was good to get my house and life back in order again.

My home is not a mansion by any stretch of the imagination but it is nice and Betty and I had worked hard and long in between medical bills and some tough times to get to where we could afford to build it. I just wish she could have enjoyed it a few more years.

When Dawn had married Dallas and moved to his house we had left the bunk beds in the boys' room. When they all moved back in with me we bought a futon for Dawn's old bedroom upstairs and Kyle moved into that room. We got him a desk with a chair and a TV stand for his television. Del took the room where the bunk beds were and Dawn and Dallas turned the study downstairs into their bedroom.

I was still writing mostly with Steve Wilkinson and some with Rob Crosby. I was writing good songs but not getting many songs recorded. My career has always been good runs then dry spells. I was in another dry spell.

Cindy was going through a lot of confusion in her life. She hated it in Canada. She couldn't afford to go back to Arizona at the time. We had talked on the phone about her coming to Nashville and the two of us finally deciding what we were going to do about each other. We had discussed marriage before but deep in my heart I wasn't wanting that. I cared about Cindy but I just didn't want to get married again. Perhaps I was gun shy now, I don't know.

Cindy drove down in that old 94 Mazda and I was surprised it was still running after so many miles. One of our favorite places to go in both Scottsdale and Nashville was Houston's. We went there one night out on West End Avenue. We dined at the bar as we usually did. Things were good and we had a nice time.

With Dawn and the boys living with me Cindy slept in the pool table room on an air mattress. I would have given my bed up to Cindy but I hate air mattresses. Air mattresses are a little like waterbeds and I don't like waterbeds either. Lying on them is like trying to keep rhythm to the wrong tempo.

After Cindy had been here for four days, she got a call from a friend about a meeting in Toronto concerning a new adventure in networking one of those, what I call, *get rich overnight quirks*. I don't recall what this one was about but I knew it would be another one of those deals where Cindy would do a lot of work and somebody else make the money, if any money was actually made.

"Cindy, when are you going to stop chasing these get rich quick schemes?" I asked her.

"It's not a get rich quick scheme," she replied, a little miffed at me for referring to it as such. "I know the guy heading this up and he makes millions doing these investments."

"Well, he may make millions," I countered. "But so far *you* haven't made a dime on one of these things."

We wound up arguing about it, that and a couple of other things, until we were arguing again about her wanting me to marry her and move to Arizona.

"I am not moving to Arizona, Cindy," I told her.

She wound up going back to Canada for the meeting, saying she would be back in a few days. I told her not to bother coming back if she left because I was tired of her always running off after some wild and crazy fortune and not wanting to live anywhere but where she wanted to live, never caring what I wanted. It was just not going to work between she and I.

I had met a songwriter/singer by the name of Todd Shea. He was also an excellent guitar player. It is hard to remember exactly where Todd is from because he was all over the place, traveling to do a show at Mount Rushmore, playing at Central Park for the military in New York, hiking through the Appalachians Mountains, spending time with his son Jason in Maryland, and visiting with his girlfriend Michelle in Florida.

Todd had written a patriotic song and wanted me to produce it for him. He had connections that got him on Fox News in New York and he performed the song one morning on Fox around 7:15 am. He had asked me to watch so I set my alarm clock for 7:00. After Todd performed the song with his acoustic guitar he told the anchorman and his lady co-anchor that he was coming to Nashville to record the song and said, "Charlie Craig is going to produce it for me."

The anchorman said, "Well, you will be in good hands with him."

I nearly fell out of my bed when the Fox News guy knew who I was.

Todd Shea had been in New York on September 11, 2001 and had seen the second plane hit the tower from his motel room. He immediately had driven his van to the scene and spent days helping at Ground Zero. I have never known anyone more giving and willing to sacrifice himself to travel anywhere in the world to help during a crisis. He would later go to Pakistan and other foreign countries to help with relief programs.

Todd came to Nashville on several occasions and stayed at my home. Besides going into the studio producing his patriotic song we later wrote a couple of new songs. He had so many interesting stories to tell. He has been in some danger zones and rough situations most people would never dare venture to. He is one tough guy and if I am ever in need of someone with real courage, Todd Shea would be the person I would call on.

Old Memories and Me

One day I called my pal Vince Gill to write another song together. We wrote at his home on this occasion. This was during the time Vince and his wife Janet were separated and eventually would divorce. Janet had moved out and the part of the house Vince and I were writing in was almost void of furniture. I recall noticing imprints in the carpet where furniture had been. It looked a little sad to me. Somehow those imprints reminded me of Betty being gone, like little memories here and there. It just made me realize, regardless of who we are, heartaches don't care who they hurt.

I had already written a song with Keith Stegall by that title but that day, just purely by coincidence, Vince and I wrote a song called *What I Knew Then*.

I wish I knew now what I knew then.

CHAPTER TWENTY-FOUR

I made a couple more trips to Sarasota to visit my friend Ruth Landers. I worked with her granddaughters Lindsay and Kristy on their vocals and had a few lunches with Audrey and Judy, as well as with Ruth of course.
One night we all went to see a circus where all of the performers were students at a school for gifted children. It was one of the most amazing things I have ever seen. The youngest performers were eight graders and the oldest seniors. Lindsey and Kristy attended school there and Kristy performed on the trapeze that night, flying out over us and letting go to catch herself with her feet and ankles in the corner of the bar and rope. She wasn't a bit scared but I was sure afraid for her.
It was like going to a Barnum and Bailey Circus. These kids did everything from walking and balancing on the tight rope to the trapeze acts. One boy, a junior, did a double somersault on the trapeze and the catcher, a senior, caught him.
Those students were as good as any professionals you see in a big top.
Ruth drove me to a marina where she once kept her boat. There were all sizes of yachts and sailboats anchored in slips there. Some of them were huge and all of them were beautiful. Ruth and I sat at a table on a wooden sidewalk of a little cantina and had refreshments, listening to a gentleman play guitar and sing, as we looked out across the blue watered harbor at the sailboats and seagulls. It was lovely there and very romantic. We talked and enjoyed each other's company.
Once again I hated to leave.
I was still writing good songs and getting a few holds at the record labels but not much was happening with my songwriting career as far as having new singles on the radio. I had started looking for songs I thought would be good for Lindsay and Kristy Landers to record. When I would find one I would mp3 in an email to Ruth Landers and Judy. I talked several times a week with Judy on the phone about the project I was working on for her daughters.
"We really like your song, *Walk On Water*," Judy told me on the phone. "We also like the one about the Wal-Mart parking lot."

Old Memories and Me

The Wal-Mart parking lot song was written by my pals Bud and Mike McGuire, along with Troy Seals.

"What do the girls think about them?" I asked Judy.

"Oh, Lindsay and Kristy love both of them," she said.

I had written a song with Steve and Amanda Wilkinson that Audrey Landers liked for herself and her son Daniel to record as a duet.

A couple of weeks later I flew back down and worked with Lindsay and Kristy on the songs *Walk On Water* and *Wal Mart Social Parking Lot*. I also spent time with Audrey working out the parts for her and Daniel on the duet, *All The King's Horses*.

Ruth, Audrey and I talked about me going to Germany and opening for Audrey in some of her shows over there. They liked my CD I had recorded a couple of years earlier, *Old Memories And Me*. We would sit out by Ruth's glass enclosed pool and I would play my guitar and sing songs from that CD.

"That would be fun," I told them. "I have never been to Germany."

"You would love it there, Charlie," Audrey told me. "It's a beautiful country and they love country music there."

"It's been a while since I have performed before a live audience," I informed them.

Ruth gave me a warm and confident smile. "You can do it, Charlie. You are a trooper, I can tell."

"Well, it sure sounds exciting," I told them with an appreciative smile.

I returned to Nashville to produce the tracks for Lindsay and Kristy's songs, as well as the duet track for Audrey and Daniel. I booked EMI Studio and called the six musicians I wanted and set the session up for two weeks later.

In the meantime Ruth sent me a video of Lindsay and Kristy performing mine, Steve Wilkinson and Illya Toshinsky song, *Walk On Water*. A filmmaker from Germany had visited Ruth and had made a video of the girls performing the song. It was home made but it was really good. There was one shot of 14-year-old Kristy turning to look at the camera as she brushed a strand of hair from her youthful and beautiful face that was priceless.

"You could shoot that scene a hundred times and never get that same magical effect," I told Ruth over the phone.

"I know," she agreed. "Those are the scenes you strive for but seldom get. It only happens when it's natural."

Just before I went into the studio I started having some health issues. I had been coughing up a little blood and since it had happened before, Dr. Friddell thought it was probably sinus drainage. Now I had begun to have some discomfort in my chest. My cardiologist, and friend, Hal Roseman, told me he rather I not fly back to Florida until we checked some things out. I had felt something was wrong for a few weeks because I got tired easily and I have always gone at everything I do wide open, around the clock. That was getting harder to do.

I did get the tracks produced and Fed-Exed them to Sarasota to Ruth Landers. Lindsay, Kristy, Audrey and Daniel were all going to record their vocals in a studio there and send the tracks back to me to mix and master in Nashville.

After the Landers had sent the tracks back to me with the vocals, I added Brittany Allyn to them with a few harmony parts. We did that at County Q Studio and T. W. Cargill mixed them. I then sent a copy to Ruth Landers.

I was tired and needed a break. Dawn, Kyle Del and me, along with Dawn's husband, Dallas, and his son, Corey, took my conversion van and drove to Myrtle Beach, South Carolina. Dawn and Dallas did a lot of the driving.

I hadn't asked my doctors about going on the trip and halfway there I knew I had made a mistake in going. I started coughing up more blood and my chest pains were getting worse. Everybody was excited about going to the beach, especially the boys, and I didn't want to spoil anything for them. I didn't say much about the pain but Dawn knew I was coughing up more blood.

"It is probably sinus," she said.

It wasn't sinus and I now knew it.

It was all I could do to walk out on the beach and back to the hotel room. I gave out of breath quickly and the pain in my upper chest was almost unbearable at times. I would take Mylanta and that would help ease the pain for a while, so I tried to tell myself the pain was coming from a reflux problem I have had for years. That didn't explain the blood I was coughing up though. By the third day at Myrtle Beach I was coughing up what looked like purple grape hulls. I called Hal Roseman.

"I want you to come back to Nashville today, Charlie," he told me. "I want to have x-rays done to see where the bleeding is coming from and also do a cardiac catheterization to check your heart."

Dawn had paid for the rooms and they were very expensive. I offered to give her the money back but she wouldn't take it. I felt really bad ending everybody's vacation two days early. They all understood and wanted to get me home to my doctors.

Once we were on our way home I called Dr. Roseman again and during the conversation he told me he couldn't perform the catheterization until they found out where the bleeding was coming from. He told me he was setting up an appointment with a lung specialist for Monday morning. Since this was Friday, I decided to try and make up for causing my family to miss two days at the beach.

"We are going to stop at Pigeon Forge," I told them. "We can spend tonight there and tomorrow we'll go to Dollywood."

"We can't do that," Dawn protested. "Let's get you home. We

Old Memories and Me

are all alright. We had four days at the beach."

"Yeah, Papa," Kyle said to me. "You are more important than anything else."

"They can't do anything until Monday anyway," I insisted. "We are going to stop at Pigeon Forge and I will pay for everything."

There was more protest but I won out. We stopped at Pigeon Forge late that afternoon even though I knew something was bad wrong with me. It even occurred to me I might be dying. I decided that if I was dying I was going to have a good time with my family before it happened, so I raced go-carts at Pigeon Forge that night, holding my chest to try and ease the pain. I love racing on the track there that goes up to a second floor, over a big hump where the go-cart leaves the floor before racing back down to the ground level. I know it was crazy to do that with my condition but I wanted to have a good time and besides, I'm a tough old bird.

We spent Saturday at Dollywood.

Dollywood is the only mountain that is uphill going up and coming back down too. I finally rented one of those little carts to ride in. I wasn't as tough as I thought.

I got to see and visit with Dolly's uncle, Lewis Owens while I was there. Lewis was the one that actually signed me to write for Dolly's publishing company, Owepar, back in the early seventies. Lewis performs with other family members on the front porch of a log house at Dollywood. It is great of Dolly to do that for her family but I've told you that she was a wonderful lady.

The next week I had a chest x-ray and it showed something the lung specialist, Dr. Aaron Esbenshade, was concerned about.

"There is a spot there that I am not sure about," he told me. "It may be scar tissue, or it could be a tumor. I just don't know, but something is there, so I want to have a CAT scan done to see what it is."

I had the CT scan and the next morning I met with a young songwriter from Oklahoma, Paul Bogart. He had found me through my website and had contacted me about helping him get started in Nashville. That day we were tossing around ideas and Paul told me about a little boy back in Oklahoma that he knew.

"Every Sunday in church he tries to put junk from his pockets in the collection plate," Paul told me.

"There ought to be a song in there somewhere," I laughed.

Paul and I discussed what a little boy would carry around in his pocket. We decided on rocks and marbles for sure and probably a frog.

Then my cell phone rang. It was Dr. Esbenshade with the CT scan results.

"There is a small tumor there and it is cancer," he told me.

Somehow I already knew that.

Dr. Esbenshade asked me to come to his office. I told

Paul Bogart I would have to leave and get back with him later. He understood.

I went straight to Esbenshade's office and after a few minutes wait, a nurse took me back to see him.

"You have been on a baby aspirin every day for quite a while, haven't you?" he asked.

"Yes," I told him. "Ever since Dr. Roseman put two stints in my heart in 1996."

"That baby aspirin saved your life," he informed me. "It caused this cancer to bleed. If that hadn't happened we wouldn't have looked for anything. Now we have found it in its infancy and I think we can get it all with surgery."

"So, it is definitely cancer," I remarked, again already knowing.

"Yes," he said. "But we have found it in time and I feel confident we can get it all with surgery.

I knew I would be laid up for quite a while recovering from the surgery. I never had liked the mattress on my bed I had bought while I was married to Brenda. It was too hard and I wanted to be as comfortable as I could while recovering. I went out and bought a new one. I didn't realize it was a pillow top and when I put it on my bed there was a drop off where the headboard on my bed had a shelf and mirror. It was a king size bed Betty and I had bought back in the late eighties.Since the bed was quite old now, and I liked the new mattress, I bought a new bedroom suite and also a 42-inch plasma television. I was going to make sure I was comfortable for my long recouping period.

It just happened that my friend Jane Bounce had to move from her furnished apartment because the owners were selling it, and she was moving into an unfurnished apartment. I gave her my old bedroom suite.

Ruth Landers called regularly to check on my condition and she told she wanted to come here when I had my surgery. I told her that wasn't necessary. I knew she had a lot going on business wise at both home and in Europe. She had a business trip already planned in Germany and her flight booked. I insisted that she not worry about me and to go on and fly to Germany. She finally conceded, telling me I would be in her thoughts and prayers.

Before they set up the lung surgery Dr. Roseman did a catheterization and found another blocked artery in my heart. They also found I had an 85 percent blockage in my neck, giving concern for a possible stroke.

Dawn was concerned and upset over these events but she hid it well, at least from the boys, but not from me. I'm her dad and know her well. Kyle was upset as well but he handled it all extremely good for a 13 year old. Del was only 8 years old and I don't think he really realized his papa was facing a life-threatening situation.

We prayed as a family and we prayed separately. My church

Old Memories and Me

family at Hermitage Hill Baptist Church started praying for me, as did my friends and other family members. I recall Wanda Vick really being concerned and showing her love and concern for me. She told me her church prayer committee was praying for me as well. Wanda plays on all of my recording sessions and has for the past 20 plus years.

I was concerned but I wasn't afraid. I knew it was in God's hands and I knew Jesus would take every step with me through it all. I was in great hands. I was 68 years old but still in pretty good shape. My hair had started to turn gray in some places but most people were still guessing me to be in my mid fifties.

In September and October of 2005, a cardiologist, Dr. Waldo, inserted two more stints in my heart. Another doctor did surgery on my neck to clear the blocked artery there and a lung surgeon then took out 2/3 of my right lung to remove the cancer.

My surgeon came into the room after I woke up and asked me how I was doing.

"Well, you were only partly truthful with me," I told him, still a bit groggy and in a lot of pain.

"Oh?" he remarked.

"Yeah," I grimaced. "You told me when I first woke up I would feel like I had been run over by a truck. That turned out to be true but what you didn't tell me it was going to come back and run over me again."

Later that afternoon two nurses came into my room.

"You need to get up and walk a little, Mr. Craig," one of them told me.

"You are kidding me," I gasped in agony.

"You just need to take a couple of steps, that's all," she said.

"I am hurting so bad I can't even turn over in this bed and you expect me to get you up and take a couple of steps?" I was astonished. "No way I can do that."

Throughout my protesting the nurses assisted me in sitting up, then getting my legs over the side of the bed and finally standing. Well, I wasn't standing straight up. I couldn't. I was sort of crouched over, my knees trying to buckle. It hurt really bad and I was weak as a little kitten. It took me what seemed like fifteen minutes to barely slide my feet those couple of steps. Then, getting back into bed was even more painful than getting up was.

"Ohhh..."

"You're alright," one of the nurses said softly, holding me and trying to help me ease back down onto my back.

I had tubes running out of me from every part of my body.

"I'm not alright," I informed her and I know I must have sounded like a baby whining.

I would whine a lot more before I got out of there. It was my pain and I could whine if I wanted too.

I was in the hospital 9 days from the lung surgery and Dawn and Kyle spent several nights there by my side, sleeping in chairs, giving me all the love and mental support in their hearts. Del came to see me several times as well. Pastor Poly Rouse from Hermitage Hills Baptist Church came by.

RCA Records and EMI both sent me nice flower arrangements. A couple of other record labels called a few days after my surgery. Jill Farrar came by to see me a couple of times. So did John Riggs. My nephew, Craig Armstrong had flown from Columbia, S.C. to Nashville for a business meeting and he came by to see me. Craig and Amy Hand came by as well. I had recently produced a 10 song CD on Craig Hand and had played it for all of the record labels to try and secure him a record deal. Several of the labels had shown an interest and had requested I bring Craig into their office for him to perform live. Of course, due to my surgery, I wasn't able to go with him so he would come by to see me and tell me how each meeting went.

My doctor had immediately put me on a breathing procedure where I had to blow into a mouthpiece and try to push a little ball up to a certain point in the tube with my breath. That was really hard to do, especially in the beginning. I was now missing 2/3 of my right lung, so nothing was easy at the time. It was like trying to learn to breath all over again. I had to do the breathing procedure several times a day and walk every morning and every afternoon.

I was getting depressed from all the pain and so much medication. I started feeling sorry for myself. This was during the Hurricane Katrina catastrophe and watching all those people helpless on television, on rooftops in New Orleans and other stricken areas, and people dying, I stopped feeling sorry for me and started feeling sorry for them.

Just when we think we are having it bad, just look around we'll see somebody having a tougher time than we are. Laying flat on my back in a hospital bed I started praying for the hurricane victims.

Finally I was dismissed from the hospital to go home and began a long process of healing.

Recovery at home was a long period of time. It was a tough surgery. They have to break your ribs and I think that is the toughest part to heal from. As I lay in bed at home I thought about Betty a lot, about her dying of lung cancer right next to where I lay. Even though I had bought a new bed, giving the old one to Jane Bounce, it was still the same room. I would look at the picture of Betty and I on the nightstand and cry. I would hold it next to my heart and cry again.

I prayed a lot and felt really close to Jesus. Although I stayed in a lot of pain for a long time, mostly confined to bed, I knew He was going to get me through all of the agony I was experiencing. Still, it wasn't easy. The pain pills would help, then they would make me nauseous. Finally, I threw them away. I had to keep using the breathing

Old Memories and Me

tube. I hated that little ball but I got to where I could push that sucker up to the level I was supposed to. It was tough but I did it.

I watched television a lot, then sometimes just laid in bed and thought about song ideas, and sometimes I just lay there and thought about my life and how fortunate I had been to have had Betty for 41 years, to have my daughter Dawn and my two grandsons, Kyle and Del. The pain was always there, the healing slow, but I was learning to endure it.

Dawn and Dallas were having problems and separated during this time. They eventually divorced and Dawn and my grandsons continued to live with me.

While I was recouping I thought about how to write the song idea Paul Bogart and I had talked about, the one about the little boy trying to put junk from his pocket in the collection plate in church. For some reason I recalled how Kyle had put a rock under Betty's hands when I had held him up to see her at the funeral home. He was only six years old at the time but Kyle had said he wanted to give his nanny a rock to help build her mansion in Heaven. Little by little I started tying the two little boys together and the things they had done into a story line. I called Paul Bogart.

"Paul," I said, "I think I know how to write the song we were working on when I got sick."

"Well, that's sounds great, Charlie," Paul responded. Are you feeling better?"

"I am still in some pain but I am doing alright," I told him. "As soon as I am able to write I will call you and we will get together and write the song."

"Sounds good," Paul said.

I already knew this was going to be a great little song.

A lot of people continued to pray for me. Monty Allen came to my home several times and brought me things and ran errands, but mostly just caring and being there for me. Monty was like a son to me and that made me feel good, especially since a couple of people I had known for years that I thought really cared about me never called once to see if I were dead or alive. I hate to say this but some people just get too big for their britches in this business and it is sad that success can do that to a person that once was down to earth and caring. I'm not ashamed to admit I shed a few tears thinking about a couple of guys that seemed to have deserted me after so many years of friendship. God gave me a tough will power but He also gave me a sentimental heart.

When I was well enough to visit an oncologist, I went to see Dr. Eric Raefsky.

"With the type of cancer you had, and the type of surgery," he told me in his office that first day, "we recommend 3-4 weeks of chemotherapy." He continued, "With the chemo treatments your chance of recovery is considered to be 70 percent, without it, 62 percent."

"They told me they got all of the cancer with the surgery," I reminded him.

"Well, they think they did, and I hope they did," Dr. Raefsky said to me earnestly. "But it could be microscopic and they can't see it."

I thought of Betty and her lung cancer. After her 31 radiation treatments they warned it could be microscopic too. And it was.

"I decided before I came here that I wasn't going to take chemo treatments," I told Dr. Raefsky. "I have had three surgeries in two months. I have been cut on, poked on, pulled on, needled and catheterized. I have had so much pain I wanted to die. I am tired and want to be left alone now."

"I understand your decision," he told me. "I really do."

From that moment on I knew Dr. Raefsky would be somebody special in my life, somebody I could trust and if my life were in danger, he would be someone I would want helping make delicate decisions on my behalf.

Dr. Raefsky told me we would do a PET Scan in six months and take things from there. I left his office feeling good about my decision not to take the chemo and I felt good about my chances of surviving. Why not, Jesus was still right beside me and He was using some great doctors to take care of me.

Old Memories and Me

CHAPTER TWENTY-FIVE

    Well into 2006 I was still healing from the lung surgery. There was a lingering pain from the nerves growing back and the rib cage under my right arm was still sore, I suppose from where they had to break my ribs. I was also having problems with my left leg hurting whenever I walked more than 30 yards and especially up stairways. While I was in the hospital having tests ran during the pre-surgery time, they had discovered I had a blocked artery in my left groin area. This was keeping a full blood flow from circulating through my leg, thus the pain. At some point in the near future I knew I was going to have to have stints inserted in that area. I already had 4 stints in my heart and sometimes kidded about setting off the alarm when I passed through security at airports.
    I hadn't seen Cindy Desotta in nearly two years but she still called several times a week from Arizona to check on how I was doing and also whenever she had a problem she called and asked me for advice. Since she and I weren't seeing each other anymore she was dating but kept having a problem finding the right guy. Seems like every time she would meet a man he would turn out to be a dud. She no longer lived in Scottsdale and had an apartment in Fountain Hills. I remembered Fountain Hills and a small lake that had a water spout that shot probably a hundred feet in the air every hour. It was really beautiful there.
    Rhonda Bulford had gotten on the Internet and opened me a *MySpace* profile in February. I had no idea what *MySpace* was. She explained it to me but I wasn't interested at that time but she finally talked me into checking my profile out a few months later.
    "Charlie, you have a bunch of emails to answer already and people are playing your songs every day on there," she informed me.
    She had downloaded *Wanted, Between An Old Memory And Me* and *I Would Like To See You Again*, all with me performing them, on *MySpace*. People were playing them on there every day and leaving me comments and sending emails. Up to that point Rhonda had been answering some of the emails and comments.
    So, in June, 2006, I went onto *MySpace* for the first time.
    Craig Hand, who I had produced a session on prior to my lung

Old Memories and Me

surgery, called me one day.

"Charlie, there is a guy that wants to start a new record label and release the CD you produced," Craig told me.

"What did you tell him?" I asked Craig.

"Well, at first I thought he might be another one of those people that claim they have money and want to get into the music business but turn out to be just blowing hot air," Craig said. "It seems this guy is legit though and owns a multimillion dollar company."

The man indeed started a new record label, called it Category 5, after category 5 hurricane Katrina, because he had met Craig when he had flown down to Florida to move his boat north to St. Augustine in order to escape the path of the storm. He had seen and heard Craig performing at a place called Hurricane Patty's in St. Augustine.

The man signed Craig Hand to the new label and flew him to California to shoot a video of the first single, Direct Connect. He bought space on two large billboards in Nashville and put Craig's picture up on each of them.

The second and third artists the man signed to Category 5 Records were two well-known artists. An introduction showcase was set up at *The Wildhorse Saloon* introduce the new label and its three newly signed artists. They showcased Craig's new video and he did a show followed with a performance by one of the known acts.

Everything was looking great, except for one thing. The guy that owned the new label didn't want to pay me producer royalties. I was working with Craig Hand on a word of mouth and honor agreement that if the session I produced was released on a record label I would get points as the producer, payable after the fee Craig had already paid me up front to produce the session was recouped. Since there was no contract the owner of the label didn't want to pay me.

I was advised by several music business executives to attain a lawyer because I was entitled to producer royalties. About all of the major labels were in support of me because they knew I had produced the session due to the fact I had played it for most of them.

"You don't come to this town and try to screw one of our own," one executive with Sony said to me. He was upset about the situation and was verbally coming to my defense, as did others at RCA and Curb.

I called an attorney that had at one time represented both Alan Jackson and Gaylord Entertainment. He instantly agreed to handle things for me and immediately contacted the attorney that represented the guy that owned Category 5.

Craig Hand was caught in the middle of the whole thing and I didn't hold him responsible. Like most legal disputes the attorneys hashed things back and forth and I was told the guy was saying he was going to work out a percentage royalties for my production. I only wanted to be paid if the CD sold anything, nothing if it didn't.

I never saw a contract but as it turned out it didn't matter anyway. Craig Hand left the label after the first single and then the label closed down some time later due to some kind of legal problem the owner was having with the government concerning the money he had used to finance the record label. I never knew the details of that but from what I was told the guy was in some serious trouble with the government.

Craig Hand and I remain good friends today and I have been back in the studio working with him on another project.

I am still writing a lot, although nobody seems to want to record great songs any more. I say that with tongue in cheek but honestly, sometimes it does appear to be true. People keep saying that country music sales are really down. My response to that is, "How do they know? We haven't had a country record out in five years."

Seriously, you take Alan Jackson, George Strait, Brad Paisley, Trace Adkins, Kenny Chesney, Gretchen Wilson, Jamey Johnson and a couple more singers out of the equation and what folks are calling country today is nothing but pop, or bubble gum music with a steel or fiddle thrown in to try and classify it as country. In my humble opinion most of the songs you hear on the radio today aren't really country at all and they say nothing that will be remembered in time. They don't stand out from the song you just heard before that one on the radio nor the next one the disc jockey will play after it. Yet they win country music awards, not because they are great songs, but mostly because they aren't competing against anything else. Sometimes I wonder who's driving the bus around here these days. It must be somebody with a learners permit.

A couple of years ago I sat at a table at the BMI Awards with legendary songwriter Marijohn Wilkin and she asked me, "Charlie, do you think many of these songs winning awards tonight will be remembered 20, 30 or 40 years from now like the songs you and I have written over the years?"

"Nope," I told her. "Nobody will remember two lines in most of these songs two years from now."

Marijohn Wilkin was writer of such classics as *Waterloo*, *Long Black Veil*, and *One Day At A Time*, among other great songs. I had known her since my days as a writer at Cedarwood Publishing. Unfortunately, she passed away since I was with her at that awards ceremony.

She and I weren't upset because we weren't receiving any awards that night. We were just somewhat depressed over what was happening to country music and wondering what was going to happen to the music we both had loved so much all of our lives. Not many of today's newer artists seem to even bother to look for the great songs and I arrived at that opinion because of what I hear on their albums. A lot of the new artists don't sound country either, yet they want to be

Old Memories and Me

called country singers. Just because you put a fiddle or a steel in a song's production doesn't necessarily make it country. These singers have a right to record the kind of songs they want to but don't try and label it as the same music that Jimmy Rogers, The Carter Family and Hank Williams pioneered, and others such as Lefty Frizzell, Merle Haggard, Patsy Cline, Loretta Lynn, George Jones and more recently Randy Travis and Alan Jackson have carried on into the history of Country Music.

    Where are all of the classics going to come from now, songs that will last a lifetime? They are still being written today but it seems this new breed of singers don't want to sing anything unless it has a pop groove and sound. *I'm So Lonesome I Could Cry* didn't have a groove, neither did *Long Black Veil* and *Ruby, Don't Take Your Love To Town*. Neither did *The Gambler*, *On The Other Hand* and *I Was Almost Home*. You just don't hear great songs like these on the radio any more so I just stopped listening.

    I sincerely believe that if *She's Single Again*, *Wanted*, *Between An Old Memory And Me* and *Leavins' Been A Long Time Coming* had never been recorded before and I pitched them today most of the artist out there wouldn't cut any of them. Not because they wouldn't recognize them as being great songs but because they are *too country* for what they do in country music today.

    We used to see country music singers presenting awards to other country music singers on award shows, but today some rock, pop, rap, or Hollywood stars are standing on a stage that should still be filled by country music singers. After all, it is our music and our award shows. You don't see George Jones or John Anderson presenting an Academy Award...

    I personally like a lot of different music styles. I have been a Lionel Ritchie fan for years. I loved the Bee Gees, The Eagles, Credence Clearwater, Ray Charles, Sheryl Crowe and I truly miss the sounds of the great Jim Croce. However, when I listen to a pop radio station I expect to hear pop music and when I tune in to a country station, I want to hear country music. I don't mix my caviar with my grits.

    The Internet is hurting all genres of music, that's for sure, but we aren't helping ourselves any by not putting enough great product out there to bring fans back to buying a full CD. I hate to keep driving that point in the ground but it is a fact. The music business is in terrible shape right now. We're struggling at every level and we're not helping ourselves by not giving the country fans what they want.

    I do commend Carrie Underwood for the magnificent job she did on the old Randy Travis hit, *I Told You So*. In my opinion if she keeps recording great country songs like that one and puts the feeling and emotion into them that she did into that song, then Carrie Underwood will not only help country music get back to the standard we used to be so proud of, but she will move her name into the category of being one of country music's all time great female singers.

Unfortunately, this is not the best time for a new singer or songwriter to try and get into the business. A songwriter new in town asked me recently, "Charlie, let's say I just arrived in Nashville, stepped off the bus and asked you for advice, what would you tell me?"
"Get back on the bus," I replied.

I lost a dear friend in 2007 when Del Reeves passed away. The only time I have performed on the Grand Ole Opry stage was when Del invited me to perform my song *I Would Like To See You Again* with him. Del sang the first verse and I sang the second verse and did harmony with him on the choruses. Del did his Johnny Cash impersonation on the last verse. Cash had the single and the hit on that song but Del was the first artist to record it on an album, then Kenny Rogers and Don Williams also recorded it on albums.

I had a lot of fun times with Del Reeves. He recorded six of my songs but my closest bond to him was our close friendship for 39 years. He was one of the greatest entertainers in our business and his impersonations of famous people were second to none. He had his own sound and recorded a number of hits over his career, including *Girl On The Billboard*, *Belles Of Southern Bell*, and *Goodtime Charlie*, among others.

Not only do I miss him, but thousands of fans around the world miss him with his charming humor and great performances.

In my 41 years of songwriting I had never written any gospel music until 2007. I don't know why it took me so long to write gospel songs since I have always believed in God and carry Jesus in my heart everywhere I go.

My old friend Moe Lytle had mentioned to me about writing a few gospel songs so I suppose that is what really got me to thinking about it. Ever since we first met back in 1973 we have been close friends and talk a lot about songs and different ideas.

Writing gospel songs all started with me sitting on the side of my bed one afternoon, strumming around on my guitar, and I started thinking about Betty being in Heaven, sitting around talking with Moses, Joshua, George Washington and all of the people we've read about in the Bible and history books, and course Jesus himself. Just before she had died she told me she would be in Heaven, free of pain, and young again, and being with Jesus. I thought about that and lines just started running through my head and I started playing my guitar and singing them.

Hello Moses, is that you Abraham
I do believe that's Ruth coming down street
Oh my goodness, there stands Jesus
I know I'm finally home cause the master is smiling at me

Old Memories and Me

I cried some tears while I was writing that song and finished it in about two hours and called it *Hello Moses*. I called Moe Lytle and sang it for him over the phone. He loved it.

I met Cynthia Hulst on *MySpace* when she emailed me one day and told me if I would help her with her songwriting she would do a photo shoot for me in return. She worked for an orthodontist as her regular job but had done both photographer work and some modeling. As usual with emails on *MySpace* her picture was attached. She was a beautiful young lady and in passing back and forth a couple more emails I learned she was friends with Johnny Bulford, so I agreed to write with her.

The day Cynthia Hulst arrived at EMI to write with me, and I saw her in person for the first time when she walked through the door, I had to do a double take of her.

With her long dark hair and dark eyes, with an eye-catching figure outlined perfectly in jeans and a sweater, she could have been Betty reincarnated, only a little taller. Cynthia entered my heart before she had said a word.

"Hi," she smiled. "You're Charlie, aren't you? I recognize you from your pictures."

"Yes," I told her and smiled back.

She was beautiful and I was instantly intrigued.

I offered her something to drink, coffee or water, but she had brought her own bottle of water.

We went downstairs to the studio where we were going to write for the day.

"So, you're from Michigan?" I said to her as we sat in chairs beside each other.

"Yes, Grand Rapids," she informed me.

You know how some people just get to you right from the start and you know you are going to like them even before you really get to know them? Cynthia Hulst had that effect on me and it was more than just her good looks. Honestly, she just had a terrific personality and charm about her.

We exchanged a few more minutes of casual conversation before we talked about writing a song.

"Well, is there any particular idea or subject you would like to write about?" I asked her at some point.

"In fact there is," she told me and opened up her notebook. She also had a laptop computer with her. "I have already written some lines and thoughts."

Cynthia went on to explain to me how she had known this elderly man, in his early eighties, and how they had become really close friends up until he had died. They had talked almost on a daily basis and the elderly man liked to refer to her as his sweetheart and she would allow him to do that. There was no actual romance between them, just a close friendship and Cynthia had developed a dear feeling for him and that is why she let him pretend she was his girlfriend in an innocent and almost playful way.

As she told me the story I watched her eyes and warm smile and knew this young lady had a tender and caring heart. I liked her even more for that. Not many 28-year-old young women would take the time to spend with an old man to give him companionship and make him happy during his last days of life. I found this to be a remarkable trait and would go on to learn in time this was just the sweet kind of person Cynthia Hulst was.

"That was really nice of you to be so kind to him," I told her. "That makes you a really special person."

"Thank you," she smiled. "He was a nice old man that lived next door and I enjoyed talking with him."

I thought about my own age and wondered if that was why she had chosen me to help her write this song. I asked her that.

"No," she assured me. "Besides, you're not that old."

"I'm 70," I informed her.

Her mouth opened and her eyes widened in disbelief. "No way."

"Afraid so," I chuckled.

"Uh uh," she said. "You look about mid to late fifties."

"You should see me trying to get out of bed in the morning and get going," I laughed. I immediately wished I hadn't said that and tried to skip right on over it.

"Well, let's see what you have started on the song," I said.

We started writing the song that morning about the older friend she had known, went to lunch and finished the song that afternoon.

"What are you doing tonight?" Cynthia asked me as we were about to leave EMI.

"Probably nothing," I replied.

"You want to have dinner and then go down town and hang out a while? I'd love to sing at the *Wannabe* karaoke place," she told me.

"I'm game if you are," I said.

We had dinner that evening at a nice restaurant on West End Avenue, then drove downtown and found a parking place. It was Friday night and the Broadway, 2nd Avenue area was pretty crowded. *The Wannabe* karaoke bar was packed. Cynthia turned in her name on the waiting list and we stood at a standup table and I had a beer while she had a mixed drink. We danced a couple of times, at least the best we could in such a crowded environment. I admit I was feeling quite intrigued with her, especially when she would throw her head back and laugh and that long dark hair would toss about her pretty face. It was nice being with her but we were just two people having a good time. I was too old for her and we weren't out on a real date. We didn't call it

Old Memories and Me

anything and just enjoyed the evening.

When they finally called her name Cynthia got onstage and sang. I was pleasantly surprised to find she had a nice voice. I stood in a chair to see over the top of the crowd and took a few pictures of her with her camera. Not long after she had performed we left the *Wannabe* and crossed Broadway to *The Stage*. It too was packed.

We didn't have any drinks there. One was enough for both us. We didn't try to dance either because it was even more crowded than the *Wannabe* had been.

"Can we write another song tomorrow?" Cynthia asked me later as we drove away from downtown.

"EMI is closed on Saturdays," I informed her. "We can write in my van though. It is a conversion van and pretty big."

The next morning, Saturday, I drove down to EMI and parked in their parking lot. Cynthia arrived and joined me in the van. She had on a pair of jeans, an orange pull over top with black stripes and a baseball cap. She looked adorable and I felt a little guilty that I kept noticing how good she looked.

There in my van that Saturday we wrote a hit song called *I Don't Always Need What I Want* and Cynthia Hulst and I became close friends for life that weekend. It was just a mutual thing between us that we liked each other from the very beginning. Several months later I took her with me to the BMI Awards and she was the belle of the ball. She was gorgeous in her low-cut black evening gown. She had called me from Michigan and told me she only had one formal dress and it was pretty low-cut.

"Wear it," I told her.

At the BMI Awards several industry men, as well as a well-known actor from Hollywood, told me I was with the best looking female there. I already knew that though.

I introduced Cynthia to my pals Vince Gill, Bill Anderson and Kris Kristofferson, and a few other stars. We met and spoke briefly with Jessica Simpson. Willie Nelson was BMI's icon recipient that night and Toby Keith, Keith Urban, Emmylou Harris, Kris Kristofferson, and Josh Turner performed some of Willie's hits. After the awards dinner Willie performed in the lobby downstairs. I was able to get Cynthia and me right on the front row, not five feet from Willie. She was ecstatic. Willie Nelson is awesome to watch perform, especially in an informal setting as it was that evening.

It was a wonderful evening and I hated for it to end. I drove Cynthia to her friend's apartment where she was staying while in town. She gave me a sweet little kiss and we said goodnight.

I drove home wishing I were forty years younger, well just for a little while anyway. I'm really contented being the age and that I am.

One day Marty Brown and I decided to drive up to Metropolis, Illinois to Harrah's Casino, which most people around here refer to as *The Boat*, because it is actually a boat docked on the Ohio River that has been converted into an elaborate casino. It's about a 2½-hour drive from Nashville.

We didn't know it until we arrived there but we learned that Merle Haggard was doing a concert that afternoon. A large portion of one of the parking areas had already been roped off for the concert. We ran into someone that was able to get us tickets right on the front row.

I hadn't seen Merle perform since the late sixties. That night when he came out onto the stage to begin his show he sang four or five songs before he ever spoke a word. Then he said into the microphone, "I'm Merle Haggard."

The crowd went nuts with applause and yells and whistling, including Marty and myself. Fans have never gotten tired of hearing and watching The Hag perform after all of these years.

I recall sitting there in awe as Merle sang one hit song after another and after about ninety minutes I was thinking, *he can't sing another one without repeating some he has already sang.* Then, he would do another classic he hadn't yet performed. The man has written so many country classics it is almost mind boggling to watch him perform one right after the other.

Merle Haggard is no doubt already a legend in his own time.

This was about the time that I went back to work for Moe Lytle to run his Power Play Music and do most of the producing for his record label, Gusto Records. Over the next few months I wrote perhaps 14 more gospel songs and I went into the studio and demoed 11 of them. Billy Joe Royal, of *Down In The Boondocks* fame, recently recorded all 11 of them and the CD will soon be released on Gusto/King Records.

Moe Lytle runs lines and ideas by me that sometimes spur me into writing some of my songs. Moe and I talk mostly late at night after Nashville has started settling down for the evening. It isn't unusual for him to call me at midnight, as he did the other night.

"Well, Charlie," Moe asked me with humor in his voice. "Do you think we'll ever sell a million records on that CD of yours?" He was referring to *The Hitmaker*, a new CD Moe had allowed me to produce on myself and he released it on Gusto Records.

"Probably not," I chuckled, propped up on about three pillows in bed, with my TV on. I turned down the volume. "I think I had over 800 plays on *MySpace* today though."

"How many of them 800 plays do you think will turn into sales?" Moe asked with a chuckle of his own.

"Probably none," I admitted.

"You know Charlie," Moe said as his mood turned more serious. "If we were thirty years younger and the record business was back like it was ten to fifteen years ago, we could probably sell a million

Old Memories and Me

records on your CD. It's a damn good CD."

I never know what to say when someone pays a compliment to me about my singing. Most times I respond with something funny.

"Since I am so old now, maybe we should put up record racks in nursing homes around the country," I told him.

Moe Lytle laughed that laugh I have come to know for more than 35 years. "Maybe so," he said. Then he told me a large distributor in England ordered copies of my CD. We are selling a few and I am very appreciative of Moe allowing me to record again. We are planning on me recording a truck driver's album soon. Moe also wants Brittany Allyn and I to do a duet album together.

Moe and I chatted for another fifteen minutes and after we hung up I went back to eating my peanut butter and crackers while I watched a video of a Vanderbilt basketball game I had recorded in 1993.

I love my peanut butter and crackers in bed at night.

CHAPTER TWENTY-SIX

One night I went to the Grand Ole Opry and visited some of my Opry friends backstage. I stopped by Porter Wagoner's dressing room to say hello and to thank him for recording my song *On The Rebound*. He had recorded a duet on the song with Pam Gadd a few months earlier. In all of the years I have been in Nashville it was the first time Porter had recorded one of my songs. I kidded him about that.

"Porter," I said to him. "Dolly cut one of my songs, *Chicken Every Sunday*, way back in 1970. Why did it take you nearly 40 years to record one of my songs?"

Porter looked at me very seriously and told me, "Well, Charlie, either Dolly is a lot smarter than me or maybe you're just writing better songs nowadays."

Great comeback Porter. I got a good laugh at that remark while Porter remained serious looking a few more minutes, then he let out that famous laugh of his and draped an arm over my shoulder and said, "I'm just kidding you, Charlie. You have always written great songs."

That's just one of the reasons I have always loved Porter, his great sense of humor. I really was grateful to him for recording my song because he is one of the all time great country music singers He also was a great songwriter himself.

I was sitting in Moe Lytle's office one night and he was playing me some of Porter Wagoner's recordings on Gusto. There was one song called *The Dream*.

"Porter came by here one night and told me about this dream he had had," Moe told me. "He said he had dreamed that he had died and gone to Heaven and saw all of his Grand Ole Opry friends that had died over the years. He saw Grandpa Jones, String Bean, Roy Acuff and Minnie Pearl and some others. He said when he woke up it was like it was real, that God had let him see his old friends one more time. Porter said he got down on his knees and prayed and thanked God for letting him see his friends again. I got chills listening to him tell me that, Charlie." Then, Moe added, "I told him he needed to go home and write all of that down before he forgot it. He did and then he wrote this song."

It was a wonderful song and I felt chills listening to Porter sing it. This was a year or so before Porter died. When Porter did pass away

Old Memories and Me

it hit both Moe and I hard. Moe had worked closely with Porter and allowed him to produce himself on several albums that were released on Gusto Records. I had known Porter since 1968 and he had been in my office a week before going into the hospital that last time. He never came home again.

On that day that Porter visited with me to listen to some of my songs for his next gospel album, I played him a song called *Singing All The Way To Heaven*. The reason I had written that song was because Porter had told me a few months earlier that Dolly Parton had called him one day crying and told him she had been listening to one of his gospel albums. He told me Dolly said to him, "What are you trying to do, sing your way into Heaven, Porter?"

I thought about Dolly telling him that and came up with the idea to write *Singing All The Way To Heaven*, especially for Porter. I co-wrote it with Derik Schumacher. When I played it for Porter that day in my office he loved it.

"I am going in the studio next week and I will record that," he told me. "Put that on hold for me."

As he left my office I walked down the long hallway with him to the front door. I could see Porter was weak and I was concerned about him. He nearly stumbled a couple of times on the carpet so I kind of held my hand under his right arm as we walked. I was really worried about him that day.

Porter did cut the tracks to *Singing All The Way To Heaven* and another song of mine but unfortunately he became ill in the studio and that is when he went to the hospital for the final time.

When Porter passed away I went to the funeral home for visitation and one of his daughters, Debbie, hugged me warmly and as she wept softly she said in a tender voice, "Oh, you're the Frog man." She was referring to my song I had written with Paul Bogart that Porter had recorded a few months earlier, *Frog For The Water*.

Debbie also told me that day that Porter had mentioned to her recently that he thought I was one of the greatest songwriters to ever come to Nashville. I was already on the verge of tears and that did it. Knowing one of the legends in country music said that about me really humbled me and touched my heart, and too, knowing I would never get to talk and spend time with my old friend ever again really saddened me even more.

There is a peace though in knowing *The Wagon Master* sings with angels now, and he really did *sing all the way to Heaven*.

Two of the nicest people in this business are Johnny Wright and Kitty Wells. I am sure that most of you know that Johnny Wright is Kitty Well's husband.

I first met Johnny and Kitty on July 29, 1968 at a package show in Greenville, South Carolina. The reason I can recall the exact date is because that was the show I performed on the night before I moved my family to Nashville, which was my daughter's sixth birthday. The Johnny Wright & Kitty Wells Show opened the concert that night and George Jones closed it. Somewhere in between was The Wilburn Brothers, Loretta Lynn, David Houston, Conway Twitty and myself. I was the unknown guy sandwiched between David Houston's and Conway Twitty's performances.

     Later on I came to know Johnny and Kitty very well and I have been proud to call them dear friends for nearly forty-one years. I visited their home about a year ago to just talk and spend some time with them. For about a year, back in the seventies, I ran their publishing company called Need A Hit. While I was working for them I needed four tires for my car but I didn't have the money. Johnny Wright paid for the tires and I tried to repay him but he would never allow me to. Johnny Wright has been known as a thrifty person but I found him to be a very generous and giving man.

     Kitty Wells has recorded several of my songs over the years and I even wrote two local television commercials for her advertising the Heritage House Smorgasbord. Two of my favorite songs she recorded that I wrote were *Every Step Of The Way* and *Nickel Bar Candy*. The legendary Owen Bradley produced both of those. Of course Kitty Well's signature hit was *It Wasn't God Who Made Honky Tonk Angels*.

     Kitty's real name was Muriel Deason and Fred Rose suggested to Johnny that they come up with a more commercial sounding name for her. Johnny heard a song called *Sweet Kitty Wells* and he told Fred Rose he thought that would be a good name for Muriel. Enter Miss Kitty Wells, soon to be Queen of Country Music and a member of the Country Music Hall Of Fame.

     I am also friends with Johnny and Kitty's son Bobby Wright. Bobby landed a part in the McHale's Navy television show and appeared in 100 episodes. In the credits of McHale's Navy his name appears as John Wright because his real and full name is John Robert Wright, Jr. He became known as Bobby Wright in country music.

     Bobby told me the way that all came about was one day Art Devine told him about an interview being held at WSM where some television producer was looking for a young southern boy that played guitar and sang, to be cast in a show about four boys living on a houseboat. Not only did Bobby Wright show up for the interview, but according to him, so did Bill Anderson, The Wilburn Brothers and Johnny Paycheck. This was in 1961.

     Bobby Wright was flown out to Hollywood for a screen test and returned home to Nashville to await the results.

     "I didn't hear anything for a few weeks," Bobby told me recently as he recalled the story. "But I eventually got a call and they told me I didn't get the part in Four Boys On A House Boat but that

Old Memories and Me

someone else was interested in me for a new 30 minute pilot for a series to be called McHale's Navy."

Bobby told me that only Ernest Borgnine, himself and one other guy were held over from the original screen test for parts in McHale's Navy. Bobby Wright recorded as an artist himself and a few chart records that did well for him.

Johnny and Kitty's two daughters are Ruby and Sue, but I never really got to know them that well. Bobby's daughter LeeAnn played softball for me one year back when I had my women's slow pitch team. LeeAnn went on to college after that year and I lost track of her.

I love the Wright family and I could search this world over and never meet better people than Johnny, Kitty and Bobby Wright.

I have been getting on *MySpace* pretty regularly for a while now and have met a lot of people on there. Most of them are singers and songwriters and a lot of them ask me for advice, some even ask me to work with them. One such person was a 15-year-old girl from Longview, Texas. Her name is Shelby Downing.

Shelby had visited my profile and emailed me to ask if I would visit her site, which I did. She was a pretty good songwriter to be so young and sang very well. I wound up talking with her mother, Debbie, on the phone and at her request I agreed to meet with Shelby to see about working with her. The Downing family came to Nashville and I met with them at my office at Gusto Records.

Shelby is a beautiful girl and looks older than fifteen, actually 16 now. She has a lot of talent that just needed fine-tuning and a little more experience. On that first visit the Downing's stayed four days in Nashville and Shelby and I wrote a few songs together. I am not a vocal coach by any means but I worked with her on her vocal delivery some. She was easy to work with and eager to learn. Her dad, Jerry, was an extremely nice man that usually stayed in the background. Debbie, Shelby's mom, constantly took pictures of Shelby and I writing together.

The Downing's' made a few more trips to Nashville for me to work with Shelby and we wrote seven or eight songs together during that period. I thought Shelby might benefit from a vocal coach and I recommended my friend Jilla Webb, formerly Jilla Roberts, and Jilla continues to work with Shelby today. They are planning on going into the studio soon to record an album on Shelby and she told me she was putting three of the songs she and I had written on the album.

I love Shelby Downing like a daughter and I hope her debut CD does well. She has worked very hard and I hope she achieves all of her dreams and goals one day.

I have gone back to writing a lot by myself but I do write quite regularly with Chuck Pinney and Donnie King from Dayton, Ohio. They come down to Nashville about once every 5 to 6 weeks and we write in my office at Gusto. They always bring down good ideas and they are both excellent writers. I co-wrote *I Married Your Sister* with them. Actually, the hook in that song was their idea. The song became popular off the *Hitmaker* CD. Naturally, most Billboard reporting radio stations wouldn't play me, due to my age and the fact my music is too country for most radio stations today.

I have received airplay from a lot of smaller and non-reporting stations and I sincerely appreciate that. I am especially grateful to Don Cronan and *The Rebel* in Middletown, Ohio and Bruce Hodge, *The Night Rider* up in Virginia. They were the first to play my record and that means a lot. Thanks guys.

I really enjoy writing with Chuck and Donnie and always look forward to them coming down for a few days.

About 6 months ago I met a beautiful lady from the Dayton, Ohio area. Her name is Connie Lee Turner. We met on *MySpace*. Actually, Shelby Downing introduced us to each other. She came down to Nashville for a visit and we had lunch together, along with one of her grandsons. I have traveled up to see her in Dayton once while on a radio tour and she frequently comes to Nashville to visit as she has done for a few years. We talk on our cell phones a few times every day and always talk at night just before going to sleep. She is a sweetheart and I enjoy her company.

Connie loves to sing and she and I go out to Rudi's at Music Valley Drive on Saturday nights whenever she is in Nashville. We get onstage and do a couple of songs each. Famed guitar player Leon Rhodes sits in at Rudi's a lot. Man, he is still a great picker and it is an honor being onstage with him.

On a recent visit to Rudi's with Connie, my old friend Jack Greene was there. I get to see Jack every now and then and it is always a pleasure to chat with him because we have known each other for over 40 years. Jack has recorded several of my songs, one of them being *Midnight Tennessee Woman* that I performed in the Robert Duvall movie, *Tender Mercies*. On that night at Rudi's, Jack performed *There Goes My Everything* and *Statue Of A Fool* magnificently, as usual. He received a standing ovation from the crowd.

Guess who was called to the stage to perform after him. Yep, unlucky me.

"Well, my life has been a lot about chasing that pot of gold but mostly stepping in potholes," I joked to the audience as soon as I sit down on a stool in front of the microphone. "And now I have to follow Jack Greene."

I performed *Wanted, Between An Old Memory And Me, I Would Like To See You Again* and *Lay A little Loving On Me*. The crowd loved those songs and I got a rewarding applause after each one, but still, there is just no way to successfully follow my friend Jack Greene right after he ends his performance with *Statue Of A Fool*. Jack Greene was

Old Memories and Me

named male vocalist of the year in 1967, which was the very first CMA Award ceremony.

The next day I dropped by Rudi's again to see another old friend and great guitar player, Steve Chapman. Steve played in clubs with me back in the seventies and also worked some of my recording sessions. Steve played on such classics as Red Sovine's *Teddy Bear*, and Barbara Fairchild's *The Teddy Bear Song*.

Connie loves to record and I recently gave her 10 tracks of some of my demos to record her vocals on. They turned out very well. Dawn is so thankful I am finally going out with someone older than she is.

I do several writer nights a year because I still enjoy performing before an audience. I love working the *Blue Bird Café* and have had some very enjoyable writer rounds there with Jim McBride, Stewart Harris and Dave Gibson. I recall on one of those rounds with Jim, Stewart and Dave, just before I went inside the Bluebird, Jami Grooms and his wife Sandi approached me in the parking lot. I was one of the first to encourage Jami with his songwriting early in his career and I suppose I became his mentor. That night in the parking lot of the Bluebird Café Jami and Sandi presented me with a brand new Martin DC16 guitar as a token of their appreciation for helping Jami get started with his songwriting career. Of course that wasn't necessary and it really surprised and humbled me. I played the Martin that night at the Bluebird and it has become my favorite guitar to write songs with. I am forever grateful to Jami and Sandi for that generous gift.

Not long ago I did another in the round I thoroughly enjoyed with James Dean Hicks, Jimmie Van Zant and Mark Preston. This one was at Douglas Corner. Connie came down for the occasion and took pictures and made a video.

"I love to watch you perform live," she told me. "I play all of your CDs in my car all the time."

She is always saying sweet things like that to me and I admit, I never get tired of hearing it.

The crowd at Douglas Corner was great that night and gave me standing ovations after each performance of *Wanted, Between An Old Memory And Me* and *Frog For The Water*. They gave James Dean Hicks the same honor after he performed his *Goodbye Time*. With Jimmie Van Zant being a member of the famous Van Zants and Lynard Skynard fame, we topped the night off with *Sweet Home Alabama*. That brought the house down and I really enjoyed playing that classic again since I used to play it with my bands in clubs over the years. We all took parts in singing it. Another standing ovation to a night that was a lot of fun.

I got a phone call from hit songwriter Jerry Foster recently and he asked me to join him, Dallas Frazier and my old friend Jim McBride for writers' round. That turned out to be a blast and one of the best rounds I have ever been a part of.

I was invited by RCA/Arista to attend a party to celebrate 50,000,000 album sales by Alan Jackson. A lot of people I knew were there, some I hadn't seen in years, like Mel Tillis. They had Alan's albums displayed in a beautiful setting in the middle of the room. RCA/BMG CEO Joe Galante hosted the gala and showed all of Alan's videos on a large screen, in the order each single and album had been released over the years. Alan made a thank you speech, being very appreciative and remaining the humble natured guy he is. He made a lot of pictures with people involved in making those albums, people who had been involved in his career, including one with me. Standing beside him for the picture, I remember thinking how it seemed like no time at all that I first met Alan in 1986, but unfortunately 22 years has a way of showing in your eyes and leaving a few travel lines on your face.

"Seems like yesterday this all started, don't it Alan?" I said to him as we both smiled for the camera.

After the picture Alan asked me, "You been doing alright?"

"I been doing OK," I told him.

We didn't get to really talk. He had to keep posing with one person, then another.

It was the first time I had seen or talked to Alan in about 8 years. Denise was there and I enjoyed a nice conversation with her. She is still as pretty as ever. I introduced myself to Alan and Denise's oldest daughter, Mattie.

"I went to your mother's baby shower when she was pregnant with you," I told Mattie with a chuckle. "It was at Marty and Sherry Gamblin's house, on the Saturday night before your dad flew out to California on Monday to shoot the video for *Wanted*."

"Of all of Dad's songs, *Wanted* is still my favorite," she told me with a smile. "I still hear it on the radio, even now."

Mattie is a very pretty young lady, as are her two sisters.

Before I left the party, I glanced back at the albums on display. Of the 50 million sold, I think I had songs on about 35,000,000. I glanced back to where Alan was still surrounded by a large crowd of people. I could still hear Betty telling me, the morning after we had seen Alan on *Nashville Now* in 1987, "Call that Jackson boy about writing with him."

I smiled to myself and walked outside to the valet service.

Kyle has really grown a lot and matured into a young man, even though he is only seventeen. He is 6 feet and weighs around 200 pounds, has a solid build, dark brown hair that he wears nearly to his shoulders in the back and his beard is heavier than mine. He has been shaving since he was 15 years old. He is a very handsome young man, with features resembling both his mom and dad.

He and I talk a lot and he has always supported my music and brags on me, paying me compliments all the time. He must tell me a

Old Memories and Me

half dozen times a day that he loves me. He has done that all of his life though.

One night, just recently, I was in my office playing some of my songs, trying to pick out the right ones for a pitch meeting at RCA Records the next day. Kyle came into the room.

"Papa, you know you're one of the best songwriters in the world, don't you? He said.

I chuckled for a moment, and then told him, "Kyle, I am glad you think so, but there are a lot of songwriters in this world better than I am."

"Not really," he said seriously. "I don't think you know how great you really are."

I stood up and gave him a big hug as he continued. "I listen to a lot of music and even though I don't like all of the country music I hear, just like I don't like all of the pop music I hear, I know enough about songs and music to be able to tell just how great you are and how far ahead of most other songwriters you are."

It really touched me that he thought so much of his papa's songwriting. I kept my hands on both of his shoulders and looked straight into his eyes, my own eyes a bit misty with proud and warm emotion.

"Kyle, do you know how much you mean to me?" I asked him.

"Yes, I know Papa," he smiled with affection. "And you know how much you mean to me too, don't you?"

"Yes, I do, and ever since you came into this world you have always made me feel good about myself. Just having you in my life means more to me than any song I have ever written or any money I have ever made. Songs have let me down, money spends and is gone, but you, you have always been there for me, and I am so proud of the young man you have grown up to be. You are such a good Christian young man."

"Thank you, Papa," he said, with a smile that was both humble and confident. "I'm a good person because I've had you to teach me, and nanny, and my mom and dad."

I just looked at my oldest grandson in silence for a moment. He was nearly as tall as me now and he looked like he should be in movies with his handsome face and striking eyes. I suppose he gets his height from me but he got those brown eyes from his mother. Dawn has those same captivating brown eyes too. She got her eyes from her mother too.

"I wish your nanny could see you now," I remarked, recalling how much he meant to Betty and the way she adored him, as I do. He was only six years old when she died.

"She can see me, Papa," he said with another Kyle smile.

Suddenly, I thought about Del.

"Where is your brother," I asked Kyle.

"Downstairs playing with his X-Box," he told me.

I walked to just outside the room and called out over the railing, "Del!"

"Yes, papa?" Del answered from downstairs.

"Come up here a minute," I called back to him.

My youngest grandson came running up the stairs. He has just turned twelve.

"What?" he asked.

"Come here," I said to him and pulled him into my arms. "I just wanted to tell you how much I love you."

"I love you too, Papa," he replied and squeezed me in return.

"I love both of my grandsons," I told them, looking from one to the other.

"We love you too," Kyle said.

"We love you too," Del echoed his brother, then asked, "Can I go back downstairs now? I'm at a place in the game I'm playing where I really need to keep going."

"Yeah," I laughed. "You can go back to your game now."

"Is it alright if Stephen comes over," Kyle asked me.

"Sure," I told him.

Kyle gave me another hug. "Love you."

"Love you too," I told him.

For some reason God just keeps on blessing me.

I still love the music business and God willing I don't suppose I will ever retire. I still love writing songs and working with new singers and songwriters. Producing has become a food that feeds my drive to create something different besides lyrics and a melody. I have continued to work with Johnny Bulford, producing a couple more sessions on him. The record labels still show a great interest in him but none of them have signed him yet.

Johnny entered the Colgate Country Showdown in 2008 and made it to the finals. On Friday night, January 15, 2009, he won the Colgate Country Showdown. I was sitting three rows from the stage and was so proud of him.

I just recently met another young singer I believe can make it one day in country music, hopefully sooner than later. His name is Dylan Robinson. Dylan is an 18-year-old Louisiana boy with a rich and deep voice that is a little reminiscent of Josh Turner, yet has a sound of its own as well.

We set up a recording session and I produced 3 tracks on Dylan. I pitched him to a few major record labels and two of them loved his vocals and have asked me to bring him in to perform live, one of them for the CEO of that label. Remember that name, Dylan Robinson, you will probably be hearing it again.

I really love working and producing in the studio, especially with new and undiscovered acts. Just recently I produced 3 sides on a pretty young lady from Tampa, Florida, Janell Wheeler, and I will be

Old Memories and Me

presenting her to the record labels as well. I also just produced a young man from Georgia, Tyler James, and one major record label has already asked me to bring him to perform live for them.

When I get in the studio, surrounded by some of the greatest musicians in the world, along with my favorite engineer, Chris Latham, and working with a singer that is hungry for stardom, my creative instincts kick into another gear and good things start to happen. It is an amazing thing to see a team of talented people in a studio feel the magic, all at the same time, and make a song come to life in a way that will touch the emotions of the world.

One of my jobs at Gusto Records is taking some of the older masters to engineer Chris Latham and have him transfer them to Pro Tools and remix everything to bring the sound up to today's standard. Recently we worked on, and released, albums by both Red Sovine and Del Reeves, as well as a various artists' CDs Gusto is about to release that includes such artists as *The Coasters, Red Sovine, Wanda Jackson, David Frizzell, Jack Greene, Terry Cobb* and yours truly. All of the artists are performing songs written by me, with Moe Lytle as co-writer on some of them. On that CD I am performing *Wate The Flowers* and *Frog For The Water*, the song that Porter Wagoner recorded of mine.

Gusto Records has it's own website called countrymusicusa.com and there you can buy albums by some of the greatest artists of all time, including *George Jones, Dolly Parton, Porter Wagoner, Dolly and Porter duets, Conway Twitty, Merle Haggard, Chet Atkins, Eddie Arnold, Jim Reeves, Waylon Jennings, Tammy Wynette* and many, many more. My own CD *The Hitmaker* is also on that website.

A lot of the artists' old masters I work with are friends I have known over the years and working with their products bring back some fond memories. One of the reasons I like working for Moe Lytle and his Gusto/Power Play companies is he won't let the good country sounds die and keeps them available for fans to hear and collect again.

On any given day you can walk into an office on record row and most of the people working there are clad in jeans. This is a blue jean town, at least the music part of it is. Even the CEOs of some of the major labels wear jeans or khaki pants, including a lot of the females.

Speaking of females, there are more women in A&R at the record labels today than any other time I can recall, and that's a good thing, because women supposedly buy most of the records out there so it stands to reason a female should know what songs other females will more than likely purchase.

Music Row is a multi-million dollar business but it really has a laid back and down home atmosphere. You see a lot of Lexus, Cadillac's and even Mercedes but a lot of the folks driving those luxury cars are just down to earth people you might see eating lunch at the Pie Wagon or a Subway.

People like Tim Dubois.

Tim Dubois is the genius that signed Alan Jackson, Brooks and Dunn and Diamond Rio to Arista Records, all within a short period of time when he first opened the label for Clive Davis, and he is often seen having lunch at the Pie Wagon, and most times he's in a pair of casual slacks or khaki pants. Tim is really a cool guy and always speaks to the lesser achievers as well as the more successful people in our business.

Tim Dubois has to be classified as one of the most successful record executives in country music and at the same time he is one of the more humble and down to earth people as well. Since the first day I met him back in 1989 he has always treated me with the utmost respect and never fails to speak to me whenever our paths cross. Tim Dubois is a good man and I feel fortunate to be able to call him my friend. In a lot of ways Tim reminds me of Jim Ed Norman because they both have a lot of the same personality traits.

Doug Johnson is the same way, down to earth and never rises above his raising. Doug has been head of Epic Records and Giant Records and is currently in an executive position with Curb Records but he is just one of the guys to all of us that know him. He has written some pretty big hit songs, especially as of late, one being *Three Wooden Crosses*, which he co-wrote with Kim Williams. Doug Johnson is like myself, about the only time you won't see him in jeans or casual pants is at an awards dinner or at the White House, which neither of us have been to, well at least I haven't. Doug and I are very close friends.

The legendary Owen Bradley falls into that same category, a nice and people caring gentleman. Mister Bradley, who is deceased now, is a member of the Country Music Hall Of Fame and would be a member of the Greatest Producers Hall Of Fame if they had one. He helped establish what is known today as the Nashville Sound, along with his brother Harold Bradley, and Bradley's Barn recording studio out in Mt. Juliet was one of the premiere sounds of country music until it burned down. I used to go out to Bradley's Barn and watch Owen Bradley work with some of the greatest names in country music history, super stars such as Loretta Lynn, Conway Twitty and Kitty Wells. I am so grateful Owen Bradley allowed me to watch him at work, although he never made it look like work. It was such a natural thing for him to be in the studio. He was one of a kind.

We are blessed with other great people in our business, good folks, a lot of them friends of mine, but I mentioned the above people because of my personal rewarding relationship and dealings with them.

There have also been some outstanding ladies in the business side of country music that have made great contributions to our industry and I need to mention a few of those; Francis Preston, retired President of BMI; Connie Bradley, President of ASCAP; the late Maggie Cavender, a songwriter's best friend; Renee Bell, formerly with MCA Records and now Vice President of A&R at RCA/BMG; and my dear friend Judy Harris, former head of CBS Songs and the best songplugger

Old Memories and Me

in Nashville. Certainly there are numerous other ladies that have made tremendous contributions to country music but these are a few that have touched my life and career in some way over the years.

I am so glad that Dawn, Kyle and Del live with me. I don't know what I would do without them. Everything I do now, I do for them. They are my three rocks to lean on and in their eyes and love I see the answers to many of my questions and also the strength to overcome most of my doubts.

My two sisters, Ruby and Dot, still live in South Carolina. I don't see them as much as I would like to but we are joined at the heart so we feel like we are together.

Dawn, the boys and I went to Carolina for Thanksgiving last year and I visited both of my sisters and spent time with Betty's twin sister, Bobbie, as well. I wish I could have seen Betty's other sister, Juanita.

I am 71 Years old now with a lot of silver in my hair and some lines in my face that I like to refer to as *character settling in*. I just had another CAT scan on my lungs to see if I am still cancer free. There has been a spot where my right lung used to be for the past six months. My oncologist, Dr. Raefsky, thinks it is inflammation. We are keeping a watch on it though and I am scheduled for another scan in August.

I walk a bit slower now and have a few aches and pains here and there. Sometimes it isn't fun being old but there sure were some fun times getting here. I just smile when most people still guess me to be in my early sixties.

It has been a long journey since Betty, Dawn and I arrived in Nashville 41 years ago, carrying everything we owned in that 1965 Mustang. I have written more than 2000 songs since then and probably 400 or more of those compositions have been recorded. *Wanted, Between An Old Memory And Me, She's Single Again* and *Leavin's Been A Long Time Coming* have all earned *BMI Millionaire Awards*, which means they have each been played on the radio a million times or more. In the case of *Wanted*, it is perhaps over 2 million airplays. My native South Carolina inducted me into the South Carolina Entertainment Hall Of Fame. I have had one Grammy nomination and two songs nominated for song of the year. I have worked with, and in some cases became friends with, some of the greatest names in the entertainment world.

There have been some wonderful times, some tough times, some sad days and lonely nights, some rain but yet a lot of sunshine, and through it all I have learned not to count on anything for sure, but I do trust and believe in everything I feel in my heart. If it comes from the heart, then I follow it, because that's where Jesus speaks to me. It is also the place where Betty lights up some precious memories.

I still travel up and down 16th and 17th Avenues quite frequently, pitching my songs to the record labels, recording in the studios, and sometimes just hanging out somewhere with old friends. In a lot of ways *Music Row* (I still call it that) has changed quite a bit since 1968, but then again, in other ways it hasn't changed at all. There are a lot of new buildings, new faces, some hard goodbyes and some easy hellos. Waylon Jennings and Conway Twitty are gone now but Alan Jackson and Brad Paisley walk where those legends once journeyed, creating their own legacies. Songs are just as hard to get recorded as they were 41 years ago but somebody will still have a #1 record every Monday in Billboard's singles chart. You just have to keep believing that next week it will be you. Invisible footprints of dreamers are still there, all up and down 16th and 17th Avenues and I can see them, because some of them are mine.

Somebody asked me the other day how long I have been in Nashville.

"Well," I replied. "When I arrived in town I sat down on a curb on 16th Avenue and waited for country music to get here."

I still have my sense of humor.

The biggest disappointment in my 41-year songwriting career is I have never been nominated for induction into the *Nashville Songwriters Hall Of Fame*. I suppose someday that will happen but I kind of wanted to be here to experience that feeling. I don't think that committee even knows who I am though, but that's alright, I know who I am.

She's been gone 11 years now, but I still visit Betty's gravesite and stare at the words inscribed on her headstone, *What A Day Yesterday Was*, then kneel and kiss the grass that covers the most beautiful gift God blessed my life with.

Would I do this music thing all over again? Well…. the answer to that is *between an old memory and me….*

Charlie & Betty's wedding day 1957

Charlie(in back)with his mother and father, Clara and Ben Craig, sisters Ruby and Dot, and brother Bill, 1958.

Charlie and Betty 1958

Charlie & Mel Tillis 1969

Charlie and Betty with friend Pat McKinnley, 1973

Betty Craig playing softball at a Memorial Day function, 1978

Charlie and Betty, 1976

Charlie(holding guitar) on the day he first signed with EMI-Screen Gems in 1979.

Charlie & Alan Jackson 1990

Charlie's grandson Del Primm, 12 (acting goofy)

Charlie's grandson Kyle Smith at the beach 2007, 15 years old

Charlie Craig 2007 at 69 years old

Dawn, Christmas, 2008

Also by Aberdeen Bay

Southern Kingdom

A Novel
Author: Don Stanford
ISBN-13: 978-1-60830-008-2
ISBN-10: 1-60830-008-0

One hears over and again that we are living in modern times. Since the day the first man walked the earth through this day, man has always lived in modern times.From the dawn of the ages when Eve was deceived by the serpent and ate the forbidden fruit to be like God, through today when men and women are eager to strike a deal with the devil to gain power and wealth, human nature has not changed.

The setting for Southern Kingdom is the nineteenth century; however, its theme is as ageless as the rising and setting of the sun. Ambition, anger, bravery, cowardice, greed, hate, love, lust, selfishness, and the struggle to survive are timeless.This novel chronicles the life – and the lives of the people his life affects – of a man who allows those forces to blacken his heart and empty his soul.

Adam Blythington relocates to America with the ambition of buying cheap land in the defeated south and living the life of a country squire.In only a few years, with the aid of a corrupt land speculator, he finds himself the owner of two vast plantations.When he acquires his first plantation, Hannah LeBlanc, the beautiful and sensuous housekeeper, offers herself as his mistress.

Although he marries the beautiful daughter of a wealthy landowner for convention's sake, and has an affair with his brother-in-law's wife, Hannah remains steadfastly loyal to him.

Together they forge the future of his empire, Southern Kingdom.They ruthlessly battle anyone, even resorting to murder, who threatens their dream of wealth and power.

Although he amasses land, riches, and power, the gratification he desired remains elusive.

Breinigsville, PA USA
02 November 2009
226885BV00002B/3/P